Critical Thinking

Richard L. Epstein

Cartoons by Alex Raffi

Wadsworth Publishing Company
I(T)P® An International Thomson Publishing Company

Belmont, CA • Albany, NY • Bonn • Boston • Cincinnati • Detroit • Johannesburg • London
Madrid • Melbourne • Mexico City • New York • Paris • Singapore • Tokyo • Toronto • Washington

Philosophy Editor: *Peter Adams*
Editorial Assistant: *Kelly Bush*
Development Editor: *Alan Venable*
Marketing Manager: *David Garrison*

Signing Representative: *Kim Johnson*
Cover Design: *Stephen Rapley*
Permissions Editor: *Robert Kauser*
Assistant Editor: *Kerri Abdinoor*

Printed in the United States of America
    4 5 6 7 8 9 10

For more information, contact Wadsworth Publishing Company,
10 Davis Drive, Belmont, CA 94002, or electronically at
http://www.wadsworth.com

International Thomson Publishing Europe
Berkshire House 168–173
High Holborn
London, WC1V 7AA, England

Thomas Nelson Australia
102 Dodds Street
South Melbourne 3205
Victoria, Australia

Nelson Canada
1120 Birchmount Road
Scarborough, Ontario
Canada M1K 5G4

International Thomson Publishing GmbH
Königswinterer Strasse 418
53227 Bonn, Germany

International Thomson Editores
Campos Eliseos 385, Piso 7
Col. Polanco
11560 México DF México

International Thomson Publishing Asia
60 Albert St.
50–01 Albert Complex
Singapore 189969

International Thomson Publishing Japan
Hirakawacho Kyowa Building, 3F
2–2–1–Hirakawacho
Chiyoda-ku, Tokyo 102, Japan

International Thomson Publishing Southern Africa
Building 18, Constantia Park
240 Old Pretoria Road
Halfway House, 1685 South Africa

Library of Congress Cataloging–in–Publication Data

Epstein, Richard L. , 1947–
    Critical thinking / by Richard L. Epstein ; cartoons by Alex Raffi .
        p.   cm.
    Includes index.
    ISBN 0–534–55839–9
    1. Critical thinking. I. Title.
BF441.E67 1998   98–22234
160—dc21

THE SLEEP OF REASON BEGETS MONSTERS

Critical Thinking
by Richard L. Epstein

THE STRUCTURE OF ARGUMENTS

AVOIDING BAD ARGUMENTS

9   Concealed Claims

10   Too Much Emotion

11   Fallacies *(A summary of bad arguments)*

Truth-Tables

Cast of Characters

Preface to the Student

You can read this book on your own. There are plenty of examples. The exercises illustrate the ideas you're supposed to master. With some effort you can get a lot out of this text.

But if you only read this book by yourself, you'll miss the discussion, the exchanges in class that make the ideas come alive. Many of the exercises are designed for discussion. That's where your understanding will crystallize, and you'll find that you can begin to use the ideas and methods of critical thinking.

You'll get the most out of discussions if you've worked through the material first. You need to know how to read this (or any) textbook.

Read the chapter through once, with a pencil in hand. Get an overview. Mark the passages that are unclear. You need to understand what is said—not all the deep implications of the ideas, not all the subtleties, but the basic definitions. You should have a dictionary on your desk.

Once the words make sense and you see the general picture, you need to go back through the chapter paragraph by paragraph, either clarifying each part or marking it so you can ask questions in class. Then you're ready to try the exercises.

You should try all the exercises. Many of them will be easy applications of the material you've read. Others will require more thought. And some you won't make sense of until you talk about them with your classmates and instructor. When you get stuck, look up the answer in the back.

By the time you get to class, you should be on the verge of mastering the material. Some discussion, some more examples, a few exercises explained, and you've got it.

That pencil in your hand is crucial. Reading shouldn't be a passive activity.

You need to master this material. It's essential if you want to write well. It's essential in making good decisions in your life. If you can think critically you can advance in your work. No matter where you start in your career—flipping hamburgers or behind a desk—when you show your employer that you are not only responsible but can think well, can foresee consequences of what you and others do and say, you will go far. As much as the knowledge of this or that discipline, the ability to reason and communicate will speed you on your way. Those skills are what we hope to teach you here.

Preface to the Instructor

This textbook is designed to be the basis of classroom discussions. I've tried to write it so that lectures won't be necessary. I've minimized the jargon while retaining the ideas. The material is more challenging than in other texts, while, I hope, more accessible.

The exercises are meant to lead to discussion, encouraging the students to compare ideas. Class time can be used to discuss homework. Instead of spending masses of time grading all the exercises, there are Quickie Exams in the Instructor's Manual that you can assign.

The chapters build on one another to the end. Rely on your students to read the material—quiz them orally in class, call on them for answers to the exercises, clear up their confusions. You can do the whole book in one semester that way.

I've chosen the material that I think is essential for a one-semester course, the fundamentals of reasoning well. I comment below on how you might rearrange the order a bit and why I've left out some subjects that are occasionally covered in a critical thinking course.

This course should be easy and fun to teach. If you enjoy it, your students will, too.

The order of the material

The Fundamentals (Chapters 1–5) is all one piece. I suggest you go through it in a direct line. It's the heart of the course. Here and throughout there is a lot of emphasis on learning the definitions.

The Structure of Arguments (Chapters 6–8) is important. Chapter 6 on compound claims—an informal version of propositional logic—is probably the hardest for most students. There's a temptation to skip it and leave that material for a formal logic course. Yet some skills in reasoning with conditionals is essential, for if you skip this chapter you'll end up having to explain the valid and invalid forms piecemeal when you deal with longer arguments. It's the same for Chapter 8 on general claims—an informal introduction to quantifiers in reasoning—except that the material seems easier. The second half of Chapter 7 can be skipped.

Avoiding Bad Arguments (Chapters 9–11) is a lot of fun. Slanters and fallacies give the students motive to look around and find examples from their own lives and from what they read and hear. It engages them. Because of that, many instructors like to put this material earlier. But then you end up teaching a hodgepodge of fallacies that won't connect and won't be retained. I've introduced the fallacies along with the good arguments they mock (e.g., slippery slope with reasoning in a chain with conditionals, *ad hominem* with a discussion of when it's appropriate to accept an unsupported claim), so that Chapter 11 is a summary and overview. You can push Chapters 9 and 10 forward to right after Chapter 5, but that leaves Chapter 11 hanging alone later. Covering this material here helps students unify the earlier material and gives them some breathing room. With the exercises in Arguments for Analysis, you can conclude a one-quarter course.

The last part, *Reasoning About Our Experience* (Chapters 12–15), covers specific kinds of arguments. Chapter 13 on numerical claims could follow directly after Chapter 5. I don't include chapters on moral reasoning, legal reasoning (there are examples of legal reasoning in the chapters and in the Instructor's Manual), or explanations. These are important subjects, and I deal with them in a second course on critical thinking. But students need to know about analogies, generalizing, and cause and effect before they tackle them. And they require introducing a lot of background: philosophical distinctions for moral reasoning, law for legal reasoning, science for explanations.

It is possible to teach students how to write good arguments. I've included two types of writing exercises. The first requires the student to write an argument for or against a given issue, where the issue and the method of argument are tied to the material that has just been presented. About midway through the book you can have your students read Composing Good Arguments, which summarizes the lessons they should learn. The writing exercises take some time to grade, but, as I discuss in the Instructor's Manual, there are shortcuts.

The second type of writing lesson presents a situation or a series of actions in a cartoon, and requires the student to write the best argument possible for a claim based on that. These lessons seem to do more to teach students reasoning than any other exercise I've used. Students have to distinguish between observation and de- duction; they have to judge whether a good argument is possible; they have to judge whether the claim is objective or subjective; they have to judge whether a strong argument or a valid argument is called for. These deserve class time for discussion.

What is new or unusual about this text

• The big difference is that I have tried to tie all the material into a single whole, a one-semester course covering the basics. The text is meant to be read and studied from one end to the other. The ideas fit together and make sense as one piece.

An example of this unity is how the principle of charity is revised into the Principle of Rational Discussion and the Guide to Repairing Arguments (Chapter 4). These play a central role in any argument analysis. They are explained and justified. They are used continuously to give shape to the analyses. They serve to organize the fallacies (Chapter 11), so that fallacies are not just a confusing list.

• There is an enormous variety and number of examples and exercises. The exercises relate to the material, and start from simply stating a definition, to relating the various ideas, to applying the concepts. There is repetition of exercises to promote mastery of the most important ideas. There are worked examples, both in the text and in the exercises, which help the students see how to proceed in their own work.

The exercises and examples are about topics students worry about all the time (their studies and grades, their love lives, their digestion, the superiority of dogs to cats, . . .). The examples from newspapers and media are focused on the material and on what will interest students. Philosophical issues are raised, but in the context of dialogues that students can imagine hearing their friends say. The text relates theory to the needs of the students to reason in their own lives.

• There is a Workbook which lays out exercises in a format that forces students to do the basic steps in argument analysis for every argument they encounter. It also makes grading a lot easier. There are many cartoon exercises in the Workbook not found in the text, including a dozen cartoon writing lessons at the end.

• Cartoons for this book have been drawn specifically to reinforce the ideas, to show relationships of ideas, and, with the writing exercises, to get students to convert nonverbal experience into arguments. The cartoons, especially the cartoon writing lessons, help students grasp the ideas much faster.

• The book has an Instructor's Manual that is extraordinarily complete. Not only have I included answers and lots of sample exams, but also a running commentary on teaching methods and why the material is presented as it is. There is also an Instructor's Disk that contains all the sample exams ready to modify and print, as well as other handouts and answers to the exams.

• Definitions and key ideas are boxed. It's easy to find the important material.

• The text is fun to read, yet challenges the very best student.

> I've tried to steer between the Scylla of saying nonsense
> and the Charybdis of teaching only trivialities. I hope
> you find the journey memorable. The water is deep.

Acknowledgments

I am grateful that so many people have been willing to give their time and ideas to help me improve this text. I am indebted to:

- Tom Bittner for a close reading of early versions of many chapters.
- Todd Jones for discussions.
- Walter Carnielli for discussions.
- Maurice Finocchiaro for discussions and the opportunity to teach this course.
- Benson Mates for discussions and correcting mistakes in an early version.
- Peter Eggenberger for discussions.
- Peter Hadreas for comments on an earlier version and many discussions.
- Stephen Epstein for a careful reading of an earlier version of the first five chapters.
- Mrs. Gertrude Epstein for her encouragement throughout.
- Vanessa Christopher for reading and checking the exercises in an earlier version.
- Neta Hoff for many discussions on the nature of the course and the organization of this material, and for reading and working through the entire text of an earlier version, not only as a proofreader but as a colleague.
- Fred Kroon, who helped a great deal by clearing up confusions in an earlier draft.
- Maria Sanders for checking the answers to the exercises.
- Ron Leonard, who did classroom testing, for a careful reading of an early version and many ideas on pedagogy.
- Jeanette Catsoulis for discussions and ideas on pedagogy from classroom testing.
- The following reviewers whose comments were crucial in clearing up confusions and shaping the text: David Adams, Phyllis Berger, Blanche Radford Curry, Betsy Decyk, Roger Ebertz, George Gale, Kevin Galvin, James W. Garson, Don Levi, Isabel Luengo, Brian J. Rosmaita, Darlene Macomber, and Kenneth Stern.
- Peter Adams for many good suggestions on how to organize and present the material, and for his help and encouragement throughout.
- Alex Raffi who contributed so much in collaboration on the cartoons.
- Alan Venable, whose careful and insightful editing improved the text enormously.
- And my students, who provided me with many examples, whose quizzical looks made me rewrite, and whose delight in the material motivated me to finish this book.

I am grateful to them all. Much of what is good in this text comes from them. What is bad is mine, all mine.

The FUNDAMENTALS

1   Critical Thinking?

A. Are You Convinced?

Everyone's trying to convince you of something: You should go to bed early. You should drop out of college. You should buy a Dodge Ram truck. You should study critical thinking . . . . And you spend a lot of time trying to decide what you should be doing, that is, trying to convince yourself: Should I take out a loan? Is chocolate really bad for my complexion? Should I really date someone who owns a cat?

Are you tired of being conned? Of falling for every pitch? Of making bad decisions? Of fooling yourself? Or just being confused?

Thinking critically is a defense against a world of too much information and too many people trying to convince us. But it is more. Reasoning is what distinguishes us from beasts, for many of them can see better, hear better, and are stronger. But they cannot plan, they cannot think through, they cannot discuss in the hopes of understanding better.

I used to go to city council meetings in the small town where I live. The public was invited to participate, and when a heated discussion took place in which I was interested, I often contributed. I was able to clarify the issues, and when I said my piece the majority often agreed with me, because I could see the issues, I could present my ideas well. That, too, is thinking critically.

An older student was in the spring term of his senior year when he took this course. He was majoring in anthropology and planned to do graduate work in the fall. Late in the term he brought me a fifteen-page paper he'd written for an anthropology class. He said he'd completed it as he usually would. Then he went through it, analyzing it as we would in class, after each paragraph asking, "So?" He found that he couldn't justify his conclusion, so he changed it and cut the paper down to eleven pages. He showed me the professor's comments, which were, roughly, "Beautifully reasoned, clear. A+." He said it was the first A+ he'd ever gotten.

I can't promise that you'll get an A on all your term papers after taking this course. But you'll be able to comprehend better what you're reading and write more clearly and convincingly.

Once in a while I'll tune into a sports talk show on the radio. All kinds of people call in. Some of them talk nonsense, but more often the comments are clear and well-reasoned. The callers know the details, the facts, and make serious projections about what might be the best strategy based on past experience. They comment on what caused a team to win or lose, they reason with great skill and reject bad arguments. I expect that you can, too, at least on subjects you consider important. What we hope to do in this course is hone that skill, sharpen your judgment, and show you that the methods of evaluating reasoning apply to much in your life.

In trying to understand how to reason well we'll also study bad ways to convince, ways we wish to avoid, ways that misuse emotions or rely on deception. You could use this knowledge to become a bad trial lawyer, but I hope you will learn a love of reasoning well, for it is not just ethical to reason well; it is, as we shall see, more effective in the long run. Critical thinking is part of the study of philosophy: the love of wisdom. We might not reach the truth, but we can be searchers, lovers of wisdom, and treat our fellows as if they are, too.

B. Claims

We'll be studying the process of convincing. Convincings depend on someone trying to do the convincing and someone who is supposed to be convinced. They fall into one of the following categories:

> • Someone tries to convince you.
> • You try to convince someone else.
> • You try to convince yourself.

It's awkward to say "convincings." Let's call an attempt to convince someone an argument.

But, you say, an argument means someone yelling at someone else. When my mom yells at me and I yell back, that's an argument. Yes, perhaps it is. But so, by our definition, is you and your friend sitting down to talk about your college finances to decide whether you need to get a job. We need a term that will cover all our attempts at reasoning, all our convincings, all our deliberations. The word "argument" has become pretty standard since about the time of Aristotle.

Still, that isn't right. Suppose the school bully comes up to you and says, "Hand over your candy bar." You don't. She hits you on the head with a stick. You give her your candy bar. You've been convinced. But that's no argument.

The kind of attempts to convince we'll be studying here are ones that are or can be put into *language*. That is, they are a bunch of sentences that we can think about. But what kind of sentences?

When we say an argument is an attempt to convince, what exactly is it that we are supposed to be convinced of? To do something? If we are to try to reason through arguments, the point has to be that something is *true*. And what is that something? A sentence, for it's sentences that are true or false. And only certain kinds of sentences: not threats, not commands, not questions, not prayers. An attempt to convince, in order to be classified as an argument, should be couched in plain language that can be true or false: declarative sentences.

You should already know what a declarative sentence is. For example:

This course is a delight.
The author of this book sure writes well.
Intelligent beings once lived on Mars.
Everyone should brush his or her teeth at least once every day.
No one knows the troubles I've seen.

The following are not declarative sentences:

Shut that door!
How often do I have to tell you to wipe your feet before you come into
  the house?
Dear God, let me be a millionaire instead of a starving student.

Still, not every declarative sentence is true or false: "Green dreams sleep peacefully" is a declarative sentence, but it's not true or false—it's nonsense. Let's give a name to those sentences that are true or false, that is, that have a ***truth-value***.

> **Claim** A *claim* is a declarative sentence that we can view as either true or false (but not both).

This definition does not say that for a sentence to be a claim we have to agree to view it as true or have to agree to view it as false. We just have to agree that it has some truth-value, though we may not know which.

One of the most important steps in trying to understand new ideas or new ways of talking is to look at lots of examples, and then try to make up your own.

Examples Are the following claims?

Example 1 Your instructor for this course is male.

Analysis This is a claim. It's either true or false.

Example 2 Your teacher is short.

Analysis Is this a claim? Probably not, since the word "short" is so vague. We'll consider problems with vagueness in Chapter 2.

Example 3 Cats are nasty.

Analysis If when I said this you disagreed, then implicitly you are accepting the example as a claim. You can't disagree unless you think it has a truth-value.

Example 4 $2 + 2 = 4$

Analysis This is a claim, though no one is going to disagree with you about it.

Example 5 I wish I were taller.

Analysis This is not a claim. It's more like a prayer or an extended sigh.

In some contexts, though, a wish might be a claim. If Dick's parents are berating him for not getting a job, he might say, "It's not that I'm not trying. I wish I could get a job." He could be lying, so in this context "I wish I could get a job" would be a claim.

Example 6 How can anyone be so dumb as to think that rats can reason?

Analysis As it stands this is not a claim; it is a question. But in some contexts we might rewrite it as "Someone must be dumb to think that rats can reason," or even "Rats can't reason." The process of rewriting and reinterpreting is something we'll consider throughout this course.

Example 7   Cada cachorro pode latir.

Analysis   Is this a claim? If you don't understand Portuguese, you better say you're not prepared to accept it as one. You shouldn't accept a sentence as a claim if you don't understand what it means.

But isn't Example 7 true or false regardless of whether you understand it? In English it means "Every dog can bark." Shouldn't we take something outside the sentence, some thought or idea the sentence expresses, to be what's true or false?

You can if you want. Still, we have to decide whether a particular use of a sentence, perhaps to express an idea or thought, is suitable for us to reason with. If it is, we'll call it a "claim," or as some say, an "assertion."

Example 8   Every mollusk can contract mixamotosis.

Analysis   If you don't know what the words mean, you shouldn't agree to view this as a claim. But that doesn't mean you should just dismiss any attempt to convince that uses language you don't understand: Get a dictionary.

Example 9   "I come to bury Caesar, not to praise him."

Analysis   This is not a claim. This is a quotation from Shakespeare's *Julius Caesar,* and lines from plays, poems, or novels aren't meant to be taken as assertions. We aren't expected to believe the sentence is true or false.

C. Arguments

We're trying to define "argument." We said it was an attempt to convince someone that a claim is true using language. The only language that we should allow in an argument, then, should be parts that are true or false: claims.

> ***Argument***   An *argument* is a collection of claims, one of which is called the ***conclusion*** whose truth the argument attempts to establish; the others are called the ***premises***, which are supposed to lead to, or support, or convince that the conclusion is true.

The point of an argument is to convince that a claim—the conclusion—is true. The conclusion is sometimes called "the point of the argument" or the ***issue*** that is being debated.

> ***Critical thinking*** is evaluating whether we should be convinced that some claim is true or some argument is good, as well as formulating good arguments.

Examples   Are the following arguments?

Example 1

Analysis   The nurse is making an argument. She's trying to convince the doctor that "Your patient in room 47 is dying" is true. She offers the premise: "He's in cardiac arrest." Sounds pretty convincing.

Example 2

Analysis   Here Dick is making an argument, trying to convince the police officer that the following claim is true: "The accident was not my fault." (I've reworded it a bit.) He uses two premises: "She hit me from the rear" and "Anytime you get rear-ended it's not your fault."

Example 3   Out? Out? I was safe by a mile. Are you blind? He didn't even touch me with his glove!

Analysis   This was spoken at a baseball game by a runner who'd just been called out. The runner was trying to convince the umpire to believe "I am safe." He used only one premise: "He didn't even touch me with his glove." The rest is just noise.

Example 4   Give me that *$!#&* wrench.

Analysis   I can remember who said this to me. He was trying to convince me. But it was no argument, just a series of commands and threats. And what he was trying to convince me of wasn't the truth of some claim.

Example 5 Follow the directions for using this medicine provided by your doctor. This medicine may be taken on an empty stomach or with food. Store this medicine at room temperature, away from heat and light.

Analysis This is not an argument. Instructions, explanations, and descriptions, though they may use declarative sentences, aren't arguments. They're not intended to convince you that some claim is true.

Example 6 You see a chimpanzee trying to get some termites out of a hole. She can't manage it because the hole is too small for her finger. So she gets a stick and tries to pull the termites out. No success. She licks the end of the stick and puts it in the hole and pulls it out with a termite stuck to it. She eats the termite, and repeats the process. Is she convincing herself by means of an argument?

Analysis This isn't an argument. Whatever the chimpanzee is doing, she's not using claims to convince herself that a particular claim is true.

But isn't she reasoning? That's a hard question you can study in philosophy and psychology courses.

Example 7

Analysis Zoe's mother is attempting to convince her, but not of the truth of a claim. So there's no argument. Perhaps we could interpret what is being said as having an unstated conclusion, "You should feel guilty for not calling your mother", and premises (disguised as questions) "Anyone who doesn't call her mother doesn't love her mother" and "If you don't love your mother, then your mother did something wrong." But it would be the interpretation that is an argument, not the original. And we would have to consider whether the interpretation is faithful to what Zoe's mother intended.

Summary   We said that this course will be about attempts to convince. But that's too much for one course. So we narrowed the topic to convincings that use language. That was still too broad. An argument, we decided, meant convincing someone that a sentence is true. So we defined a claim as a sentence that could be true or false. Arguments, we decided, will be attempts to convince that use only claims.

Now we'll begin to look at methods and make distinctions. Because your reasoning can be sharpened, you can understand more, you can avoid being duped. And, we can hope, you will reason well with those you love and work with and need to convince, and you will make better decisions. But whether you will do so depends not just on method, not just on the tools of reasoning, but on your goals, your ends. And that depends on virtue.

Exercises for Chapter 1

1. What's this course about?

2. How did I try to convince you in this book that this course is important? Can you pick out at least two *ways* I tried to convince you? Were they arguments?

3. Explain how to divide up all convincings depending on who is trying to convince whom.

4. Which of the following are claims?
   a. Lassie is a dog.
   b. I am 2 meters tall.
   c. Is any politician not corrupt?
   d. Power corrupts.
   e. Feed Ralph.
   f. Did you feed Ralph?
   g. A friend in need is a friend indeed.
   h. Why can't the English teach their children how to speak?
   i. Strike three!
   j. "Love is not love which alters when it alteration finds."
   k. No se puede vivir sin amar.
   l. Whenever Juney barks, Ralph gets mad.
   m. Wayne Newton lives in Las Vegas.
   n. You believe that Wayne Newton lives in Las Vegas.
   o. If the author of this book teaches in Las Vegas, then he lives in Nevada.
   p. $2 + 2 = 5$
   q. I feel cold today.
   r. $\int_{1}^{7} \frac{1}{t}\, dt = \ln 7$
   s. There is an odd number of stars in the universe.

5. Write down five sentences, four of which are claims and one of which is not. Exchange with a classmate and see if he or she can spot which are the claims.

6. How did I try to convince you that my definition of "claim" is a good definition?

7. What is the goal of an argument?

8. What is an argument?

9. What is a premise? What is a conclusion?

10. Why is not every attempt to convince you an argument? Give an example.

11. Give two examples of arguments that you have encountered outside class in the last two days.

12. Bring in a short article from the front page of a newspaper. Are all the sentences used in it claims? Is it an argument?

Here are two samples of exercises done by Tom, along with my comments.

> **Sheep are the dumbest animals. If the one in front walks off a cliff, all the rest will follow it. And if they get rolled over on their backs, they can't right themselves.**
>
> *Argument?* (yes/no) Yes.
> *Conclusion:*   Sheep are the dumbest animals.
> *Premises:*   If a sheep walks off a cliff, all the rest will follow it.
>   If a sheep gets rolled over on its back, it can't right itself.
>
>   *This is good work, Tom.*

> **How can you go to the movies with Sarah and not me? Don't you remember I helped you fix your car last week?**
>
> *Argument?* (yes/no) Yes.
> *Conclusion:*   You should go to the movie with me.
> *Premises:*   I helped you fix your car last week.
>
> *Is what you are given an argument? No: There are just two questions, and questions aren't claims. So it can't be an argument. And if there's no argument, there are no premises and no conclusion. Sure it seems that we ought to interpret what he's saying as an argument—as you have done. But before we go putting words in someone's mouth, we ought to have rules and a better understanding of when that's justified.*

Do each of Exercises 13–27 in the same way: State whether it is an argument. If it is an argument, identify the premises and conclusion.

13. You liked that movie? Boy are you dumb. I guess you just can't distinguish bad acting from good. And the photography was lousy. What a stupid ending, too.

14. Cats are nasty. They smell bad, they urinate in the house, they kill songbirds, they cause allergies so your friends can't come over. Why not just get a piece of wool with a recorder in it that will "miaou" when you stroke it?

15. If it's O.K. to buy white mice to feed a pet boa constrictor, why isn't it O.K. to buy white mice for your cat to play with?

16. You shouldn't eat at Zee-Zee Frap's restaurant. I heard they did really badly on their health inspection last week.

17. If you don't take a course on critical thinking you'll always end up being conned, a dupe for any fast-talker, an easy mark for politicians. So you should take a course on critical thinking. You'd be especially wise to take one from the instructor you've got now— (s)he's a great teacher.

18. Whatever you do, you should drop the critical thinking course from the instructor you've got now. (S)he's a really tough grader, much more demanding than the other professors that teach that course. You could end up getting a bad grade.

19. (Advertisement for Roundup®, a herbicide) Using Roundup® in your backyard makes gardening easy as well as effective. That's what gardening experts such as zoo horti-culturists have learned through years of using the product. Since it can be used in areas where kids and pets are going to play, gardening experts have a high comfort level in using Roundup® in areas from backyards to zoo habitats. That's because any Roundup® not used by the sprayed plant quickly binds to the soil and breaks down into naturally occurring elements.

    Roundup® works by preventing production of certain proteins, special only to plants, which are needed for growth. Extensive tests show that it will not move in or on the soil to affect nearby plants. So this spring and summer, do what many zoos do–use Roundup® to beautify your surroundings. (© 1996 Monsanto Company)

20. Look Dick! Look Zoe! See Spot. See Spot run.

21. Bad dog, bad dog. If you jump over this fence again I'll get a newspaper and hit you.

22 Zoe: I don't love you.
    Dick: Don't be ridiculous. Of course you do. Why just yesterday you said you couldn't live without me. What would you do without me?

23. Letter to the editor:
    Recently, there was an article in The Spectrum concerning pets being poisoned by antifreeze. If this were intentional, what an awful thing to do. I do wonder about the owners of these pets. Why have you allowed your pets to wander the neighborhood unleashed in the first place? Most pets are considered a member of the family. If you cared at all for these animals, why are they allowed to run in the streets to be hit by a passing vehicle? While driving through my neighborhood early one morning, I almost hit three dogs because they ran up to my car barking.

    Pet owners need to take responsibility for their animals. Not only is it unsafe for these pets to wander, it is very inconsiderate to other neighbors. Many of us are tired of the end-less, nauseating piles we have to shovel from our lawns and dead flowers caused by dogs passing by. Children in our neighborhoods cannot walk to a friend's house to play for fear of aggressive dogs. Pets should be in a fenced yard or on a leash, not just to protect pets, not just out of consideration for your neighbors, but also because it is the law.

Claudia Empey, *The Spectrum,* April, 1996

24. Homosexuality can't be hereditary: Homosexual couples can't reproduce, so genes for homosexuality would have died out long ago.

25. Letter to the editor:

I'm 45, a mother and a postal worker. I also happen to be in a long-term relationship with a woman. We both work, pay taxes, vote, do volunteer work, and lead full, productive lives.

My partner Sara and I have been together for over four years and we formalized our lifetime commitment to each other in a ceremony several years ago. In a fair and non-discriminating society, we would be able to obtain the same benefits for each other that heterosexual Americans obtain when they marry.

I've worked for the postal service for 10 years, yet I can't obtain health insurance for Sara, nor can I use family leave to care for or be with her if she's ill, has had surgery or has been injured.

Heterosexual employees who are married or get married can get benefits for a spouse and any number of children, including adopted, foster and stepchildren.

Even when we have legal papers drawn up to protect our rights, property and relationships, it often takes lengthy and expensive court battles to get other people to honor our wishes and instructions. Sometimes we lose those battles, and some rights (like family health insurance coverage) we simply can't get.

No one should be surprised that we want the right to marry.

Kathy Worthington, *The Spectrum,* May 26, 1996

26. You may own stocks or securities which are selling at a lower price than whenpurchased. Tax considerations might call for a sale of such securities in order to create a currently deductible tax loss. However, if it is desired to still own the securities while producing a tax loss, you can't just sell securities at a loss and then buy them right back. Any purchase of the same securities within 30 days before or after the sale negates any losses. To get around this restriction, you can purchase similar but not identical securities to the ones sold. Or, in the case of bonds, you can achieve the same result by making a swap through a brokerage house. *1994 Tax Guide for College Teachers*

27. Oven Light Bulb

The light bulb is located in the upper left corner of the oven. Before replacing the bulb, disconnect electric power to the range at the main fuse or circuit breaker panel or unplug the range from the electric outlet. Let the bulb cool completely before removing it. Do not touch a hot bulb with a damp cloth as the bulb will break.

To remove: Hold hand under lamp bulb cover so it doesn't fall when released. With fingers of same hand, firmly push down wire bail until it clears cover. Lift off cover. Do not remove any screws to remove this cover. Replace bulb with a 40-watt home appliance bulb.

To replace cover: Place cover into groove of lamp receptacle. Lift wire bail up to center of cover until it snaps into place. When in place, wire holds cover firmly. Be certain wire bail is not below depression in center of cover.

How to get the best from your range, Hotpoint

28. Dr. E is out for a walk with his dog. He gets ahead of her, comes to a fork in the path and goes along one side of it. His dog comes up to the fork and runs down the wrong side looking for him. Soon she re-appears at the fork and runs down the other side after him. Is Dr. E's dog using an argument? Explain.

29. Your friend goes outside, looks up at the sky and sees it's cloudy. She returns home and gets her raincoat and umbrella. Is she engaged in an argument? Explain.

30. Bring an advertisement to class that uses an argument. State the premises and conclusion.

31. In order to choose good courses of action in our lives we need not only knowledge of the world and the ability to reason well, but what else?

32. You've seen some arguments. What do you think should be the definition of "good argument"?

Key Words

truth-value	conclusion
true	premise
false	critical thinking
claim	issue
argument	

Further Study   There is much more to learn about the nature of claims, truth, falsity, and the relation of language to our experience. We'll touch on some of those in the next chapter. An introductory philosophy course would be the next place to go.

Attempts to convince that use language but aren't arguments, such as fables and examples, are studied in courses in rhetoric. Courses in marketing or advertising or psychology study both verbal and non-verbal ways to convince that aren't arguments. And convincing using body language is at the heart of acting classes.

A place to begin reading about whether animals can reason is *The Animal Mind,* by James and Carol Gould, Scientific American Library.

Writing Lesson 1

Write an argument either for or against the following:

"Student athletes should be given special leniency when the instructor assigns course marks."

Your argument should be at most one page long.

2   What Are We Arguing About?

In Chapter 1 we learned that arguments are attempts to convince using claims. So we need to distinguish different kinds of claims and be aware of sentences that look like claims but aren't.

A. Vague Sentences

1.   Too vague?

Zoe heard a radio advertisement that said Snappy detergent gets clothes whiter. So when she was in the supermarket, she bought a box. She's not very happy.

> **Vague Sentence**   A sentence is *vague* if it is unclear what the speaker intended.

We hear vague sentences all the time:

You can win a lot playing blackjack.
Our dish soap is new and improved.
People are more conservative now than they used to be.
Freedom is the greatest good.

They sound plausible, yet how can anyone tell whether they are true?

But isn't everything we say somewhat vague? After all, no two people have identical perceptions, and since the way we understand words depends on our experience, we all understand words a little differently. There has to be a little wiggle-room in the meaning of words and sentences for us to be able to communicate. You say, "My English professor showed up late for class Tuesday." Which Tuesday? Who's your English professor? What do you mean by late? 5 minutes? 30 seconds? How do you determine when he showed up? When he walked through the door? At exactly what point? When his nose crossed the threshold?

That's silly. We all know "what you meant," and the sentence isn't too vague for us to agree it has a truth-value. *The issue isn't whether a sentence is vague, but whether it's too vague, given the context, for us to be justified in saying it has a truth-value.*

2. Drawing the line   (*Bad arguments*)

Everyday we need to rely on words that are somewhat vague. Sometimes people get confused (or try to confuse you) by demanding more precision than is reasonable.

> If a suspect who is totally uncooperative is hit once by a policeman, then that's not unnecessary force. Nor twice, if he's resisting. Possibly three times. If he's still resisting, shouldn't the policeman have the right to hit him again? It would be dangerous not to allow that. So, you can't tell me exactly how many times a policeman has to hit a suspect before it's unnecessary force. So the defendant did not use unnecessary force.

This argument convinced the jury in the first trial of the policemen who hit Rodney King. But it's a bad argument. We may not be able to draw a precise line that always discriminates between unnecessary and necessary force, but we can distinguish extreme cases.

You should suspect any argument that relies on this premise:

If you can't make the difference precise, there is no difference.

It's called the fallacy of ***drawing the line***.

In a very large auditorium lit by a single candle at one end, there is no place where we can say it stops being light and starts being dark. But that doesn't mean there's no difference between light and dark. That we cannot draw a line does not mean there is no obvious difference in the extremes.

It's a bad argument, a bad way to convince, to say that because you can't draw a line there is no difference.

3. Vagueness and standards

Sometimes the problem with a sentence that appears to be vague is that we're not clear what standards are being used. Suppose Dick hears Harry say,

"New cars today are really expensive."

Harry might have some clear standards for what "expensive" means, perhaps that the average price of a new car today is more than 50% of what the average person earns in a year.

Or Harry might just mean that new cars cost too much for him to be comfortable buying one. That is, Harry has standards, but they're personal, not necessarily shared by anyone else. They're how he thinks or believes or feels.

Or Harry might have no standards at all. He's never thought very hard about what it means for a car to be expensive.

It's convenient to have terms for these different possibilities.

> ***Objective Claim*** A claim is *objective* if it is true independently of what anyone or any thing thinks/believes/feels.
>
> ***Subjective Claim*** A claim is *subjective* if it is not objective.

So Harry might have objective standards, or he might have subjective standards, or he might have no standards at all. Until we know what he meant, we shouldn't accept what he said as a claim.

If I say, "It's cold outside," is that objective or subjective? If it's meant as shorthand for "I feel cold when outdoors," then it's subjective, and it's a claim. But if it's meant as objective, that is, I mean to assert that it's cold independently of me or anyone, then it's too vague for us to consider it to have a truth-value. A sentence that's too vague to be an objective claim might be perfectly all right as a subjective claim, if that's what the speaker intended. After all, we don't have very precise ways to describe our feelings.

Whether a claim is subjective or objective doesn't depend on whether it's true or false, nor on whether someone knows if it's true: "$2 + 2 = 5$" is objective; "There are an even number of stars in the sky" is not subjective, even though there's no way we could know whether it's true. A subjective claim can be false, as when your co-worker says, "I felt sick yesterday, and that's why I didn't come in to work."

You might think that it's harder to know whether a subjective claim is true compared to an objective one. After all, you need to know someone's thoughts or feelings. But when it's well below freezing outside and I see my dog whining and shivering, and she feels cold to the touch, I'm almost certain that she feels cold. On the other hand, no one has a clue whether $2^{24^{483}} - 3$ is prime.

4. Moral claims

Suppose Tom says to Suzy, "Abortion is wrong."

If Suzy starts into a debate on this, she's viewing it as objective: It has a truth-value independently of what she or Tom thinks. On the other hand, Suzy might say, "Maybe abortion is wrong to you, but it's O.K. for me." Then she's taken the sentence to be a subjective claim. There's no sense arguing a subjective claim about your own feelings. If "Abortion is wrong" just means "Abortion is wrong to me," then there's nothing to debate. Suzy wouldn't be disagreeing with *that* claim, since there would be no contradiction for Suzy to say, "Abortion is not wrong to me."

But if Tom intends the sentence to be taken as an objective claim, there's a problem: What does he mean by "wrong"? In disagreement with the commands of the Bible? In disagreement with what a priest said? In disagreement with the Koran? Contravenes moral principles that are not codified but are well-known by everyone? Or something else? The sentence is too vague.

Sentences that appear to state a moral position are not easy to classify or debate. If they're meant as objective, then we need to be clear what standards are being invoked. To take a claim about morality as objective, we need to be fairly precise if we want to try to resolve apparent disagreements.

Sometimes when you challenge people to make things clearer, they'll say, "I just mean it's wrong (right) to me." Then when you press them, it turns out they're not so happy when you disagree. They're just being defensive, and what they really mean is "I have a right to believe that." Of course they do. But do they have a *reason* to believe it? It's rare that people intend moral views to be subjective.

I've got a right to believe. ≠ I have a good reason to believe.

Often when people say "That's just your opinion" they mean "You don't have any good reason to believe that, do you?" It's a challenge to provide reasons or standards.

Examples   Are the following too vague to be taken as claims? What standards are intended?

Example 1   Men are stronger than women.

Analysis   Don't bother to argue about this one until you clarify it, even though it may seem quite plausible. What's meant? Stronger for their body weight? Stronger in that the "average man" (whoever that is) can lift more than the "average woman"? Stronger emotionally?

Example 2   On the whole, it seems that people are much more conservative than they were 30 years ago.

Analysis   We get into disagreements about sentences like this and make decisions based on them. But that's a mistake: The example is too vague to have a truth-value. What does "people" mean? Everyone? What does "conservative" mean? That's *really* vague. Is George Bush conservative? Pat Buchanan? David Duke? Pat Boone?

Example 3   (Chef to new dishwasher) You should wash your hands after visiting the toilet.

Analysis Sentences with words like "should" and "ought to" presuppose some standards, much as moral claims. But often enough those standards are relatively clear. If the chef were asked to explain why the dishwasher should wash his hands (that is, if he were asked to give an argument to support the claim), then the premises he'd put forward would make explicit the standards he's invoking. So we can view the sentence as a claim

Example 4

Analysis Sure "too loud" is vague. It's subjective, too. But it serves its purpose here. We understand what he means.

Example 5 (Advertisement) Irritating skin rash? Only Cortaid® is recommended most by doctors.

Analysis How could we tell if this is true? What doctors? Recommended for what? Determined by an impartial survey? Or did they just ask doctors on their mailing list? This isn't a claim.

Example 6 (Advertisement) If you think all light yogurts are the same, we suggest you do a little *light* reading. Read light yogurt labels and you'll find that you can count on Dannon to give you 8 big ounces for 100 little calories.

Analysis The second sentence is a claim. There's no vagueness there, though it does suggest, without proof, that other light yogurts have more calories.

Example 7 Capricorn: This is the time to finalize travel and higher education plans. You are vibrant with friends and group projects. This will be a progressive period of unexpected change.

Heather Subran, *It's in the stars!* September 18, 1997

Analysis Ever notice how vague horoscopes are? It's no accident. How could you tell if this horoscope came true? There's no claim here.

Example 8 I'm feeling romantic tonight.

Analysis It's only Harry's second date with her and she said this. What in the world does she mean? This is too vague even to be a subjective claim.

Example 9 *Greeks, Turks spar over islet*
> Greek and Turkish warships faced off Tuesday in the Aegean Sea, escalating a dispute over a tiny barren island 3.8 miles off the Turkish coast.
> Both Greece and Turkey claim sovereignty to the uninhabited islet, called Imia in Greek and Kardak in Turkish.
> State Department spokesman Glynn Davies called the situation "hot and heavy . . . a little tense. The message we're sending to both governments is to please calm down and to draw back." . . .
>
> Marilyn Greene, *USA Today,* January, 1996

Analysis What's a situation that is "hot and heavy . . . a little tense"? What does it mean to say warships "faced off"? These are sentences masquerading as claims.

Example 10 Dick weighs 215 lbs.

Analysis This is an objective claim. It doesn't depend on what anyone thinks or believes.

Example 11 Dick is overweight.

Analysis If Dick's doctor says this, he's probably thinking of some standards for being overweight, and he *intends* it as an objective claim. If you or I say it, it's probably subjective, just as if we were to say someone is ugly or handsome.

Example 12 Dick is fat.

Analysis "Fat" isn't a technical term of a doctor. It's a term we use to classify people as unattractive or attractive, like "beautiful." The claim is subjective.

But what if Dick is so obese that *everyone* would agree with you that he's fat? Is this still subjective? Yes. It isn't whether we know or agree that a claim is true which determines what standards are being used.

5. Confusing objective and subjective (*Bad arguments*)

It's easy to confuse what the standards are.

Lee:	I deserve a higher mark in this course
Dr. E:	No you don't. Here's the record of your exams and papers. You earned a C.
Lee:	That's just your opinion.

Lee is treating an objective claim, "I deserve a higher mark in this course," as if it were subjective. But if it really were subjective, then there'd be no point in arguing it with Dr. E, any more than arguing whether Dr. E feels cold.

Often it's reasonable to question whether a claim is really objective. But sometimes it's just a confusion. All too often people insist that a claim is subjective— "That's just your opinion"—when they are unwilling to examine their beliefs or engage in dialogue.

Treating a subjective claim as if it were objective can also be a mistake:

> Zoe: That tie is hideous. I'm not going to the party with you wearing that.
> Dick: What are you talking about? This tie is great! It's the new style.
> Zoe: You're crazy. It's ugly.

What are Dick and Zoe arguing about? He likes the tie, she doesn't.

Exercises for Section A

1. What does it mean to say a sentence is vague?

2. Give an example of a vague sentence someone tried to pass off to you as a claim.

3. Bring to class instructions on medication or instructions from your doctor. Are they too vague?

4. Which of the following are too vague to be considered claims? (You may have to suggest a context in which it is spoken.)
   a. John always gets irritable when it's cold outside.
   b. Margery is the best cook in this school.
   c. Richard looks like he has a cold today.
   d. Dogs are better pets than cats.
   e. Public animal shelters should be allowed to sell unclaimed animals to laboratories for experimentation.
   f. Tuition at state universities should cover the entire cost to the university of a student's education.
   g. All unnatural sex acts should be prohibited by law.
   h. All citizens should have equal rights.
   i. People with disabilities are just as good as people who are not disabled.
   j. Boy are you lucky to get a date with Jane. On a scale of 1 to 10, she's at least a 9.
   k. Zoe has beautiful eyes.
   l. Dog food is cheaper at Lin's grocery store than at Smith's grocery.
   m. Alpo is cheaper at Lin's grocery store than at Smith's grocery.
   n. Spot is a big dog.
   o. Cholesterol is bad for you.
   p. English should be the official language of the United States.
   q. (spoken by Richard Nixon) "I am not a liar."
   r. Parents should be held responsible for crimes their children commit.

5. If someone wants to debate a sentence that you think is too vague to be treated as a claim, what should you do?

6. All the following are vague, but are they too vague for their intended purpose?
   a. Waiter, take back this steak and cook it longer. I asked for it medium.
   b. You call this painting job done? Don't come back until you've got it right.
   c. (On a TV weather report) There's a good chance of rain tomorrow.
   d. (On a TV weather report) There's a 70% chance of rain tomorrow.
   e. (Doctor's instructions) Your health will improve if you get more exercise.
   f. Harmful if swallowed.
   g. (Patient to doctor) Every time I swallow I get a burning sensation in my throat.

7. You hear the checkout clerk at your supermarket say, "Picasso is a better painter than Rembrandt." Comment on the possible ways we could take this depending on what standards you think she has.

8. Find an advertisement that treats a vague sentence as a claim.

9. Explain why horoscopes are vague. Does the same apply to weather forecasts?

10. What's wrong with the following attempt to convince?

    Look officer, if I were going 36 in this 35 m.p.h. zone, you wouldn't have given me a ticket, right? What about 37? But 45 you would? Well, isn't that saying that the posted speed limit is just a suggestion? Or do you write the law on what's speeding?

11. What is an objective claim? What is a subjective claim?

12. a. Give an example of a true objective claim.
    b. Give an example of a false objective claim.
    c. Give an example of a true subjective claim.
    d. Give an example of a false subjective claim.

13. Explain why a sentence that is too vague to be taken as an objective claim might be acceptable as a subjective claim.

14. Classify the following as objective or subjective. In some cases you may have to imagine who is saying it and the context. Where possible, explain your answer in terms of the standards you imagine are being used.
    a. Wool insulates better than rayon.
    b. Silk feels better on your skin than rayon.
    c. Pablo Picasso painted more oil paintings than Norman Rockwell.
    d. Bald men are more handsome.
    e. All ravens are black.
    f. Gorillas have opposable thumbs.
    g. You intend to do your very best work in this course.
    h. Murder is wrong.
    i. Your answer to Exercise 3 in Chapter 1 of this book is wrong.

    j.   Demons caused Jeffrey Dahmer to cut up and cannibalize people.

    k.   (In a law court, said by the defense attorney) The defendant is insane.

    l.   He's sick, he's got the flu.

    m. He's sick. How could anyone say something like that?

    n.   (Said to the professor after grades come out) I deserve a B not a D.

    o.   Suzy believes that the moon does not rise and set.

    p.   Dick's dog is hungry.

    q.   God exists.

15. Make up a list of five claims for your classmates to classify as objective or subjective.

16. a.   Give an example of someone treating an objective claim as if it were subjective.
    b.   Give an example of someone treating a subjective claim as if it were objective.

17.   Dick: If you don't slow down, we're going to get in an accident.
                You nearly went out of control going around that last corner.
    Zoe: That's just what you think.

    Is Zoe right? How should Dick respond?

18. Suppose you're talking with a friend and he says that abortion is wrong. You ask him what he means: Wrong according to the Bible? According to the Koran? . . . And he responds, "I mean just plain *wrong*. Not wrong according to some standard. Just wrong." How should you reply?

19. Bring to class two advertisements, one that uses only subjective claims and another that uses only objective claims.

20. Find one of the ten articles of the Bill of Rights that uses vague words and explain why the vague language is not bad.

21. Do you think that the proposed law described in the following is too vague? Explain.

    Yvette Melanson grew up in Brooklyn believing she was white and Jewish.

    It wasn't until last month that she learned she was one of the so-called "Lost Birds"–Indian children often taken illegally and adopted by white families from the 1950s to the 1970s. . . .

    Melanson and her twin brothers were whisked away from their parents' hogan by a public health nurse when they were two days old. . . .

    The (Navajo) tribe also believes that Melanson's story underscores the importance of the 1978 Indian Child Welfare Act, which is under attack in Congress. The House-passed version of the bill would remove child custody proceedings from tribal courts if the cases involve children whose birth parents did not maintain "significant social, cultural or political affiliations with the tribe."

    Tribes say the vague language could open the door for state courts to decide that some children are not "Indian enough," allowing them to be adopted by white families.   Associated Press, June 2, 1996

22. A few years ago the National Football League allowed teams to challenge a referee's call by requiring a head referee to view an instant replay of a disputed call and make a final

determination. A few years later that practice was discontinued. Once again whatever the referees on the field decide is the final call. Comment on this in terms of the distinction between objective and subjective standards.

B. Ambiguous Sentences

1. Which do you mean?

Sometimes the problem isn't that there's no clear way to understand a sentence, but that there's more than one clear understanding, and we're not sure which is intended.

> ***Ambiguous Sentence*** A sentence is *ambiguous* if there are at least two clear ways to understand it.

We cannot treat an ambiguous sentence as a claim until we agree on which reading we mean. We can tolerate some vagueness; we should never tolerate ambiguity in reasoning. For example, suppose I say:

Dogs smell better than horses.

You disagree, thinking of the lovely odor of horses in a barn on a rainy day. Then I say, "You've got to be kidding—dogs smell a lot better, because they have to in order to track game." We aren't disagreeing at all. We can replace the sentence in question by another that eliminates ambiguity, "Dogs smell better with their noses than horses do."

Vagueness = Huh?
Ambiguity = Do you mean this or do you mean that?

Sometimes it's not so easy to see that ambiguity is infecting an argument:

Saying that having a gun in the home is an accident waiting to happen is like saying that people who buy life insurance are waiting to die. We should be allowed to protect ourselves.

The speaker is trading on two ways to understand "protect": physically protect vs. emotionally or financially protect. It's easier than you might think to get confused and start scratching your head and accepting unreasonable conclusions when an ambiguous sentence is used as a premise.

2. Pronouns and quotation marks

Suppose Tom says:

I am over 6 feet tall.

Then Tom has made a claim that's true. However, if you were to say the same sentence, it might be false. And a claim has to have just one truth-value, not two. Words such as "I," "you," "it," "this," "that," and others make the truth-value of the sentence depend on who uttered it or to whom it is spoken or what you're pointing at. They create the same problems that ambiguous sentences do. Whenever these words show up, let's be sure we know what they refer to.

The device I just used of putting *quotation marks* around a word or phrase is a way of naming that word or phrase. We need quotes because there can be ambiguity whether a word or phrase is being used *as* a word or phrase. For example, suppose I say:

The Taj Mahal has eleven letters.

I don't mean the building has eleven letters, but that the name of it does, which I should indicate with quotation marks: "The Taj Mahal" has eleven letters.

We also use quotation marks as an equivalent of a wink or a nod in conversation, a nudge in the ribs indicating that I'm not to be taken literally, or that I don't really subscribe to what I'm saying. When used this way quotation marks allow us to get away with "murder."

Examples   Is there any ambiguity in the following passages?

Example 1 There is a reason I haven't talked to Robert [my ex-lover] in seventeen years (beyond the fact that I've been married to a very sexy man whom I've loved for two-thirds of that time). Laura Berman, *Ladies' Home Journal,* June, 1966

Analysis The rest of the time she just put up with him?

Example 2 Your mother says you shouldn't argue with your elders. Your instructor is older than you, and he says that this course is about arguing. How can you possibly pass this course and still be a good son or daughter?

Analysis Don't drop this course! Your mother is saying you shouldn't disagree in a disagreeable manner with your elders, while your professor is trying to teach you how to reason. There's the colloquial understanding of "argue," and then the understanding common to philosophy and English composition.

Example 3 Homosexuality can't be hereditary: Homosexual couples can't reproduce, so genes for homosexuality would have died out long ago.

Analysis The argument appears good, but only because it trades on an ambiguity in the premise "Homosexual couples can't reproduce." That's true if understood as "Homosexuals can't reproduce *as couples,*" but it is false in the sense needed to make the argument good: "Homosexuals, who happen to be in couples, each can't reproduce."

Example 4 Dr. E's dogs eat over 10 pounds of meat every week.

Analysis Is this true or false? It depends on whether it means: "Each of Dr. E's dogs eats over 10 pounds of meat every week" (big dogs!), or "Dr. E's dogs altogether eat over 10 pounds of meat every week." *It's ambiguous whether the individual or the group is meant.* That's the same problem as in Example 3.

Exercises for Section B

1. a. Can a claim be ambiguous?
    b. Can a claim be vague?

2. Decide whether each of the following sentences is a claim. If it is ambiguous, give at least two sentences corresponding to the ways it could be understood.
    a. Zoe saw the waiter with the glasses.
    b. I was invited to go to the movies a week ago.
    c. Americans bicycle thousands of miles every year.
    d. (Sign in laundromat) Customers are required to remove their clothes when the machine stops.
    e. That psychiatrist helps torture victims.
    f. Zoe is cold.
    g. The players on the basketball team had a B average in their courses.
    h. Herman Melville wrote Moby-Dick.
    i. The judge let him get away with murder.
    j. This is a civilized nation.

3. How much ambiguity can we tolerate in an argument?

4. Give an example of an ambiguous sentence you've heard recently.

5. Give an example of an ambiguous sentence from an advertisement. Is the use of ambiguity intentional? Misleading?

6. Each of the following arguments depends on ambiguity or vagueness to sound convincing. Rewrite at least one of the sentences to eliminate the ambiguity.
    a. Zoe says that nothing is better than an ice cream cone on a hot summer's day. It's a hot summer's day. So, I'd better give Zoe nothing rather than this ice cream cone.

    b. In some places, golden eagles have used the same nesting site for hundreds of years. So golden eagles live longer than humans.

    c. Dick to Zoe: Anything that's valuable should be protected. Good abs are valuable—you can tell that because everyone is trying to get them. A layer of fat will protect my abs. So I should continue to be 5 lbs. overweight.

    d. Croesus: Should I wage war on the Persians?
        Oracle at Delphi: If Croesus should wage war against the Persians, a great empire will be destroyed.

So Croesus went to war against the Persians. When he lost he returned.
Croesus: You lied! I waged war against the Persians and I lost.
Oracle at Delphi: So a great empire was destroyed.

7. Ambiguous sentences are sometimes classified by the way in which they are ambiguous.

   a. A sentence is *semantically ambiguous* if the various meanings we can assign to it arise because a word or phrase has two standard meanings. For example, "Dogs smell better than horses." The problem is with the word "smell." Give two examples from a newspaper or magazine of semantically ambiguous sentences.

   b. A sentence is *syntactically ambiguous* if the various meanings we can assign to it arise because of the placement of the words in the sentence. For example, "Police help torture victims." Is the word "torture" used here as an adjective modifying "victims," or as a verb with "Police" as subject? You can usually figure that the ambiguity is syntactical if it can be cleared up by the way you say the sentence out loud. Give two examples from a newspaper or magazine of sentences that are syntactically ambiguous.

C. Definitions

We've seen that we can get into problems, waste our time, and generally irritate each other through misunderstandings. It's always reasonable and usually wise to ask people we are reasoning with to be clear enough that we can agree on what it is we are discussing.

The general methods of making what we say clear are:

1. Replace the entire sentence by another that is not vague or ambiguous.
2. Use a definition to make a specific word or phrase precise.

Definition   A *definition* explains or stipulates how to use a word or phrase.

For example,

"Dog" means "domestic canine."

Puce is the color of a flea, purple brown or brownish purple.

"Puerile" means boyish or childish, immature, trivial.

There are several ways we can make a definition. One way, as with the definition of "dog," is to give a synonym, a word or phrase that means the same and that could be substituted for "dog" wherever that's used.

Another way is to describe: A lorgnette is a kind of eyeglass that is held in the hand, usually with a long handle.

Or we can explain, as when we say a loophole is a means of escaping or evading something unpleasant.

Or we can point:

THAT'S WHAT I MEAN BY A ST. BERNARD.

And sometimes we can infer a definition from context: He must understand "rutabaga" to mean some kind of vegetable, because otherwise what he said wouldn't make sense.

A dictionary is not an encyclopedia. When you look up a definition in a dictionary you do not find a claim that is true or false, you find an explanation of how to use a word or phrase. Dictionaries are instruction manuals.

> *Definitions are not claims.* We add them to an argument so that we can understand each other. They are not premises.

Lots of times a dictionary won't be much help, or we don't have one handy and we have to make our own definitions. But to be able to engage in reasoned discussion we don't want our definitions to be tendentious or ***persuasive definitions***. If someone defines abortion as the murder of unborn children, he's made it impossible to have a reasoned discussion on whether abortion is murder and whether a foetus is a person. *A persuasive definition is not a definition—it is a claim masquerading as a definition.*

> If you call a tail a leg, how many legs has a dog? Five? No, calling a tail a leg don't *make* it a leg.
>
> attributed to Abraham Lincoln

Examples   Which of the following are definitions? Persuasive definitions?

Example 1 Friendship: A ship big enough to carry two in fair weather, but only one in foul.

Analysis Ambrose Bierce (*The Devil's Dictionary*) may have hit on a home truth, but this is a persuasive definition.

Example 2 A dog is a man's best friend.

Analysis This is not a definition: It doesn't tell us how to use the word "dog." Not every sentence with "is" in it is a definition.

Example 3   —Maria's so rich, she can afford to pay for your dinner.
                —What do you mean "rich"?
                —She's got a Mercedes.

Analysis This is not a definition, since by "rich" we don't mean "has a Mercedes." There are lots of people who are rich who don't have a Mercedes, and some people who own Mercedes aren't rich. What we have here is an argument: "Maria has a Mercedes" is given as evidence that Maria is rich.

I just tried to convince you that "has a Mercedes" is not a good definition of "rich." How? I pointed out that someone could own a Mercedes and not be rich.

For a *good definition*, the words being defined and the words doing the defining have to work interchangeably: It's correct to use the one exactly when it's correct to use the other.

Example 4 Maria: Dr. E has an Australian shepherd.
              Manuel: What's that?
              Maria: A kind of dog they breed in Australia to herd sheep, the black and tan kind, about the size of a border collie.

Analysis Maria's defined "Australian shepherd." But Manuel probably wouldn't be able to recognize one if he's never seen one before. Breeds of dogs, colors, shapes, and many other kinds of words are often best explained by pointing.

Example 5 "Coitus" means "sexual intercourse."

Analysis Definition by synonym, the simplest, most reliable definition you can get, *if* we know the synonym.

Example 6 AIDS means "Acquired Immune Deficiency Syndrome."

Analysis This is just spelling out what the acronym stands for. A definition should tell you that AIDS is a disease and the nature of that disease.

Example 7 Getting good marks in school means that you are intelligent.

Analysis Getting good marks in school is not what the word "intelligent" means. Here, "means" is used in the sense of "If you get good marks in school, then you're intelligent."

Example 8 Microscope: an instrument consisting essentially of a lens or combination of lenses, for making very small objects, as microorganisms, look larger so that they can be seen and studied.
Webster's New World Dictionary

Analysis This is from the dictionary, so it's got to be a good definition. But if you're trying to convince someone that what she sees through a microscope is actually there—that it's not in the lens or inside the microscope like a kaleidoscope—then this definition won't do. "See, there really are microorganisms. After all, it's part of the definition of a microscope that it's just enlarging what's there." What counts as a persuasive definition can depend on the issue.

Example 9 A Pittman Elementary School teacher won a narrow Supreme Court [of Nevada] victory Tuesday allowing her to bring a service dog in training to her music class.
    One dissenting justice warned, however, that the majority opinion could have far-reaching consequences for public employers ranging from hospitals to bakeries.
    The majority decision, written by Justice Cliff Young, interprets a state law prohibiting a public place from refusing admittance to a person training a service dog as applying to employees as well as the public. The majority also found the school is a public place.
Las Vegas Review-Journal, September, 1996

Analysis The court has to decide the meaning of vague language by giving definitions. The definition can be explicit. Or the definition can be implicit: After enough cases have been decided it becomes pretty clear what the court thinks the words (ought to) mean.

Steps in making a good definition
1. Show the need for a definition.
2. State the definition.
3. Make sure the words make sense.
4. Give examples where the definition applies.
5. Give examples to show where the definition doesn't apply.
6. If necessary, contrast it with other likely definitions.
7. Revise your definition if necessary.

Summary In Chapter 1 we learned that arguments are attempts to convince using claims. So we need to distinguish different kinds of claims and be aware of sentences that look like claims but aren't.

A sentence is vague if it's unclear what the speaker intended. Vagueness is something we have to live with, but we can learn to recognize when a sentence is too vague to reason with. It's a bad argument, however, to claim that just because we can't draw a precise line there's never any clear meaning to a word.

Often the problem with a vague sentence is to determine what standards are being assumed. They could be objective—independent of what anyone or anything thinks/believes/feels, or they could be subjective, or there might not be any standards at all. A sentence that's too vague to be an objective claim might be all right as a subjective claim.

Thinking whether a claim is objective or subjective can save us a lot of heartache: We won't debate someone else's feelings. On the other hand, confusing subjective and objective leads to bad arguments.

Our reaction to a vague sentence is "Huh?"; our reaction to an ambiguous sentence, one that has two or more clear meanings, is "Which do you mean?" Ambiguous sentences should never be taken as claims.

We need to eliminate excessive vagueness and ambiguity if we are to reason together. We can do so by rewriting our arguments or speaking more precisely. Or we can be very explicit and define the words that are causing the problem. A definition isn't a claim, but is something added to an argument to clarify. Definitions shouldn't prejudge the issue; if one is a concealed claim, we call it a "persuasive definition."

Exercises for Section C

1. Which of the following are definitions? Which are persuasive definitions? Which are neither?

    a. "Dog" means "a canine creature that brings love and warmth to a human family."

    b. Domestic violence is any violent act by a spouse or lover directed against his or her partner within the confines of the home of both.

    c. A feminist is someone who thinks that women are better than men.

    d. A conservative, in politics, is one who believes that we should conserve the political structure and laws as they are as much as possible, avoiding change.

    e. A liberal is someone who wants to use your taxes to pay for what he thinks will do others the most good.

    f. Love is blind.

    g. Sexual intercourse is when a man and a woman couple sexually with the intent of producing offspring.

2. For each of the following, give both a definition and a persuasive definition:
    a. Cat litter box
    b. Spouse
    c. School cafeteria

3. For each of the following, replace "believes in" with other words that mean the same:
    a. Zoe believes in free love.
    b. Dick believes in God.
    c. Zoe believes in the Constitution.
    d. Zoe believes in herself.

4. What is a good definition?

5. Give *definitions* that make the following subjective claims objective.
    Don't rewrite the sentences.

    a. It's hot outside.
    b. Eating more than 100 grams of fat every day is unhealthy.

6. Why should we avoid persuasive definitions?

7. Give an example of a definition used in one of your other courses.

8. *Mother defends decision to let daughter fly plane*
    Jessica Dubroff's mother Friday defended her decision to allow her 7-year-old daughter to make the flight that ended in tragedy, saying, "You've no idea what this meant to Jess."

    "She had a freedom which you can't get by holding her back." a crying Lisa Blair Hathaway told NBC's "Today" while cradling her 3-year-old daughter Jasmine.

    Jessica, in an effort to become the youngest person to fly cross-country, was killed Thursday when her single-engine plane crashed in driving rain and snow shortly after takeoff, barely missing a house. Her father and flight instructor also died.

    At the site of the crash in a commercial-residential section of north Cheyenne, an impromptu memorial was set up as people dropped off flowers, teddy bears and even framed poems. By this morning the pile of teddy bears had grown to a row about 3 feet long by 8 feet wide. Someone placed a yellow flower on the driveway where the airplane's tail section came to rest.

    "I did everything so this child could have freedom and choice and have what America stands for," Hathaway said. "Liberty comes from . . . just living your life, . . . I couldn't bear to have my children in any other position."

    Hathaway said that if children were forbidden to do anything unsafe, "they would be padded up and they wouldn't go anywhere. They wouldn't ride a bicycle. My God they wouldn't do anything."   Associated Press, 1996

    Show how Ms. Hathaway's argument relies crucially on the use of vague words.

We've learned a lot about how to classify claims and what passes for a claim but isn't. Here are a few of Tom's attempts to do some exercises that use all the ideas we've learned in this chapter, along with my corrections. He's supposed to underline the terms that apply.

Dogs bark.

<u>claim</u>   subjective   ambiguous or too vague

not claim   objective   definition   persuasive definition

Yes, it's a claim. But if it's a claim, then it has to be either objective or subjective.

Cats are nasty.

<u>claim</u>   <u>subjective</u>   <u>ambiguous or too vague</u>

not claim   objective   definition   persuasive definition

No–if it's ambiguous or too vague, then it's not a claim. This is an example of a subjective claim.

Rabbits are the principal source of protein for dogs in the wild.

<u>claim</u>   subjective   ambiguous or too vague

not claim   <u>objective</u>   <u>definition</u>   persuasive definition

No–if it's a definition it's not a claim. And this is not a definition—what word is it defining? Certainly not "rabbit."

Dogs are canines that bring warmth and love to a family.

claim   subjective   ambiguous or too vague

<u>not claim</u>   objective   definition   <u>persuasive definition</u>

No. If it's a persuasive definition, then it is a claim—just masquerading as a definition.

For each of 9–19, state which of the following terms apply. More than one may apply.

claim   subjective   ambiguous or too vague

not claim   objective   definition   persuasive definition

9. Rats do not have tails longer than 37% of their body length.

10. Marriage is the legal union of a man and a woman.

11. A mark of A in this course means you know how to parrot what the professor said.

12. Steffi Graf is the best female tennis player in history.

13. This candy bar has 45% less fat than the average of the 25 leading chocolate brands, to be exact.

14. China has the largest land mass of any single country.

15. I've already seen the movie *Splash*.

16. There are 13 planets in our solar system.

17. It's cold outside.

18. Though legalizing drugs could cut taxes, as McKenna suggests, they destroy brain cells.

19. Administrators have no hearts.

20. Definitions can be classified according to their purpose.
    a. A *stipulative definition* is one that is used to give a particular meaning to a familiar word. For example, suppose we define "dog" to mean "a domestic canine that barks." Then "All dogs bark" becomes true *by definition*. Give two examples of stipulative definitions.
    b. An *explanatory definition* has the purpose of making a concept clear that may simply not be well-known to someone. For example, a carburetor is a device that mixes air and gasoline to the proper proportions for ignition before injecting the mixture into the cylinder in an internal combustion engine. Find two explanatory definitions in your other textbooks.
    c. A *precising definition* has the purpose of making a very general or vague word precise. For instance, by "cold" let's understand "below freezing." Give two examples of precising definitions.

Key Words
vague sentence	ambiguous sentence
objective claim	definition
subjective claim	persuasive definition
drawing the line	good definition

Further Study   Much of philosophy is concerned with attempts to give criteria that will turn apparently subjective claims into objective claims. A course on ethics will study whether claims about what's wrong or right can be made objective; relativism is the view that all moral claims are subjective. A course on aesthetics will analyze whether all claims about what is beautiful are equally subjective. And a course on the philosophy of law or criminal justice will introduce the methods the law uses to give objective criteria for determining what is right or wrong.

Some people believe that all there is to a claim being objective is that it is believed by enough people. That is, objectivity is just collective subjectivity. Philosophy courses deal with that debate.

Courses in nursing discuss how to deal with subjective claims by patients and vague instructions by doctors.

Some courses in English deal with definitions, particularly the correct forms and uses of definition. Courses on the philosophy of language or linguistics study the nature of definitions, ways in which definitions can be made, and misuses of definitions. Ambiguity and vagueness are also covered in English composition and rhetoric courses.

Writing Lesson 2

We know that before we begin deliberating we should make the issue precise enough that someone can agree or disagree. Vague or ambiguous sentences are not claims.

Make the following sentence sufficiently precise that you could debate it:

"Student athletes should be given special leniency when the instructor assigns course marks."

Your definition or explanation should be at most one page long. That's at most one page, not at least or exactly one page.

To give you a better idea of what you're expected to do, I've included Tom's homework, along with my comments. He's still struggling.

Tom Wyzyczy
Critical Thinking
Section 4
Writing Lesson 2

"All unnatural sex acts should be prohibited by law."

Before we can debate this we have to say what it means. I think that "unnatural sex act" should mean any kind of sexual activity that most people think is unnatural. And "prohibited by law" should mean there's a law against it.

You've got the idea, but your answer is really no improvement. You can delete the first sentence. And you can delete "I think." We can guess that because you wrote the paper.

Your proposed definition of "unnatural sex act" is too vague. It's reminiscent of the standard the U.S. Supreme Court uses to define obscenity: prevailing community standards. In particular, what do you mean by "sexual activity"? Does staring at a woman's breasts count? And who are "people"? The people in your church? Your neighborhood? Your city? Your state? Your country? The world?

Of course "legally prohibited" means there's a law against it. But what kind of law? A fine? A prison sentence? A penalty depending on severity of the offense? How do you determine the severity?

Mary Ellen has a better idea how to do the assignment.

Mary Ellen Zzzyzzx
Critical Thinking
Section 4
Writing Lesson 2

"All unnatural sex acts should be prohibited by law."

By "unnatural sex act" I shall mean any sexual activity involving genitals, consensual or not, *except* between a man and a woman who are both over sixteen and in a way that could lead to procreation if they wanted it to and which is unobserved by others.

By "prohibited by law" I shall mean it would be a misdemeanor comparable to getting a traffic ticket.

I don't really think that everything else is unnatural, but I couldn't figure out any other way to make it precise. Is that what we're supposed to do?   Mary Ellen

You did just fine. Really, the burden to make it precise would be on the person suggesting the sentence be taken as a claim. Most attempts are going to seem like a persuasive definition. But at least you now have a claim you could debate. If the other person thinks it's the wrong definition, that would be a good place to begin your discussions.

---

3   What is a Good Argument?

A. What is a Good Argument?

An argument is a collection of claims. But not every collection of claims is an argument. There must be some intention to connect the premises to the conclusion: The premises are meant to "lead to" or "establish" or "give support for" the conclusion.

What makes an argument good? We don't want to say a good argument is one that actually convinces someone. Who's being convinced? Me? You? Maybe you're in a bad mood and nothing would convince you, or your friend is drunk and you can't convince him. Does that mean the argument is bad?

No, an argument is good or bad independently of you or me.

> **Good Argument**   A *good argument* is one in which the premises give good reason to believe the conclusion is true.

Most of this course will be about what qualifies as "good reason": We want a definition that will make sentences like "This is a good argument" objective claims. It's not a matter of taste.

39

We can start by noting that for an argument to be good, it should pass two tests:

1. There should be good reason to believe the premises are true.
2. The premises lead to, support, establish the conclusion.

These tests are independent of each other, as the next two examples show.

Premises and conclusion true, but premises don't support the conclusion.

Your instructor is paid to teach at this school.

You are a student at this school.

Therefore, your instructor teaches critical thinking.

Premises support the conclusion, but one of the premises is false.

Your instructor is a teacher.

All teachers are men.

So your instructor is a man.

If one of the premises is false, or we don't know it's false but it doesn't seem very plausible, then we have no reason to accept the conclusion. From a false premise we can derive both true claims and false claims. For example,

---

False premise, true conclusion.

The author of this book is a dog.

Dogs bark.

So the author of this book barks.

The conclusion follows and is true. Arf arf.

False premise, false conclusion.

The author of this book is a dog.

Dogs lick people.

So the author of this book licks his students.

The conclusion follows in this case, too. But the conclusion is false. Believe me, it's false.

We say a claim is **dubious** or **implausible** if we have no good reason to believe it's true, yet we're not sure it's false. If we know that a claim is true, or we have very good reason to believe it's true, we'll say the claim is *highly plausible*.

An argument is no better than its least plausible premise.

To pass the first test for an argument to be good, we have to ask whether we have good reason to believe the premises are true. In Chapter 5 we'll consider that.

Should we be interested in the second test if we don't know if the premises are true? Yes. Compare the evaluation of an argument whose premises aren't known to be true to applying for a home loan. A couple goes in and fills out all the forms. The loan officer looks at their answers. She might tell them right then that they don't qualify. That is, even though she doesn't know if the claims they made about their income and assets are true, she can see that even if those claims are true, the couple won't qualify for a loan. So why bother to investigate whether what they said is true? On the other hand, she could tell them that they'll qualify if those claims are true. Then she goes out and makes phone calls, checks credit references, etc., and finds out if the couple was lying.

Good reasoning is concerned with what follows from what, as well as what is true. In this chapter we will try to decide what we mean by "the conclusion follows from the premises."

B. The Connection Between the Premises and Conclusion

We want to give some explicit, clear criteria for what we mean when we say that one claim *follows from* some other claims.

It's not enough that both the premises and conclusion are true, as the first example showed. And we might not know whether the premises are true. We have to consider the ways that the premises *could be true.*

We can't go to an encyclopedia to look up all the ways a claim could be true, nor ask the manager of a supermarket. They can only tell us, perhaps, what is true. To survey all ways the premises *could be* true we have to imagine those ways.

Then we ask: Among all the ways the premises could be true, is there one in which the conclusion is false? Suppose we find that there is no way the premises could be true and conclusion false. In that case if the premises are true the conclusion is true.

> All dogs bark.
> Ralph is a dog.
> Therefore, Ralph barks.

It's impossible for the premises to be true and conclusion false.

Valid Argument   An argument is *valid* if it is impossible for the premises to be true and the conclusion false (at the same time). We say an argument is *invalid* if it is not valid.

From the examples above we know a valid argument can have a false premise.

Valid ≠ Good

A valid argument that has true premises must have a true conclusion. Yet suppose we're given an argument and find that there is a way the premises could be true and conclusion false, but only in preposterous situations. Then the premises would give us very good reason to believe the conclusion. They just wouldn't give us certainty.

For example, suppose you've heard there are parakeets on sale down at the local mall. You know your neighbor has a birdcage in his garage, and you wonder if it will be big enough for one of those parakeets. You make the following argument:

> All parakeets anyone anyone I know has ever seen or heard or read about
>   are under 2' tall.
> Therefore, the parakeets on sale at Boulevard Mall are under 2' tall.

Surveying all the ways the premise could be true, we think that yes, a new supergrow bird food could have been formulated and the parakeets at the local mall are really 2' tall, we just haven't heard about it. Or a rare giant parakeet from the Amazon forest could have been discovered and brought here. Or a UFO might have abducted a parakeet by mistake, hit it with growing rays, and the bird is gigantic.

All of these ways the premise could be true and conclusion false are *so very unlikely,* almost preposterous, that we would have very good reason to believe the conclusion if the premise is true. We just wouldn't have absolute certainty. The conclusion might be false.

> ***Strong and Weak Arguments***   We classify invalid arguments on a scale from very strong to weak. An argument is *very strong* if it is almost impossible for the premises to be true and the conclusion false (at the same time). An argument is *weak* if it is likely that the premises could be true and conclusion false (at the same time).

Either an argument is valid or it isn't. There are no degrees to it. But whether an argument is strong is a matter of degree.

Here's how Lee thinks through the steps in evaluating whether the conclusion follows from the premises.

Lots of people think that to reason logically and be critical in your thinking you have to squelch your imagination. They think that "She's logical" is the opposite of "She's creative." But they're wrong. To evaluate arguments, you have to imagine all possible ways the premises could be true. You have to be creative.

Suppose we find that the argument is valid or strong. Does that mean it's a good argument? No. To be a good argument, there must also be good reason for us to believe the premises are true. It may be that we can delete a false premise and still have a strong or valid argument, but that would be a recasting of the original argument. In the next chapter we'll study when we're justified in rewriting what is said.

But if the conclusion doesn't follow—if the argument is not valid or strong—then the premises don't give us good reason to believe the conclusion.

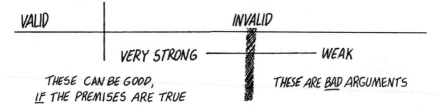

- Only invalid arguments are classified from very strong to weak.
- Every weak argument is bad.
- Not every valid or strong argument is good.

C. The Tests for an Argument to Be Good

A valid or strong argument with true premises can still be a bad argument:

> Dogs have souls.
> Therefore, you should treat dogs humanely.

This is bad because the premise is more dubious than the conclusion. The premises of an argument have to be more plausible than the conclusion for an argument to give us good reason to believe the conclusion.

Suppose you overhear:

> —God exists.
> —How do you know?
> —'Cause the Bible says so.
> —But why do you think that's true?
> —'Cause God wrote the Bible.

The first person is arguing in a circle. Ultimately, his premises are no more plausible than the conclusion. It's a bad argument.

Here's another example from the first writing lesson:

> Student athletes should not be given special leniency in assigning their course marks because that wouldn't be fair to the other students.

What does "fair" mean? It means "treat everyone the same way." So the argument is: You shouldn't treat athletes differently, because you should treat everyone the same way. The premise may be true, but it's just a restatement of the conclusion.

These arguments are deceptive because they seem to say something significant. Generally, we can say an argument ***begs the question*** if it's circular, or a premise just restates the conclusion, or both the premise and conclusion assume the truth of the same dubious claim.

> She: You're mean.
> He: Why?
> She: 'Cause you're not nice.
> One of my students told her boyfriend this and she convinced him.
> I hope for her sake he doesn't read this book.

> ### Tests for an Argument to be Good
> - There should be good reason to believe the premises are true.
> - The argument must be valid or strong.
> - The premises are more plausible than the conclusion.

The rest of this course will be devoted to learning how to decide if an argument passes these tests, and whether every argument that passes these tests really is good.

Examples   Are the following arguments valid? If not valid, where on the scale from very strong to weak does the example lie? If the example is valid or very strong, is it good?

Example 1   Dick: Maria is divorced.
            Zoe: I didn't know that. So Maria was married.

Analysis   Zoe makes a valid argument: Maria is divorced, so Maria was married. It is impossible for the premise to be true and conclusion false. It's valid because that's what the word "divorced" means. Still, we don't know if the argument is good, because we don't know if the premise is true.

Example 2   Dr. E is a philosophy professor. All professors prefer dogs to cats. So Dr. E prefers dogs to cats.

Analysis   The argument is valid. But even though the conclusion is true, it's a bad argument because the second premise is false. The premises give us no good reason to believe the conclusion more than just stating the conclusion.

Example 3   Dick is a bachelor. So Dick was never married.

Analysis   This is not valid: Dick *could have been* divorced. This argument is weak: It's not all that unlikely that the premise could be true and conclusion false.

Example 4   Good teachers give fair exams, and Dr. E gives fair exams. So Dr. E is a good teacher.

Analysis   The premises of the argument are true. And the conclusion is true, too. But is it a good argument? Can we imagine a way in which the premises could be true and conclusion false? Yes: Dr. E might bore his students to tears and just copy good exams from the instructor's manual of the textbook. So the argument is weak. For the argument to be valid, we need more than that good teachers give fair exams; we need that *only* good teachers give fair exams.

> How do we show that an argument is not valid? *We give an example, a possible way in which the premises could be true and conclusion false.*

Example 5   Mary Ellen's hair is naturally brown. Today Mary Ellen's hair is red. So Mary Ellen dyed her hair.

Analysis   Could the premises be true and conclusion false? Perhaps: Mary Ellen might be taking a new medication that has a strong effect, or she might have gotten too close to the machinery when they were painting her car, or . . . These are all pretty preposterous, but still possible. So the argument is strong, not valid. And if the premises are true, it's a good argument.

Example 6 Harry: Every time I can remember eating eggs I've broken out in a rash. It couldn't be the butter or oil they're fried in, 'cause I remember it happening when I had hard-boiled eggs, too. I must be allergic to eggs.

Analysis   This is a strong argument, with good evidence for the conclusion. But it is not valid: There could be a strange new virus that Harry caught whose only symptom is that it makes him sick when he eats eggs. In a week or two he might be fine.

Example 7 Prosecuting attorney: The defendant intended to kill Louise. He bought a gun three days before he shot her. He practiced shooting at a target that had her name written across it. He staked out her home for two nights. He shot her twice.

Analysis   The argument is strong: The prosecuting attorney gives good evidence that the conclusion is true, an argument that establishes beyond a reasonable doubt "The defendant intended to kill Louise." If the premises are true, it's a good argument. But it's not valid: We don't know the defendant's thoughts, and the conclusion might be false.

Example 8 (Continuing Example 7)

I DIDN'T MEAN TO KILL LOUISE. I ONLY WANTED TO SCARE HER. THAT'S WHAT WAS IN MY MIND, ONLY THAT, I SWEAR.

Analysis   The defendant may be telling the truth. All he says may be true, yet the argument is weak: We have no good reason to believe the conclusion. What he says wouldn't create reasonable doubt.

---

2 OJ Verdicts?

The standard in a criminal case is that the government has to prove the defendant guilty "beyond a reasonable doubt." For a civil case, however, brought by one person against another, the standard is much lower. To collect damages you only have to prove with "a preponderance of evidence" that the other side did you harm. That's why there's no contradiction in finding O.J. innocent of murder, but liable for the death of his ex-wife.

Consider classifying arguments from strong to weak as a bet: If you know the premises are true, would it be a great bet, a 50-50 chance, or an awful bet that the conclusion is true? How likely is it that the premises could be true and conclusion false?

Example 9	Tom:	You didn't have eggs in the house this morning, did you?
	Dick:	No. Why?
	Tom:	Well, you've got some in the refrigerator now.
	Dick:	Zoe must have bought eggs, since she knew we were out.

Analysis   This isn't valid. Zoe's mom could have brought over the eggs; when they were out the landlord might have brought them over; a guest who was staying with them might have bought them; . . . There are so many likely possibilities for the premises to be true and conclusion false that the argument is weak.

Example 10	Tom:	You didn't have eggs in the house this morning, did you?
	Dick:	No. Why?
	Tom:	Well, you've got some in the refrigerator now.
	Dick:	Zoe must have bought eggs, since she knew we were out.
	Tom:	Are you sure?
	Dick:	Sure. No one else has a key to the apartment. And Zoe didn't plan to have any guests over today.

Analysis   This argument is stronger than the last one, because some of the possible ways the premises could be true and conclusion false have been ruled out. But it's still not very strong.

Yet if we can't tell exactly where this lies on the scale from very strong to weak, isn't the whole business of classifying arguments worthless? No, that's a *drawing the line fallacy*. There may be some fuzziness in the middle, but we can distinguish strong arguments from weak ones.

Example 11	Tom:	You didn't have eggs in the house this morning, did you?
	Dick:	No. Why?
	Tom:	Well, you've got some in the refrigerator now.
	Dick:	Zoe must have bought eggs, since she knew we were out.
	Tom:	Are you sure?
	Dick:	Sure. No one else has a key to the apartment. And we never let anyone else in.
	Tom:	But didn't your neighbor Mrs. Zzzyzzx say she had some eggs from her cousins' farm?
	Dick:	Yes, but Zoe said we should only bring food into the house that we'd purchased ourselves at the health-food store. And she always keeps her word.

Analysis   This argument is a lot stronger because so many of the ways have been ruled out in which the premises could be true and conclusion false. But it's still not valid: The landlord could have gotten a locksmith to open the door, and then before he went out put eggs in the refrigerator; or a burglar could have broken in and left some eggs behind; or Zoe could have bought a chicken and left it in the refrigerator and it laid eggs there; or . . . These are possible ways that the premises could be true and conclusion false, but they are all so preposterous that the argument is very strong: Tom and Dick have good reason to believe that Zoe bought the eggs.

We've seen good arguments and we've seen bad arguments. A good argument gives us good reason to believe the conclusion. *A bad argument tells us nothing about whether the conclusion is true or false.* If we encounter a bad argument, we have no more reason to believe or disbelieve the conclusion than we had before. *A bad argument does **not** prove that the conclusion is false or even dubious.*

Exercises for Sections A–C

1. What is an argument?

2. What is a good argument?

3. What does it mean to say an argument is valid?

4. What does it mean to say an argument is strong?

5. If an argument is valid or strong, does that mean it is a good argument? Explain.

6. How can you show that an argument is not valid?

7. If an argument is valid and its premises are true, is its conclusion true, too? Explain.

8. If an argument is bad, what does that show about its conclusion?

9. If an argument is strong and its premises are true, is its conclusion true, too? Explain.

10. To be classified as good, an argument must pass three tests. What are they?

11. a.   Make up an example of an argument that is valid and good.
    b.   Make up an example of an argument that is valid and bad.

12. a. Make up an example of an argument that is strong and good.
    b. Make up an example of an argument that is strong and bad.

13. Make up an example of an argument that is weak.

14. Can we show that an argument is not valid by showing that its conclusion is false? Example or explanation.

15. To decide whether an argument is good, does it depend on whether it convinced anyone?

16. Can an argument be both valid and strong?

17. What do we call an argument with a false premise?

18. Which, according to the definitions we're using, are incorrect uses of "valid" or "invalid"? For incorrect ones, rewrite the sentence without that word.

    a. Your parking sticker is invalid.
    b. That's not a valid answer to my question.
    c. Your reasoning is invalid.
    d. I can't believe the referee made that decision. It's completely invalid.
    e. Tom has a valid reason for showing up late to football practice.
    f. That's not a valid excuse.

For exercises 19–24, select the claim that makes the argument valid. (You're not supposed to judge whether the claim is plausible, just whether it makes the argument valid.)

19. The dogs are drinking a lot of water today. It must be hot.

    a. Dogs always drink when they are hot.
    b. Every dog will drink when the weather is hot.
    c. Hot weather means dogs will drink.
    d. Only on hot days do dogs drink a lot of water.
    e. None of the above.

20. Every color monitor I've had either was defective and had to be returned or else burned out in less than two years. So you'd be foolish to buy a color monitor.

    a. You should do what I tell you to do.
    b. Every color monitor will be defective or go bad.
    c. All monitors that are reliable are not color.
    d. None of the above.

21. Puff is a cat. So Puff meows.

    a. Anything that meows is a cat.
    b. Dogs don't meow.
    c. All cats meow.
    d. Most cats meow.
    e. None of the above.

22. Spock is a Vulcan. So Spock doesn't feel emotion.

    a. Vulcans aren't humans.
    b. Humans can't spot Vulcan emotions.

   c. No Vulcan has emotions.

   d. Most Vulcans feel no emotion most of the time.

   e. None of the above.

23. The President is on every channel on television. So he must be making an important speech.

   a. Only Presidents make important speeches on television.

   b. When the President makes an important speech on television, he's on every channel.

   c. When the President is on every channel on TV, he's making an important speech.

   d. Presidents only make important speeches.

   e. None of the above.

24. If Spot gets into the garbage, Dick will hit him with a newspaper. So Dick hit Spot.

   a. The garbage is a bad thing for Spot to get into.

   b. Whenever Spot gets into the garbage, Dick hits him.

   c. Whenever Dick hits Spot, Spot was in the garbage.

   d. Spot got into the garbage.

   e. None of the above.

25. In a civil case one person or company attempts to collect damages from another. According to the instructions the judge gives in California,

> The plaintiff has the burden of proving by a preponderance of the evidence all of the facts necessary to establish . . .

"Preponderance of evidence" means:

> Such evidence as, when weighed with that opposed to it, has more convincing force and the greater probability of truth.

For a criminal case, the government must prove the issue of guilt beyond reasonable doubt. In the California Code "reasonable doubt" is defined:

> It is not mere possible doubt; because everything relating to human affairs, and depending on moral evidence, is open to some possible or imaginary doubt. It is that state of the case, which, after the entire comparison and consideration of the evidence, leaves the minds of jurors in that condition that they can not say they feel an abiding conviction, to a moral certainty, of the truth of the charge.

   a. Do these definitions give objective criteria for the jury?

   b. How would you rewrite these two definitions to put them on the scale from weak to strong (as in the diagram on p. 43)?

   c. In some trials of cases concerning mortgages, separate property in a marriage, naturalization questions, and others, a different standard of proof is required:

> The plaintiff has the burden of proving by clear and convincing evidence.

"Clear and convincing evidence" is understood in California as:

> Clear, explicit and unequivocal; so as to leave no substantial doubt; sufficiently strong to command the unhesitating assent of every reasonable mind.

How does this compare to the standards for criminal and civil cases?

D. Strong vs. Valid Arguments

We know that we can't always rely on valid arguments. But when should we expect to use a strong argument?

A strong argument with true premises is sometimes better than a valid argument with the same conclusion when we reason from experience. For example,

(A)   All parakeets are under 2' tall.
          Therefore, the parakeets on sale at Boulevard Mall are under 2' tall.

(B)   All parakeets anyone in this class has ever seen or heard or read about
              are under 2' tall.
          Therefore, the parakeets on sale at Boulevard Mall are under 2' tall.

Which is the better argument? The first is valid; the second is strong.

Here (B) is the better argument, because its premise is clearly true. It gives us good, though not certain reason to believe that its conclusion is true. We do not know if the premise of (A) is true. What good is validity if the premise is dubious? The only way I know to establish the premise of (A) is with the argument:

All parakeets anyone in this class has ever seen or heard or read about
    are under 2' tall.
Therefore, all parakeets are under 2' tall.

But this reduces the valid argument (A) to the strong argument (B). Sometimes a strong argument is preferable to a valid one.

Folks often indicate when they make an argument that they think it's valid or that it's strong. For example,

Dick says he was in the circus. He knows all the lingo and I've seen him juggle. And when the circus people were in town they all knew him. So Dick really was in the circus.

Dick says he was in the circus. He knows all the lingo and I've seen him juggle. And when the circus people were in town they all knew him. So maybe Dick was in the circus.

The words "maybe" and "really" just tell us the speaker's attitude toward the claim. These are the *same argument*: They have the same premises, and the conclusion of both is "Dick was in the circus." Using "so really" instead of "so" lets us know that the speaker thinks the argument is valid, but that doesn't make the argument valid. You can't make an argument strong by calling it strong, anymore than I can make you a horse by calling you a horse.

Words like "so" or "therefore" are not part of a claim. They serve to tell us that the conclusion is coming up.

Whether an argument is valid or strong:
  Does not depend on us.
  Does not depend on whether the premises are true.
  Does not depend on whether we know the premises are true.
It depends only on the relation between the premises and conclusion.

Summary   We said that a good argument is one that gives good reason to believe that the conclusion is true. We wanted an objective standard for what "good reason" means, so that judging an argument won't be a matter of taste.

We saw that we could split into two questions the evaluation of an argument: Are the premises highly plausible? Do the premises lead to the conclusion? In this chapter we considered only the second.

The best connection the premises can have to the conclusion is if it's impossible for the premises to be true and conclusion false: The argument is valid. But valid ≠ good. The premises could be false. Or they could be true, but no more plausible than the conclusion.

Or the premises could be true and conclusion false, but only in preposterous situations. Then the premises do give us good reason to believe the conclusion, and we call the argument "strong."

In the end, then, there are three tests an argument must pass to be good:

There should be good reason to believe its premises.
It must be valid or strong.
Its premises must be more plausible than its conclusion.

Some arguments fail the last test by being circular or restating a premise in a concealed way as the conclusion. We call those "begging the question."

Valid arguments give us certainty, if the premises are true. Strong arguments give us high likelihood but not certainty that the conclusion is true, if the premises are true. Depending on the conclusion we're trying to prove, and the evidence we have, we have to decide whether it's best to make a valid argument or a strong argument.

Exercises for Chapter 3

1. Is it always better to make our arguments valid rather than strong? Explain.

2. Identifying the conclusion of an argument is important. Words like "therefore" or "so" indicate a conclusion is coming up. List at least five more words or phrases that we use to introduce a conclusion. List five words that indicate premises.

3. If an argument is bad, what does that tell us about the conclusion?

4. A mathematician suspects that an extremely abstruse mathematical claim is true. He isn't sure, but he decides to investigate its consequences. He finds after some investigation that using the claim as a premise he can prove that a well-known theorem of

mathematics is false. What should he conclude?

5. If we want to give a good argument with a subjective claim as conclusion, would it be better for it to be valid or strong?

6. To prove an objective claim should we always give an argument that is valid? Explanation or example.

7. Which subjects in your school would employ only valid arguments? Which would employ primarily strong arguments? Which would rely on a mix of the two?

We've learned a lot about how to classify arguments. Here are some of Tom's answers to exercises that require all the ideas we've learned in this chapter. He's supposed to answer the italicized questions. I've left my comments attached.

Ralph is a dog. So Ralph barks.

Argument? (yes or no) Yes.

Conclusion: Ralph barks.

Premises: Ralph is a dog.

Classify: <u>valid</u>   very strong ——————— weak

If not valid, show why:

Good argument?

    It's good (passes the three tests). √

    It's bad because a premise is false.

    It's bad because it's weak.

    It's bad because a premise is more dubious than the conclusion.

    It's valid or strong, but you don't know if the premises are true, so you can't say if
       it's good or bad.

    *No! This isn't valid. Ralph might be a basenji. But it's fairly strong, so a pretty good
    argument if the premise is true—which you don't know for sure.*

Whenever Spot barks, there's a cat outside. Since he's barking now, there must be a cat outside.

Argument? (yes or no) Yes.

Conclusion: Whenever Spot barks, there's a cat outside.

Premises: Spot's barking now. There must be a cat outside.

Classify: valid   very strong ————X——— weak

If not valid, show why: Maybe he's barking because the garbageman's there.

Good argument?

    It's good (passes the three tests).

    It's bad because a premise is false.

    It's bad because it's weak. √

    It's bad because a premise is more dubious than the conclusion.

    It's valid or strong, but you don't know if the premises are true, so you can't say if
       it's good or bad.

    No. The conclusion is: "There's a cat outside." Ask yourself where you could put "therefore" in the argument. Which claims are evidence for which others? The argument is valid. But the premise "Whenever Spot barks, there's a cat outside" is implausible. As you point out, what about the garbageman? So it's not a good argument.

Alison is Kim's sister, so Alison and Kim have the same mom and dad.

Argument? (yes or no) Yes.

Conclusion: Alison and Kim have the same mom and dad.

Premises: Alison is Kim's sister.

Classify: valid   very strong ————————X— weak

If not valid, show why: One of them might be adopted. Or they are half-sisters.

Good argument?

> It's good (passes the three tests).
> It's bad because a premise is false.
> It's bad because it's weak. √
> It's bad because a premise is more dubious than the conclusion.
> It's valid or strong, but you don't know if the premises are true, so you can't say if
>   it's good or bad.
>
> *Good work!*

Bob has worked as a car mechanic for twenty years. Anyone who works that long at a job must enjoy it. So Bob enjoys being a car mechanic.

Argument? (yes or no) Yes.

Conclusion: Bob enjoys being a car mechanic.

Premises: Bob has worked as a car mechanic for twenty years. Anyone who works
    that long at a job enjoys it.

Classify: valid   very strong ————————X— weak

If not valid, show why: Bob might not be able to get any other job.

Good argument?

> It's good (passes the three tests).
> It's bad because a premise is false.
> It's bad because it's weak. √
> It's bad because a premise is more dubious than the conclusion.
> It's valid or strong, but you don't know if the premises are true, so you can't say if
>   it's good or bad.
>
> *Wrong! The argument is <u>valid</u>. What you showed is that the second premise is false or at least very dubious. So the argument <u>is</u> bad, but not for the reason you gave.*

For Exercises 8–34 answer the following questions:

Argument? (yes or no)

Conclusion:

Premises:

Classify: valid   very strong ———————— weak

If not valid, show why:

Good argument? (choose one)

It's good (passes the three tests).

It's bad because a premise is false.

It's bad because it's weak.

It's bad because a premise is more dubious than the conclusion.

It's valid or strong, but you don't know if the premises are true, so you can't say if it's good or bad.

8. Your hair was long. Now it's short. So you must have got a hair cut.

9. All cars have wheels. My bicycle has wheels. Therefore, my bicycle is a car.

10. Intelligent students study hard. Zoe studies hard. So Zoe is intelligent.

11. Dogs bark. Spot barks. So Spot is a dog.

12. All cats meow. Puff is a cat. So Puff meows.

13. All licensed drivers in Utah have taken a driver's test. Dick has taken a driver's test in Utah. So Dick is a licensed driver in Utah.

14. No dog meows. Puff meows. So Puff is not a dog.

15. No cat barks. Spot is not a cat. So Spot barks.

16. All students who study hard are liked by their teachers. Zoe is liked by all her teachers. Therefore, Zoe studies hard.

17. Spot is a black and white dog. Therefore, Spot is a dog.

18. Dick: I got sick after eating at the school cafeteria this week.
    Zoe: Me, too. What happened?
    Dick: Runs and dizziness.
    Zoe: Exactly the same for me.
    Dick: You know, the same thing happened to me last week.
    Zoe: It must be the food at the school cafeteria that's making us sick.

19. Dick missed almost every basket he shot in the game. He couldn't run, he couldn't jump. He should give up basketball.

20. All people who haven't gone to college are bad company. The students in this class have gone to college. So no students in this class are bad company.

21. I'm telling you I'm not at fault. How could I be? She hit me from the rear. Anytime you get rear-ended it's not your fault.

22. What do you want to eat for dinner? Well, we had fish yesterday, and pasta the other day. We haven't eaten chicken for awhile. How about some chicken with potatoes?

23. Dick: I just heard you on the phone to the travel agent. What's up? I thought we were going to drive to San Francisco.
    Zoe: Look, your car's broken down twice in the last two weeks. It would be stupid to take it on a long trip to San Francisco.

24. Maria: Almost all the professors I've met at this school are liberals.
    Manuel: So to get a teaching job here it must help to be a liberal.

25. —Either Sam is a professor or he has learned a lot on his own from reading.
    —He's not a professor, he's a restaurant owner.
    —So Sam has learned a lot on his own.

26. Tom: If Dick bought a new car, he must have had more money than I thought.
    Harry: Well, look, there's the new hatchback he bought.
    Tom: So Dick must have had more money than I thought.

27. Suzy: Mary Ellen wasn't home last night when I called.
    Zoe: She said she was going to stay home last night to study.
    Suzy: She's been pretty interested in Harry. I bet she went out with him.

28. Suzy: Mary Ellen wasn't home last night when I called.
    Zoe: She said she was going to stay home last night to study.
    Suzy: She's been pretty interested in Harry. I bet she went out with him.
    Zoe: Do you really think so?
    Suzy: Sure. She's so serious about her studies. Only a good-looking guy could drag
           her away from her books.

29. Suzy: Mary Ellen wasn't home last night when I called.
    Zoe: She said she was going to stay home last night to study.
    Suzy: She's been pretty interested in Harry. I bet she went out with him.
    Zoe: Do you really think so?
    Suzy: Sure. She's so serious about her studies. Only a good-looking guy could drag
           her away from her books. And Harry told me he was planning to call her.
    Zoe: You're probably right. I talked with her mom this morning, and if there'd been
           some sort of emergency at her place, she would have said.
    Suzy: And Harry's the only guy she's even talked about in the last month.

30. Every student who has ever taken a critical thinking course from this instructor has
    gotten an A. Therefore, I will get an A in this course.

31. Dick was dressed. Now Dick is naked. So Dick removed his clothes.

32. Your instructor was born. Therefore, your instructor will die.

33. No one will live forever. So your instructor will die.

34. There are 30 seconds left in the football game. The 49ers have 35 points. The Dolphins
    have 7 points. So the 49ers will win.

Key Words   good argument   strong argument
                   plausible claim   weak argument
                   dubious claim   tests for an argument to be good
                   valid argument   begging the question

Writing Lesson 3

We've been learning how to analyze arguments. Now it's time to try to write one.

You know what tests a good argument must pass. It must be composed of claims, and claims only. It shouldn't contain any vague or ambiguous sentences. It must be valid or strong, or at least as strong as the issue allows. And the premises should be plausible.

Write an argument either for or against the following:

"Everyone should use a bicycle as his or her main form of transportation."

Your argument should be at most one page long.
Just list the premises and the conclusion. Nothing more.
Check whether your instructor has chosen a *DIFFERENT TOPIC* for this assignment.

It doesn't matter if you never thought about the subject, or whether you think it's terribly important. This is an exercise, a chance for you to sharpen your skills in writing arguments. It's the process of writing an argument that should be your focus.

If you have trouble coming up with an argument, think how you would respond if you heard someone say the claim at a city council meeting or if someone in class said it. Make two lists: *pro* and *con*. Then write the strongest argument you can.

Don't get carried away. You're not expected to spin a one-page argument into three pages. You can't use any of the literary devices you've been taught are good fillers. List the premises and conclusion—that's all. And remember, premises and conclusion don't have those words "therefore" or "I think" attached. Once you can write an argument in this outline form, you can worry about making your arguments sound pretty. It's clarity we want first.

To give you a better idea of what you're expected to do, I've included Tom's argument on a different topic.

Tom Wyzyczy
Critical Thinking
Section 4
Writing Lesson 3

Issue: Students should be required to take a course on critical thinking.

Definition: I'll understand the issue as "College students should be required to take a course on critical thinking before graduating."

Premises:

A critical thinking course will help students to write better in their other courses.

A critical thinking course will help students to read assignments in all their other courses.

A critical thinking course will make students become better informed voters.

Most students who take a critical thinking course appreciate it.

Professors will be able to teach their subjects better if they can assume their students know how to reason.

Critical thinking is a basic skill and should be required, like Freshman Composition.

Conclusion: College students should be required to take a course on critical thinking before graduating.

Tom, it's good that you began by making the issue precise. Even better is that you realized the definition wasn't a premise. You've learned a lot from the last assignment.

Your argument is pretty good. You've used claims for your premises. Some of them are a bit vague. But only the fourth is so vague you should delete it or make it more precise. All of your premises support your conclusion. But the argument's not strong as stated. You're missing some glue, something to fill the gap. You're piling up evidence, but to what end? To your third premise, I'd just say "SO?" And you never used that you're talking about <u>college</u> students. Won't your argument work just as well for high school? Is that what you want?

We'll look at how to fill in what you've missed in the next chapter.

Writing Lesson 4

For each of the following write the best argument you can that has as conclusion the claim that accompanies the cartoon. List only the premises and conclusion. If you believe the best argument is only weak, explain why.

Do not make up a story about the cartoon—this isn't a course in creative writing. Use what you see in the cartoon and your common knowledge.

1.

Spot ran away.

2.

Spot chased a cat.

3.

Professor Zzzyzzx is cold.

4.

Dick should not drink the coffee.

4　Repairing Arguments

A. The Need to Repair Arguments.

> Maria:　Mary Ellen had to go to the hospital with asthma, right after
> visiting a friend who has a cat. She was really sick. She must
> be allergic to cats.
>
> Tom:　Maria, you're not reasoning well. That's not a valid argument.

Maria shouldn't clobber Tom. Tom's going through a normal phase when we begin
to analyze arguments: If the argument isn't perfect as stated, we think it's bad.

But Maria did make a good argument. She just left out an obvious premise:
"Almost anyone who gets asthma immediately after being exposed to a cat is allergic
to cats." Why bother to say it when everyone knows that, and it's obvious that's
what is left out?

And recall Exercise 25 of Chapter 1. It seemed obvious, though it was never
stated, that the conclusion, the point of the argument, was "Homosexuals should
have the right to marry each other." You couldn't even make sense out of what was
said if you didn't spot that.

We normally leave out so much that if we look only at what is said, we will be missing too much. We can and must rewrite many arguments we get by adding an **unstated premise** or even an **unstated conclusion**.

But when are we justified in adding an unstated premise? How do we know whether we've rewritten an argument well or just added our own prejudices? How can we recognize when an argument is beyond repair?

B. The Principle of Rational Discussion

It doesn't make sense to repair an argument if the other person isn't being rational. But what does it mean to say someone is rational?

Suppose an argument appears to be good, but you still think the conclusion is false. Then you have to show the conclusion doesn't really follow from the premises or that one of the premises is false. Otherwise you are denying the entire point of rational deliberation. Judging that an argument is good is not a matter of taste.

> **Rationality and Arguments**   If you recognize that an argument is good, then it is irrational to believe the conclusion is false.

What if you hear an argument for both sides, and you can't find a flaw in either? Then you should **suspend judgment** on whether the claim is true until you can investigate more.

I can't tell you exactly what it means to be rational, but there are some assumptions we're entitled to make about anyone with whom we wish to deliberate.

> **The Principle of Rational Discussion**   We assume that the other person who is discussing with us or whose arguments we are reading:
> 1. Knows about the subject under discussion.
> 2. Is able and willing to reason well.
> 3. Is not lying.

What justification do we have for invoking this principle? After all, not everyone fits all three criteria all the time.

Consider (1). Dr. E leaves his car at the repair shop because it's running badly, and returns later in the afternoon. The mechanic tells him that he needs a new framistam. Dr. E asks, "Are you sure I need a new one?" That sounds like an invitation for the mechanic to give an argument. But he shouldn't. Dr. E doesn't have the slightest idea how his engine runs, and the mechanic might as well be speaking Greek. He should try to educate Dr. E, or he'll have to ask Dr. E to accept his claim on trust.

Consider (2). Sometimes people intend not to reason well. Like the demagogic politician or talk-show host, they want to convince you by nonrational means and will not accept your arguments, no matter how good they may be. There's no point in holding a discussion with such a person.

Or you may encounter a person who is temporarily unable or unwilling to reason well: a person who is upset or in love. Again, it makes no sense at such a time to try to reason with such a person. Calm him or her, address his or her emotions, and leave discussion for another time.

Then again, you might find yourself with someone who wants to reason well but just can't seem to follow an argument. Why try to reason with him? Give him a copy of this book.

What about (3)? If you find that the other person is lying, not just a little white lie, but continuously lying, there's no point in reasoning with him, unless perhaps to catch him in his lies. Walk away.

The Principle of Rational Discussion, then, does not instruct us to give other people the benefit of the doubt. It summarizes the necessary conditions for any rational discussion. Compare it to playing chess with someone: What's the point if your opponent doesn't understand or won't play by the rules?

Still, you say, most people don't follow the Principle of Rational Discussion. They don't care if your argument is good. Why should you follow these rules and assume them of others? If you don't:

- You are denying the essentials of democracy.
- You are likely to undermine your own ability to evaluate arguments.
- You are not as likely to convince others.

A representative democracy is built on the idea that the populace as a whole can choose good men and women to write laws by which they can agree to live. If any appeal to the worst in people will succeed, then a democracy will degenerate into the rule of the mob, as it did in ancient Athens. It is only by constantly striving to base our political discussions on rational arguments that we have any hope of living in a just and efficient society.

And if you start using shoddy means of convincing others, it won't be long before you won't distinguish good arguments from bad yourself. Your standards will degenerate.

But most of all, you're wrong if you think that in the long run convincing with clever ads, sound bites, or appeals to prejudice really work better than good arguments. They don't. I've seen the contrary in my city council meetings. I've seen it with my friends. I've seen it with my students. With a little education, most people prefer most of the time to have a sensible, good argument to think about.

> If you once forfeit the confidence of your fellow citizens, you can never regain their respect and esteem. It is true that you may fool all the people some of the time; you can even fool some of the people all the time; but you can't fool all of the people all the time.
>
> Abraham Lincoln

C. The Guide to Repairing Arguments

When are we justified in repairing an argument? When the other person satisfies the Principle of Rational Discussion.   But how do we repair an argument?

> *The Guide to Repairing Arguments*   Given an (implicit) argument that is apparently defective, we are justified in *adding* a premise or conclusion if it satisfies all three of the following:
>
> 1. The argument becomes stronger or valid.
> 2. The premise is plausible and would seem plausible to the other person.
> 3. The premise is more plausible than the conclusion.
>
>   If the argument is then valid or strong, yet one of the original premises is false or dubious, we may *delete* that premise if the argument remains valid or strong.

For example, suppose we hear:

—I was wondering what kind of pet Dick has. It must be a dog.
—How do you know?
—Because I heard it barking last night.

We shouldn't dismiss this as worthless reasoning just because as stated the link from premises to conclusion is missing. We ask what claim(s) are needed to make it strong, since by the Principle of Rational Discussion we assume the speaker intends to and is able to reason well. The obvious would be:

Almost all pets that bark are dogs.

Nothing very much different from this would make the argument strong. The claim is true. So we're justified in adding it to the argument. We do not add "All pets that bark are dogs" because we know that's false (seals, foxes), and can assume the other person does, too.

We don't need to know what the speaker was thinking in order to find a claim or claims that make the argument strong or valid, and that's why we take (1) to have precedence over (2). It is much less clear what the other person thinks is obviously true. We first fix the relation between premises and conclusion, then ask if the claims are true.

> By first trying to make the argument valid or strong, we can show the other person what he or she needs to assume to make the argument good.

It's the same problem when you make your own arguments. You have premises and conclusion, and you ask yourself: Is it possible for the premises to be true and conclusion false? When you find a possible way for the premises to be true and conclusion false, you try to eliminate it by adding a premise. As you eliminate ways in which the premises could be true and conclusion false, you make the argument stronger.

In repairing arguments we have to be faithful to what the speaker actually said. We should pay special attention to *indicator words* like "so" or "therefore." They tell us the conclusion is coming up. Words like "since" or "because" indicate a premise follows.

> **Indicator word** An *indicator word* is a word or phrase added to a claim to tell us the role of the claim in an argument or what the speaker thinks of the claim or argument.

Indicator words are flags put on claims—they are not part of a claim. Here are some common ones:

Conclusion indicators	Premise indicators
therefore	since
hence	because
so	for
thus	in as much as
consequently	given that
we can then derive	suppose that
it follows that	it follows from

Examples   Are the following good arguments? Can they be repaired?

Example 1 No dog meows. So Juney does not meow.

Analysis "Juney is a dog" is the only premise that will make this a valid or strong argument. So we add that. Then, if this new claim is true, the argument is good.

We don't add "Juney barks." That's true and certain to seem obvious to the person who stated the argument, but it doesn't make the argument any better. So adding it violates (1) of the Guide. We repair only as needed.

Example 2 All dogs barks. So Ralph is a dog.

Analysis We've seen lots of arguments of the following form:

> All dogs bark.
> Ralph barks.
> So Ralph is a dog.

They are not valid; they're usually weak. In this case, note that foxes, seals, and some critical thinking instructors bark, too.

It's arguments of the following form that are valid:

> All dogs bark.
> Ralph is a dog.
> So Ralph barks.

It seems, though, that the person who's speaking here is making the first argument. That's evidence he or she can't reason well. All we can do is point it out. The argument can't be repaired because the obvious premise to add makes it weak.

Example 3 Anubis is a dog. So Anubis barks.

Analysis This isn't valid, since Anubis might be a basenji that doesn't bark.

You could make it a stronger by adding "Anubis is not a basenji" and "Anubis didn't have her vocal cords cut." Those would rule out a lot of possibilities where Anubis is a dog but Anubis doesn't bark. And why not add, "Anubis scares away the electric meter reader every month"? Or you could add . . . But this isn't a course in creative writing. You can't make up just anything to add to the argument to make the argument stronger. You have no reason to believe those claims are true.

The only premise we can add here is a blanket one that rules out lots of possibilities without specifying any one of them: "Almost all dogs bark." Then the argument is good.

Example 4 Dr. E is a good teacher, because he gives fair exams.

Analysis The unstated premise needed here is "Almost any teacher who gives fair exams is a good teacher." That gives a strong argument. But it's very dubious, since a teacher could copy fair exams from the instructor's manual. (If you thought the claim that's needed is "Good teachers give fair exams," then reread Example 2.) The argument can't be repaired because the obvious premise to add to make the argument strong or valid is false or dubious.

But can't you make it strong by adding, say, "Dr. E gives great explanations," "Dr. E is amusing," "Dr. E never misses class," . . . ? Yes, all those are true, and perhaps obvious to the person. But adding those doesn't repair this argument—it makes a whole new argument. *Don't put words in someone's mouth.*

Example 5 Your instructor teaches critical thinking. You have to pay tuition for this course. Therefore, you will get a passing grade in critical thinking.

Analysis The argument is weak—and it *is* an argument: The word "therefore" tells us that. But there's no obvious way to repair it. The person doesn't seem to understand how to reason.

Example 6 (advertisement) Doctors recommend aspirin more than any other pain reliever.*

> * Of physicians who were asked, more recommended aspirin than Tylenol, Ibuprofen, or other pain relievers.

Analysis There is no conclusion here, but implicit in the form of advertising is: "You should buy aspirin." Some link is missing, because the argument is neither strong nor valid. Perhaps we should add "If more doctors recommend aspirin than other pain relievers, it must be the best pain reliever for me." Nothing short of this will give a good argument. Is it true? We have no reason to believe it. What if it's false? The advertiser could say that he never actually stated that premise. But then we can see that the advertiser had no intention of reasoning well or was lying, both reasons to reject this attempt to convince us. The argument is unrepairable because the obvious premise to add to make the argument either strong or valid is dubious.

Example 7 You shouldn't eat the fat on your steak. Haven't you heard that cholesterol is bad for you?

Analysis The conclusion is right up front here: It's the first sentence. But what are the premises? The speaker's question is rhetorical, meant to be taken as an assertion: "Cholesterol is bad for you." But that alone won't give us the conclusion. We need something like "Steak fat has a lot of cholesterol" and "You shouldn't eat anything that's bad for you." Premises like these are so obvious we don't bother to say them. The argument is O.K.

Example 8 You're going to vote for the Socialist Party candidate for President? Don't you realize that means your vote will be wasted?

Analysis Where's the argument here? These are just two questions. Again, the questions are rhetorical, meant to be taken as assertions: "Don't vote for the Socialist Party candidate" (the conclusion) and "Your vote will be wasted" (the premise). This sounds pretty reasonable, though something is missing. A visitor from Denmark may not know "The Socialist Party candidate doesn't have a chance of winning." But she may also question why that matters. We'd have to fill in the argument further: "If you vote for someone who doesn't have a chance of winning, then your vote will be wasted." And when we add that premise we see the argument that used such "obvious" premises is really not very good. Why should we believe that if you vote for someone who doesn't stand a chance of winning then your vote is wasted? If that were true, then who wins is the only important result of an election, rather than, say, making a position understood by the electorate. At best we can say that when the unstated premises are added in, we get an argument one of whose premises needs a substantial argument to convince us that it is true.

Example 9 My eyes are getting tired and I'm getting headaches every time I work on the computer. This hasn't happened much before, but I remember a few years ago when it happened I needed a new prescription for my glasses. I'd better see the optometrist next week.

Analysis The conclusion here is "I'd better see the optometrist next week." But it's arrived at in two steps. First, we add "I need a new prescription for my glasses" as the conclusion of the premises that are given. That plus "If I need a new prescription, then I should see the optometrist" will yield this conclusion.

   The first argument is fairly strong, the second valid, and all the premises are true. So it's a pretty good argument. But, as it turned out, the conclusion was false: After getting new glasses with a slightly different prescription I found that my computer monitor was defective and giving me headaches. I hadn't been creative enough to imagine that possibility.

Example 10   Cats are more likely than dogs to carry diseases harmful to humans. Cats kill songbirds and can kill people's pets. Cats disturb people at night with their screeching and clattering in garbage cans. Cats leave pawprints on cars and will sleep in unattended cars. Cats are not as pleasant as dogs and are owned only by people who have satanic affinities. So there should be a leash law for cats just as much as for dogs.

Analysis This letter to the editor is going pretty well until the next to last sentence. That claim is a bit dubious, and the argument will be just as strong without it. So we should delete it. Then we have an argument which, with some unstated premises you can supply, is pretty good.

Example 11 Affirmative action will not correct the problems that blacks face from their history. They're just like any other minority group, and they should fend for themselves.

Analysis Let us assume that this example is part of an argument made by someone whom we know to be a racist (I'm not suggesting that only a racist would make these remarks). Then we would not be justified in adding as an unstated premise "Blacks suffered greatly under the institution of slavery in the eighteenth and nineteenth centuries in America." That may be plausible to you and me. But unless that claim is essential to his reasoning, there's no reason to think he finds it plausible. We do not dismiss his reasoning, but hope that rational discussion may lead us to understand the differences in our beliefs. The repair to this incomplete argument must be made by the speaker.

Example 12 Harry's new dog is a pit bull. So it must be dangerous.

Analysis The question here is whether we should try to make this argument valid or strong. The word "must" strongly suggests that the speaker thinks the argument he's making is valid. Unless we have good reason to think otherwise, "must" and "have to" will signal to us that we should repair the argument as valid.

But then the only premise we could add is "All pit bulls are dangerous." And that's false. So the argument is unrepairable.

Example 13 In a famous speech, Martin Luther King Jr. said:

> I have a dream that one day this nation will rise up and live out the true meaning of its creed: "We hold these truths to be self-evident—that all men are created equal." . . . I have a dream that one day even the state of Mississippi, a desert state sweltering with the heat of injustice and oppression, will be transformed into an oasis of freedom and justice. I have a dream that my four little children will one day live in a nation where they will not be judged by the color of their skin but by the content of their character. [Quoted from *Let the Trumpet Sound,* by Stephen B. Oates.]
>
> . . . King is also presenting a logical argument . . . the argument might be stated as follows; "America was founded on the principle that all men are created equal. This implies that people should not be judged by skin color, which is an accident of birth, but rather by what they make of themselves ('the content of their character'). To be consistent with this principle, America should treat black people and white people alike."

> *The Art of Reasoning,* David Kelley, W.W. Norton & Company, 1988, pp. 114–115

Analysis The rewriting of this passage is too much of a stretch—putting words in someone's mouth—to be appropriate. Where did David Kelley get the premise "This implies . . ."? Stating my dreams and hoping others will share them is not an argument. Martin Luther King, Jr. knew how to argue well and could do so when he wanted. We're not going to make his words more respectable by pretending they're an argument.

Example 14 Lee: None of Dr. E's students are going to beg in the street. 'Cause only poor people beg. And Dr. E's students will be rich because they understand how to reason well.

Analysis This is a superb argument.

We've seen how to repair some arguments. And just as important, we've seen that some arguments can't be repaired. Often the value of the Guide is to isolate what's wrong with an argument.

> ***Unrepairable Argument*** We can't repair an argument if any one of the following hold:
>
> • There's no argument there.
> • The argument is so lacking in coherence that there's nothing obvious to add.
> • The premises it uses are false or very dubious and cannot be deleted.
> • The obvious premise to add would make the argument weak.
> • The obvious premise to add to make the argument strong or valid is false.
> • The conclusion is clearly false.

D. Relevance (*Bad arguments*)

If we take the second question as rhetorical, Tom is making an argument:

> Environmentalists should not be allowed to tell us what to do.
> The federal government should not be allowed to tell us what to do.
> Therefore, we should go ahead and allow logging in old-growth forests.

When the argument is put this way, it seems obvious to us that Tom has confused whether we have the right to cut down the forests with whether we should cut them down. Tom's proved something, just not the conclusion.

Sometimes people say an argument like Tom's is bad because his premises are irrelevant to the conclusion. They say an argument is bad if in response to one or more premises your reaction is: "What's that got to do with anything?" or "So?"

What would you do if someone told you that a claim you made is irrelevant? You'd try to show that it is relevant by adding more premises to link it to the conclusion. The trouble is that the premises needed to make the claim relevant are not obvious to the other person. When we say that a premise is irrelevant to the conclusion, all we're saying is that it doesn't make the argument any stronger, and we can't see how to add anything plausible that would link it to the conclusion. And when we say that all the premises are irrelevant, we're saying that we can't even imagine how to repair the argument.

> A premise is ***irrelevant*** if you can delete it and the argument isn't any weaker.

Exercises for Sections A–D

1. Why add premises or a conclusion? Why not take arguments as they are?

2. State the Principle of Rational Discussion and explain why we are justified in adopting it when we reason with others.

3. What should you do if you find that the Principle of Rational Discussion is not applicable in a discussion you are having?

4. You find that a close friend is an alcoholic. You want to help her. You want to convince her to stop drinking. Which is more appropriate, to reason with her or take her to an Alcoholics Anonymous meeting? Explain why.

5. Since most people don't really satisfy the Principle of Rational Discussion, why not just use bad arguments to fit the circumstances?

6. You're talking to your doctor about why you're feeling ill.
   a. In analyzing what you say, should your doctor assume the Principle of Rational Discussion?
   b. In telling you what to do for your illness, should your doctor assume the Principle of Rational Discussion?

7. State the guide we have in judging when to add or delete a premise and what would count as a suitable unstated premise.

8. When can't you repair an argument?

9. Which is riskier, adding unstated premises or an unstated conclusion? Why?

10. Find a letter to the editor with an argument that depends on at least one unstated premise.

11. Find a letter to the editor with an argument that has an unstated conclusion.

12. a. What is an indicator word?
    b. List at least five words or phrases not in the chart that indicate a conclusion.

   c. List at least five words or phrases not in the chart that indicate premises.

   d. Some indicator words tell us what a speaker thinks of a claim or argument. For example, when the conclusion is introduced by "probably" we understand that the speaker thinks the argument is strong, not valid. List five more words or phrases that show an attitude toward a claim.

   e. Bring in an argument from some source that uses indicator words.

13. Mark which of the blanks below would normally be filled with a premise (P) and which with a conclusion (C).

   a. i_____, ii_____, iii_____, therefore, iv _____.

   b. i_____, since, ii_____, iii_____, and, iv _____.

   c. Because i_____, it follows that ii_____ and iii_____.

   d. Since i_____, and ii_____, it follows that iii_____, because iv_____.

   e. i_____ and ii_____, and that's why iii_____.

   f. Due to i_____ and ii_____, we have iii_____.

   g. In view of i_____, ii_____, and iii_____, we get iv _____.

   h. From i_____ and ii_____, we can derive iii_____.

   i. If i_____, then it follows that ii_____, for iii_____, and iv _____.

14. Rewrite the following argument using indicator words.

A college education will be useful to you later in life. You'll probably earn more money. You'll certainly have a better chance at doing work you enjoy. You'll understand the world better, especially if you've taken a critical thinking course. And you'll be able to get a better mate. And impress your friends. And it'll make your mother happy.

15. How should we understand the charge that a premise in an argument is irrelevant?

16. a. Make up an argument against the idea that lying is a good way to convince people.

   b. Convert your argument in (a) to show that reasoning badly on purpose is not effective or ethical.

17. Look at the Gettysburg Address and determine if it is an argument.

We've learned that arguments often need to be repaired. Tom's trying to apply that idea to some exercises. He's supposed to answer the italicized questions. I'll let you see what I've written about his answers.

> **I'm telling you I'm not at fault. How could I be? She hit me from the rear. Anytime you get rear-ended it's not your fault.**
>
> *Argument?* (yes or no) Yes.
>
> *Conclusion*: I'm not at fault.
>
> *Premises*: She hit me from the rear. Anytime you get rear-ended it's not your fault.
>
> *Additional premises needed to make it valid or strong* (if none, say so): She was speeding.
>
> *Classify* (with the additional premises): valid very strong ——X——— weak
>
> *Good argument?* (Choose one with an explanation.)

√ It's good (passes the three tests).   with the added premise.

It's valid or strong, but you don't know if the premises are true, so you can't say
 if it's good or bad.

It's bad because it's unrepairable (state which of the reasons apply).

No! The argument as originally stated was valid. Why try to repair it? And if you do add a premise, then you must check either "valid or very strong"—there's no other point in adding a premise. Besides, why do you think this premise would seem plausible to the speaker? You're making up a story, not repairing this argument.

Anyone who studies hard gets good grades. So Zoe studies hard.

Argument? (yes or no) Yes.

Conclusion: Zoe must study hard.

Premises: Anyone who studies hard gets good grades.

Additional premises needed to make it valid or strong (if none, say so):
   Zoe gets good grades.

Classify (with the additional premises): <u>valid</u> very strong ———————— weak

Good argument? (Choose one with an explanation.)

 √ It's good (passes the three tests).   with the added premise.

It's valid or strong, but you don't know if the premises are true, so you can't say
 if it's good or bad.

It's bad because it's unrepairable (state which of the reasons apply).

No! Zoe could get good grades and not study hard if she's very bright. It's the obvious premise to add, all right, but it makes the argument weak. The argument is unrepairable. See Example 2.

Celia must love the coat I gave her. She wears it all the time.

Argument? (yes or no) Yes.

Conclusion: Celia loves the coat I gave her.

Premises: She wears it all the time.

Additional premises needed to make it valid or strong (if none, say so): Anyone
   who wears a coat all the time loves it.

Classify (with the additional premises): valid very strong ——X—— weak

Good argument? (Choose one with an explanation.)

 √ It's good (passes the three tests).   with the added premise.

It's valid or strong, but you don't know if the premises are true, so you can't say
 if it's good or bad.

It's bad because it's unrepairable (state which of the reasons apply).

You've confused whether an argument is valid or strong with whether it's good. With your added premise, the argument is indeed valid. But the premise you added is clearly false. Weakening it to make the argument just strong won't do—the person making the argument intended it to be valid (that "must" in the conclusion). So the argument is unrepairable because the obvious premise to add to make it valid is false.

I got sick after eating shrimp last month. Then this week again when I ate shrimp I got a rash. So I shouldn't eat shellfish anymore.

Argument? (yes or no) Yes.

Conclusion: I shouldn't eat shellfish anymore.

Premises: I got sick after eating shrimp last month. This week again when I ate shrimp I got a rash.

Additional premises needed to make it valid or strong (if none, say so):
None.

Classify (with the additional premises): valid very strong X——————— weak

Good argument? (Choose one with an explanation.)

    It's good (passes the three tests).

√ It's valid or strong, but you don't know if the premises are true, so you can't say if it's good or bad. Sounds very strong to me. I sure wouldn't risk eating shrimp again.

    It's bad because it's unrepairable (state which of the reasons apply).

I agree, I wouldn't risk eating shrimp again, either. But that doesn't make the argument strong—there are lots of other possibilities for why the person got a rash. The argument is only moderate. <u>Risk may determine how strong an argument we're willing to accept, but it doesn't affect how strong the argument actually is.</u>

Our congressman voted to give more money to people on welfare. So he doesn't care about working people.

Argument? (yes or no) Yes.

Conclusion: Our congressman doesn't care about working people.

Premises: Our congressman voted to give more money to people on welfare.

Additional premises needed to make it valid or strong (if none, say so):
I can't think of any that are plausible.

Classify (with the additional premises): valid very strong ———————X weak

Good argument? (Choose one with an explanation.)

    It's good (passes the three tests).

    It's valid or strong, but you don't know if the premises are true, so you can't say if it's good or bad.

√ It's bad because it's unrepairable (state which of the reasons apply).

    The only premise I can think of that would even make the argument strong is something like "Almost anyone who votes to give more money to people on welfare doesn't care about working people." And I know that's false. So the argument is unrepairable, right?

Right! Excellent work.

When I get near a cat, my tongue swells. I sneeze 10 times in a row, and I get a rash all over my body. I must be allergic to cats.

Argument? (yes or no) Yes.

Conclusion: I am allergic to cats.

Premises: When I get near a cat, my tongue swells.

When I get near a cat I sneeze 10 times in a row.

When I get near a cat, I get a rash all over my body.

Additional premises needed to make it valid or strong (if none, say so): Anyone whose tongue swells, sneezes 10 times in a row, and gets a rash whenever he is near a cat is allergic to cats.

Classify (with the additional premises): <u>valid</u> very strong ————— weak

Good argument? (Choose one with an explanation.)

√ It's good (passes the three tests).   The added premise is plausible, and makes the argument valid.

It's valid or strong, but you don't know if the premises are true, so you can't say if it's good or bad.

It's bad because it's unrepairable (state which of the reasons apply).

Great! You've clearly got the idea here.

I'm sure you can do more of these now if you'll just remember that sometimes the correct answer is that the argument is unrepairable. Review those five conditions on p. 70.

Analyze the following exercises by answering the following questions.

Argument? (yes or no)

Conclusion:

Premises:

Additional premises needed to make it valid or strong (if none, say so):

Classify: valid   very strong ————— weak

Good argument? (Choose one with an explanation.)

It's good (passes the three tests).

It's valid or strong, but you don't know if the premises are true, so you can't say if it's good or bad.

It's bad because it's unrepairable (state which of the reasons apply).

18. George walks like a duck. George looks like a duck. George quacks like a duck. So George is a duck.

19. If you're so smart, why aren't you rich?

20. You caught the flu from me? Impossible! I haven't seen you for two months.

21. You caught the flu from me? Impossible! You got sick first.

22. Mary Ellen just bought a Mercedes. So Mary Ellen must be rich.

23. All great teachers are tough graders. So Dr. E is a great teacher.

24. No dog meows. So Spot will only eat dry dog food.

25. This banana is green, so it's not ripe.

26. All green bananas are not ripe. So this banana is not ripe.

27. All dogs that are half-wolf are great hunters. So Anubis is half-wolf.

28. No cat barks. So Ralph is not a cat.

29. You're blue-eyed. So your parents must be blue-eyed.

30. All professors are required to have office hours, and Dr. E is a professor.

31. Dick: Harry got into college because of affirmative action.
    Suzy: Gee, I didn't know that. So Harry isn't very bright.

32. All students who study hard are liked by their teachers. So Zoe studies hard.

33. They should fire Professor Zzzyzzx because he has such a bad accent that no one can understand his lectures.

34. —That masked man saved us.
    —Did you see he has silver bullets in his gunbelt?
    —And he called his horse Silver.
    —Didn't he call his friend Tonto?
    —He must be the Lone Ranger.

35. My buddies Tom, Dick, and Harry all took Dr. E's Philosophy 102 class and did well. So I should sign up for it, too. I need a good mark.

36. Suzy: Did you see how that saleslady treated Harry?
    Tom: Yeah, she just ignored him.
    Suzy: She must be racist.

37. Our college president should spend more time with the students here. Otherwise (s)he'd be neglecting one of the most important duties as president of the college.

38. These exercises are impossible. How do they expect us to get them right? There are no right answers! They're driving me crazy.

39. These exercises are difficult but not impossible. Though there may not be a unique right answer, there are definitely wrong answers. There are generally not unique best ways to analyze arguments you encounter in your daily life. The best this course can hope to do is make you think and develop your judgment through these exercises.

40. (Advertisement)

E. Inferring and Implying

Suppose your teacher says in class:

> All of my best students hand in extra written arguments for extra credit.

She hasn't actually said you should hand in extra work. But you *infer*:

> If I want to do well in this class, I'd better hand in extra credit work

She has *implied* this, you have *inferred* it.

> **Inferring and Implying**   When someone leaves a conclusion unsaid, he is
> *implying* the conclusion. When you decide that an unstated claim is the
> conclusion, you are *inferring* that claim.
>   We can also say someone is implying a claim if in context it's clear he
> believes the claim. In that case we infer that the person believes the claim.

This implying and inferring is risky business. If you complain to the department head that your teacher is demanding more than she asked for on the syllabus, your teacher could say she wasn't, you just inferred incorrectly. She might say:

> I've observed that my best students hand in extra credit work—that's all
> I was saying. I had no intention of making an argument.

You, however, could say that in the context in which she made the remark it was fairly obvious she was implying that if you wanted her to believe you are a good student, you should hand in extra work.

In law, there is a theory of implied contracts. You shake hands with a buddy and give him $100, and he gives you the keys to his car and tells you he'll meet you next week for the rest of his money. You have a contract to buy his car, even if it's not written down and nothing was said about exactly when you'd pay him. A landlord gives you the keys to an apartment and tells you he'll be by tomorrow to fill out the lease; you have an implied contract. If there's a dispute, the courts will have to decide what the terms of that contract are, since it wasn't exactly specified.

When Suzy was home for vacation, her father said to her before she went out Saturday night, "Don't forget we're going to be leaving very early for the beach tomorrow." Suzy got home at 3:30 a.m., and the next morning her father was livid when she said she was too tired to help with the driving. "I *told* you we were leaving very early," he said. To which Suzy replied, "So?" Her father believed that he had clearly implied, "You should get home early and rest enough to help with the driving." Suzy says he should have been more explicit.

The trouble is, we aren't always explicit, we often leave the conclusion unstated because it seems so obvious. And what is obvious to you may not be obvious to me: One man's intelligent inference is another's jumping to conclusions.

Examples   What's being implied? What's being inferred?

Example 1 I'm not going to vote, because no matter who is president nothing is going to get done.

Analysis   An unstated claim is needed to make sense of what is said: "If no matter who is president nothing is going to get done, then you shouldn't vote for president." We infer this from the person's remarks; he has implied it.

Example 2 Dick is working in the computer lab at school. He's been there for an hour and a half. He looks up and notices that all the students who have come in lately are wearing raincoats and are wet. He figures it must be raining outside.

Analysis   We can say that Dick inferred "It is raining outside." But where's the argument? This is the kind of inferring that psychologists and scientists and lawyers do all the time. They have evidence, but not stated verbally, and proceed as if they had an argument.

  We often infer from our experience, but we can't analyze those inferences nor discuss them with others until we have verbalized them into arguments.

Example 3 Your teacher makes a sexual innuendo the first day of class. You figure she must have meant something harmless, you just didn't get it. But it happens again. And again. You start taking notes on all the remarks. Finally, after four weeks you are fed up and go to the head of the department. You say, "My teacher is making sexually suggestive remarks in class. It's not an accident. It's intentional."

Analysis   The argument you'd need to make to the department head might be: "My teacher made many remarks over a long period of time that could be taken sexually. This could not be an accident, because it happened too often. Therefore, she intended to make sexually suggestive comments."

  This may or may not be a strong argument, depending on exactly what remarks were said. It has a subjective claim as a conclusion, one you have inferred from the teacher's actions, not from an incomplete argument she might have made. And subjective claims are especially difficult to prove, since we can never know with certainty what she intended. I knew one lady who was constantly making sexually suggestive remarks, and on each occasion did not realize it until someone pointed it out to her. Freud would have loved her.

Exercises for Section E

1. Suzy says, "I find fat men unattractive, so I won't date you."
    a. What has Suzy implied?
    b. What can the fellow she's talking to infer?

2. Tom: Hey, your pants have a rip in them.
   Lee: Yeah. A lot of my clothes need sewing. I'm hopeless at it.
   Tom: You ought to get a girlfriend.

   What claim has Tom implied?

3. Tom: Where are you from?
   Rudy: New York.
   Tom: Oh, I'm sorry.

   What has Tom implied here?

4. The following conversation is ascribed to W.C. Fields at a formal dinner party. What can we say he implied?

   W. C. Fields: Madame, you are horribly ugly.
   Lady: Your behavior is inexcusable. You're drunk.
   W. C. Fields: I may be drunk, but tomorrow I'll be sober.

5. President Clinton said, "I smoked marijuana, but I never inhaled it." What can we infer from his remarks? Be explicit in constructing the *entire* argument.

6. Give a recent example where you inferred a claim.

7. Give a recent example where you implied a claim.

Summary   Most arguments we encounter are flawed. But they aren't necessarily bad. They can often be repaired by adding claims that are common knowledge.

   By reflecting on the conditions for us to enter into a rational discussion, we can formulate a guide for how to repair apparently defective arguments. We assume the other person is knowledgeable about the subject, is able and willing to reason well, and is not lying. So we add premises that make the argument stronger or valid and which are plausible and plausible to the other person.

   Of course, not everyone can reason well, or wishes to reason well. And lots of arguments can't be repaired, which is something we can discover when we try to add premises. That, too, helps us evaluate arguments.

   Our actions, as well as our words, can lead people to think we believe some claim. We talked about how people imply claims by their actions or words, and how others infer claims from them.

Key Words   unstated premise   indicator word
                unstated conclusion   unrepairable argument
                rationality   irrelevant claim
                suspend judgment   imply
                The Principle of Rational Discussion   infer
                The Guide to Repairing Arguments

Further Study   To follow up on the idea that rational discussion is necessary for a democracy, you can read Plato's dialogue *Gorgias* in which Socrates castigates those who would convince without good arguments.

Writing Lesson 5

Write an argument either for or against the following:

"No one should receive financial aid their first semester at this school."

Your argument should be at most one page long.
Just list the premises and the conclusion. Nothing more. Look at the instructions for Writing Lesson 3.

Check whether your instructor has chosen a *DIFFERENT TOPIC* for this assignment.

To give you a better idea of what you're expected to do, I've included Manuel's argument on a different issue.

Manuel Luis Andrade y Castillo de Pocas
Critical Thinking
Section 2
Writing Lesson 5

Issue: The chance of contracting AIDS through sexual contact can be significantly reduced by using condoms.

Definition: "AIDS" means "Acquired Immunodeficiency Syndrome"
     "significantly reduced" means by more than 50%
     "using condoms" means using a condom in sexual intercourse rather than having unprotected sex

Premises:

- AIDS can only be contracted by exchanging blood or semen. *A*

- In unprotected sex there is a chance of exchanging blood or semen.

- Condoms are better than 90% effective in stopping blood and semen.*

- 90% is bigger than 50%.

- AIDS has never been known to have been contracted from sharing food, using a dirty toilet seat, from touching, or from breathing in the same room with someone who has AIDS. *B*

- If you want to avoid contracting AIDS you should use a condom. *C*

Conclusion: The chance of contracting AIDS through sexual contact can be significantly reduced by using condoms.

*I'm not sure of the exact figure, but I know it's bigger than 90%.

Good. Your argument is indeed valid. But it could easily be better. You don't need "only" in A, which is what makes me uneasy in accepting that claim. And without a reference to medical literature, I'm sure not going to accept B. But you don't need it. You can delete it and your argument is just as strong.

*   And the last claim, C, is really irrelevant—delete it. This isn't an editorial: You're not trying to convince someone to <u>do</u> something; you're trying to convince them an objective claim is true.*

Writing Lesson 6

For each of the following write the best argument you can that has as conclusion the claim that accompanies the cartoon. List only the premises and conclusion. If you believe the best argument is only weak, explain why.

Do not make up a story about the cartoon. Use what you see in the cartoon and your common knowledge.

1.

The fellow stole the purse.

2.

A. The man at the car in the parking lot is the person who ran over the bicycle.

B. The man in the car knew he ran over the bicycle and purposely didn't stop.

3.

Crows ate farmer Hong's corn.

4.

The mother is scolding her child for breaking the flower pot.

5   Is That True?

A. Evaluating Premises

Recall the three tests that an argument must pass for it to be good:

1. There must be good reason to believe the premises.
2. The premises lead to, support, establish the conclusion.
3. The premises must be more plausible than the conclusion.

In the last two chapters we looked at how to evaluate whether the premises support the conclusion. Now we'll ask when we have good reason to believe the premises.

But why just believe the premises? This course is about methods of convincing. Shouldn't every claim be backed up with an argument? We can't do that. If we want a justification for every claim, we'd have to go on forever. We'd never get started. When someone makes a claim, we have to decide if we believe it.

Three Attitudes We Can Take Towards the Truth of a Claim
Accept the claim as true.
Reject the claim as false.
Suspend judgment.

We needn't pretend to be all wise, nor force ourselves to make judgments. Rejecting a claim means to say that it is *false*. Sometimes it's best to suspend judgment and evaluate the argument as best we can. If we find that the argument is valid or strong, we can then worry about whether the premise is true.

---

not believe ≠ believe is false
lack of evidence ≠ evidence that it's false

B. Criteria for Accepting or Rejecting Claims

There are no absolute rules for when we should accept, when reject, and when suspend judgment about a claim. It's a skill, weighing up the following in order of importance.

1. *Reject*: The claim contradicts our personal experience

What would you think of someone who never trusted his own experience, who always deferred to authority? He goes to a priest and asks him if it's daytime. He looks up in an atlas whether his hometown is in Nevada. He asks his teacher whether the room they're standing in is painted white.

You'd say he's crazy. You'd have to be crazy not to trust your own experience as the most reliable source of information you have about the world.

We need to trust our own experience because that's the best we have. Everything else is second-hand. Should I trust my buddy, my spouse, my priest, my professor, my president, the dictator, when what they say contradicts my own experience? I certainly hope not. That way lies demagoguery, religious intolerance, and worse. We are not sheep, led to believe whatever the authorities say. Remember that—because too often leaders have manipulated the populace: All Jews are tight with their money? But what about my neighbor who's Jewish, the shoe salesman, who's as generous as can be? You have to forget your own experience to believe the Big Lie. That's what happens. They repeat it over and over and over again until you begin to believe it, even when your own experience says it isn't so.

Oh, we get the idea. Don't trust the politicians. No. It's a lot closer to home than that. Every rumor, all the gossip you hear, compare it to what *you* know about the person or situation. Don't repeat it. Be rational, not part of the humming crowd.

So trust your own experience.

Except our memories are not always reliable. Quick, answer these questions:

What color is the ceiling in your kitchen?
What is the pattern of the tile on your bathroom floor?
Are your mother's eyebrows the same level?
What was the last dog you saw?

You've probably come up with answers. But are you sure of them? Experiment with a friend. You'll be surprised how often you're sure of something you don't know.

We all think eyewitnesses are the best evidence we can get if we're looking for a criminal. But as Sgt. Carlson of the Las Vegas Police Department says, "Eyewitnesses are terrible. You get a gun stuck in your face and you can't remember anything." The police do line-ups, putting a suspect among 6 other people taken from the jail who look a bit similar to be identified by a witness. The police have to remind the witness that hair length, hair color, facial hair, all may have changed. The police have to be very careful not to say anything that may influence the witness, because memory is malleable.

So what's the moral? Trust your own experience, but be aware of the tricks that memory can play. Still . . .

There are times we rightly don't trust our own experience. You go to the circus and see a magician cut a lady in half. You *saw* it, so it has to be true. Yet you don't believe it. Why? Because it contradicts too much else you know about the world.

Or stranger still: Day after day after day we see the sun rise in the east and set in the west, yet we say the earth revolves around the sun. We don't accept our own experience because there's a long story, a theory of how the earth turns on its axis. And that story explains neatly and clearly so many other phenomena, like the seasons and the movement of stars in the skies, that we accept it. A convincing argument has been given for us to reject our own experience, and that argument builds on other experiences of ours. It's rational then to accept this claim that contradicts some of our experience.

> We reject a claim of our own experience if:
> - We have good reason to doubt our memory.
> - The claim contradicts other experiences of ours, and there is a good argument (theory) against the claim.

There is one other problem with trusting our experience: Often it's not our experience at all that we remember, but what we've deduced from our experience. Think of Writing Lesson 6. Typically you would have looked at the situation and said, for example, "The fellow stole the purse" or "Spot chased the cat," when that was what you deduced, not what you saw. Or consider the person who's met only two Chinese, both of whom are good at math, and then says that all Chinese are good at math. He's generalizing (badly, as we'll discuss in Chapter 14); all he's justified in saying from his own experience is that all Chinese he's met are good at math.

Exercises for Sections A and B.1

1. Why can't we require that every claim made in an argument be backed up?

2. What are the three attitudes we can take toward whether a claim is true?

3. Explain why in a court of law you are sworn "to tell the truth, the whole truth, and nothing but the truth," rather than just sworn to tell the truth.

4. If the conclusion of a valid argument is false, why must one of the premises be false?

5. Give an example of a rumor or gossip you heard in your personal life recently that you believed. Did you have good reason to believe it?

6. We can tell that a rumor or gossip is coming up when someone says, "Did you hear that . . .".   Give five other phrases that alert us similarly.

7. Shouldn't you trust an encyclopedia over your own experience? Explain.

8. Give at least one example of a claim that someone made this week that you knew from your own experience was false.

9. Give an example of a claim which you believed was true from memory, but really you were making a deduction from your experience.

10. When is it reasonable for us to accept a claim that disagrees with our own experience? Give an example (not in the text) of a claim that it is reasonable for you to accept even though it appears to contradict your own experience.

11. Remember the last time this class met? Answer the following about your instructor.
    a. Male _____ or Female _____
    b. Hair color _____
    c. Eye color _____
    d. Approximate height _____
    e. Approximate weight _____
    f. Was he wearing jeans? _____ Was she wearing a skirt? _____
    g. Did he/she bring a backpack to class? _____ If so, describe it.
    h. Did he/she use notes? _____
    i. Did he/she get to class early? _____
    j. Did he/she wear a hat? _____
    k. Is he/she left-handed or right-handed? _____

12. Remember the last time this class met? Answer the following about the room:
    a. How many windows? _____
    b. How many doors? _____
    c. How many walls? _____
    d. Any pictures? _____
    e. How high is the ceiling? _____
    f. What kind of floor (concrete, tile, linoleum, carpet)? _____
    g. How many chairs? _____
    h. How many students showed up for class? _____
    i. Chalkboard? _____
    j. Lectern? _____
    k. Faucet? _____
    l. Wastebasket? _____
    m. Did you get out of class early? _____

13. Which of your answers to Exercises 11 and 12 were from actual memory, and which were inferences?

14. The state of the world around us can affect our observations and make our personal experience unreliable. You could honestly say you were sure the other driver didn't put on a turn signal, when it was the rain and distractions that made you not notice. List at least five ways that the *physical conditions around us* can affect our observations.

15. Recollections of our observations can be colored by tricks of our memory, but our observations can be colored at the time by our mental state, too. (For example, if you're terrified by a gun pointed at you, you might not remember the length of hair of the assailant.) List at least five ways that your *mental state* could affect your observations.

16. Our personal observations are no better than _____ ?

17. What does a bad argument tell us about its conclusion?

18. If an argument has one false premise and thirteen true premises, what attitude should we take towards its conclusion?

19. The thrust of Western culture has been: Seeing is believing. The thrust of Eastern culture has been: Believing is seeing. Explain the difference and give examples from your own experience.

2. *Reject*: The claim contradicts other claims we know are true

You're thinking of going to the Post Office to buy stamps and mail a letter, but your friend tells you not to bother. She says it's closed on Saturdays. You don't believe her, because you know it's open until noon on Saturdays.

You don't know that from personal experience—calling the Post Office or going there that day—but from reading or an authority, or common knowledge. That's not as reliable. Even going there last Saturday doesn't show for sure it's open this Saturday. But that's how we know most of what we know.

Someone tries to convince you that you shouldn't go to the restaurant with a friend because there's a chance she has AIDS, and you could catch it from eating at the same table with her. You reject the claim that you can catch AIDS in that manner, because it's common knowledge that AIDS can be transmitted only through contact with bodily fluids. You make your own argument: AIDS can only be transmitted through contact with bodily fluids; when eating at a restaurant with a friend, it is extremely unlikely that you'll share bodily fluids with her; so it's safe to go to a restaurant with a friend who might have AIDS.

3. *Don't accept*: The claim contradicts one of the other premises

We don't have to know a lot about the world to say an argument is bad that has premises that contradict one another. One of the claims must be false, and we know that false premises give us no reason to believe the conclusion. You hear someone on radio saying:

> The streets aren't safe. We need to get tougher on crime. We should lock up more of those drug-pushers and scare people into obeying the law. Get more police, lock the criminals up, and throw the key away.
>
> And we also need to reduce taxes. We can't afford that new bond proposition to build a new prison.

Perhaps there is a way to salvage these claims as consistent, but on the face of it they are contradictory: You can't increase the prison population a lot and not build new prisons. From these contradictory claims you could prove that the sun rises in the west.

4. *Accept*: The claim is given as personal experience of someone we know and trust, and the person is an authority about that kind of claim

Zoe tells Harry to stay away from the area of town around S. 3rd. She's seen people doing drugs there and knows two people who have been held up in that neighborhood. He'll believe those premises and likely accept the conclusion that follows from those (and other unstated) premises. It makes sense. Zoe is reliable, and the claims she's making are the sort that her knowledge would matter.

On the other hand, your mother tells you that you should major in business so you can get ahead in life. Should you believe her? She can tell you about her friends' children. But what are the chances of getting a good job with a degree in business? It'd be more reasonable to check at the local colleges where they keep records on the hiring of graduates. Don't reject her claim. Suspend judgment until you get more information.

5. *Accept*: The claim is offered by a reputable authority whom we can trust as an expert about this kind of claim and who has no motive to mislead us

The Surgeon General announces that smoking is bad for your health. He's got no axe to grind. He's a physician. He's in a position to survey the research on the subject. It's reasonable to believe him.

But the doctor hired by the tobacco company says there's no proof that smoking is addictive or causes lung cancer. Is he an expert on smoking-related diseases? Or perhaps an allergist or pediatrician? It matters in whether to trust his ability to interpret the epidemiological data. And he has a motive for misleading, being paid by the tobacco companies. There's no reason to accept his claim, and some motive for rejecting it.

The new Surgeon General says that marijuana should be legal. What kind of authority is she on this subject? Is she a politician? A lawyer? What kind of expertise does she have on matters of law and public policy? She is an authority figure, but not an expert on *this* kind of claim. No reason to accept it.

President Nixon tells the country during the Vietnam War that we are not bombing Cambodia. He'd know if anyone would. But he has a motive for misleading us, since we have no declaration of war against Cambodia. Don't trust him (it turned out he was lying through his teeth).

Which authorities we trust and which we disregard change from era to era. It was the lying by Presidents Johnson and Nixon that led us to distrust all pronouncements from the government. It was the Chicago police killing the Black Panthers in their beds and calling it self-defense that convinced many of us not to accept what big city police say. I remember growing up in Iowa before the Vietnam War. When

I visited Denmark as an exchange student, they asked me who I thought killed Kennedy. I said, "Oswald." They asked me why I believed that. I said because the FBI said so. They all shook their heads in sadness, right after they stopped laughing.

The moral is that some authorities are more trustworthy than others, even in their own areas of expertise. Some may have motive for misleading. And the more you tell the truth, the more likely you are to be believed; but even one lie can ruin your reputation for reliability.

What are you to do if the authorities disagree? Suspend judgment—except that you don't always have that option. If you're on a jury where two ballistics experts disagree on whether the bullet that killed the victim came from the defendant's gun, what should you do? You have to make a decision. Even if you think an authority has the expertise to speak on a subject and has no motive for misleading, you will still have to use your judgment.

Exercises for Sections B.2–B.5

1. Give an example of an argument that uses claims you know to be false, though not from personal experience. (Letters to the editor in a newspaper are a good source.)

2. a. Describe three people you encounter regularly whose word you trust and why you believe them.

   b. Give an example of a claim that one of them made that you shouldn't accept because the knowledge or expertise he or she has does not bear on that claim.

3. Describe two people you encounter regularly whose word you do not trust and why you do not believe them.

4. List three *categories* of authorities you feel you can trust. State for which kind of claims those kind of authorities would be experts.

5. Give a recent example from some media source of an authority being quoted whose claims you accepted as true.

6. Give an example from some media source of an authority being quoted whose expertise does not bear on the claim being put forward, so you have no reason to accept the claim.

7. Give an example of an authority who made a claim recently that turned out to be false. Do you think it was a lie? Or did the person just not know it was false?

8. You're on a jury where two ballistics experts disagree on whether the bullet that killed the victim came from the defendant's gun.
   a. How would you decide which to believe?
   b. What consequences would there be for suspending judgment?

9. You tell your friend who's experimenting with heroin that he should stop. It's dangerous. He says you're no expert. Besides, you've never tried it. How do you respond?

10. Give an example of an argument that uses contradictory premises. If you can't get one from listening to your friends, try the letters to the editor.

6. *Accept*: **The claim is put forward in a reputable journal or reference source**

The New England Journal of Medicine is regularly quoted in newspapers, and for good reason. The articles in it are subjected to peer review: Experts in the subject are asked to evaluate whether the research was done to scientific standards. That journal is notable for having high scientific standards.

The National Geographic has less reliable standards, since they pay for their own research. But it's pretty reliable about natural history and ethnography.

What about the *Dictionary of Biography*? There's probably no motive for bias in it, though it may be incomplete. Yet it's often hard to get a better source of information about, say, a 19th century physician.

On the other hand, anyone can incorporate into a nonprofit corporation called "The Institute for Advanced Thinking on Cybernetics," or any other title you like. A name is not enough to go by.

There are good sources in your library for checking about the history and reputation of an institute, for example, *Research Centers Directory,* or *Encyclopedia of Medical Organizations and Agencies.* Still, you're not going to go run to the library every time you read in the newspaper about some experiment. Yet if you're not careful, you're likely to remember what you hear as "fact." There's no reason to accept a claim made by an "institute" you're not familiar with.

7. *Accept*: **The claim is in a media source that's usually reliable and has no obvious motive to mislead**

With newspapers, television, radio, magazines, and other media sources it's partly like trusting your friend and partly like trusting an authority. The more you read a particular newspaper, for instance, the better you'll be able to judge whether to trust its news gathering as reliable or not. The more you read a particular magazine, the better you'll be able to judge whether there's an editorial bias.

What are some factors you can use to evaluate a news report?

a. The source has been reliable in the past

A local paper seems to get the information correct about local stories most of the time. It's probably trustworthy in its account of a car accident. *The National Enquirer* gets sued a lot for libel, so it may not be reliable about the love life of a movie star.

b. The source doesn't have a bias on this topic

A television network consistently gives a bias against a particular presidential candidate. So when it says that the candidate contradicted himself twice yesterday, you should take it with a grain of salt. That may be true, but it may be a matter of interpretation. Or it may be plain false.

Clinton proposes 'wanted' list for deadbeat dads

Picking on an easy political target, President Clinton urged states Monday to post "Wanted" lists on the Internet and in Post Offices to track down "deadbeat" parents who refuse to pay child support.

"If you deliberately refuse to pay it," Clinton warned, "you can find your face posted in the Post Office. We will track you down with computers . . . We will find you through the Internet."

Paying his 25th visit to California as president, Clinton devoted himself to promoting an election-year grab bag of family-values themes popular with middle-class voters.

Associated Press, July 23, 1996

Who said newspapers are impartial?

---

c. The source being quoted is named

Do you know who wrote the articles you read in your newspaper? "From our sources" or no by-line at all often indicates that the article was a publicity hand-out.

Remember those Department of Defense unnamed sources? Don't trust them. *There's never good reason to accept a claim from an unnamed source.* "Usually reliable sources" are not even as reliable as the person who is quoting them, and anyway they've covered themselves by saying "usually."

8. *Suspend judgment*: Plausibility isn't truth

You encounter the claim "Whales migrate to the Southern Hemisphere every northern winter." It sounds plausible. But that doesn't mean it's true. Plausibility isn't truth. A claim that sounds true is good enough for you not to reject it. But you should try to confirm or disconfirm that claim if the conclusion of the argument is important to you.

It's the plausible claims, repeated and repeated, that you're most likely to believe are true without any good reason. They come in advertisements, from the government, from your family, in rumors and gossip. Don't close your mind to them: Suspend judgment. Remember, there are *three* attitudes we can take to a claim: accept, reject, or suspend judgment.

> They said that the crash in which Princess Di was killed was an accident. Ha! Can you imagine letting someone that drunk drive their car? And the royal family wanted her dead. They didn't like the idea of Prince Charles' sons being raised by her new Arab boyfriend. They wanted her dead, and they had the power to make it happen. They have the power to cover up, too—the British royal family has more money than the entire state of Nebraska. It was murder.

This conspiracy theorist hasn't proved anything. At best, she's brought up some reasons, and not very good ones at that, to *suspend judgment* on the claim "The crash was an accident." Possibility isn't truth.

9. Advertising?

The truth-in-advertising laws weren't written because all the advertisers were always telling us the truth. Many advertisements are arguments, with the (often unstated) conclusion that you should buy the product, or frequent the establishment, or use the service. Sometimes the claims are accurate, especially in advertising for medicines. But sometimes they are not. There's nothing special about them, though. They should be judged by the criteria we've already considered. If you think there should be more stringent criteria for ads, you're not judging other claims carefully enough.

10. Arguing backwards: Don't believe the premises just because the conclusion is true

Someone gives an argument that sounds pretty reasonable, the conclusion of which we're sure is true. So we think it must be a good argument with true premises.

> All dogs bark.
> Spot is a dog.
> So Spot barks.

The conclusion is true. And the premises are reasonable. So it's a good argument? No. Wild dogs don't bark. In Africa there's some breed of dogs that don't bark. The first premise isn't true, and the argument is bad.

It's easy to think that when someone gives reasons to believe a claim is true, and the claim is true, and the reasons are plausible, it must be that those reasons are true. But they needn't be; the argument may be defective. *An argument is supposed to convince us that its conclusion is true, not that its premises are true.* Don't argue backwards.

The only time we can go back from the conclusion to the premises is when the conclusion is false and the argument is valid. Then we know that one of the premises is false.

Summarizing: When to accept and when to reject

Here is a list of the criteria for when to accept or reject an unsupported claim. They're listed in the order in which you should apply them.

Reject:	The claim contradicts personal experience.
	(Exceptions: Our memory is not good; there's a good argument against our understanding of our experience; it's not our experience at all, but what we've concluded from it.)
Accept:	The claim is known by personal experience.
Reject:	The claim contradicts other claims we know to be true.
Don't accept:	The claim contradicts one of the other premises.
Accept:	The claim is given as personal experience by someone we know and trust, and the person is an authority on that kind of claim.
Accept:	The claim is offered by a reputable authority whom we can trust as an expert about this kind of claim and who has no motive to mislead.
Accept:	The claim is put forward in a reputable journal or reference source.
Accept:	The claim is in a media source that's usually reliable and has no obvious motive to mislead.

Exercises for Section B

1. Give an example of a plausible claim you've heard repeated so often you think it's true, but which you really have no reason to believe is true.

2. What three attitudes can we adopt towards whether a claim is true?

3. a. Give five criteria for accepting an unsupported claim.
   b. Give three criteria for rejecting or not accepting an unsupported claim.

4. What is our most reliable source of information about the world?

5. What do we mean when we say that someone is arguing backwards?

6. Explain why we should apply the criteria listed in the summary in the order in which they are listed.

7. Your friend who's an avid fan tells you that the baseball game on Saturday has been cancelled. Five minutes later you hear on the radio that tickets are on sale for the game on Saturday. Whom do you believe? Why?

8. Your doctor tells you that the pain in your back can't be fixed without surgery. You go to the health-food store and the clerk tells you that they have a root extract that's been formulated especially for back pain and is likely to do you some good. Whom do you believe? Why?

9. Tom: I'm going to start taking steroids.
   Zoe: What? You're crazy. They'll destroy your body.
   Tom: No way. My coach said it'll build me up. And my trainer at the health club said he can get them for me.

   Comment on Tom's reasons for believing that steroids don't harm your body.

I asked Tom to try his hand at using the criteria we've learned in this chapter. He's supposed to decide whether to accept, reject, or suspend judgment on the claims, and give an explanation of what criteria he's using. I haven't made any comments, because all his answers are good. Like most people, Tom is better at thinking critically about what other people say.

Suzy prefers to go out with athletes.

accept   *reject*   *suspend judgment*

criteria: Personal experience. She told me so.

Japanese are good at math.

accept   *reject*   *suspend judgment*

criteria: I know everyone thinks this is so, but it's just a stereotype isn't it? I know a couple who aren't <u>real</u> good at math, but maybe they mean "almost all"? It just seems so unlikely.

Crocodiles are found only in Asia and Africa.

accept   *reject*   *suspend judgment*

criteria: I think this is true. At least I seem to remember hearing it. Crocodiles are the ones in Africa and alligators in the U.S. But I'm not sure. So I guess I should suspend judgment.

Evaluate the claims in Exercises 10–29 by saying whether you accept, reject, or suspend judgment, and what criteria you are using to make that decision.

10. Smoking is bad for your health. (said by the Surgeon General)

11. Toads give you warts. (said by your mother)

12. Toads give you warts. (said by your doctor)

13. The moon rises in the west.

14. Almost all dogs bark.

15. The Pacers beat the Knicks 92–84 last night. (heard on your local news)

16. Mike Tyson is in better shape than Evander Holyfield for their title bout next week. (heard on ESPN)

17. It will take a 90% average in this course to get an A. (said by your instructor)

18. You were speeding. (said by a police officer)

19. Smoking gives you bad breath. (said to someone who smokes after a kiss)

20. Boise-Cascade has plans to log all old-growth forests in California. (said by a Sierra Club representative)

21. I still don't get it. Our instructor said that the argument in Exercise 47 was valid. I guess I'll just have to believe it.

22. The United States government was not involved in the recent attempt to invade Cuba. (unnamed sources in the Defense Department, quoted in an Associated Press story)

23. Cadillac is the best-selling luxury car in California. (in an advertisement)

24. Cadillac is the best-selling luxury car in California. (in Consumer Reports)

25. Cats are the greatest threat to public health of any common pets. (said by the author of this book)

26. Cats are the greatest threat to public health of any common pets. (said by the Surgeon General)

27. Cats are the greatest threat to public health of any common pets. (said by the Pope)

28. You left the water running when you left home today. (said by someone who lives with you)

29. The Big Bang with which the universe began was the work of God. (said by a noted astronomer)

30. Look at the front page of your local newspaper and the first page of the local section of your newspaper and see if you can determine who wrote each article. Can you do the same with your local TV newscast?

31. Pick a magazine you often read and tell the class what biases you expect from it. That is, for what kinds of claims in it should you suspend judgment rather than accept?

32. Which section of your local newspaper do you think is most reliable? Why?

33. a.   What part of the national newscast do you think is most likely to be true?
    b.   Which part do you think is least reliable?

34. Give an example of a news story you heard or read that you knew was biased because it didn't give the whole story.

35. What difference is there between how we evaluate an advertisement and how we evaluate any other (implicit) argument?

36. Find an advertisement and evaluate the claims in it.

37. Here are two articles. At the end of the chapter I'll tell you where they're from. Which, if either, of these do you find believable? Cite the criteria you're using.

a. **Half-Man Half-Dog Baffles Scientists**

Half-man, half-dog Kent Morley has baffled scientists who say that he has the genetic makeup of both man and canine in spite of the fact that his mother and father were human–and normal in every way!

That's the word from geneticist William Cramer, who says that the 38-year-old Morley is currently being studied at Minnesota's famed Mayo Clinic, where doctors are trying to figure out just what he is–and why Mother Nature made him that way.

"This is one of the most intriguing medical mysteries of all time," declared Dr. Cramer, who is widely considered to be one of the world's top authorities on genetic abnormalities and mutations.

"Mr. Morley has the head of a dog, the body and brain of a human being, and the behavioral characteristics of both species. Some people might be inclined to dismiss him as an ordinary freak of nature," he continued, "but nothing could be further from the truth.

"Ma Nature might make mistakes, but she doesn't make mistakes like this. Mr. Morley turned out the way he did for a reason. And some of the best minds in the field are bound and determined to find out what that reason is."

Spokesmen for the Mayo Clinic declined to comment on Dr. Cramer's report.

But the Washington-based geneticist not only stands by his story, he says clinic staffers have consulted him almost daily since the half-man, half-dog was admitted for testing and evaluation under an assumed name on March 14.

He added that Morley, who was born in Florida and now earns a very good living as a computer programmer, is extremely intelligent–with an IQ in the range of 125.

"Judging from the many tests that have been conducted to date, his brain would appear to be predominantly human," said Dr. Cramer. "On the other hand, he exhibits some canine behavior, including a powerful hunting instinct.

"Like most dogs, he is wary of strangers. But once he gets to know you, he is extremely friendly and loyal. He also offers something that most dog owners prize in their pets–unconditional love."

Morley has been unavailable for comment. But interviews that appeared in science and medical journals over the past few years indicate that he suffered emotionally for most of his life. As a child, he was shunned by "normal" children and forced to endure the stares and comments of complete strangers who considered him to be a freak. He reportedly found both comfort and anonymity in his study of computers and related technologies.

And in recent years, he seems to have come to terms with his appearance and learned to accept himself for what he is.

In fact, Dr. Cramer says Morley met and married a 28-year-old woman who "loves his looks," late last year. And while the couple would like nothing more than to have children, they want assurances that their babies will be 100 percent human.

"It appears that Mr. Morley can father normal children but we can't be sure until the results of a few more tests are in and analyzed," Dr. Cramer said.

[There are pictures of Mr. Morley and Dr. Cramer.]

b. **Two-headed calf born in Minersville**

It would have made a great side show for a circus.

The heifers at Gillins dairy in Minersville, Utah were averaging about a calf a day recently, but Monday dairy owner Wayne Gillins witnessed something he has not seen in his 50 years of dairy farming.

One of the heifers was ready to calf when, Gillins said, he and his son began to help the cow. They reached inside and could feel two hind legs. They began to try and pull the cow out, but as they got further along in aiding the birth, they found something else.

"We reached up there and could feel two tails," Gillins said. He thought for sure the heifer was having twins. They continued to try to birth the calf, but the back was too big. It became apparent they would have to take the animal to the veterinarian for a caesarean section delivery.

After some prodding with a pitch fork, Gillins and his son loaded the cow into a trailer and took it to Dr. H. Nielsen in Delta, Utah, 80 miles away. Nielsen began the operation to deliver the calf, but it was not what he had expected.

"He said to me I've got a head . . . and another head," Gillins said. But, surprise, the heifer was not delivering twins.

When it was removed, the new calf had two heads, two tails, six legs and two spinal cords. It looked like a single animal with one body. The calf was the width of two newborn calves and died shortly before it was delivered.

The calf had two back legs and two legs in front that appeared to be normal size for a newborn calf. Two more underdeveloped legs were on the inside between the necks of the calf.

Gillins said the calf was an embryo transplant, but he said that should not have had anything to do with the abnormal birth, because many of his calves come from such transplants and arrive with no birth defects.

The heifer had to be cut a longer length than usual to deliver the calf. Tuesday afternoon, the animal had a paralyzed right front leg. Nielsen said he was unsure what caused the paralysis.

"It's kind of different, isn't it?" Gillins said, pointing at the calf. "I've been in this business for 50 years, and I've never seen anything like this."

Nielsen said he was planning to dissect the calf Tuesday to see if the internal organs were separate as well. He said he assumed it had two hearts and other vital organs because of the structure, but he could not tell for sure without opening it up.

Nielsen said he has been practicing veterinary medicine for more than 20 years and he has seen only one other birth like this one.

He said a Scipio, Utah, beef cow gave birth to a two-headed calf with eight legs. It also died shortly after birth. While he had seen this type of birth before, Nielsen said it is still not an everyday occurrence.

"It's not real common, but it's not real uncommon, either," he said. Nielsen said if he had to guess, he would say that about one in every 100,000 births are like this one.

"It is clear that the tissue did not separate completely, but there is no indication what caused it." Nielsen said he has talked to other veterinarians who have witnessed these types of births and most of them concur that the calf dies after a few hours if it lives through the birthing process.

"They are not survivors," he said. "Even if they do survive the birth they don't live long." [There is a picture of the calf.]

38. The following was in the advertising section of a magazine. It wasn't clear if it was a paid ad or an article. Evaluate the claims by the criteria of this chapter.

Sam Louie, Pet Psychic

"Animals and people share a commonality of soul and spirit. We all search for love and we all seek to connect."

Using the same tools that many other psychics use–clairvoyance, feelings, and intuition received through the seventh chakra–Sam Louie communicates with animals. A practicing psychic since 1987, Louie found that he was increasingly "picking up" on animals and two years ago decided to focus on bridging the gap between pets and their humans.

Louie consults with pets and owners, usually via the telephone. "When someone calls, I ask for a description of the animal (color, weight, age, breed) then I focus in and contact the animal. I ask permission to communicate, tell them who I am, and then ask them if they want to talk."

People generally call with specific questions regarding their pets' behavior or health. He works with several clients who race horses, helping them to understand the animal's anxieties and needs. Many people call for a consultation when their pet is dying, asking Louie to express to the animal their love and gratitude and hoping for a final "word" from a beloved companion.

In addition to his consultations, Louie also conducts workshops in basic, intermediate and advanced animal communication. "I encourage people to develop their Buddha nature, to understand that there is no separation between souls, that we can all understand each other." Using guided meditations, imaging and other techniques, Louie teaches animal lovers to visualize communication, then helps them to re-open their innate psychic abilities and to recognize true communication when it occurs. He describes the process this way: "You have to bring forth creative imagination coupled with belief in reality."   *Catalyst,* May, 1996

39. Discuss the following advertisement in terms of the criteria given in this chapter.

> $250,000 is what you can make per year playing CRAPS
> Finally: a two-part video and book written by a top Las Vegas
> gaming expert that is easy to follow. In fact it's
> CRAP$ MADE EASY
> You do not need a large bankroll to get started.
> Order toll free 1-800-xxx-xxxx and receive
> - 1 hour instructional video   • Regulation dice and playing chips
> - 150 page book with graphs charts, and inside tips,
> - Pocket-sized game card for quick reference   . . . $59.95 . . .
> - Felt layout for home play

40. Find an article that has quotes from some "think tank" or "institute." Find out what bias that group would have.

C. It's Not Who Said It (*Bad arguments*)

1. Mistaking the person for the argument

Suppose Dr. E gives an argument in class that a critical thinking course should be required of every college freshman. His students are not convinced. So he makes the same argument tap dancing on his desk while juggling bean bags, between each claim whistling "How much is that doggy in the window?" Is the argument any better? Suppose someone in class just found out that he sicked his dogs on a kitten. Is the argument any worse?

We have standards for whether an argument is valid or strong, good or bad. It may be more memorable if Dr. E stands on his head; you may be repulsed by him if he sicked his dogs on a kitten. But the argument is good or bad—independently of how Dr. E or anyone presents it and independently of their credentials.

Mistaking the Person for the Argument   An argument *mistakes the person for the argument* if it uses or requires as premise:

(Almost) any argument that _____ gives about _____ is bad.

Mistaking the person for the argument is always bad.

> Maria: I went to Professor Zzzyzzx's talk about writing last night. He said that the best way to start on a novel is to make an outline of the plot.
> Lee: Are you kidding? He can't even speak English.

Lee makes an (implicit) argument: "Don't believe what Professor Zzzyzzx says about writing a novel because he can't speak English well." To make that strong you'd need the implausible premise, "(Almost) any argument that someone who doesn't speak English gives about writing a novel is bad."

We can also mistake a *group* for an argument:

> Dick: This proposed work corps program for the unemployed is a great idea.
> Zoe: Are you kidding? Wasn't that on the Democratic Party platform?

Mistaking the group for the argument is a favorite ploy of demagogues. It's an important tool in establishing stereotypes and prejudice. It's led to war and the misery of many.

2. Mistaking the person for the claim

Still, we know that sometimes we are justified in accepting a claim because of who said it. That's an **appeal to authority**. It's a mistake, however, a bad appeal to authority, when we accept a claim because we give too much credence to someone who's not really an authority.

Dick: What do you think of the new seat belt law?

Zoe: It must be bad, 'cause William Buckley said so.

We often treat our friends as authorities. We accept their claims because we're sure they're authorities on just about everything, or because we'd be embarrassed not to. "Come on, have a drink. Everyone's doing it." Sometimes it's the conviction that if everyone else believes it or does it, it must be true or right.

Suzy: Grab me some taco sauce, about 20 packets, so I can take some home.

Zoe: You're only supposed to eat the sauce inside Taco Bell.

Suzy: C'mon, Zoe. Are you going to reform the whole United States?

Appeal to Common Practice   An argument is an *appeal to common practice* if it uses or requires as premise:

If (almost) everyone else (in this group) does it, then it's O.K. to do.

Appeal to Common Belief   An argument is an *appeal to common belief* if it uses or requires as premise:

If (almost) everyone else (in this group) believes it, then it's true.

An appeal to common practice or common belief is usually bad, but not always. When Mary Ellen went to Japan she reasoned that since everyone there was driving on the left-hand side, she should, too. That's a real good appeal to common practice.

We can sometimes accept a claim because of who said it. But it is always a mistake to reject a claim as false because of who said it.

Mistaking the Person for the Claim   An argument *mistakes the person for the claim* if it uses or requires as premise:

(Almost) anything that _____ says about _____ is false.

George Orwell and his colleagues detested the British minister in charge of foreign affairs, Lord Halifax. But Orwell agreed with Halifax that atrocities were being committed by foreign governments. In exasperation he said to his colleagues, "They happened even though Lord Halifax said they happened."

---

3. Phony refutation

Harry: We should stop logging old-growth forests. There are very few of them left in the U.S. They are important watersheds and preserve wildlife. And once cut, we cannot recreate them.

Tom: You say we should stop logging old-growth forests? Who are you kidding? Didn't you just build a log cabin on the mountain?

Tom's rejection of Harry's argument seems reasonable: Harry's actions betray the conclusion he's arguing for. But whether they do or not (perhaps the logs came from the land Harry cleared in a new-growth forest), Tom has not answered Harry's argument. Tom is not justified in ignoring an argument because of Harry's actions.

If Harry were to respond to Tom by saying that the logs for his home weren't cut from an old-growth forest, he's been suckered. Tom got him to change the subject, and they will be deliberating an entirely different claim than he intended. It's a phony refutation—it's just missing the point.

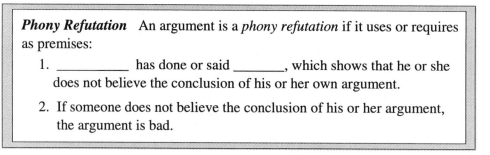

> **Phony Refutation** An argument is a *phony refutation* if it uses or requires as premises:
>
> 1. _____ has done or said _____, which shows that he or she does not believe the conclusion of his or her own argument.
>
> 2. If someone does not believe the conclusion of his or her argument, the argument is bad.

We have a desire for consistency in actions and words. We don't trust hypocrites. But when you spot a contradiction between actions and words, at most you can lay a charge of hypocrisy or irrationality. The argument might still be good. In any case, the contradiction is often only apparent, not real.

> Dick: Hey, did you see, Ted Kennedy has come out in support of a new federal law on drunk-driving.
> Suzy: Oh, yeah. Like I'm going to listen to him about drunk-driving.

Even Ted Kennedy can learn from his mistakes.

All these ways of mistaking a person for a claim or argument are sometimes referred to under the Latin term *ad hominem* (against the person).

Exercises for Section C

1. a. What is an appeal to authority?
   b. Is every appeal to authority bad? Explanation or example.

2. Why should you never mistake the person for the argument?

3. When are we justified in rejecting a claim because of who said it?

4. a. What is an appeal to common belief?
   b. How does it differ from an appeal to common practice?
   c. Give an example of either an appeal to common belief or practice that you heard this last week.

5. What do we call it when someone gives too much deference to an authority?

6.   Hypocrisy is bad. So why shouldn't we reject anything that smacks of hypocrisy?

7.   What does it mean to say that a person has made a phony refutation?

Here are some more of Tom's exercises. He's trying to see if he can distinguish between good and bad reasons for accepting or rejecting claims. I'm including my comments.

> **Doctor Ball said that for me to lose weight I need to get more exercise, but he's so obese. So I'm not going to listen to him.**
> This person is mistaking the person for the claim. Looks like a phony refutation to me.
> > *That's right.*

> **Lucy said I shouldn't go see Doctor Williams because he's had problems with malpractice suits in the past. But Lucy also believes in herbs and natural healing, so she's not going to like any doctors.**
> Looks O.K. to me. The speaker is just questioning the authority of Lucy and deciding not to accept her claim.
> > *No. It's a case of mistaking the person for the argument. The speaker isn't suspending judgment on a claim, but is rejecting Suzy's argument.*

> **Zoe: Everyone should exercise. It's good for you. It keeps you in shape, gives you more energy, and keeps away depression.**
> **Dick: Are you kidding? I've never seen you exercise.**
> Phony refutation.
> > *Right!*

For Exercises 8–20 answer:
a. Does it fit into one or more of the classifications of this section?
b. Is it a bad argument?

8.   Suzy: I played doubles on my team for four years. It is definitely a more intense game than playing singles.
    Zoe: Yesterday on the news Michael Chang said that doubles in tennis is much easier because there are two people covering almost the same playing area.
    Suzy: I guess he must be right then.

9.   Mom: You shouldn't stay out so late. It's dangerous, so I want you home early.
    Son: But none of my friends have curfews and they stay out as long as they want.

10. Manuel: Barbara said divorce'll hurt her kids' emotions.
    Maria: But she goes out with her boyfriend every night leaving the kids and her husband at home. She doesn't divorce, but she's already hurt her kids. So it doesn't matter if she gets divorced or not.

11. I can't solve this math question. It's too hard for a high school student. But my math teacher says the answer is 3. So the answer must be 3.

12. The Surgeon General said that smoking is bad for your health, so you should give up smoking.

13. The Surgeon General said that marijuana should not be legal, so I'm going to write my congresswoman and urge her not to support the bill legalizing marijuana.

14. Zoe: You should be more sensitive to the comments you make around people.
    Dick: Of course you'd think that, 'cause you're a woman.

15. Zoe: The author of this book said that bad people always make wrong decisions. You need to have virtue to make good use of critical thinking.
    Suzy: What does he know about virtue?

16. Suzy: Why don't you try to straighten out the problem with Dick?
    Zoe: Everyone knows it's best to let a sleeping dog lie.

17. Zoe: That program to build a new homeless shelter is a great idea.
    Suzy: How could you say that? You don't even give money to the homeless who beg on street corners.

18. Zoe: Don't throw that candy wrapper out the window. That's terrible. It makes a mess someone else will have to clean up.
    Dick: What are you talking about? Everyone does it. Do you want to reform the whole world?

19. Tom: What do you think about requiring kids at school to wear uniforms?
    Lee: It must be good because my mother said so.

20. —We should tax cigarettes much more heavily.
    —I can't believe you said that. Don't you smoke three packs a day?

In the Exercises for Section B, Exercise 37:
  a.   Was by Nick Mann/ Special Correspondent, *Weekly World News,* April 20, 1993.
  b.   Was by Tyson Hiatt, *The Spectrum,* St. George, Utah, July 17, 1996.

Summary We can't prove everything. We must take some claims as given or we'd never get started. But when should we accept a claim someone puts forward without proof, and when should we suspend judgment?

We don't have hard and fast rules, but we can formulate some guidelines. Most important is experience: If a claim disagrees with what we have experienced, we should reject it. Or if it disagrees with what we all know, though not from personal experience, we should reject it.

We are inclined to accept claims from people we trust who know what they're talking about and from respected authorities. But we can give too much deference to an authority. And it's wrong to think a claim is false because of the source. We can argue badly by rejecting anything that a particular person or group says. Worse is when we reject an argument because of who said it. Arguments are good or bad irrespective of who made them.

Key Words   personal experience   appeal to authority
                     suspend judgment   mistaking the person for the claim
                     arguing backwards   appeal to common practice
                     mistaking the person   appeal to common belief
                         for the argument   phony refutation

Further Study   Courses in psychology deal with the reliability of witnesses and the
nature of memory. Courses in journalism or communications will discuss the
reliability of various sources in the media and bias in the media. A short course on
how to use the library is offered at most colleges in order to help you find your way
through reference sources.

A book about the psychology of why people believe claims for bad reasons is
How We Know What Isn't So, by Thomas Gilovich, The Free Press.

Writing Lesson 7

Write an argument either for or against the following:

"No spacecraft landed on Mars in 1997; the photos were faked."

Your argument should be at most one page long.

Just list the premises and the conclusion in the format of the sample arguments. Nothing more.

Check whether your instructor has chosen a *DIFFERENT TOPIC* for this assignment.

You know whether you believe this claim. But why do you believe it or doubt it? Make your argument based on the criteria we studied in Chapter 5.

But what if you're unsure? You write pro and con lists, yet you can't make up your mind. You're really in doubt.

Then write the best argument you can for why someone should suspend judgment on the claim. That's not a cop-out; sometimes suspending judgment is the most mature, reasonable attitude to take. But you should have good reasons for suspending judgment, based on conflicts in the criteria of Chapter 5.

To give you a better idea of what you're expected to do, I've included arguments by Tom and Suzy on different topics.

Tom Wyzyczy
Critical Thinking
Section 4
Writing Lesson 7

Issue: Elvis is still alive.

Definition: By "Elvis" I understand Elvis Presley.
Premises:

Elvis Presley was reported to have died a number of years ago.

All the reputable press agencies reported his death.

Many people went to his funeral,^{A} which was broadcast live.^{B}

His doctor signed his death certificate, according to news reports.

There have been reports that Elvis is alive.

No such report has been in the mainstream media, only in tabloids.

No physical evidence that he is alive has ever been produced.

No one would have anything to gain by faking his death.^{C}

If Elvis were alive, he would have much to gain by making that known
to the public.

Conclusion: Elvis is not alive.

Good. But it could be better. First, split the third premise into two (A and B). I don't know if it was broadcast live, yet I can accept part A.

Second, the phrase "mainstream media" and "tabloid" are too vague. You should cite real sources if you want someone to accept your argument.

And premise C is very dubious: Any of his heirs had lots to gain.

Finally, you take for granted that the reader knows why some of your premises are important. But it isn't obvious. Why is A important? To explain, you need to add the glue, a premise or premises linking it to the conclusion. You're still leaving too much unstated. Don't rely too much on the other person making your argument for you. Review Chapters 3 and 4.

Still, I think you have the idea from Chapter 5 and won't be suckered by the conspiracy theorists.

Suzy Queue
Critical Thinking
Section 2
Writing Lesson 7

Issue: The CIA started the cocaine epidemic in the ghettos in order to control and pacify blacks.

Premises:

The CIA has lied to us a lot in the past.

Riots in the past in the ghettos have been a serious problem in the U.S.

The government wants to control blacks, so they won't make any trouble.

Black people in the ghetto had too much to ~~loose~~ *lose* to start.

Many people in the ghettos believe that the CIA introduced cocaine to the U.S.

It was reported on national news that the CIA was involved with drug running from Latin America.

Conclusion: The CIA started the cocaine epidemic in the ghettos in order to control and pacify blacks.

At best you've given reason to <u>suspend judgment</u>. You haven't given me any reason to believe the claim is <u>true</u>, only that it isn't obviously false.

Some of your premises are way too vague ("national news," "serious problems"). And I can't see how they link to the conclusion. Are you suggesting that if the CIA lied to us in the past that makes it highly probable that they introduced cocaine into the ghettos? That's pretty weak. And big deal that a lot of people in the ghettos believe the CIA introduced cocaine there. A lot of people think the moon doesn't rise or that it rises in the west—that doesn't make it true. Are they authorities?

Review the criteria in Chapter 5.

Review Chapters 1–5

Let's review what we've done.

We began by saying we would study attempts to convince. But that was too broad, so we restricted ourselves to convincing through arguments: collections of claims used to show a particular claim is true.

We said a claim was any declarative sentence that we can view as true or false. But to use that definition took practice. We learned to recognize sentences that posed as claims but were ambiguous or too vague for us to deliberate. Definitions were one way to clear up confusions. And we differentiated among claims, noting that unstated standards could make a claim objective or subjective.

We saw that there are two aspects of an argument that have to be evaluated. We should have good reason to believe the premises, and we looked at criteria for that. But even if the premises are true, it might not be enough to convince. The conclusion has to follow from the premises. We decided that meant the argument must be either valid or strong.

Often there's a gap between the premises and conclusion. We needed a guide for when it's reasonable to repair an argument and when an argument is unrepairable. We based the guide on the assumptions we need in order to deliberate with someone.

You should now be able to analyze an attempt to convince:

> - Is it an argument?
> - What's the conclusion?
> - What are the premises?
> - Are any further premises needed?
> - Is it valid? If not, where is it on the scale from very strong to weak?
> - Is it a good argument?
> - Can it be repaired?

Along the way, we also saw various types of bad arguments that you should be able to spot.

You'll get a lot more practice in analyzing arguments in the following chapters. The review exercises here are designed to make sure you know the *definitions*. You can't apply ideas you only half-remember. Recall the steps in understanding a definition:

- Know what the words mean and be able to recall the definition.
- Know an example of the definition.
- Know an example of something that doesn't fit the definition.
- Practice classifying with the exercises.
- Relate the definition to other concepts you've learned.

The last step is the crucial one in putting the material together. You may have learned the definition of "valid" and know how to recognize whether an argument is valid, but you don't really understand that definition until you know how it relates to others, such as "strong" and "good argument."

Review Exercises for Chapters 1–5

1. What is an argument?

2. What is a claim?

3. a. What is an objective claim?
   b. Give an example of an objective claim.
   c. Give an example of a subjective claim.

4. What does it mean to say a sentence is ambiguous?

5. Can a vague sentence be a claim? Explain.

6. Is a definition a claim? Explain.

7. a. What is a persuasive definition?
   b. Give an example.

8. What is the definition of a "good argument"?

9. What three tests must an argument pass for it to be good?

10. a. What is a valid argument?
    b. Give an example of a valid argument that is good.
    c. Give an example of a valid argument that is bad.

11. a. What does it mean to say an argument is strong?
    b. Give an example of a strong argument that is good.
    c. Give an example of a strong argument that is bad.

12. Is every weak argument bad? Explain.

13. How do you show an argument is not valid?

14. If an argument has fourteen true premises and one false premise, should we accept the the conclusion? Explain.

15. If an argument is bad, what does that tell us about its conclusion?

16. Is every valid or strong argument with true premises good? Explain.

17. Should we always prefer valid arguments to strong arguments? Explain.

18. What is the main mark of irrationality?

19. State the Principle of Rational Discussion.

20. State the Guide to Repairing Arguments.

21. Give five circumstances in which we shouldn't repair an argument.

22. a. What is an indicator word?
    b. Is an indicator word part of a claim?

23. What is our most reliable source of information about the world?

24. What three attitudes can we take to whether a claim is true?

25. Give five criteria for accepting an unsupported claim.

26. Give three criteria for rejecting or not accepting an unsupported claim.

27. What does it mean to say that someone is arguing backwards?

28. What does it mean to say someone is mistaking the person for the argument?

29. When are we justified in rejecting a claim because someone said it?

30. When are we justified in rejecting an argument because someone said it?

31. What is a phony refutation?

The STRUCTURE
of ARGUMENTS

6   Compound Claims

A. It's Just One Claim

1. Compound claims

Suppose your neighbor says:

> "I'll return your lawn mower or I'll buy you a new one."

Has he promised to return your lawn mower? No. Has he promised to buy you a new lawn mower? No. He's promised to do one or the other. We have one claim, not two.

> **Compound Claim**   A *compound claim* is one composed of other claims, but which has to be viewed as just one claim.

Here are some examples using "or":

Either a Democrat will win the election or a Republican will win.
Either some birds don't fly or penguins aren't birds.
Columbus landed in South Carolina or on some island near there.

Each "or" claim, though just one claim, is made up of two claims. The last one, for instance, contains:

Columbus landed in South Carolina.
Columbus landed on some island near South Carolina.

Alternatives   *Alternatives* are the claims that are the parts of an "or" claim.

Now suppose your instructor says to you:

"If you do well on the final exam, then I'll give you an A in this course."

This is *one* claim. If it shows up in an argument, we don't say one premise is "You do well on the final exam" and another is "I'll give you an A in this course." Rather *if* you do well, *then* your instructor will give you an A in this course. There is no promise to give you an A, only a *conditional* promise. If you do poorly on the final, your instructor is not obligated to give you an A.
Or consider:

If Maria calls in sick today, then Dick will have to go to work.

Either this whole "if . . . then . . ." claim is true or not. To decide whether it is true we ask whether Dick is obligated to work if Maria calls in sick. If she could call in sick and he's not obligated to work, then the claim is false.
Sometimes "then" is left unsaid, or the order of the two parts is reversed:

a. If Dick loves Zoe, he will give her an engagement ring.

b. If they're serving beef stroganoff in the cafeteria, I won't eat there.

c. I'll meet you at the cafeteria if they're not serving beef stroganoff.

And sometimes, neither "if" nor "then" is used, yet it's clear that the claim makes sense as an "if . . . then . . ." claim. For example,

d. Bring me an ice cream cone and I'll be happy.

Conditional Claim   A claim is called a *conditional* if it can be rewritten as an "if . . . then . . ." claim that must have the same truth-value.

Antecedent and Consequent   In a conditional rewritten as "If A, then B", the claim A is called the *antecedent,* and the claim B is called the *consequent.*

In (a), the antecedent is "Dick loves Zoe," and the consequent is "He will give her an engagement ring."

In (b) the antecedent is "They're serving beef stroganoff in the cafeteria," and the consequent is "I won't eat there."

In (c), though the order is reversed, it is the part that follows "if " that is the antecedent, "They're not serving beef stroganoff," and the consequent is "I'll meet you at the cafeteria."

In (d) the antecedent is "Bring me an ice cream cone," and the consequent is "I'll be happy."

There is one way to connect claims that looks like a compound, and could be treated as a compound, but is simpler not to view as a compound—namely, when we join two claims with "and." Suppose you hear Lee say,

> Tom's coming over this afternoon, and Maria is going out.

When is this true? Well, exactly when both "Tom is coming over" is true and "Maria is going out" is true. So in an argument we'd have to treat each of those claims independently anyway. It's just the same with "but."

> Manuel wants to go out, but Maria has the van.

This is true when both parts are true. So we might as well view each claim independently. "But" works just like "and" in an argument—it's a stylistic variation that shows some surprise.

2. The contradictory of a claim

Because a compound claim is made up of other claims, we often get confused in trying to say it's false.

> **The Contradictory of a Claim**   The *contradictory* of a claim is one that always has the opposite truth-value. Sometimes a contradictory is called the *negation* of a claim.

The contradictory of "Spot is a doberman" is "Spot is not a doberman." But you don't always have to add "not" to a claim to make the contradictory. The contradictory of "You will never learn how to drive" is "You will learn how to drive"— and "not" doesn't appear in it.

claim	*contradictory*
Spot barks.	Spot doesn't bark.
Dick isn't a student.	Dick is a student.

It's easy to make the contradictory of an "or" claim:

claim

Suzy will go to the movies
  or she will stay home.

Tom or Suzy will pick up
  Manuel for class today.

contradictory

Suzy won't go to the movies
  and she won't stay home.

Neither Tom nor Suzy will pick up
  Manuel for class today.

The Contradictory of an "or" Claim

A or B *has contradictory*   not A and not B.

We can also make the contradictory of "A or B" by saying "*Neither* A *nor* B."
    Here I've used the capital letters "A" and "B" to stand for any claims. And I've written "not A" and "not B" to stand for "the contradictory of A" and "the contradictory of B." For example, the following fits into this form:

Either Lee will pick up Manuel, or Manuel won't come home for dinner.
contradictory:
Lee won't pick up Manuel, and Manuel will come home for dinner.

But how do we form the contradictory of a conditional? Listen to Suzy and Zoe.

Zoe: I'm so worried. Spot got out of the yard. If Spot got out of the
       yard, then the dogcatcher got him, I'm sure.
Suzy: Don't worry. I saw Spot. He got out of the yard, but the
       dogcatcher didn't get him.

IF    **THEN**

contradictory:

   **BUT**

> ### The Contradictory of a Conditional
> If A, then B *has contradictory*   A, but not B

The contradictory of a conditional is not another conditional. For example:

(‡)   If Suzy studies three hours every day, she will pass critical thinking.

Neither of the following contradicts (‡):

> If Suzy doesn't study three hours every day, she will pass critical thinking.
> If Suzy studies three hours every day, she will not pass critical thinking.

Both those and (‡) can all be false. The contradictory of (‡) is:

> Suzy studies three hours every day *and* she does *not* pass critical thinking.

Sometimes, when we reason about how the world might be, we use a conditional with a false antecedent:

> If cats had no fur, they would not give people allergies.

We could form the contradictory as for any conditional. But more commonly we use words like "although," or "even if":

> Even if cats had no fur, they would still give people allergies.

In "even if" the "if" *doesn't* make a conditional. "Even if" means the same as "although" or "despite that."

Exercises for Section A

1. What is a compound claim?

2. Why can we take both A and B to be premises when someone says "A and B"?

3. a.   What is a conditional?
    b.   Is a conditional a compound claim?

4.   Make a conditional promise to your instructor you believe you can keep.

5.   What do we call the parts of an "or" claim?

For each of Exercises 6–9, if it is an "or" claim, identify the alternatives.

6.   Either Dick loves Zoe best, or he loves Spot best.

7.   You're either for me or against me.

8.   You'd better stop smoking in here or else!

9.   AIDS cannot be contracted by touching nor by breathing air in the same room as a person infected with AIDS.

10.   What is the antecedent of a conditional?

11.   Give five examples (not from the text) of conditional claims that don't use the word "if" or don't use the word "then." At least one should have the consequent first and antecedent last. Exchange with a classmate to identify the antecedents and consequents.

12.   What is the contradictory of a claim?

13.   How do you say the contradictory of "A or B"?

14.   How do you say the contradictory of "If A then B"?

15.   Write the contradictory of:
    a.   Inflation will go up or interest rates will go up.
    b.   Maria or Manuel will pick up Dick at the airport.
    c.   Zoe will serve either mustard greens or brussels sprouts at dinner.
    d.   Manuel won't take the exam on Tuesday.
    e.   Maria will go shopping and Manuel will cook.
    f.   If Maria goes shopping, then Manuel will cook.

16.   Make up two conditionals and two "or" claims. Exchange them with a classmate to write the contradictories.

Here are two examples of Tom's work on conditionals.

> **Getting an A in critical thinking means that you studied hard.**
> *Conditional?* (yes or no) Yes.
> *Antecedent*: You get an A in critical thinking.
> *Consequent*: You studied hard.
> *Contradictory*: You got an A in critical thinking but you didn't study hard.
>   (or   Even though you got an A in critical thinking, you didn't study hard.)
> *Good work.*

Spot loves Dick because Dick plays with him.
Conditional? (yes or no) No.
Antecedent: Spot loves Dick. *No*
Consequent: Dick plays with him. *No*
Contradictory: Spot loves Dick but Dick doesn't play with him. *No*

> *You're right, it's not a conditional: the word "because" tells you it's an argument. But if it's not a conditional, then there is no antecedent and no consequent. And there can't be a contradictory of an argument.*

For Exercises 17–28 answer the following:
Conditional? (yes or no)
Antecedent:
Consequent:
Contradictory:

17. If the Israelis and Palestinians agree on the next step of the peace process, then Syria will make peace with Israel.

18. If you don't apologize I'll never talk to you again.

19. Neither Maria nor Manuel will travel at Christmas.

20. Loving someone means you never throw dishes at them.

21. Lee never writes to his brother.

22. Since 2 times 2 is 4, and 4 times 2 is 8, I should be ahead $8, not $7.

23. Spot is a good dog, even though he attacked your cat.

24. "If Spot attacked your cat, then I'll pay for the funeral," said Dick.

25. Dick or Zoe will go to the grocery to get eggs.

26. If it's really true that if Dick takes Spot for a walk he'll do the dishes, then Dick won't take Spot for a walk.

27. If Dick goes to the basketball game, then he either got a free ticket or he borrowed money for one.

28. Dick will love Zoe so long as she treats Spot well.

B. Consider the Alternatives

1. Reasoning with "or" claims

We can often recognize that an argument is valid or weak just by the role that a compound claim plays in it. For example,

> Either there is a wheelchair ramp at the school dance, or Manuel stayed home. But there isn't a wheelchair ramp at the school dance. Therefore, Manuel stayed home.

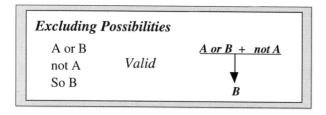

The argument is valid: It's impossible for the premises to be true and conclusion false. That's the same for any argument like the one above.

> ### Excluding Possibilities
>
> A or B
> not A   *Valid*
> So B
>
> $\underline{A \ or \ B \ + \ not \ A}$
>
> $\downarrow$
>
> B

This form of argument is sometimes called the "disjunctive syllogism."
    Of course, we could negate either claim. This is valid, too:

A or B, not B, therefore A.

And there's no reason to have just two alternatives:

Somebody's cat killed the bird that always sang outside. *1*
Either it was Sarah's cat or the neighbor's cat or some stray. *2*
Sarah says it wasn't her cat, *3* because hers was in all day. *4*
My neighbor says her cat never leaves the house. *5*
So it must have been a stray. *6*

First, it seems we get from *3* and *4* :

Sarah's cat didn't kill the bird. *a*

And from *5* we get:

My neighbor's cat didn't kill the bird. *b*

(As before, lower case letters mark claims that are added to an argument.)

No one of *2, a,* or *b* by itself would give us *6*. But *a* and *b* together with *2* do. With *2* rewritten as "Either Sarah's cat killed the bird, or the neighbor's cat killed the bird, or some stray cat killed the bird," this has the form:

A or B or C + *not A* + *not B*

↓

C

When arguing by excluding possibilities, sometimes we can only eliminate some of the alternatives:

> Either all criminals should be locked up forever, or we should put more money into rehabilitating criminals, or we should accept that our streets will never be safe, or we should have some system for monitoring ex-convicts. *1* (*this is all one claim*)
>
> We can't lock up all criminals forever *2*, because it would be too expensive. *3*
>
> We definitely won't accept that our streets will never be safe. *4*
>
> So either we should put more money into rehabilitating criminals, or we should have some system for monitoring ex-convicts. *5*

The argument is valid, because *2* and *4* eliminate some of the possibilities given in *1*. But even if *1* is true (really lists all possibilities), all we get from this argument is another "or" claim—we've reduced the possibilities.

A or B or C or D + *not A* + *not C*

↓   *Valid*

B or D

Reasoning with compound claims that use "or" seems simple. But there's a problem: The word "or" in English is ambiguous. Sometimes we use it in the *inclusive* sense: "One or the other or both." Sometimes we use it in the *exclusive* sense: "One or the other, but not both." An example of the exclusive sense is:

> Suzy: Where's Dick tonight?
> Zoe: He went out with Tom and Harry. They're either at the movies or at the bar.

If an argument fails to be good on one reading, try the other sense of "or"; maybe that was intended.

2. False dilemmas (*Bad arguments*)

Excluding possibilities is a valid form of argument. But valid arguments need not be good. We get a bad argument when the "or" claim doesn't list all the possibilities.

Zoe has made a valid argument, but it isn't a good one. She's posed a false dilemma: "You're either going to have to stop smoking those nasty expensive cigars or we'll have to get rid of Spot" is false. Dick could respond that Zoe could give up talking to her mother long distance every day.

> **False Dilemma**   An "or" claim that seems to be true but isn't, because there is another possibility it does not state.

To avoid false dilemmas, you have to use your imagination for the other possibilities. Even the argument about Manuel going to the dance was a false dilemma:

Often a false dilemma relies on an unstated "or" claim:

Tom: Both Lee and I think they should allow logging on Cedar Mountain. You do, too—don't you, Dick?

Dick: Actually, no, . . .

Tom: I didn't know you were one of those environmentalist freaks.

The unstated claim is "Either you're for allowing logging on Cedar Mountain, or you're an environmentalist freak." This is one of those "If you're not with us, you're against us" arguments.

Exercises for Section B

1. Give an "or" claim that you know is true, though you don't know which of the alternatives is true.

2. State the form of valid arguments that use "or" claims.

3. What is a false dilemma?

4. Give an example of a false dilemma you've used or had used on you recently.

5. Why is using a false dilemma so good at making people do what you want them to do? Is it a good way to convince?

6. Sometimes a false dilemma is stated using "if . . . then . . .":

    > If you don't stop smoking, you're going to die.
    >> (Either you stop smoking or you will die.)

    > Mommy, if you don't take me to the circus, then you don't really love me.
    >> (Either you take me to the circus or you don't love me.)

    > If you can't remember what you wanted to say, it's not important.
    >> (Either you remember what you want to say or it's not important.)

    Give two examples of false dilemmas stated using "if . . . then . . ." Give them to a classmate to rewrite as "or" claims.

7. A particular form of false dilemma is the *perfectionist dilemma,* which assumes:

    > Either the situation will be perfect if we do this, or we shouldn't do it.
    > (*All or nothing at all.*)

    For example,

    > — I'm voting for raising property taxes to pay for improvements to the schools.
    > — Don't be a fool. No matter how much money they pour into the schools, they'll never be first rate.

    Give an example of a perfectionist dilemma you've heard or read.

8. a. Give two examples of "or" claims that are best understood as meaning that the alternatives exclude each other (*exclusive* "or").
    b. An argument that relies on a dubious claim that says it has to be one or the other but not both is a *false exclusive dilemma.* Give an example.

    Evaluate Exercises 9–13 by answering the following questions:
    Argument? (yes or no)
    Conclusion (if unstated, add it):
    Premises:
    Additional premises needed (if none, say so):
    Classify (with the additional premises): valid   very strong ————— weak
    Good argument? (yes or no, with an explanation) (If it's a false dilemma, say so.)

9. Either Suzy loves Tom or she's putting on a good show. But she's a lousy actress. So she must really love Tom.

10. Dick : It's time. Either we get married or we should stop living together.
    Zoe: What do you mean "It's time"?
    Dick: I mean we both know that just living together is awkward.
    Zoe: Well, I don't want to live alone. Do you?
    Dick: No. So we'll have to get married.
    (Evaluate the whole dialogue as one argument.)

11. Zoe: We should get rid of Spot. He keeps chewing on everything in the house.
    Dick: But why does that mean we should get rid of him?
    Zoe: Because either we train him to stop chewing or get rid of him. And we
           haven't been able to train him.
    Dick: But I love Spot. We can just make him live outdoors.
    (Evaluate what Zoe says as an argument. Consider Dick's answer in doing so.)

12. Zoe: Either you do the dishes and take out the trash or I'm leaving you.
    Dick: Hey, I'm a man, that's not man's work.
    Zoe: Then I'm leaving you.

13. I'm not going to vote, because no matter who is president I still won't get a job.

C. Conditionals

1. Valid and invalid forms of arguments using conditionals

> If Spot barks, then Dick will wake up.
> Spot barked.
> So Dick woke up.

That's valid. It's impossible for the premises to be true and conclusion false.

> If Suzy calls early, then Dick will wake up.
> Suzy called early.
> So Dick woke up.

This is valid, too.

Did you notice that these arguments are similar? They have the same *form*:

If <u>Spot barks</u>, *then* <u>Dick will wake up</u>. 　　　A　　　　　　　B	*If* <u>Suzy calls early</u>, *then* <u>Dick will wake up</u>. 　　　　A　　　　　　　　　B
<u>Spot barked</u>. 　　A	<u>Suzy called early</u>. 　　　A
So <u>Dick woke up</u>. 　　　B	*So* <u>Dick woke up</u>. 　　　B

Any argument of this form is valid (though not necessarily good, since a premise could be false).

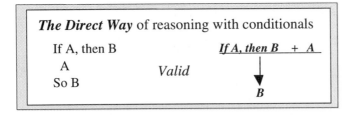

This way of reasoning is sometimes called *modus ponens.*
    We can also reason:

    If Spot barks, then Dick will wake up.
    Dick didn't wake up.
    So Spot didn't bark.

That's valid. After all, if Spot had barked, Dick would have awoken. Similarly:

    If <u>Suzy calls early</u>, *then* <u>Dick will wake up</u>.
           A   B

    <u>Dick didn't wake up</u>.
        not B

    So <u>Suzy didn't call early</u>.
        not A

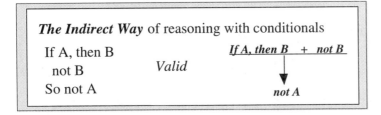

This way of reasoning is sometimes called *modus tollens.*
    Here, again, "not A" and "not B" are shorthand for "the contradictory of A"
and "the contradictory of B." For example, this argument also uses the Indirect Way:

    If Suzy doesn't call early, then Zoe won't go shopping.
    Zoe went shopping.
    So Suzy called early.

    Recognizing this form can be hard if there are several "nots" or the order of the
antecedent and consequent is reversed. For example, this uses the Indirect Way:

    Zoe won't go shopping if Dick comes home early.
    Zoe went shopping.
    So Dick didn't come home early.

Zoe won't go shopping *if* Dick comes home early.
        B   A

Zoe went shopping.
     not B

So Dick didn't come home early.
       not A

Here's what Dick has to face every morning:

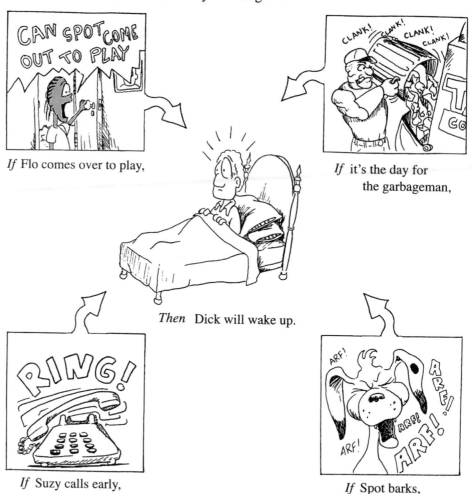

If Flo comes over to play,

If it's the day for
the garbageman,

Then Dick will wake up.

If Suzy calls early,

If Spot barks,

There are many ways that Dick could be woken. And if he doesn't wake up, then we know that none of those happened.

But it's wrong to reason that if Dick did wake up, then Spot barked. Maybe Suzy called early. Or maybe Flo came over to play. It's reasoning backwards, over-looking possibilities, to reason: If A, then B, B, so A. Yet it's easy to get confused and use this way of reasoning as if it were valid, because it's so similar to the Direct Way of reasoning with conditionals.

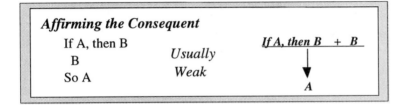

Affirming the Consequent

If A, then B
  B
So A

Usually Weak

If A, then B + B
        ↓
        A

Just as there's an invalid form that's easy to confuse with the Direct Way, there's an invalid form that's easy to confuse with the Indirect Way.

If it's the day for the garbageman, then Dick will wake up.
It's not the day for the garbageman.
So Dick didn't wake up.

This, too, is reasoning backwards. Even though the garbageman didn't come, maybe Flo came over to play, or Spot barked. You can't overlook other possibilities.

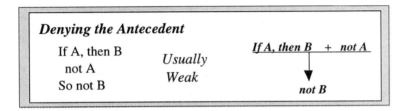

Denying the Antecedent

If A, then B
  not A
So not B

Usually Weak

If A, then B + not A
        ↓
      not B

With this form, too, we have to be alert when "not" shows up in the conditional.

If Maria doesn't call Manuel, then Manuel will miss his class.
Maria did call Manuel. So Manuel didn't miss his class.

If Maria doesn't call Manuel, *then* Manuel will miss his class.
          A   B

Maria did call Manuel.
      not A

So Manuel didn't miss his class.
        not B

But if Dick woke up, can't we at least say that one of those four claims from the picture are true? No, there could be another possibility.

From this discussion and the picture on page 132 we can see an equivalence.

> ***Contrapositive***   The *contrapositive* of "If A, then B" is "If not B, then not A."
> The contrapositive is true exactly when the original conditional is true.

Sometimes it's easier to understand a conditional via its contrapositive:

If you get a speeding ticket, then a policeman stopped you.
If a policeman didn't stop you, then you didn't get a ticket.

Here's a picture to summarize what we've discussed.

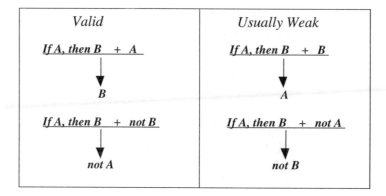

> The invalid forms of arguing are obviously confusions with valid forms,
> mistakes a good reasoner doesn't make. When you see one, *don't bother*
> *to repair the argument.*

For example, suppose you hear someone say,

If Suzy called early, then Dick woke up.
So Dick didn't wake up.

The obvious premise to add is "Suzy didn't call early." But that makes the argument
weak. So the argument is unrepairable.

Exercises for Section C.1

1. If Dick and Zoe get another dog, then Spot will be happy.
    If Dick buys Spot a juicy new bone, then Spot will be happy.
    If Dick spends more time with Spot, then Spot will be happy.
    If Spot finally learns how to catch field mice, then Spot will be happy.

    Assume all these conditionals are true. Using them:

    a. Give two examples of the Direct Way of reasoning with conditionals.

    b. Give two examples of the Indirect Way of reasoning with conditionals.

    c. Give two examples of Affirming the Consequent. Explain why each is not valid in terms of other possibilities.

    d. Give two examples of Denying the Antecedent. Explain why each is not valid in terms of other possibilities.

2. Give an example (not from the text) of the Direct Way of reasoning with conditionals.

3. Give an example (not from the text) of the Indirect Way of reasoning with conditionals.

4. Give an example (not from the text) of Affirming the Consequent. Show it's not valid.

5. Give an example (not from the text) of Denying the Antecedent. Show it's not valid.

6. State the contrapositive of:

    a. If Flo plays with Spot, then she has to take a bath.

    b. If Manuel doesn't get his wheelchair fixed by Wednesday, he can't attend class on Thursday.

    c. If Maria goes with Manuel to the dance, then Lee will be home alone on Saturday.

For Exercises 7–12, if there's a claim you can add to make the argument valid according to one of the forms we studied, add it. If the argument is unrepairable, say so.

7. If Flo comes over early to play, then Spot will bark. So Spot barked.

8. Whenever Flo comes over to play, Spot barks. So Flo didn't come over to play.

9. Tom: Zoe will cook spaghetti if Dick remembered to buy tomato paste.
    Harry: So it's definitely spaghetti tonight.

10. Zoe will wash the dishes if Dick cooks. So Dick didn't cook.

11. Lee: Dr. E gives multiple choice exams when he has no time to grade regular exams.
    Suzy: So Dr. E won't give a multiple choice exam today.

12. If Flo does her homework, then she can watch TV. So Flo did her homework.

13. Here's another valid form of reasoning with conditionals:

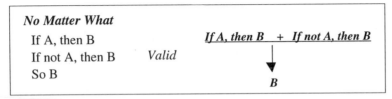

    Dick: If I study for my math exam this weekend we won't be able to have a good time at the beach.

    Zoe: But if you don't study for your exam, you'll worry about it like you always do, and we won't be able to have a good time at the beach. So it looks like this weekend is shot.

    Give another example of this form.

2. "Only if"

Look again at the picture on page 132. Dick could wake up for lots of reasons. But in the morning there's no way that Spot could bark and Dick not wake up: "If Spot barks, then Dick will wake up" is true. That is, Spot barks *only if* Dick wakes up.

> Dr. E: I'll give you an A in this course only if you show up for every class.
>
> Suzy: O.K.
>
> Suzy: (*later*) What happened, Dr. E? I attended every single class, and I didn't get an A.
>
> Dr. E I said I'd give you an A *only if* you showed up. Don't you understand? If you didn't show up, you wouldn't get an A. You also needed to pass all the exams, and . . .

"A only if B" just means "If not B, then not A." That's straightforward. Yet we know that the contrapositive is equivalent to "If A, then B." So we have:

> A only if B *can be replaced by* If A, then B.

So all the following have the same truth-value:

You can get a speeding ticket *only if* you are going over the speed limit.

If you don't go over the speed limit, then you won't get a speeding ticket.

If you get a speeding ticket, then you went over the speed limit.

3. Necessary and sufficient conditions

What's necessary for getting a driver's license?

Being of legal age to drive.   Taking the written test.
Paying the fee.   Taking the driving test.

Each of these (and more) is required. But none by itself is sufficient to get a driver's license.

Distinguishing what is a necessary condition and what is sufficient is easy using conditionals.

> "If A, then B" is always true
>
> means   A is *sufficient* for B
>   B is *necessary* for A

Dick's predicament in the morning can illustrate this:

Flo coming over early is sufficient for Dick to wake up.

Zoe being noisy making breakfast is sufficient to get Dick to wake up.

Dick waking up is necessary (required, inevitable) when Zoe is noisy.

Dick waking up is necessary (required, inevitable) when Spot barks.

The translation between necessary and sufficient conditions and conditionals makes it a snap. So what's the big deal? People get mixed up and argue for a condition being sufficient, when what they should be showing is that it is necessary.

Manuel:　It's just wrong that Betty didn't make the basketball team.

Lee:　　Yeah. I watched the tryouts and she was great. She hit a couple three-pointers, and she can really jump.

Manuel:　And the coach chose only girls who could jump well and hit three-pointers.

Lee:　　She had everything you need to get on the team.

Lee is confused. He thinks that jumping well and hitting three-pointers are *sufficient* for getting on the team. But what Manuel pointed out was that they were *necessary*. Lee is arguing backwards.

Exercises for Sections C.2 and C.3

1. We know that the following are equivalent:

    Dick will go to the movies only if he gets home before 6 p.m.

    If Dick didn't get home before 6 p.m., then he didn't go to the movies.

    If Dick went to the movies, then he got home before 6 p.m.

    Rewrite each of the following in two ways:

    a. You can pass this course only if you study hard.
    b. I'll love you only if you love me.
    c. You can get AIDS only if you're stupid or unlucky.

2. a. Give two examples (not from the text) of "only if" claims that you know are true.
    b. Rewrite them in the form "if A, then B."
    c. Rewrite them in the form "if not B, then not A."

For Exercises 3–10 state which of the following hold:

    (i) is necessary for (ii)　　　　(i) is both necessary and sufficient for (ii)

    (i) is sufficient for (ii)　　　　(i) is neither necessary nor sufficient for (ii)

3. (i) The ground outdoors is wet.　(ii) It's raining hard.

4. (i) The Packers scored a touchdown.　(ii) The Packers are winning.

5. (i) Zoe won $47 at blackjack.　(ii) Zoe was gambling.

6. (i) Suzy is lying.　(ii) Suzy isn't telling the truth.

7. (i) Maria has a restraining order on her ex-husband.

(ii) Maria's ex-husband is prohibited by law from approaching her.

8. (i) Ralph is a dog. (ii) Ralph chases cats.

9. (i) Suzy is over 21. (ii) Suzy can legally drink in this state.

10. (i) Tom was charged with DUI. (ii) Tom was found guilty of DUI.

Often we say that one condition is necessary or sufficient for another, like "Being over 16 is necessary for getting a driver's license." That means that the general conditional is true: "If you can get a driver's license, then you're over 16." For Exercises 11–15 state which condition is necessary or sufficient, as for Exercises 3–10.

11. (i) being a dog (ii) being an animal

12. (i) being a U.S. citizen (ii) being born in the U.S.

13. (i) being a U.S. citizen (ii) being allowed to vote in the U.S.

14. (i) having the ability to fly (ii) being a bird

15. (i) being a sister (ii) being a female

16. What is a necessary condition for there to be a fire?

17. What is a necessary condition for being a father?

18. What is a sufficient condition for passing this course?

19. What is a necessary condition for performing open heart surgery?

For each of Exercises 20–28, rewrite it as an "if . . . then . . ." claim if that is possible. If it's not, say so.

20. Flo will go over to play with Spot only if her mother lets her.

21. Eating nutritious dog food is necessary for Spot to be healthy.

22. Paying the garbageman $5 is necessary for Dick to sleep late.

23. Only if Zoe's mother doesn't come for the holidays will Dick and Zoe go to Mexico.

24. Suzy will get an A in critical thinking only if Dr. E is drunk when he fills out grades.

25. Suzy will get an A in critical thinking if Dr. E reads his grade sheet wrong and confuses her with Maria, who's next on the list.

26. Tom loves Suzy even though she hasn't a clue in the critical thinking class.

27. Of course, Suzy loves Tom despite the coach suspending him for a game.

28. For Tom to get back on the team, he has to do 200 push-ups.

29. Give an example in which someone has argued for a condition being necessary, when what he or she should be arguing for is that it is sufficient.

30. A *if and only if* B means if A then B, and if B then A.

    For example, suppose Dick is such a heavy sleeper that the only way he will wake up is if Spot barks. Then there's only one route to "Dick will wake up." We have both:

If Spot barks, then Dick will wake up.
If Dick wakes up, then Spot barked.

So we can say:

Spot will bark *if and only if* Dick wakes up.

Give an example of an "if and only if " claim from your own life that you know is true.

4. Reasoning in a chain and the slippery slope

Suppose we know:

If Dick takes Spot for a walk, then Zoe will cook dinner.
And if Zoe cooks dinner, then Dick will do the dishes.

We can conclude:

If Dick takes Spot for a walk, then he'll do the dishes.

We can set up a chain of reasoning, a chain of conditionals. For example,

If Dick and Zoe get a new dog, then Spot will have company every day.
If Spot has company every day, then Spot will not get bored.
If Spot does not get bored, then Spot will be happy.
So if Dick and Zoe get a new dog, then Spot will be happy.

The conclusion is another conditional.

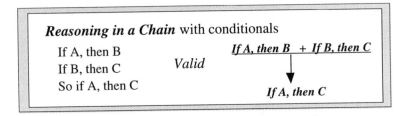

Reasoning in a Chain with conditionals

If A, then B		*If A, then B* + *If B, then C*
If B, then C	*Valid*	
So if A, then C		*If A, then C*

Reasoning in a chain is important. We go by little steps. Then if A is true, we can conclude C.

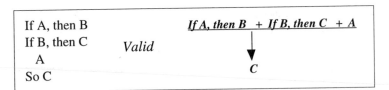

If A, then B		*If A, then B* + *If B, then C* + *A*
If B, then C	*Valid*	
A		
So C		*C*

But this valid form of argument can be used badly. Here's what Lee said to Maria last week:

Don't get a credit card! If you do, you'll be tempted to spend money you don't have. Then you'll max out on your card. Then you'll be in real debt. And you'll have to drop out of school to pay your bills. You'll end up a failure in life.

This isn't stated as a series of conditionals, but it's easy to rewrite it as such (that's Exercise 6 below). Then it will be valid. But it's not a good argument. If you take the first step (accept the antecedent of the first conditional), then the chain of conditionals forms a slippery slope for you to slide all the way to the conclusion. But you can stop the slide: Just point out that one of the conditionals is dubious. The second one is a good candidate. Or perhaps each one is only a little dubious, but your reason to believe the conclusion becomes thinner and thinner as the doubt of each one adds to the doubt of the previous ones.

> ***Slippery Slope Argument***   A *slippery slope* argument is one that uses a chain of conditionals some or many of which are false or dubious.

Zoe:	Don't go out with a football player.
Suzy:	Why not?
Zoe:	You're crazy about football players, and if you go out with one you're sure to sleep with him.
Suzy:	So?
Zoe:	Then you'll get pregnant. And you'll marry the guy. But those guys are such jerks. You'll end up cooking and cleaning for him while he and his buddies watch football on TV. In twenty years you'll have five kids, no life, and a lot of regrets.
Suzy:	Gosh. I guess you're right. I'll go out with a basketball player instead.

Summary   Some claims are made up of other claims. We need to recognize that such claims must be treated as just one claim.

We looked at two kinds of compound claims in this chapter that involve possibilities for how things could be: "or" claims and conditionals. The variations on conditionals were confusing: how to say they are false, "only if" claims, necessary and sufficient conditions. But we need to master them because they are the ways we talk about how things could turn out under certain conditions.

We found that compound claims are an important way to construct valid arguments. We can reason with "or" claims by excluding possibilities. We can reason with conditionals the direct or indirect way, or with a chain of conditionals.

There are typical mistakes people make using these valid forms. Some use dubious or false premises, like false dilemmas or slippery slope arguments. Others argue backwards about the possibilities by affirming the consequent or by denying the antecedent.

Exercises for Chapter 6

1. Make a list of the valid argument forms we studied in this chapter.

2. Make a list of the invalid argument forms we studied in this chapter.

3. Make a list of the bad argument types we studied in this chapter.

4. What does it mean to say someone is reasoning in a chain with conditionals?

5. What's a slippery slope argument?

6. Rewrite the credit card argument in Section C.4 to show that it is Reasoning in a Chain.

7. If Dr. E wins the lottery, then Dr. E will be rich.
   If Dr. E's book sells one million copies, then Dr. E will be rich.
   If Dr. E marries a rich woman, then Dr. E will be rich.

   Assume that the three claims above are true. Using them:
   a. State all the true "only if" claims.
   b. Rewrite each "if. . .then . . ." claim as its contrapositive.
   c. Write the contradictory of each "if . . . then . . ." claim.
   d. Give an example using these claims of each of the valid and invalid forms using conditionals.
   e. Give an example using these claims of each of the valid and invalid forms except that in each you use an "only if" claim.
   f. State which claims are sufficient for which others.
   g. State which claims are necessary for which others.
   h. Explain why you enjoyed this exercise so much. Do not use any four-letter words. ⌊

8. Make up flash cards to learn how to recognize the forms of arguments we studied in this chapter. On the back of a card, put the form (for example, If A then B, not A, so not B). Write whether it's valid or invalid. On the front put an example you've made up. Make three cards for each form, each card showing a different example. Some of the examples should have a conditional that isn't already in "if . . . then . . ." form. Practice with your own cards. Trade with a fellow student. If you're not sure that your examples illustrate the forms, ask your instructor.

Here are more of Tom's homeworks with my comments. He's supposed to evaluate the argument, noting whether it uses a particular valid or invalid or bad argument form.

> **Suzy: If you apologize to Zoe, I'm sure she'll help you go look for Spot.**
> **Dick: It's her fault he got loose. I won't apologize.**
> **Suzy: Then she won't help you look for Spot.**

Argument? (the whole dialogue) (yes or no) Yes.
Conclusion (if unstated, add it): Zoe won't help Dick look for Spot.
Premises: If you apologize to Zoe, she'll help you go look for Spot. It's Zoe's fault Spot got loose. Dick won't apologize to Zoe.
Additional premises needed (if none, say so): None.
Classify (with the additional premises): Valid.

Good argument? (yes or no, with an explanation) Good. It's the direct way of reasoning with conditionals.

> *No. It's a case of denying the antecedent. The premises are true, all right, but Zoe did go help Dick. She felt guilty.*

Zoe: **I'll go hiking with you only if you'll go to this movie with me.**
Dick: **O.K., I'll go to the movie.**
   (***A week later, after Dick's gone to a Jane Austen movie with Zoe***)
Zoe: **I'm not going to go hiking with you. You ruined my dinner party.**

Did Zoe go back on her word? Yes. It's the direct way of reasoning with conditionals. Zoe made a conditional promise and didn't follow through.

> *No. Zoe said she's go <u>only if</u> Dick went to the movie, not <u>if</u> he went to the movie. Review <u>only if</u> vs <u>if</u>.*

If you don't give to charity you're selfish. If you pay all your bills on time with nothing left over, you can't give to charity. Since you don't want to be selfish, you shouldn't pay all your bills on time.

Argument? (yes or no) Yes.

Conclusion (if unstated, add it): You shouldn't pay all your bills on time.

Premises: If you don't give to charity you're selfish. If you pay all your bills on time with nothing left over, you can't give to charity. You don't want to be selfish.

Additional premises needed (if none, say so): When you pay your bills, you have nothing left over.

Classify (with the additional premises): Valid. Reasoning in a Chain and Indirect Way.

Good argument? (yes or no, with an explanation) It looks O.K., if the premises apply to the person, but something seems wrong.

> *Good work. You recognized the form, and you're getting good at spotting what unstated premises are needed. What's wrong here is that "selfish" is too vague or ambiguous. The first premise isn't true. What is true, perhaps, is "If you don't give to charity when you have more money than you need for your essentials, then you're selfish."*

For Exercises 9–23, answer the following questions. If the argument has one of the forms we studied, say so.

Argument? (yes or no)
Conclusion:
Premises:
Additional premises needed to make it valid or strong (if none, say so):
Classify: valid   very strong ——————— weak
One of the forms we studied in this chapter? (state which one)
Good argument? (check one)

   It's good (passes the three tests).

   It's valid or strong, but you don't know if the premises are true, so you can't say if it's good or bad.

   It's bad because it's unrepairable (state which of the reasons apply).

9. Mr. Ensign is a congressman who shows up for every vote. If someone is a good congressman, he shows up for every vote in congress. So Mr. Ensign is a good congressman.

10. Tom: Dick said he would go to the basketball game only if he could get a free ticket.
    Harry: I see he's at the game.
    Tom: He must have gotten a free ticket.

11. Dick: If Freud was right, then the only things that matter to a man are fame, riches, and the love of beautiful women.
    Zoe: But Ralph is poor, single, never married and uninterested in women (or men), and certainly not famous. Yet he's happy. So Freud was wrong.

12. Dick: If Tom isn't a football player, then Suzy won't go out with Tom.
    Zoe: But Suzy went to the movies with Tom.
    Dick: So I guess Tom is a football player.

13. Only if Columbus landed in a place with no people in it could you say that he discovered it. But the Americas, especially where he landed, were populated. He even met natives. So Columbus didn't discover America. He just discovered a route to America.

14. Tom: If Dick loves Zoe, he'll give her an engagement ring.
    Harry: But Dick loves Spot a lot more than Zoe.
    Suzy: So Dick won't give Zoe an engagement ring.

15. Maria: Professor, professor, why wouldn't you answer my question in class?
    Professor Zzzyzzx: I do not allow questions in my class. If I allow one student to ask a question, then I must allow others, too. Und then I vill have lots and lots of questions to answer. Und I won't have time for my lecture.

16. Zoe: This critical thinking book by Epstein is great. If you have a sense of humor you should buy it.
    Dick: Even if you don't have a sense of humor, you should buy Epstein's book.
    Tom: So I should buy Epstein's book.

17. We shouldn't require uniforms in public schools. No one will like them. If you're poor, you'll resent having to spend the extra money on them. If you're rich, you'll resent not being able to flaunt your wealth.

18. If Dick has a class and Zoe is working, there's no point in calling their home to ask them over for dinner. Spot can't answer the phone.

19. Gun control should not be allowed. If laws requiring registration of all guns are passed, then they'll start investigating people who have guns. They'll tap our phones. They'll look at what we check out of the library. They'll tap our Internet records. It'll be a police state.

20. If murder is the killing of someone with the intent to kill that person, and if Jeffrey Dahmer really did kill all those people they say he did, then, since it seems clear that he would have had to intend to kill them, Jeffrey Dahmer was guilty of murder.

21. Dick: I heard that Tom's going to get a pet. I wonder what he'll get?
    Zoe: The only pets you're allowed in this town are dogs or cats or fish.
    Dick: Well, I know he can't stand cats.
    Zoe: So he'll get a dog or fish.
    Dick: Not fish, he isn't the kind to get a pet you just contemplate.
    Zoe: So let's surprise him and get him a leash.

22. Every criminal is either already a hardened repeat offender or will become one because of what he'll learn in jail. We don't want any hardened criminals running free on our streets. So if you lock up someone, he should be locked up forever.

23. Aid to third world countries? Why should we care more about starving children there than here?

24. You've worked hard enough. Take some time off. Go to a bar or a party or a church social. Listen. And bring back examples of the valid and invalid forms of reasoning we studied in this chapter.

Key Words

compound claim	direct way
"or" claim	of reasoning with conditionals
alternative	indirect way
conditional	of reasoning with conditionals
antecedent	affirming the consequent
consequent	denying the antecedent
contradictory of a claim	contrapositive
excluding possibilities	only if
inclusive "or"	sufficient condition
exclusive "or"	necessary condition
false dilemma	reasoning in a chain with conditionals
	slippery slope argument

Further Study   Propositional logic is the study of how to analyze arguments solely in terms of their structure as composed of compound claims using "and," "or," "not," "if . . . then . . .". The appendix on truth-tables is a short introduction to it. Beyond that is a course on formal logic, or you can read my *Propositional Logics,* Oxford University Press.

Writing Lesson 8

You've learned about filling in unstated premises, indicator words, what counts as a plausible premise, and reasoning with compound claims.

Write an argument either for or against the following:

"For any course at this school, if a student attends every class, takes all the exams, and hands in all the assignments, then the professor should give the student a passing mark."

Check whether your instructor has chosen a *DIFFERENT TOPIC* for this assignment.

In order to make sure you use your new skills, the directions for this assignment are a little different. You should hand in two pages.

One page: A list of premises and the conclusion.

One page: The argument written as an essay with indicator words.

We should be able to see at a glance from the list of premises whether your argument is good. The essay form should read just as clearly, if you use indicator words well. Remember, there should be no claims in the essay form that aren't listed as premises.

Note that the topic is a conditional. You need to understand how to form the contradictory in order to make up your pro and con lists and to write your argument. Be very clear in your mind about what you consider to be necessary as opposed to sufficient conditions to get a passing mark.

To show you some of the problems students have, I'm including Suzy's argument on a different topic, as well as Tom's. Lee wrote a better one, so I've included his, too.

Suzy Queue
Critical Thinking

Issue: If a professor's colleagues do not consider his exams to be well written, then marks for the course should be given on a curve, not on percentage.

Premises:
1. A grade on a test reflects just how students are doing on that subject. If a test is not clearly understood, then the reflection of the scores will be lower.
2. Every student deserves to be treated fairly if the test is not clearly written the opportunity is not equal.
3. Due to the unclear test, the grading should start with the highest scored test in the class and the other test scores behind that.
4. Unclear tests should not be given in the first place, so to compensate for the strain on your brain for trying to decipher the test, grades should be curved to compensate.
5. The test is a direct reflection of how the teacher is getting through to his students, so in order to have an accurate idea, grading on the curve would show him the relation of all the students scores together.

Conclusion: Teachers who give poorly written exams should grade on the curve.

A grade on a test reflects just how students are doing on that subject. If the test is not clearly understood, then the reflection of the scores will be lower. Every student deserves to be treated fairly if the test is not clearly written the opportunity is not equal. Due to the unclear test, the grading should start with the highest scored test and the other test score behind that. Unclear tests should not be given in the first place, so to compensate for the strain on your brain for trying to decipher the test, grades should be curved to compensate. The test is a direct reflection of how the teacher is getting through to his students, so in order to have an accurate idea, grading on a curve would show him the relation of all the students scores together. Teachers who give poorly written exams should grade on the curve.

Some serious problems here. For (1), what does "reflect" mean? And "clearly understood"? By whom? That's the point. Besides, it's not one premise—it's two claims. For (2) you apparently have two claims, but it's incoherent. Your (4) is an argument (that word "so" is the clue), not a premise. And (5) is two claims, too.

You almost proved the conclusion you've stated. But you missed the point. It's a lot easier to prove what you stated than the issue you were supposed to write on. Who decides what "poorly written" means? Where is anything about his colleagues?

It's pretty clear to me that you wrote the essay first, and then tried to figure out what you said.

Also, you were supposed to use two pages. And where is your section number?

Tom Wyzyczy
Critical Thinking
Section 4
Writing Lesson 8

Issue: Every student should be required to take either critical thinking or freshman composition, but not both.

Definition: I'll understand the issue as "University students should be required to take either a freshman course on critical thinking or freshman composition, but not both."

Premises:

Critical thinking courses teach how to write. *1*

Freshman composition teaches how to write. *2*

Critical thinking courses teach how to read an essay. *3*

Freshman composition teaches how to read an essay. *4*

Credit should not be given for taking two courses that teach roughly the same material. *5*

If credit shouldn't be given for taking a course, students shouldn't be required to take it. *6*

Conclusion: Every student should be required to take either critical thinking or freshman composition, but not both.

continued on next page

This is sloppy work compared to what you've done in the past. You've shown, more or less, that a student should not have to take both courses. But you haven't shown that he should take one or the other, which is also part of the issue [(A or B) and not C]. So you've established neither the original claim nor its contradictory.

You need a claim that links 1–4 with 5 and 6, like "Freshman composition and critical thinking courses teach the same material." (I see on the next page you do have that claim.)

But worse is that 6 is at best dubious: How about those students who have to take remedial math for which no credit is given? And 1 and 2 are too vague. Both courses teach "how to write," but quite different aspects of that. Ditto for 3 and 4.

Tom Wyzyczy, writing lesson 8, page 2

Both critical thinking courses and freshman composition courses teach how to write. Both critical thinking courses and freshman composition courses teach how to read an essay. Since they both teach roughly the same material, they shouldn't both be required, because credit should not be given for taking two courses that teach roughly the same material. And if credit shouldn't be given for taking a course, students shouldn't be required to take it.

Good use of indicator words. It was O.K. to put two claims together in the first sentence as you did, since you recognized in your list of premises that they were two claims.

But you did what I specifically asked you not to do. You added a claim here you didn't have on the previous page: "Both courses teach roughly the same material."

The argument looks so good when it's written this way, but the previous page shows its weaknesses.

You should re-do this whole assignment.

Lee Hong-Nakamura O'Flanagan

Issue: If critical thinking were not a required course, a lot fewer people would take it.

Definition: I assume that "a lot fewer" is purposely vague.

Premises: ‡ Critical thinking is required of all students now.
‡ Critical thinking is one of the harder core requirement courses.
‡ A lot of students prefer to take easy courses, rather than learn something.
‡ Students in engineering and architecture have more courses to take than they can finish in four years.
‡ Students don't want to spend more time at their studies than they have to.^{1}
‡ Money is a problem for many students.^{2}
‡ For most students, if they have more courses to take than they can finish in four years, they will not take courses that aren't required.^{3}
‡ Students think they already know how to think critically.^{4}
‡ If critical thinking weren't required, then students who prefer easy courses and students who want to finish as quickly as they can, which are a lot of students, will not take it.

Conclusion: If critical thinking were not a required course, a lot fewer people would take it.

Critical thinking is required of all students now. And critical thinking is one of the harder core requirement courses. A lot of students prefer to take easy courses, rather than learn something. So many of them won't take critical thinking.^{5} Besides, students in engineering and architecture have more courses than they can finish in four years. Why would they take critical thinking if they didn't have to? After all, we all know that students don't want to spend more time at their studies than they have to. After all, money is a problem for most students. So for most students, if they have more courses to take than they can finish in four years, they will not take courses that aren't required. Anyway, students think they already know how to think critically. Thus we can see that if critical thinking weren't required, then students who prefer easy courses and students who want to finish as quickly as they can, which are a lot of students, will not take it. That is, if critical thinking were not a required course, a lot fewer people would take it.

This is good, but there are a few problems. 1 isn't tied into 3, though the unstated premise is pretty clear. But 2 definitely needs to be tied into 3 better. And 4 is left dangling—what's the connection you intend? Finally, you use 5 and it should be on the list of premises. Nonetheless, this is pretty good work.
But DOUBLE SPACE and put your SECTION NUMBER on the sheet!

Writing Lesson 9

For each of the following write the best argument you can that has as conclusion the claim below the cartoon. List only the premises and conclusion. If you believe the best argument is only weak, explain why. Do not make up a story about the cartoon. Use what you see in the cartoon and your common knowledge.

1.

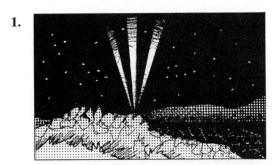

There are searchlights behind the hill.

2.

Someone has walked here since the snow began falling.

3.

This is a school for the handicapped.

151

4.

Spot escaped by digging a hole under the fence.

7   Complex Arguments

A. Raising Objections

Everyone should ride a bicycle for transportation. *1*   Cars are expensive
to buy and maintain and cause much pollution. *2*   A bicycle is better for
your health and also for everyone else's. *3*   Bicycles also look better
than cars. *4*

When asked to evaluate this argument, most students think it's good. To which I
respond, "Why do you drive a car?" Remember, it is irrational to say that an argument is good and then deny its conclusion.

Some students, rather than evaluating the argument directly, raise objections:

Bicycles aren't good for people who are handicapped or weak. *5*
Bikes aren't useful for carrying groceries or lots of kids. *6*
It's dangerous to ride a bike in downtown traffic. *7*

Then they say the argument is bad. They have good reason not to believe the
conclusion (*1*).

Raising objections is a standard way to show that an argument is bad. In doing
so, we are making another argument that either calls into question one of the

153

premises directly or shows that an unstated premise is dubious.

In this example, *5* shows that *3* is dubious, while *6* and *7* make us doubt the unstated premise needed to make the argument good: "Anything that's cheaper to buy and maintain than a car, causes less pollution than a car, and is better for your health and everyone else's should be the form of transportation for everyone." (We might as well ignore *4*, since it's subjective and dubious.)

Raising objections is common.

Dick:	Zoe, we ought to get another dog.
Zoe:	What's wrong with Spot?
Dick:	Oh, no, I mean to keep Spot company.
Zoe:	Spot has us. He doesn't need company.
Dick:	But we're gone a lot. And he's always escaping from the yard, 'cause he's lonely. And we don't give him enough time. He should be out running around more.
Zoe:	But think of all the work! We'll have to feed the new dog. And think of all the time necessary to train it.
Dick:	I'll train him. We can feed him at the same time as Spot, and dog food is cheap. It won't cost much.

Dick is trying to convince Zoe to believe, "We should get another dog." But he has to answer her objections.

We ought to get another dog.
  (*objection*) We already have Spot.
The other dog will keep Spot company.
  (*objection*) Spot already has us for company.
We are gone a lot. (*answer*)
He is always escaping from the yard. (*answer*)
He's lonely. (*answer*)
We don't give him enough time. (*answer*)
He should be out running around more. (*answer*)
  (*objection*) It will be a lot of work to have a new dog.
  (*objection*) We will have to feed the new dog.
  (*objection*) It will take a lot of time to train the new dog.
Dick will train him. (*answer*)
We can feed him at the same time as Spot. (*answer*)
Dog food is cheap. (*answer*)

Argument. Counterargument. Counter-counterargument. This is how we reason every day. Objections are raised: Someone puts forward a claim that, if true, makes one of our claims false or at least doubtful. We then have to answer that challenge to sustain our argument. *Knocking off an objection is a mini-argument within your argument—if it's not a good (though brief) argument, it won't do the job.*

Or you could say, "I hadn't thought of that. I guess you're right."

Or you could say, "I don't know. I'll have to think about that."

In making an argument of your own, you'll want to make it strong. You might think you have a great one. All the premises seem obvious and they glue together to get the conclusion. But if you imagine someone objecting, you can see how to give better support for doubtful premises. And answering counterarguments in your own writing allows the reader to see you haven't ignored some obvious objections. All you have to do, as in the earlier writing lessons, is make a list of the pros and cons. Then answer the other side.

B. Refuting an Argument

1. Refuting directly

| It's useless to kill flies. The ones you kill will be the slowest, because the fast flies will evade you. | So you will be killing off the slowest ones and the fastest ones will remain. Over time, then, the genes for being fast will predominate. | Then with super-fast flies, it will be impossible to kill them anyway. So it's useless to kill flies. |

Zoe can't let it pass. But how do you refute an argument?

Zoe might object to one of the premises, saying Dick won't be killing the slowest, but only the ones that happen to come into their house.

Or she could agree with the premises, but note that "over time" could be thousands of years, so the conclusion doesn't follow.

Or she could attack the conclusion, saying that it's not useless to kill flies, because she does it all the time and it keeps their home clean.

> ### *Direct Ways of Refuting an Argument*
> 1. Show that at least one of the premises is false.
> 2. Show that the argument isn't valid or strong.
> 3. Show that the conclusion is false.

When you attack the conclusion directly, ignoring the argument, you're just showing that the argument is weak: Even if the premises were true, the conclusion is false.

Refuting directly is no more than showing that an argument is unrepairable by the standards we've already adopted.

2. Refuting indirectly

Sometimes you can't point to any one premise that is false or dubious, but you know there's something wrong with the premises. They might get the conclusion that's argued for, but they get a lot more, too. So much more that you can see the premises are inconsistent or lead to an absurdity. For example,

> You complain that taxes are already too high and there is too much crime. And you say we should permanently lock up everyone who has been convicted of three felonies. In the places where this has been instituted it hasn't reduced the crime rate. So we will have many, many more people who will be incarcerated for their entire lives. We will need more prisons, many more, because these people will be in forever. We will need to employ more guards. We will need to pay for considerable health-care for these people when they are elderly. Thus, if you lock up everyone who has been convicted of three felonies, we will have to pay substantially higher taxes. Since you are adamant that taxes are too high and crime is too prevalent, you should abandon your claim that we should permanently lock up everyone who has been convicted of three felonies.

Here the speaker isn't refuting an argument. He's showing that the other person's beliefs lead to an unwanted conclusion: You'll have to raise taxes.

> **Reducing to the Absurd**   To *reduce to the absurd* is to show that at least one of several claims is false or dubious, or collectively they are unacceptable, by drawing a false or unwanted conclusion from them.

Reducing to the absurd is an expanded version of the idea that if the conclusion of a valid argument is false, then one of the premises must be false.

> You have to be sure the argument you use to get the false or absurd conclusion is really strong or valid and doesn't use any other dubious claims. Only then is there good reason to believe that there's a problem with the original collection of claims.

One way to reduce to the absurd is to use similar premises in an argument that sounds just like the original, yet leads to an absurd conclusion. Then by analogy (Chapter 12), the original argument is bad.

LOOK, YOUR ARGUMENT AGAINST KILLING FLIES IS BAD. I COULD USE THE SAME ARGUMENT AGAINST KILLING BACTERIA, OR AGAINST KILLING CHICKENS FOR DINNER FROM AUNT MARGERY'S HENHOUSE. THOSE CONCLUSIONS WOULD BE ABSURD.

3. Attempts to refute that are *bad arguments*

Some attempts to refute are just bad arguments.

In Chapter 5 we studied *phony refutations*. They're bad versions of reducing to the absurd: Here's the conclusion, here's what the speaker believes, they're contradictory, so the argument is bad.

Or an attempt to reduce to the absurd can lead to a *slippery slope*. Consider:

Gun control should not be allowed. If laws requiring registration of all guns is passed, then they'll start investigating people who have guns. They'll tap our phones. They'll look at what we check out of the library. They'll tap our Internet records. They'll come gunning for us. It'll be a police state.

This person has argued that gun control legislation is the first step on a slippery slope that will end in a disaster for us all. That doesn't refute the original, because the slippery slope adds false or dubious premises.

And then there's *ridicule*.

Dr. E: I hear that your department elected a woman as chairman.
Professor Zzzyzzx: Jah, jah, dat is right. Und now we is trying to decide vat we should be calling her—"chairman" or "chairwoman" or "chairperson."
Dr. E: "Chairperson"? Why not use a neutral term that's really appropriate for the position, like "chaircreature"?

In rational discussion, ridicule is a device to end arguments, belittle your opponent, and make enemies. No argument has been given for why "chairman" shouldn't be replaced by "chairperson," though Dr. E thinks he's shown the idea's absurd.

REDUCE TO THE ABSURD

$\{A, B, ..., C\}$ — THE OTHER PERSON'S CLAIMS

(OTHER PLAUSIBLE CLAIMS)

D — CONCLUSION, FALSE OR ABSURD

RIDICULE

A — THE OTHER PERSON'S CLAIM

HA! HA! HA! HA! HA!

In theory there's a big difference between reducing to the absurd and ridicule, but in practice it's difficult to distinguish them. Not enough of an argument is given to see how the absurd conclusion follows, so it sounds like ridicule. If someone wants us to see his comments as an argument, it's his responsibility to make that clear. Otherwise, let's classify it as ridicule.

When judging whether something is ridicule, an attempt to reduce to the absurd, a slippery slope, or an unwillingness to acknowledge distinctions because they are a bit vague, think less of rejecting what the other person says and more of taking his comments as a challenge to make your own arguments clearer.

The worst of the bad ways to refute is to attack an argument the other person didn't even say. When someone makes a claim, and the other person tries to refute it by putting words in his mouth, that's a **strawman**. It seems to be the norm in political discourse:

> The incumbent congressman is against gun control. Clearly, he doesn't care about violence on the streets.

Excuse me? What's the connection here? The congressman never said he wasn't against violence in the streets.

The only reasonable response to a straw man is to say calmly that it isn't what you said:

> Tom: Unless we allow the logging of old-growth forests in this county, we'll lose the timber industry and these towns will die.
> Dick: So you're saying that you don't care what happens to the spotted owl and to our rivers and the water we drink?
> Tom: I said nothing of the sort. You've misrepresented my position.

Note that Tom did not say, "You've misrepresented my position, you jerk." Let's keep alive some hope of rational discourse.

Summary (Sections A and B) When we make an argument, we should be prepared to defend it. Think ahead and imagine what objections might be raised, then answer them.

There are legitimate ways to refute an argument: Attack a premise, show that the argument isn't valid or strong, or attack the conclusion directly.

We can also refute an argument by showing that a false or absurd conclusion follows from the premises. To do that, we must be sure that any other claims we use to get the false or absurd conclusion are plausible, and that the argument we give is strong or valid.

But remember: Refuting an argument does not show that the conclusion is false.

There are three bad ways to reason that imitate reducing to the absurd: phony refutation, slippery slope arguments, and ridicule. And then there's the worst: putting words in someone's mouth.

Exercises for Sections A and B

1. In my first comment after the argument about bicycling on p. 153 I challenge the student. Have I shown that the argument is bad?

2. What is a counterargument?

3. If you show an argument is bad, what have you shown about its conclusion?

4. How should you respond to a counterargument?

5. a. Why are counterarguments useful in your own writing?
    b. Give three phrases you can use to introduce objections to your own argument in your writing.

6. Find an article in which the author answers a counterargument.

7. Explain the role of each claim in the following discussion.

    Zoe: I think sex is the answer to almost everyone's problems.
    Dick: How can you say that?
    Zoe: It takes away your tensions, right?
    Dick: Not if you're involved with someone you don't like.
    Zoe: Well, anyway, it makes you feel better.
    Dick: Not if it's against your morals. Anyway, heroin makes you feel good, too.
    Zoe: But it's healthy, natural, just like eating and drinking.
    Dick: Sure, and you can catch terrible diseases. Sex should be confined to marriage.
    Zoe: Is that a proposal?

8. Write a short argument against drinking alcohol that acknowledges why some people want to drink alcohol.

9. If you can show that a collection of claims leads to a false conclusion, do you know that the claims are inconsistent or one of them is false? Explain.

10. Refuting an argument directly is just showing that the argument is _____ .

11. What is reducing an argument to the absurd?

12. Which of the ways of refuting an argument is best? Why?

13. What's the difference between ridicule and reducing to the absurd?

14. Why isn't a phony refutation really a refutation of an argument?

15. Why won't a slippery slope argument do as a way to reduce to the absurd?

16. a. What is a strawman?
    b. Bring in an example.

Evaluate the following attempts to refute arguments by answering the following questions:
What is the method of refutation?
Is the refutation a good argument? (Explain)

17. There is no value at all in Heidegger's philosophy, especially his ethics, since he collaborated with the Nazis in running German universities in the 1930s, and fired all the Jews.

18. You say you want to raise tuition again? Why not raise the parking fees, too? And the dorm contracts. And raise prices at the cafeteria, while you're at it. Or maybe even charge students for using the library. You could balance the college's budget for sure that way.

19. Look, I agree with you. We have too much violence in the streets, too many drug pushers, too little respect for the law. But our prisons are overflowing, and that's costing us a fortune. So we've got to reduce our prison population. Yet you say we should be even tougher on crime. The answer is simple: Institute a lottery among all convicted felons in jail and execute one of them every month, no appeals. That'll instill a real fear of being arrested. And it'd be fair, too.

20. Lee: I'm going to vote for that initiative to eliminate discrimination against homosexuals in hiring and getting places to live. They should be treated like everyone else. They deserve a chance to get jobs and homes.
    Tom: Are you kidding? I'm voting against it. You should, too. They don't deserve any preference over the rest of us.

Refute the following arguments. Say whether you are showing a premise is dubious, attacking an unstated premise, showing the argument is weak, or reducing to the absurd.

21. Single parents should get special assistance from the government. After all, a two-parent family has two paychecks and twice the attention to give to their children. Some single parent families end up having to use the welfare system because they can't afford child care. Therefore, the government should give free child care to single-parent families.

22. Multiple-choice examinations are the best way to examine students. The grading is completely objective. Students know how to prepare for them. And professors don't have to spend a lot of time grading them.

23. You should keep a gun in your home. This is a dangerous neighborhood, and a gun is the best protection you can get. Think of what could happen if someone broke in.

C. Arguments within Arguments

Arguments are usually more complex than those we've looked at so far. We support one premise from which we derive others, leaving as little as possible to be taken without support.

> None of Dr. E's students are going to beg in the street. 'Cause only poor people beg. And Dr. E's students will be rich because they understand how to reason well.

First we should number the claims. The last sentence is two claims: "because" is an indicator word showing that a premise comes next. So we have:

> None of Dr. E's students are going to beg in the street. *1*
> Only poor people beg. *2*
> Dr. E's students will be rich. *3*
> They understand how to reason well. *4*

The conclusion is claim *1*. Claim *4* supports *3* (though some premise is missing), so only *4* and 2 are unsupported. But as it stands the argument is neither strong nor valid. So we should try to repair it. We need a claim to get us from *4* to *3*. I suggest:

> Almost anyone who reasons well will be rich. *a*

(Here, as throughout, let's use numbers for the original argument, and lower case letters for claims we add.)

Only this premise or something awfully like it will make the argument from *4* to *3* strong, which is the first step we take according to the Guide to Repairing Arguments. But that premise is not believable (although it's better than "Anyone who reasons well will be rich"). So the argument is unrepairable.

Does that mean that some of Dr. E's students will beg in the streets? No! A bad argument does not prove that the conclusion is false. A bad argument proves nothing.

Here's another example:

Whatever you do, don't take the critical thinking course from Dr. E. *1* He's a really tough grader *2*, much more demanding than the other professors who teach that course. *3*   You could end up getting a bad grade. *4*

I've numbered every sentence or clause that might be a claim. But *1* isn't a claim, so we rewrite it as "You shouldn't take the critical thinking course from Dr. E." We can rewrite *3* as "He's much more demanding than the other professors who teach that course." Now what is the structure of this argument? There aren't any indicator words.

It seems to me, *1* is the conclusion. Why do I say that? If I believed *2*, *3*, and *4*, then I would have some reason to believe *1*. Not awfully good reason, since some unstated premise(s) are needed to make the argument strong or valid. But it makes sense to say, "You shouldn't take the critical thinking course from Dr. E, *because* he's a really tough grader"; while it seems silly to say, "You shouldn't take the critical thinking course from Dr. E. *Therefore* he's a really tough grader."

When there are no indicator words ask:

If I believed this claim, would I have more reason to believe that one?
Can I put *therefore* or *because* between these two claims?

If it's not clear which claim is meant to support which other, that's a fault of the argument. In this argument, even with the conclusion identified, we still have two ways to interpret it:

(A)   Dr. E is more demanding than the other professors who teach that course.
           Therefore, he's a really tough grader.
           Therefore, you could end up getting a bad grade.
           Therefore, you shouldn't take the critical thinking course from Dr. E.

(B)   Dr. E is more demanding than the other professors who teach that course, and he's a really tough grader.
           Therefore, you could end up getting a bad grade.
           Therefore, you shouldn't take the critical thinking course from Dr. E.

To choose between these, we need to use the Guide to Repairing Arguments to make the argument valid or strong. For (A) we'd need an unstated premise like:

(Almost) anyone who's more demanding than other professors who teach critical thinking is a really tough grader.

That's plausible. For (B) we'd need something like:

If you take critical thinking from someone who's more demanding than other professors who teach that course and who is a really tough grader, then you could end up getting a bad grade. *a*

That's a lot more plausible. It looks like (B) is a better choice, though we still need to get from *4* to *1*. We can use:

You shouldn't take any course where you might get a bad grade. *b*

That's what we need, though it's not clearly true. In the end, then, this argument is only as good as the unsupported premise *b*.

Even if there's no one right way to interpret this argument, that doesn't mean there aren't wrong ways. If you said that *4* supports *2*, that would be wrong.

D. Dependent and Independent Premises

Sometimes people use several premises hoping the combined weight of them will somehow bring about the conclusion. For example:

These are separate premises meant to support the conclusion. But someone who likes cats could just say, "So?" after each of *1* through *4*. Compare:

Cats smell bad. *1*
Anything that smells bad is unpleasant. *2*
Cats kill songbirds. *3*
Anything that kills songbirds is nasty. *4*
Thus, cats are nasty and unpleasant creatures. *5*

Here we're not just piling up "facts" to support the conclusion. Claims *1* and *2* work together, as do claims *3* and *4*. If either of *1* or *2* is false, then the other of the pair doesn't give any support at all to the conclusion; similarly for *3* and *4*.

Dependent Premises Two or more premises are called *dependent* if they are meant together to support another claim, in the sense that if one is false, the other(s) do not give support.

Premises are *independent* if they are not dependent.

More than two premises can be dependent on each other:

Here *3* would be of no use in deriving *4* if *1* and *2* are not both true. And *1* and *2* can't do their work in deriving *4* if we don't have *3*.

Some people think it's just fine to give an argument with many independent premises supporting the conclusion. There are lots of reasons to believe the conclusion—if you don't like this one, take that one. I've got a bag full of 'em.

That may convince some folks, but it shouldn't convince you. You're sharp enough to spot that after each independent premise you could ask, "So?" If it's not linked to the conclusion, the argument is still weak. When someone keeps piling up reasons with no glue, it just means you have to ask "So?" oftener. It doesn't make the argument strong. (The only exception, as we'll discuss in Chapter 14, is proving generalizations like "All parakeets are under 2' tall.") When you spot independent premises in an argument, you know it's ripe for repair.

Exercises for Sections C and D

1. a. What does it mean to say that premises are dependent? Independent?
    b. Can we say that a conclusion is dependent? Explain.
    c. Give an argument all of whose premises are independent.
    d. Repair your argument in (c) by adding premises.

2. Give an example (not from the text) of a strong argument with just one premise supporting a conclusion. That is, no unstated premise is missing. (Hint: Look in Chapter 3.)

I've asked Tom to analyze the structure of a few arguments. Here's some of his work.

> **The dogcatcher in this town is mean.** *1* **He likes to kill dogs.** *2* **He is overzealous, picking up dogs that aren't really strays.** *3* **Some people say he beats the dogs.** *4* **So the position of dogcatcher should be eliminated.** *5*

Argument? (yes or no) Yes.

Conclusion: The position of dogcatcher should be eliminated.

Number the claims

Additional premises needed? If someone likes to kill dogs, picks up dogs that aren't really strays, and beats dogs, then he is mean. *a* If someone is mean, he shouldn't be dogcatcher. *b*

Identify any subargument, saying which claims are independent: 2, 3, and 4 are independent and support 1. Then *1* supports the conclusion, 5.

Good argument? Looks good to me.

You haven't been critical enough. The argument is really pretty bad. First, I agree that 2, 3, and 4 are independent. You can say they support 1, but 1 is vague and no improvement on 2, 3, and 4. I think it's too vague to be a claim. We do need something like your a . But for that we need a further premise, one you're always overlooking, "If people say that the dogcatcher beats dogs, then he does beat dogs." And that's pretty dubious. So instead of a let's take: "If someone likes to kill dogs and picks up dogs that aren't strays, then he should not be a dogcatcher." That's true. But that doesn't get you the conclusion. What you then need is, "If the person who is now dogcatcher shouldn't be dogcatcher, then the position of dogcatcher should be eliminated." And that is implausible. Still, it's just your first try.

Harry wants to get a dog. *1* **Harry's friends Celia and Emily have puppies they want to give away.** *2* **Celia's is a border collie** *3* **and Emily's is a dalmatian.** *4* **Harry likes border collies better than dalmatians.** *5* **So he'll probably take Celia's puppy.** *6*

Argument? (yes or no) Yes.

Conclusion: Harry will probably take Celia's puppy.

Additional premises needed? If Harry wants to get a dog, then he'll get one of his friends' puppies.

Identify any subargument, saying which claims are independent: 1, 2, 3, 4, and 5 are independent and support the conclusion, 6.

Good argument? Very strong, and I know the premises are true. So it's good.

Much better. The conclusion, however, doesn't have the word "probably" in it—that's an indicator word.

You're still having trouble identifying what's dependent. Look, 3, 4, and 5 work together to support an unstated claim: "If Harry picks one of Celia or Emily's puppies, it'll be Celia's." Then that plus the unstated premise you added make the argument moderately strong. Perhaps some other friend has puppies to give away, too.

For the following arguments, answer the following:

Argument? (yes or no)

If an argument, number each part that might be a claim.

Conclusion:

Additional premises needed?

Identify any subargument, stating which claims are dependent:

Good argument?

3. Dr. E is a teacher. All teachers are men. So Dr. E is a man.

4. Sheep are the dumbest animals. If the one in front walks off a cliff, all the rest will follow him. And if they get rolled over on their backs, they can't right themselves.

5. I'm on my way to school. I left five minutes late. Traffic is heavy. Therefore, I'll be late for class. So I might as well stop and get breakfast.

6. Pigs are very intelligent animals. They make great pets. They learn to do tricks as well as any dog can. They can be housetrained, too. And they are affectionate, since they like to cuddle. Pigs are known as one of the smartest animals there are. And if you get bored with them or they become unruly, you can eat them.

7. Smoking is disgusting. It makes your breath smell horrid. If you've ever kissed someone after they smoked a cigarette you feel as though you're going to vomit. Besides, it will kill you.

8. Dr. E: I took my dogs for a walk last night in the fields behind my house. It was very dark. They started to chase something: I could hear it running in front of them. It seemed like it was big because of the way the bushes were rustling, and they came back towards where I was in a U turn, which suggests it wasn't a rabbit. Rabbits almost always run in more or less one direction. I think they killed it, because I heard a funny squeaky "awk" sound. It didn't sound like a cat, but it didn't sound like a big animal either. And I don't think rabbits make that kind of sound. I'm puzzled what it was, but one thing I am sure of after the dogs returned: It wasn't a skunk.

9. Las Vegas has too many people. There's not enough water in the desert to support more than a million people. And the infrastructure of the city can't handle more than a million: The streets are overcrowded and traffic is always congested; the schools are overcrowded and new ones can't be built fast enough. We should stop migration to the city by tough zoning laws in the city and county.

10. (Charlie Graven speaking on Geraldo about Nicole Simpson calling 911 and not following up on it)

    She didn't file charges, she didn't get a restraining order, therefore . . . If I were getting harassed, I would file charges, I would get a restraining order.

E. Analyzing Complex Arguments

Many arguments we encounter are more complex than the ones we've looked at. Here's an example from a letter to the editor:

> Pet owners need to take responsibility for their animals. *1* Not only is it unsafe for these pets to wander, *2* it is very inconsiderate to other neighbors. *3* Many of us are tired of the endless, nauseating piles we have to shovel from our lawns and dead flowers caused by dogs passing by. *4* Children in our neighborhoods cannot walk to a friend's house to play for fear of aggressive dogs. *5* Pets should be in a fenced yard or on a leash, *6* not just to protect pets, *7* not just out of consideration for your neighbors, *8* but also because it is the law. *9*
> Claudia Empey, *The Spectrum*, 1996

I've labeled every clause that might be a claim.

First we need to identify the conclusion without the aid of an indicator word. The choice seems to be between *1* and *6*. Looking at all the other claims, it seems to me they best support *6*. If I believed all the others, I'd have more reason to believe *6*. Indeed, *1* supports *6*, though weakly.

We have the conclusion, but that doesn't give us the structure. First, let's see if there's any noise or problematic sentences.

Sentence *2* is ambiguous: Does it mean "unsafe for the pets" or "unsafe for people"? Those two readings are made separately in *5* and *7*, so we can ignore *2*. Also *3* and *8* are the same, so let's ignore *8*.

What do we have? Just lots of independent premises. But the weight of them doesn't give the conclusion. We are missing the glue. Why should we care about our neighbors? Why protect the pets? Each of these independent premises needs some further premise to help us get *6*. In Exercise 2 below I ask you to finish this analysis by trying to repair the argument.

A debate about affirmative action by Betsy Hart and Bonnie Erbe, which appeared in the newspaper, gives a more complex example still. Here is the introduction and Betsy Hart's argument. Bonnie Erbe's argument is in the exercises.

Affirmative action debate heads for ballot box
Question: Affirmative action is under attack. In California and Texas, such programs have been largely ended in state university systems–pending court challenges–by school regents or the lower courts. A fall ballot initiative will determine whether other such programs in California should go. Affirmative action will be a hot topic everywhere on the campaign trail. What's going on? (Bonnie Erbe and Betsy Hart provide differing views on current issues. Erbe is host of the PBS program "To the Contrary." Hart is a frequent commentator on CNN and other national public affairs shows.)
Scripps Howard News Service, March, 1996

Betsy Hart: What's going on is that affirmative action is counterproductive or useless, *1* and it's time for it to end. *2*

First, consider its legacy for blacks. Since the civil rights laws of 1964 were passed, aggregate black-white unemployment gaps haven't contracted, and they've expanded in some markets! *3* That's because holding a space open at Yale or a prestigious law firm for a minority doesn't help the people who need help most—the inner-city drop-out with no future. *4*

Why not fight the real problems instead? *5* For instance, rampant crime in the inner-city. *6* Studies repeatedly show crime is one of the biggest inhibitors to business and job creation where it's most needed. *7* But liberals are loathe to truly fight this insidious destroyer of lives and futures. *8*

Solid education is fundamental to helping disadvantaged minorities. *9* That means early on in life, as well as at the college level. *10* Yet today, the publicly run inner-city schools, which the education establishment refuses to honestly reform, *11* are rarely anything but violence-ridden cesspools. *12*

Families, too, have to be repaired. *13* The No. 1 indicator of crime rate in any neighborhood is not income or education, but the level of single-parent headed households. *14* The high-rates of such families in the inner city show why many such kids are prepared for a life of violence, not a life of achievement. *15*

All the affirmative action programs in the world can't fix these problems. *16* But focusing on affirmative action allows the liberal do-gooders to avoid doing anything about the real issues facing the disadvantaged. *17*

Middle-class minorities and women no longer need affirmative action programs, if they ever did. *18* (Black college educated women, for instance, make more than their white counterparts in the aggregate. *19* When factors such as age and their own parental status are controlled for, women make 98 percent of what men do. *20*) And disadvantaged minorities are hurt by these programs *21* because their real problems are overlooked. *22*

Yes, it's time for affirmative action programs to go. *23*

The first thing to do in analyzing this passage is decide if it's an argument. I think it is, with conclusion, "It's time to end affirmative action." So we need to number every sentence or clause that might be a claim.

But already there is a problem. What exactly does Betsy Hart mean by "affirmative action"? Does it mean different standards for entrance into university? Does it mean that some places should be reserved for minorities in universities and businesses? Does it mean that contracts should be set aside for minority businessmen? Unless we are clear about that, she's whistling in the wind. What exactly are we encouraged to end? This is a problem that is fatal to her argument unless we can deduce how we should interpret those words from the rest of what she says.

1 Affirmative action is counterproductive or useless.

This is a claim. If she can prove this, then the conclusion, *2*, will follow. But we have to ask "Counterproductive of what?" Let's hope she makes that clear.

3 Since the civil rights laws of 1964 were passed, aggregate black-white unemployment gaps haven't contracted, and they've expanded in some markets.

This is a claim, and if true would be some support for affirmative action being useless or counterproductive, if we add as a premise: "One of the goals of affirmative action is to lessen the unemployment gap between blacks and white." Do we have any reason to believe *3*? Betsy Hart doesn't back it up. Maybe it's true, maybe not. We should suspend judgment.

4 Holding a space open at Yale or a prestigious law firm for a minority doesn't help the people who need help the most—the inner-city drop-out with no future.

This is a claim. It sounds plausible, but what reason do we have to believe it? For it to be true, the word "help" must be understood as "help immediately financially" or something like that. Is that the goal of affirmative action?

5 We should fight the real problems instead.

I've taken the rhetorical question as a claim. I guess from context and *6* we can understand "real problems" to be the financial and crime problems of minorities in the ghettos. But are those the only problems we should deal with? This is an implicit *false dilemma*: We can fight the real problems or continue affirmative action, but not both.

Claim *7* we can dismiss, because we don't know what studies she's talking about. And *8* is just noise: Who are these liberals?

Claims *9* and *10* are highly plausible. But then we have *11*: The education establishment refuses to honestly reform inner city-schools. This is just noise: What is the "education establishment"? What does "honestly reform" mean? And *12*, highly overstated, is what a lot of people believe. But how does that support the conclusion? Its only value is through the false dilemma, just as with *13–15*.

But now we come to the crucial part. Betsy Hart is going to show that her argument isn't based on a false dilemma. First, affirmative action can't fix these "real" problems (*16*) (as if the problems that affirmative action can fix are "false"). And then the most important part of her argument:

17 Focusing on affirmative action allows the liberal do-gooders to avoid doing anything about the real issues facing the disadvantaged.

This is supposed to show that there isn't a false dilemma. But who are these "liberal do-gooders"? Can she name anyone who avoids trying to deal with these "real" problems because he or she supports affirmative action? That's implausible, and without some serious support for this very vague sentence, we shouldn't even consider it a claim.

Finally, Betsy Hart tries to show that affirmative action isn't needed anyway (*18*), assuming as unstated premise, "The *only* goal of affirmative action is immediate financial equality" (*a*). The "immediate" came earlier; now it's beginning to look like a perfectionist dilemma. But she doesn't tell us where the statistics in *19* and *20* come from, and she's not an unbiased source.

Finally, *21* and *22* rehearse what she's already said, and *23* restates her conclusion.

In summary, much of what Betsy Hart has said is too vague to be taken as a claim, is unsupported, or relies on a false dilemma she hasn't managed to prove. Nor do we ever find out what she means by "affirmative action," though it seems to be *a*. It's a weak argument, if it's an argument at all.

What can we learn from this analysis? Can we formulate some general procedures for analyzing complex arguments? Here are some guidelines:

1. Read the entire passage and decide if it's an argument. If so, identify the conclusion.

2. If it is an argument, then number every sentence or clause that might possibly be a claim.

3. For each numbered part, decide if it is a claim:
   a. Is it too vague or ambiguous?
   b. If it's vague, could we clear that up by looking at the rest of the argument? Are the words implicitly defined?
   c. If it's too vague, scratch it out as noise.
   d. If it's written in highly charged language, reword it neutrally. (We'll study how to do this in Chapter 9.)

4. Identify the claims that lead directly to the conclusion.

5. Identify any subarguments that are meant to support the claims that lead directly to the conclusion.

6. See if the obvious objections have been considered.
   a. List ones that occur to you as you read the passage.
   b. See if they have been answered.

7. Note which of the claims in the argument are unsupported, and evaluate whether they are plausible.

8. Evaluate each subargument on the scale from valid to strong through weak.
   a. Note if the argument is one of the bad types or valid types we've discussed.
   b. If it is not valid or strong, can it be repaired?
   c. If it can be repaired, do so and evaluate any added premises.

9. Evaluate the entire argument as valid, strong, or weak.
   a. Note if the argument is one of the bad types or valid types we've discussed.
   b. If it is not valid or strong, can it be repaired?
   c. If it can be repaired, do so and evaluate any added premises.

10. Decide whether the argument is good.

That's a lot to do. But not all the steps are always needed. If you spot that the argument is one of the bad types we've discussed, you can dismiss it. If key words are too vague to consider the conclusion or crucial parts as claims, you can dismiss the argument. But often you will have to go through all these steps. Or you could just go with your gut reaction—throwing out all the work you've done in this course.

Summary (Sections C–E) Most arguments we encounter require us to analyze their structure before we can evaluate them: Which claims are unsupported, and which act as premises of a subargument? Which premises are independent?

We can't proceed to determine the structure unless we have a strong grasp on how to repair arguments: the Guide; what's a plausible unsupported premise; what arguments are valid, strong, or weak; what argument types we know are bad or valid. It takes some work and some time, but the result is a deeper understanding of the issue and the support for it. Often by analyzing another's argument we can see better how to formulate our own.

Exercises for Section E

1. On pages 239–241 Tom has tried his hand at analyzing a long argument. Though it uses a few ideas from Chapter 9, it ought to be clear enough. Read through it and say if he's followed the steps above.

2. Finish the analysis of the first argument of this section.

3. Find an editorial or a letter to the editor from your local newspaper and analyze it.

4. Here is the reply to Betsy Hart by Bonnie Erbe that appeared in the same feature. Analyze it.

    Bonnie Erbe: Before my colleague takes off on such wild tangents, she needs to define affirmative action. The term has come to mean different things to different people, ranging from strict, unbending quotas to mild incentive programs.

    My definition of affirmative action is as follows: institutions and corporations that have extremely small percentages of women and/or minority group members among their ranks should take gender and race into account, along with a panoply of other factors (i.e., intelligence, job or grade performance, geographic distribution, economic disadvantage) when recruiting new talent.

    Using that definition, affirmative action will undoubtedly be outmoded in some institutions, but decidedly necessary in others.

    For example, there's clearly no need to pay special attention to admit more Chinese- or Japanese-Americans to the University of California at Berkeley.

    But blacks and Hispanics are still underrepresented on some campuses in the University of California system.

    Similarly, some federal agencies—most notably the FBI, the CIA and the State Department—are woefully short on women agents and diplomats. Yet the Justice Department's No. 1 and No. 2 lawyers (Janet Reno and Jamie Gorelick) are women. Hence, affirmative action for women is unneeded in some federal agencies, while not in others.

    Besides, if we are going to eliminate affirmative action entirely, we ought to eliminate all preferences throughout society.

    No more special admissions to Harvard for the young man with a B minus average just because his grandfather's name is on a Harvard dorm.

    Fathers should no longer be able to hire sons (or sons-in-law) to help run the family company simply because they're related.

    I'm being hyperbolic, but my point is this: Preferences (based on who you know and how much money you have) are still rampant in society. If we eliminate one, in fairness we should eliminate them all.

If we actually, really eliminated preferences–all forms of affirmative action–upper-class white children would be much more thoroughly vitiated than lower-class minority children.

Key Words   direct ways of refuting   strawman
                     reducing to the absurd   dependent premises
                     ridicule   independent premises

Writing Lesson 10

Now you know that you should include the other side when arguing for a controversial claim. Argument, counterargument, counter-counterargument. Remember, to knock off an objection, you need a mini-argument that will be judged by the same standards as any argument.

Write an argument either for or against the following:

"Students in public high schools should be required to wear uniforms."

Check whether your instructor has chosen a *DIFFERENT TOPIC* for this assignment.

In order to make sure you use your new skills, the directions for this assignment are the same as for Writing Lesson 8. You should hand in two pages:

One page: A list of premises and the conclusion.

One page: The argument written as an essay with indicator words.

We should be able to see at a glance from the list of premises whether your argument is good. The essay form should read just as clearly, if you use indicator words well. Remember, there should be no claims in the essay form that aren't listed as premises. And you should include the other side.

> For this issue and generally, there is a trade-off: You can make your argument very strong, but perhaps only at the expense of a rather dubious premise. Or you can make all your premises clearly true, but leave out the dubious premises that are needed to make the argument strong. Given the choice, *opt for making the argument strong*. If it's weak, no one should accept the conclusion. And if it's weak because of unstated premises, it is better to have those premises stated so they can be the object of debate.

Tom's so embarrassed about his last writing assignment that he's asked me not to include any more. But he's doing much better now, and I'm sure he'll do well in the course. Maria's done such a good job, though, that I'm including her essay on a different issue.

Maria Schwartz Rodriguez
Critical Thinking, Section 6
Writing Lesson 10

Issue: If a woman has a baby, then she should not work outside the home until the child reaches the age of four.

Definition: I take "work outside the home" to mean the woman takes a job that requires her to be away from her home and child at least 15 hours/week.

Premises:

1. Some women who have a child under the age of four are single mothers.

2. Some women who have a child under the age of four have husbands who do not earn enough money to support them and the child.

3. Some women who have children have careers from which they cannot take time without stopping them permanently or for a very long time from advancing.

4. Some women who have children do not have extended families or lots of friends.

5. A woman who has only her family can go stir-crazy if she is just with her child all the time.

6. A woman who is going stir-crazy, or who is too poor to provide for her child, or is unsatisfied because her child is stopping her from getting along in her career will make a bad mother and companion for her child who is under four.

7. Mothers who are not with their children do not deserve to have children.

8. Whether they deserve to have them or not, they do have them.

9. Children who are not with their mothers will not develop proper intellectual and emotional skills.

10. What studies I have seen contradict that claim. Until reliable studies are produced for it, we should not accept it.

11. Day-care can be dangerous.

12. The mother can screen day-care providers, and besides, a bitter, unsatisfied mother can be dangerous, too.

Conclusion: Under some circumstances it is acceptable for a woman to work outside the home when she has a child under the age of four.

Maria Schwartz Rodriguez
Critical Thinking, Section 6
Writing Lesson 10, page 2

Under some circumstances it is acceptable for a woman to work outside the home when she has a child under the age of four. After all, some women who have a child under the age of four are single mothers. And other women who have a child under the age of four have husbands who do not earn enough money to support them and the child. We can't forget women who have children and have careers from which they cannot take time without stopping them permanently or for a very long time from advancing. And think of the women who have children who do not have extended families or lots of friends. She could go stir-crazy if she is just with her child all the time.   These women should be allowed to take work outside the home, for a woman who is going stir-crazy, or who is too poor to provide for her child, or is unsatisfied because her child is stopping her from getting along in her career will make a bad mother and companion for her child who is under four.

But lots of people say that mothers who are not with their children do not deserve to have children. Well, whether they deserve to have them or not, they do have them.

But children who aren't with their mothers will not develop proper intellectual and emotional skills, it is said. Well, what studies I have seen contradict that claim. Until reliable studies are produced for it, we should not accept it.

One objection is that mothers who work outside the home often need day-care.^{A} And day-care can be dangerous. But the mother can screen day-care providers, and besides, a bitter, unsatisfied mother can be dangerous, too.

So despite the obvious objections, we can see that under some circumstances it is acceptable for a woman to work outside the home when she has a child under the age of four.

This is really excellent. Bravo! A few points where you could improve:

You must include the definition in the essay, right after the first sentence giving the conclusion.

The grammar on premise 3 is not right.

You missed a possible response to 8 that the state or a church should take the child, and you'd need to come up with a response to that.

Some variety in putting in the objections might be good, for example, stating (9) as a question.

You left A out of your list of premises. And (12) is two premises, not one.

I see you avoided entirely the issue of welfare. Have you asked other students to look at your paper to see if they can think of objections or support because of that?

If you can write like this in your other courses you'll do great all through college!

8 General Claims

A. "All" and "Some"

> All good teachers give fair exams. Professor Zzzyzzx gives fair exams.
> So Professor Zzzyzzx is a good teacher.

This may seem to be valid, but it's not. The premises could be true, yet Professor Zzzyzzx could be a terrible teacher and give fair exams from an instructor's manual.

> Some dogs like cats. Some cats like dogs.
> So some dogs and cats like each other.

This may seem valid, too. But it's not. It could be that all the dogs that like cats are abhorred by the cats as too wimpy. Yet these arguments sound reasonable. How are we to avoid getting lured into belief?

We need to be clear about what "all" and "some" mean. "All" means "every single one, no exceptions." But then is the following true?

> All polar bears in Antarctica can swim.

There are no exceptions: There's not one polar bear in Antarctica that can't swim. Of course, there aren't any polar bears in Antarctica that can swim. There just aren't any polar bears in Antarctica.

Some people will say the claim is false: There has to be at least one for us to be right when we say "all" in ordinary conversation. Others will say that the claim is true. People disagree on how "all" is to be understood.

Dr. E: At the end of this term, some of my students will get an A.

At the end of the term one student in all of Dr. E's classes got an A. Was Dr. E right? If you say "no," then how many is "some students"? At least 2? At least 8? At least 10%? More than 18%?

"Some" is purposely vague. We use it when we can't or don't want to be precise. When we say "some" we are only guaranteeing that there has to be at least one.

Dr. E: Some of you will pass my next exam.

All Dr. E's students pass. Was Dr. E right? For this claim to be true don't some also have to fail? We're not consistent in how we use "some" in our ordinary conversations. Often we mean "at least one, but not all." But not always. "Some" and "all" can be ambiguous.

> *All* means "Every single one, no exceptions." Sometimes *all* is meant as "Every single one, and there is at least one." Which reading is best may depend on the argument.
>
> *Some* means "At least one." Sometimes *some* is meant as "At least one, but not all." Which reading is best may depend on the argument.

There are lots of ways we can say "all" or "some":

All dogs bark.
Every dog barks.
Dogs bark.
Everything that's a dog barks.

Some dogs are affectionate.
There is a dog that's affectionate.
At least one dog is affectionate.
There exists an affectionate dog.

> *Universal Claim*   A claim is *universal* if it can be rewritten as an "all" claim that must have the same truth-value.
>
> *Existential Claim*   A claim is *existential* if it can be rewritten as a "some" claim that must have the same truth-value.

We use the term "existential" because "some" can be read as "there exists."

B. Contradictories

One of the most common mistakes with universal and existential claims is getting the contradictory wrong. Recall that a *contradictory* of a claim is one that always has the opposite truth-value.

At the end of an advertisement for electric razors you read:

This product may not be available in all stores.

What? Why are they advertising their razors if you might not be able to get them anywhere? They've got the contradictory wrong for "This product is available in all stores." It should be: "This product may not be available in some stores."

And the contradictory of "All dogs bark" isn't "All dogs don't bark." Both claims are false. The contradictory is "Some dogs don't bark."

The contradictory of "Some foxes are affectionate" isn't "Some foxes are not affectionate." Both claims are true. Rather it's "Not even one fox is affectionate" or "All foxes are not affectionate." Or better still, "No fox is affectionate."

> **Negative Universal Claim** A *negative universal claim* is one that can be rewritten as a "no" claim or an "all not" claim that must have the same truth-value.

So the following are all equivalent:

No dog likes cats.
All dogs do not like cats.
Nothing that's a dog likes cats.
Not even one dog likes cats.

Here are some examples of claims and their contradictories:

Claim	Contradictory
All dogs bark.	Some dogs don't bark.
Some dogs bark.	No dogs bark.
Some dogs don't bark.	All dogs bark.
No women are philosophers.	Some women are philosophers.
Every Mexican likes vodka.	Some Mexicans don't like vodka.
Some Russians like chili.	No Russian likes chili.
Some whales eat fish.	Not even one whale eats fish.

Because there are so many ways we can make universal and existential claims, it's hard to give set formulas for contradictories. With some practice you ought to be able to use your common sense to get the contradictory right. But as an aid here is a very rough guide:

Claim	Contradictory
All —	Some are not — Not every —
Some —	No — All are not — Not even one —
Some are not —	All are —
No —	Some are —

C. "Only"

"Only" has its own typical mistake:

> Only dogs bark.
> Ralph is a dog.
> So Ralph barks.

This is *not* valid. Only dogs bark doesn't mean that all dogs bark. It means that anything that barks has got to be a dog.

> *Only* S are P   means   All P are S

The contradictory of "Only S are P" is either of:

> Not every P is S.
> Some P are not S.

If we want to say that just exactly dogs bark and nothing else, we should say that, or:

> Dogs and only dogs bark.

The contradictory of that is:

> Either some dogs don't bark or some things that bark aren't dogs.

Exercises for Sections A–C

1. Give three other ways to say "All cars use gasoline."

2. Give three other ways to say "Some dogs bark."

3. Give two other ways to say "All students are smart."

4. Give three other ways to say "Some women are married."

5. Give at least one other way to say "Only birds fly."

6. Give three other ways to say "No teacher is illiterate."

7. Give another way to say "Everything that's a dog is a domestic canine and everything that's a domestic canine is a dog."

8. Give two other ways to say "No pig can fly."

9. What is a universal claim?

10. What is an existential claim?

11. What is a negative universal claim?

Judging from your experience, which of the claims in Exercises 12–19 are true? Be prepared to defend your answer.

12. Only dogs bark.

13. All blondes are dumb.

14. Some cars are designed to fall apart after six years.

15. Crest toothpaste is not available in all supermarkets.

16. Some critical thinking professors are women.

17. Every outhouse is made of wood.

18. Dictionaries are the only way to learn the meaning of new words.

19. No student can register for this course after the first week of classes.

For Exercises 20–40 give a contradictory claim.

20. All dogs bark.

21. No teacher is friendly.

22. Some dogs bite mailmen.

23. Every cat has clawed its owner.

24. Some rats aren't unpleasant.

25. Cat owners need regular physical examinations.

26. No dog owner is truly unhappy.

27. If some dog owner likes cats, then he or she is mentally unbalanced.

28. This exam will be given in all of the sections of critical thinking.

29. No exam is suitable for all students.

30. Some exams don't really test a student's knowledge.

31. Not all foxes are red.

32. Students who play up to their teachers get good grades.

33. Only philosophy professors know how to teach critical thinking.

34. All policemen and only policemen carry guns.

35. Nothing both barks and meows.

36. These exercises are boring.

37. Every subscriber to this magazine is gullible.

38. Decisions about abortion should be left to the woman and her doctor.

39. The Lone Ranger was the only cowboy to have a friend called "Tonto."

40. Only Dr. E, of all teachers, knows how to bark.

D. Some Valid and Invalid Forms

Recall the first argument in this chapter:

> All good teachers give fair exams.
> Professor Zzzyzzx gives fair exams.
> So Professor Zzzyzzx is a good teacher.

We saw it wasn't valid. Here's a picture that summarizes the discussion:

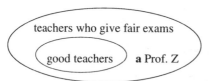

Professor Zzzyzzx could be among the bad teachers who give fair exams. It's a weak argument. It's a confusion of valid and invalid forms. Briefly, where "a" stands for the name of some thing, we have:

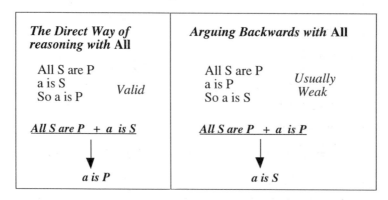

The Direct Way of reasoning with All	**Arguing Backwards with All**
All S are P a is S So a is P *Valid*	All S are P a is P So a is S *Usually Weak*
<u>All S are P + a is S</u> ↓ *a is P*	<u>All S are P + a is P</u> ↓ *a is S*

Valid: All dogs bark.   *Weak*: All dogs bark.
Ralph is a dog.   Ralph barks.
So Ralph barks.   So Ralph is a dog.

The second argument is arguing backwards again. One way to be something that barks is to be a dog, but there may be other ways (seals and foxes).

   The picture I drew is an example of a general way to check whether certain kinds of arguments that use universal and existential claims are valid.

Checking for Validity with Pictures

- A collection is represented by an enclosed area.
- If one area is entirely within another, then everything in the one collection is also in the other.
- If one area overlaps another, then there is something that is common to both collections.
- If two areas do not overlap, then there is nothing common to both.
- We use an "a" or dot to mark that a particular object is in an area.
- Draw the areas to represent the premises as true while trying to represent the conclusion as false. If you can, then the argument is invalid. If there's no way to represent the premises as true and conclusion as false, the argument is valid.

For example,

All dogs bark.
Everything that barks is a mammal.
So all dogs are mammals.

How can we use pictures to check whether this is valid? We draw the picture to represent the premises as true.

   The "dogs" area is completely inside the "things that bark" area:
      All dogs bark.

   The "things that bark" area is completely inside the "mammals" area:
      All things that bark are mammals.

   (not drawn to scale)

So the "dogs" area ends up being inside the "mammals" area. There's no way it couldn't be. That represents that all dogs are mammals. So if we represent the premises as true, we are forced to represent the conclusion as true. The argument is valid.

This argument is an example of a general form of argument that is valid:

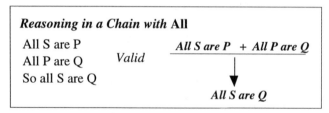

Reasoning in a Chain with **All**

All S are P
All P are Q   *Valid*
So all S are Q

$$\underline{\textit{All S are P} \;+\; \textit{All P are Q}}$$

↓

All S are Q

Here's another kind of argument:

All dogs bark.
No professor is a dog.
So no professor barks.

How do we check if this is valid? We do what we've always done: Look for all the possible ways that the premises could be true, only now we can use pictures to represent those possibilities. We know that the "dogs" area must be entirely within the "things that bark" area (All dogs bark). So we just have to figure out where to put the "professors" area. We know that there must be no overlap of the "professors" area and the "dogs" area (No professor is a dog). So here are the possibilities:

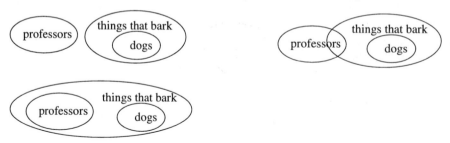

These (schematically) represent all the ways the premises could be true. Yet both the right and the bottom picture represent the conclusion as false. It's possible for there to be a professor who barks, even though he (she?) isn't a dog. The argument is invalid.

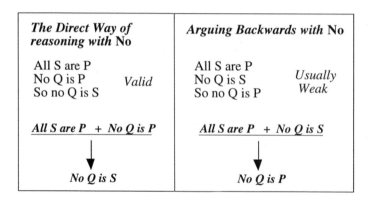

The Direct Way of reasoning with **No**	*Arguing Backwards with* **No**
All S are P No Q is P *Valid* So no Q is S	All S are P No Q is S *Usually Weak* So no Q is P
All S are P + No Q is P ↓ *No Q is S*	*All S are P + No Q is S* ↓ *No Q is P*

Here's an argument with a different form we can check with diagrams:

Some foxes are affectionate.
Some creatures that are affectionate are loyal.
So some foxes are loyal.

Is the argument valid? What do we have to have in a picture?

The "foxes" area must overlap the "affectionate" area:
Some foxes are affectionate.

The "loyal" area must overlap the "affectionate" area:
Some creatures that are affectionate are loyal.

Now it's easy to come up with a picture that represents the premises as true and conclusion false:

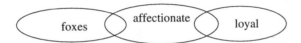

We were able to draw the picture to represent both premises as true, yet there's no overlap between the "foxes" area and the "loyal" area, so the conclusion is false: It's possible that no foxes are loyal. The argument is invalid.

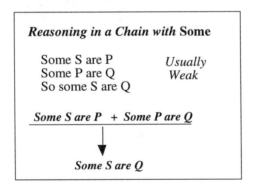

Drawing pictures to check validity is just another way to look for possibilities that make the premises true and conclusion false. The method works for some arguments that use universal or existential claims, but not for all. Even the simple argument about dogs that like cats which began the chapter can't be analyzed using pictures this way. You'll just have to think your way through all possible ways the premises could be true when you do some of the exercises.

Let's see how Lee and Maria have been using pictures to check for validity. (There are more examples in the Workbook of Lee and Maria applying this method.)

Exercises for Section D

Which of the argument forms in Exercises 1–6 are valid? Justify your answer. Then give an argument of that form.

1. All S are P.
    No Q is S.
    So some Q aren't P.

2. All S are P.
    a is S.
    So *a* is P.

3. Some S are P.
    All P are Q.
    So some S are Q.

4. Only S are P.
    a is S.
    So *a* is P.

5. Some S aren't P.
    So no P are S.

6. All S are P.
    No Q is P.
    So no Q is S.

For exercises 7–13, select the claim that makes the argument valid. (You don't need to judge whether the claim is plausible, just whether it makes the argument valid.)

7. All turtles can swim. So turtles eat fish.
   a. Anything that eats fish swims.
   b. Fish swim and are eaten by things that swim.
   c. Anything that swims eats fish.
   d. None of the above.

8. Every teacher at this school gets a free parking space. So Ms. Fletcher is a teacher at this school.
   a. Ms. Fletcher has a free parking space at this school.
   b. Ms. Fletcher is at this school every day.
   c. Both (a) and (b).
   d. None of the above.

9. Dogs bark. So dogs eat meat.
   a. Anything that eats meat barks.
   b. Dogs don't meow.
   c. Anything that barks eats meat.
   d. None of the above.

10. All heroin addicts cannot function in a 9–5 job. So no one who teaches is a heroin addict.
    a. Teachers usually don't take drugs.
    b. Teachers can work hard.
    c. All teachers can function in a 9–5 job.
    d. None of the above.

11. Every policeman must pass a physical fitness examination. So no person with heart-disease can pass a physical fitness examination.
    a. No person with heart-disease is a policeman.
    b. No person with heart-disease is physically fit.
    c. If you're a policeman, you can pass a physical fitness exam.
    d. None of the above.

12. Some dogs chase cats. So some cats are bitten.
    a. Some dogs catch cats.
    b. Some things that chase cats bite them.
    c. Some dogs bite cats.
    d. None of the above.

13. Every dog chases cats. So Spot chases Puff.
    a. Spot is a dog.
    b. Puff is a cat.
    c. Puff irritates Spot.
    d. Both (a) and (b).
    e. None of the above.

Which of Exercises 14–31 are valid arguments? (You are not expected to determine whether it is good, only whether it is valid.) Check by doing *one* of the following:

- Give an example in which the premises are true and conclusion false.
- Draw a diagram.
- Point out that the argument is in one of the forms we have studied.
- Explain in your own words why it's valid.

14. Not every student attends lectures. Zoe is a student. So Zoe doesn't attend lectures.

15. No students are enthusiastic about mathematics. Dr. E is not a student. So Dr. E is enthusiastic about mathematics.

16. No students are enthusiastic about mathematics. Harry is enthusiastic about mathematics. So Harry is not a student.

17. Some dogs bite mailmen. Some mailmen bite dogs. So some dogs and mailmen bite each other.

18. Everyone who is anxious to learn works hard. Dr. E's students work hard. So Dr. E's students are anxious to learn.

19. All lions are fierce, but some lions are afraid of dogs. So some dogs aren't afraid of lions.

20. All students who are serious take critical thinking in their freshman year. No heroin addict is a serious student. So no heroin addict takes critical thinking his freshman year.

21. No student who cheats is honest. Some dishonest people are found out. So some students who cheat are found out.

22. Some people who like pizza are vegetarians. Some vegetarians will not eat eggs. So some people who like pizza will not eat eggs.

23. Only ducks quack. George is a duck. So George quacks.

24. Everyone who likes ducks likes quackers. Dick likes ducks. Dick likes cheese. So Dick likes cheese and quackers.

25. No dogcatcher is kind. Anyone who's kind loves dogs. So no dogcatcher loves dogs.

26. Some things that grunt are hogs. Some hogs are good to eat. So some things that grunt are good to eat.

27. Every newspaper Dr. E reads is published by an American publisher. All newspapers published by an American publisher are biased against Muslims. So Dr. E reads only newspapers that are biased against Muslims.

28. Not every canary can sing. So some canaries can sing.

29. Some art students aren't good at math. John is an art student. So John isn't good at math.

30. Every dog loves its master. Dr. E has a dog. So Dr. E is loved.

31. Every cat sheds hair on its master's clothes. Dr. E does not have a cat. So Dr. E has no cat hair shed on his clothes.

32. Arguing backwards with "all" and arguing backwards with conditionals are related.
    We can rewrite:

All dogs bark.		If anything is a dog, then it barks.
Ralph barks.	as	Ralph barks.
So Ralph is a dog.		So Ralph is a dog.

Rewrite the following universal claims as conditionals:

> All good teachers give fair exams.
> Every horse loves attention.
> Ducks like water.

E. Between One and All

1. Precise generalities

There are a lot of quantities between one and all. For example,

> 72% of all students who take critical thinking from Dr. E think he's the best teacher they've ever had. Harry took Dr. E's critical thinking course last year. So Harry thinks Dr. E is the best teacher he's ever had.

This is not valid. Where does it land on the strong–weak scale? We can say exactly: There's a 28% chance the premises could be true and conclusion false. Not very strong. If the percentages are very high or very low, though, we can get a strong argument:

> 95% plus-or-minus 2% of all cat owners have cat-induced allergies. Dr. E's ex-wife has a cat. So very probably Dr. E's ex-wife has cat-induced allergies.

> Only 4% of all students who take Dr. E's class fail his final exam. Mary Ellen took Dr. E's class. So Mary Ellen almost certainly passed Dr. E's final exam.

Both of these are strong.

2. Vague generalities

There are a lot of ways we make general claims without specifying a number:

> *All* dogs bark.
> *Almost all* dogs bark.
> *Most* dogs bark.
> *A lot of* students at this school will vote.
> *Some* foxes are affectionate.

A few foxes are affectionate.
Very few students dislike Dr. E.
At least one fox is affectionate.

Despite the ambiguity of the words "all" and "some," we can analyze whether arguments using universal and existential claims are valid. We have enough precision.

The rest of these quantity words are too vague to figure in valid arguments. *Most of them are too vague even to be used in a claim.* How could we tell if "A few students dislike Dr. E" is true? Or "A lot of students will vote"?

There are two vague generalities, though, that we can use in *strong* arguments:

Almost all parakeets are under 2' tall.
So the parakeets at Boulevard Mall are under 2' tall.

Very few dogs don't bark.
Spot is Dick and Zoe's dog.
So Spot barks.

These conclusions don't follow with absolute certainty, yet the premises give us good reason to believe them. The following are the "almost all" versions of the forms for "all":

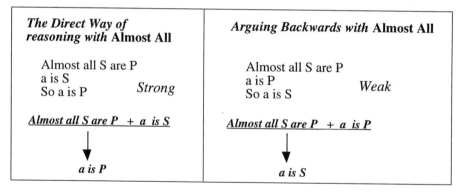

The Direct Way of reasoning with **Almost All**	*Arguing Backwards with* **Almost All**
Almost all S are P a is S So a is P *Strong*	Almost all S are P a is P So a is S *Weak*
<u>Almost all S are P + a is S</u> ↓ *a is P*	<u>Almost all S are P + a is P</u> ↓ *a is S*

Now consider:

Almost all dogs like peanut butter.
Almost all things that like peanut butter don't bark.
So almost all dogs don't bark.

The premises are true and the conclusion false, and there's nothing improbable about that. This form of argument is usually weak.

Almost all S are P.
Almost all P are Q.   *Usually Weak*
So almost all S are Q.

An argument of this form might be strong if you could specify exactly which S aren't P, and which P aren't Q. But that's just to say you need further premises to make it strong.

Exercises for Section E

1. Give two other ways to say, "Almost all dogs bark."

2. Give two other ways to say, "Only a few cats bark."

Which of the argument forms in Exercises 3–6 are strong? Justify your answer.

3. Very few S are P.
   a is S.
   So *a* is not P.

4. Very few S are P.
   a is P.
   So *a* is not S.

5. Most S are P.
   Most P are Q.
   So most S are Q.

6. Almost all S are P.
   Every P is Q.
   So almost all S are Q.

Which of the following arguments are strong? Check by doing one of the following:

- Give enough examples in which the premises are true and conclusion false.
- Point out that the argument is in one of the forms we have studied.
- Explain in your own words why it's strong or weak.

7. Very few college students use heroin. Zoe is a college student. So Zoe doesn't use heroin.

8. Almost no students are enthusiastic about mathematics. Harry is enthusiastic about mathematics. So Harry is not a student.

9. Only a very few dogs like cats. Almost no cats like dogs. So virtually no dogs and cats like each other.

10. A majority of people who are anxious to learn work hard. Dr. E's students work hard. So a majority of Dr. E's students are anxious to learn.

11. No student who cheats is honest. Almost all dishonest people are found out. So almost all students who cheat are found out.

12. Almost all people who are vegetarians like pizza. Almost all vegetarians will not eat eggs. So all but a few people who like pizza will not eat eggs.

13. Mostly ducks quack. George is a duck. So George quacks.

14. Most things that grunt are hogs. Almost all hogs are good to eat. So most things that grunt are good to eat.

15. All but a very few canaries can sing. So not many canaries can't sing.

16. Very few art students are good at math. John is an art student. So John isn't good at math.

17. Almost every dog loves its master. Dr. E has a dog. So Dr. E is loved.

Summary   How do we reason with words that indicate how many?

We studied ways to use "all" and "some" in arguments. We began by saying how we'll understand those words, and then noted that there are lots of equivalent ways to say them or to form their contradictories, including using the words "no" and "only." Then we looked at a few valid and invalid forms of arguments using those words. We also saw how sometimes we could use pictures to decide if an argument is valid.

Other precise general claims that lie between one and all normally don't figure in valid arguments, but we saw that sometimes they can figure in strong arguments.

Then we looked at vague generalities. Most don't figure in good arguments. Most don't even belong in claims. But "almost all" and "a few" can be used in strong arguments. We looked at some strong and weak argument forms using them.

Key Words

all	reasoning in a chain with "all"
some	direct way of reasoning with "no"
universal claim	arguing backwards with "no"
existential claim	reasoning in a chain with "some"
contradictory	precise generalities
negative universal claim	vague generalities
only	direct way of reasoning with
direct way of reasoning	"almost all"
with "all"	arguing backwards with "almost all"
arguing backwards with "all"	

Further Study   An introductory course on *formal logic* will devote a lot of time to studying the roles of universal and existential claims in valid arguments.

Writing Lesson 11

Write an argument either for or against the following:

> "All students at this school who are physically able should be required to take a course in physical education."

Check whether your instructor has chosen a *DIFFERENT TOPIC* for this assignment.

The issue is simple. There's nothing subtle that you're supposed to do here that you haven't done on the previous assignments. You just need to know how to argue for or against a universal claim. And for that you must be sure you can form the contradictory of it.

By now you should have learned a lot about writing arguments. You don't need more examples, just practice using the new ideas presented in the chapters. You can use as a guide Composing Good Arguments at the end of the text (p. 339), which summarizes many of the lessons you've learned.

Review Chapters 6–8

In Chapters 1–5 we established the fundamentals of critical thinking. In this part we looked at the structure of arguments.

Compound claims have their own structure. We saw that a compound claim, though made up of other claims, has to be viewed as just one claim. We saw that some arguments are valid solely because of their form relative to the compound claims in them.

For example, excluding possibilities is a form of valid argument using "or" claims. But if the "or" claim doesn't list all the possibilities, we get a bad argument, a false dilemma.

Conditionals took more care. We saw how to form their contradictories and considered how true conditionals expressed necessary or sufficient conditions.

We noted the direct and the indirect ways to make valid arguments using conditionals. Two forms are similar to valid conditional arguments, but are invalid: affirming the consequent and denying the antecedent. We decided that any argument using those shouldn't be repaired.

Reasoning in a chain with conditionals is valid, too. But if some of the conditionals are false or enough of them are dubious, the result can be a bad argument, a slippery slope.

Counterarguments are important to distinguish in the structure of arguments. Counterarguments are useful in our own writing, because they help us see what assumptions we may have missed. Looking at counterarguments led us to consider the ways we can refute an argument: directly or by reducing to the absurd. We also saw four bad ways to attempt to refute an argument: phony refutations, slippery slopes, ridicule, and the worst, putting words in someone's mouth.

We also looked at more complex arguments, and devised a rough strategy for analyzing them.

Perhaps the most common mistakes we make in our reasoning come from using "all" and "some." We made sure how to understand those words and saw other ways of saying them. Then we saw how to form contradictories of universal and existential claims. We looked at a few valid and invalid forms using "all" and "some," finding that sometimes we could use pictures to check for validity. But with vague generalities we had less scope. They don't figure in valid arguments, and only "almost all" and "a very few" seemed to yield strong argument forms.

You should now be able to use the methods of Chapters 1–5 on arguments that have more complicated structure. In the next part we work on spotting bad arguments. Then you can try your hand at evaluating lots of real arguments.

Review Exercises for Chapters 6–8

1. What is an argument?

2. What is the definition of a "good argument"?

3. What is a valid argument?

4. What does it mean to say an argument is strong?

5. Is every valid argument good? Explain.

6. How do you show an argument is not valid?

7. Is every valid or strong argument with true premises good? Explain.

8. What is a compound claim?

9. a. What is a conditional?
    b. Give an example, then rewrite it four ways, one of which uses "only if".

10. a. What is a contradictory of a claim?
    b. Give an example of an "or" claim and its contradictory.
    c. Give an example of a conditional and its contradictory.
    d. Give an example of an "only if" claim and its contradictory.

11. Give an example of arguing by excluding possibilities. Is it valid?

12. What is a false dilemma? Give an example.

13. Give an example of the direct way of reasoning with conditionals. Is it valid?

14. Give an example of the indirect way of reasoning with conditionals. Is it valid?

15. Give an example of affirming the consequent. Is it valid?

16. Give an example of denying the antecedent. Is it valid?

17. Is every argument that uses reasoning in a chain with conditionals good? Explain.

18. a. What does it mean to say that A is a necessary condition for B?
    b. Give examples of claims A and B such that:
        i.   A is necessary for B, but A is not sufficient for B
        ii. A is sufficient for B, but A is not necessary for B
        iii. A is both necessary and sufficient for B
        iv. A is neither necessary nor sufficient for B

19. Why is it a good idea to include a counterargument to an argument that you are writing?

20. What are the three ways of directly refuting an argument?

21. When you use the method of reducing to the absurd to refute an argument, does it show that one of the premises is false?

22. Give an example of a phony refutation.

23. How does a slippery slope argument differ from reducing to the absurd?

24. How does ridicule differ from reducing to the absurd?

25. a. What is a universal claim?
    b. Give an example and a contradictory of it.

26. a. What is an existential claim?
    b. Give an example and a contradictory of it.

27. Give an example of arguing backwards with "all." Is it valid?

28. Give an "only" claim and rewrite it as a universal claim.

29. Give an example of a strong method of reasoning with vague generalities.

30. Give an example of a weak method of reasoning with vague generalities.

31. List the valid forms of arguments we studied.

32. List the invalid forms we said indicated that an argument is not repairable.

33. List the strong forms of argument we studied.

34. List the weak forms of argument we said indicated an argument is not repairable.

AVOIDING

BAD ARGUMENTS

9 Concealed Claims

A. Where's the Argument?

Someone tries to convince us by his choice of words rather than by an argument—the subtleties of rhetoric in place of reasoned deliberation.

We've already seen an example: persuasive definitions. Someone tries to close off the argument by making a definition that should be the conclusion. When a person defines "abortion" to mean "the murder of an unborn child," he's made it impossible to debate whether abortion is murder and whether a foetus is a human being. Those conclusions are built into the definition.

There are lots of ways we conceal claims through our choice of words. Collectively, we call them "slanters."

> **Slanter** A *slanter* is any literary device that attempts to convince by using words that conceal a dubious claim.

Slanters are bad because they try to get us to assume a dubious claim is true without reflecting on it. Let's look at some.

B. Loaded Questions

"When did you stop beating your wife?"

Don't answer. Respond, instead, by pointing out the concealed claim: "What makes you think I have been beating my wife?"

> **Loaded Question**   A *loaded question* is a question that conceals a dubious claim that should be argued for rather than assumed.

> When are you planning to start studying in this course?
> Why don't you love me anymore?
> Why can't you dress like a gentleman?
> *What Do Dogs Dream About*? (the title of an actual book)

The best response to a loaded question is to point out the concealed claim and begin discussing *that.*

C. What Did He Say?

1.   Making it sound nasty or nice

President Reagan called the guerillas fighting against the Nicaraguan government in the 1980's "freedom fighters." The Nicaraguan government called them "terrorists." The labels they chose slanted the way you viewed any claim about those people. Each label concealed a claim:

> "Freedom fighter"—the guerillas are good people fighting to liberate
>   their country and give their countrymen freedom

> "Terrorist"—the guerillas are bad people, inflicting violence on
>   civilians for their own partisan ends without popular support

> **Euphemism** (yoo'-fuh-mizm) A *euphemism* is a word or phrase that makes something sound better than a neutral description.
>
> **Dysphemism** (dis'-fuh-mizm) A *dysphemism* is a word or phrase that makes something sound worse than a neutral description.

> In 1985 a State Department spokesman explained why the word "killing" was replaced with "unlawful or arbitrary deprivation of life" in its human rights report: "We found the term 'killing' too broad."

The descriptions in the personals ads are full of euphemisms. Women describe themselves as "petite," "full-figured," "mature." But not every description involves a euphemism. One man described himself as "attractive, fun, and fit." He may have lied, but he didn't use a nice word in place of a neutral one. Nor is every euphemism bad. We don't want to get rid of every pleasant or unpleasant description in our writing and speech. We just want to be aware of misuses where we're being asked to buy into a dubious concealed claim.

> "Self-comforting patterns help a child get herself back down between sleep cycles."
> *Family Circle*, November 19, 1996
>
> That's a nice way to say thumb sucking, nose picking, holding of genitals.

2. Downplayers and up-players

Zoe: What is this lipstick on your collar? What did you and Suzy do?
Dick: Nothing.
Zoe: Nothing! Nothing!
Dick: Oh, I kissed her just one time.

"Just"? That's downplaying the significance of what happened.

Zoe: Hey Mom. Great news. I managed to pass my first French exam.
Mom: You only just passed?

Zoe has up-played the significance of what she did, concealing the claim "It took great effort to pass" with the word "managed." Her mother downplayed the significance of passing by using "only just," concealing the claim "Passing and not getting an A or a B is not commendable."

> ***Downplayer***   A word or phrase that minimizes the significance of a claim.
> ***Up-player***   A word or phrase that exaggerates the significance of a claim.

> "Yes, I have cheated in a class although it has never been off someone else. Just crib notes."   *U. The National College Magazine*, November, 1996

The extreme version of an up-player is called an ***hyperbole*** (hi-purr'-buh-lee):

Zoe: I'm sorry I'm late for work. I had a terrible emergency at home.
Boss: Oh, no. I'm so sorry. What happened?
Zoe: I ran out of mousse and had to go to the store.

> Chilly 58-degree days normally happen in December and January, but they blew in early to make Sunday teeth-chattering.   *Las Vegas Review-Journal*

One way to downplay is with words that restrict or limit the meaning of others, what we call *qualifiers*—like the asterisks in advertisements.*

(*On approved credit and $500 down and the right to your first-born child).

> The city will install stop signs this week for a four-way stop at the corner of St. George Boulevard, attempting to cut down accidents and prepare motorists for a stoplight at the intersection.
>   "The city has recorded six accidents at the intersection in the past four months, and there may have been more that were not reported," said city traffic engineer Aron Baker.   *The Spectrum,* September 23, 1996

What did he say? Were there more accidents? No: There *may have been* more. But then there may not have been more. Or aliens may have landed at the intersection. The qualifiers "may" and "might" allow someone to suggest what he's not willing to say. In a badly written history book you can find these used to make lots of claims almost meaningless, "Thomas Jefferson may have thought that . . ."

In the extreme someone can weasel right out of what he's apparently saying:

Dick (to his boss): I am truly sorry that it has taken so long for you to
                    understand what I have been saying.

Dick isn't sorry at all. We call a *weaseler* a claim that's qualified so much that the apparent meaning is no longer there.

We also downplay by using quotes or a change in voice:

He got his "degree" from a beauty school.

The hidden claim is "A degree from a beauty school is not really something worth calling a degree."

3. Where's the proof?

By now you must have been convinced what a great textbook writer I am. It's obvious to anyone. Of course, some people are a little slow. But surely you see it.

In the last paragraph I didn't *prove* that I was a great textbook writer, though I made it sound as if I were proving something. I was just reiterating the claim, trying to browbeat you into believing it with the words "obvious," "some people are slow," "surely," "must have been convinced."

> ***Proof Substitute***   A *proof substitute* is a word or phrase that suggests the speaker has a proof, but no proof is actually offered.

When I was an undergraduate I had a famous teacher for an upper-division mathematics course, Professor Fröelich. One day he wrote a claim on the board and said, "So the following is obvious." Then he stopped and looked puzzled. He went to the end of the blackboard and looked at the wall for a few minutes. Then he returned and said, "Yes, it is obvious," and continued.

I always say I prefer a student who asks questions. It's better to be thought dumb and learn something than to sit on your ignorance. If someone tells you it's obvious, or conceals a lack of proof with flowery language, don't be cowed—ask for the proof. In some recipes you can substitute corn syrup for sugar, but there's no substitute for a proof.

> Existing research substantiates this: nearly 50% of all injuries in some sports are acute in nature and involve either muscle or tendon tissue.
> *Concepts of Athletic Training* by Brent C. Mangus, p. 79
>
> That's the whole passage.

Ridicule is a particularly nasty form of proof substitute: That's so obviously wrong it's a joke.

> Send aid to Russia? Sure, why not just put your money in a barrel and burn it! Or better yet, give it to me.

No argument has been given for why aid should not be sent to Russia.

Another way to conceal that you have no support for your claim is to ***shift the burden of proof***.

> Mom: You should become a lawyer.
> Dick: Why?
> Mom: Why not?

The burden of proof should be on the person putting forward the claim. The implausible assumption here is:

> I don't have to support my assertions, you have to show why they aren't true.

This is a variation on the theme that whatever's plausible must be true. For example, we hear the CIA was involved in drug running, and soon people are saying:

> The CIA introduced crack cocaine into the inner-cities in order to hook young blacks on it.

Whoever is asserting this has the burden of proof to show it's true. Plausibility isn't truth. The CIA and government don't have to show it's false, except maybe to calm people's fears.

D. Innuendos

Any concealed claim is an ***innuendo***. But usually we use that term for concealed claims that are really unpleasant.

> Zoe: Where are you from?
> Harry: New York.
> Zoe: Oh, I'm sorry.

Just to belabor the point, the concealed claim is "You deserve pity for having had to live in New York."

Innuendos imply nasty claims (Chapter 4.D). They are the bread of the sandwich of political discourse.

I agree. My opponent is telling the truth this time.

Look for the meat.

E. Slanters and Good Arguments

You may be tempted to use slanters in your own writing. Don't. Slanters turn off those you want to convince—it's like preaching to the converted. Worse, though they may work for the moment, they don't stick. Without reinforcement, the other person will remember only the joke or jibe. A good argument can last and last—the other person can see the point clearly and reconstruct it. And if you use slanters, your opponent can destroy your points not by facing your real argument, but by pointing out the slanters.

> If you reason calmly and rationally you will earn the respect of the other, and may learn that the other merits your respect, too.

When evaluating someone else's argument, acknowledge that he or she may have been a bit emotional. Get rid of the noise—ignore the slanting, interpret the claims neutrally, and see if there is a good argument.

If there are just too many slanters, though, used time and again, then it's clear the other person can't or won't reason well. The Principle of Rational Discussion doesn't apply.

Summary   The point is to recognize slanters. Names and classifications, like "downplayer," "weaseler," or "innuendo" are aids to help you learn how to recognize something bad is going on in an argument. Often not just one, but two or more names apply.

You know the material in this chapter when you can take an argument and point out the concealed claims in it, rewriting to eliminate slanted language. The names are just shorthand for explanations you can give in your own words.

Exercises for Chapter 9

1. a. Why is it wrong to use a persuasive definition?
    b. Give an example (not from the text) of a persuasive definition. What claim(s) is it concealing?

2. Come up with a loaded question you might pose to an instructor to try to make him or her give you a better grade.

3. Give a loaded question you might ask a policeman when he stops you.

4. Give an example of politically correct language and rephrase it in neutral language.

5. Give a euphemism and a dysphemism for each of the following. Be sure your word or phrase can be used in a sentence in place of the original.
    a. Used car
    b. Sexually explicit books
    c. Cat
    d. Handicapped person
    e. Unemployed

6. Bring in an example of a euphemism from a network news broadcast.

7. Bring in an example of a dysphemism from a network news broadcast.

8. Bring in an example of a downplayer. Say what the hidden claim is.

9. Bring in an example of hyperbole from a network news broadcast.

10. Typical proof substitutes are "Obviously," "Everyone knows that . . ." List six more.

11. Bring in an example from *another* textbook in which it sounds like the author is giving an argument but there's really no proof.

12. Bring in an example from a political speech in which it sounds like the speaker is giving an argument but there's really no proof.

13. Write a neutral description of someone you know well, one that a third party could use to recognize him or her. Now write a slanted version by replacing the neutral terms with euphemisms and/or dysphemisms, adding downplayers or up-players.

14. Rewrite the following in neutral language. All are actual quotes.
    a. "The president misspoke himself."
        (Attributed to Ron Ziegler, press secretary for Richard Nixon.)
    b. "Our operatives succeeded with the termination with extreme prejudice."
        (Reported by the CIA.)
    c. "There was a premature impact of the aircraft with the terrain below."
        (Announced by the FAA.)

Say what, if anything, is wrong with the following. Make any concealed claim explicit:

15. Dick: That was really rotten, making me wait for an hour.
    Zoe: I'm sorry you feel that way.

16. I was only three miles over the speed limit, officer.

17. (Ron Ziegler was the press secretary for Richard Nixon's administration.)
    Ziegler: So it was a really terrific year except for the downside.
    Interviewer: What downside?
    Ziegler: Watergate.

18. Can't you ever get to class on time?

19. Lee: I used to find Peruvian women attractive, until I learned Spanish.

20. Those hippies are protesting the war again.

21. Students should be required to wear uniforms in high schools. It has been well documented that wearing uniforms reduces gang violence.

22. A book on Hopi prophecies by a former Lutheran minister [Rev. Thomas Mails] has reignited a battle between tribal members and the author about the sanctity of his actions.
    Mails claims he and Evehema recently deciphered a symbol on an ancient Hopi stone tablet that revealed the next world war will be started by China at an undisclosed time.
    "If what they told me is true, it's the most important message in the world today," Mails said.

    Associated Press, September 30, 1996

23. Why won't those tree huggers let us get on with logging?

24. Did you hear that the lumber company is planning to cut down the forest?

25. I'm surprised your readers took offense at the truth.

26. The gaming industry in Nevada recorded another record year of profits.

27. Your instructor teaches pretty well for someone his (her) age.

28. Probably your instructor just forgot to write down your grade. Certainly she wouldn't have lied to you about it.

29. An alcoholic is someone with a lack of willpower to stop drinking alcohol.

30. Tom: Hey Dr. E, did you read in the newspaper what Madonna said after she had her first child this week? "This is the greatest miracle that's ever happened to me."
    Dr. E: The biggest miracle that ever happened to Madonna is that she had a career in music.

31. The so-called reform in taxes is nothing more than a redistribution of wealth from the poor to the rich.

32. That corporation wants to erect a hotel in an unspoiled wilderness area.

33. I'm sorry to hear your dog passed away.

34. (Catcatcher) Hey, lady, I'm paid to terminate cats.

35. Doctors are just legal drug-pushers.

36. **Experts say too many get too little sleep**

    Many Americans will happily snooze through the extra hour provided by Sunday's shift into daylight-saving time.

    But researchers say the annual luxury scarcely dents the national sleep deficit. Too many Americans are on the verge of nodding off.

    "I think most experts would agree that self-imposed sleep deprivation is a major problem for many people," said Mark Chambers, a psychologist and clinical director of The Sleep Clinic of Nevada in Las Vegas. "Sleep seems to be the lowest priority on people's list."

    Charlotte Huff, *Las Vegas Review-Journal,* October, 1996

37. The National Rifle Association intends to arm every man, woman, and child in this country. Only by forcefully countering their arguments can we stop these gun-pushers from destroying our society.

38. Those ACLU freaks will defend anyone: They even defended the free-speech rights of Nazis in Chicago.

39. That male chauvinist pig won't stop "complimenting" me.

40. What's a nurse? A nurse is someone who does the doctor's job, cleans up after his messes, and gets paid a tenth of what he gets paid.

41. The United States has no plans at present for invading Cuba.

42. Alan Boss, an astronomer at the Carnegie Institution in Washington D.C., remarked on the discovery of a large planet orbiting a nearby star: "It's a very nice discovery. Even a single discovery like this can make people stop and rethink everything that's happened so far."

43. (Headline for AP story by Marc Rice, *The Spectrum*, October 29, 1996, concerning the guard, Richard Jewell, who discovered the bomb at the Olympics)
    No Hard Evidence Linking Jewell to Olympic bombing

44. The county sanitation workers are threatening to go out on strike.

45. At last our government has decided to give compensation to the Japanese who were resettled in internment camps during WWII.

46. Politician: I know that some of you are concerned about my little run-in with the law. But I can assure you that my record speaks for itself.

47. **Blondes aren't dumb—they're just slow**

    Berlin—Blonde women are not dumber than brunettes or redheads, a reassuring study shows—they are just slower at processing information, take longer to react to stimuli and tend to retain less information for a shorter period of time than other women.

    "This should put an end to the insulting view that blondes are airheads," said Dr. Andrea Stenner, a blonde sociologist who studied more than 3,000 women for her doctoral research project.

    Weekly World News, October 15, 1996

48. (Pat Buchanan is a U.S. politician who advocates restricting immigration and ending

welfare. During his campaign for the presidency in 1996 the following was said.)
Pat Buchanan's speeches are better in the original German.

49. **One injured in one-car rollover**

A West Valley, Utah, woman was injured Sunday when she apparently fell asleep at the wheel on Interstate 15.

Utah Highway Patrol dispatch reports that 18-year-old Jennifer Gustin was heading north on I-15 Sunday morning about 7:30 a.m. when she fell asleep at the wheel.

Gustin drifted off to the right and then over-corrected to the left. The vehicle rolled and then came to rest on its top in the median. Gustin was not wearing a seat belt and was partially ejected from the vehicle.

UHP reports state she suffered from internal injuries.

She was taken to Valley View Medical Center in Cedar City following the accident and was later transferred to Pioneer Valley hospital in West Valley, Utah.

Nancy Camarena, 19, also of West Valley, was in the car, but received no injuries despite not wearing a seat belt.

Tyson Hiatt, *The Spectrum,* April 30, 1996

50. On the day that Wislawa Symborski was awarded the Nobel Prize for Literature, there were orders for 12,000 copies of her most recent book. The publicist for her American publisher, Harcourt Brace, Dori Weintraub, said, "For a Polish poet, that's not bad."

51. (Advertisement)

If you love eggs, you'll love this news.
New studies say eggs are okay.

If you haven't heard the news, allow us to break it to you.

If you have normal cholesterol, follow a low-fat diet and love eggs, go ahead and enjoy them. Your cholesterol probably won't go up enough to notice.

Two recent studies published in a leading scientific journal showed that 20 healthy young men and 13 healthy young women with normal blood cholesterol levels could eat up to two eggs a day while on a low-fat diet without significantly boosting their blood cholesterol levels. Up to two eggs a day!

Research also shows that the amount of cholesterol consumed by the average American (300 mg to 400 mg a day) does not significantly boost blood cholesterol levels in most healthy people.

And how about this news?

Over the past 25 years, 227 studies conducted among 23,686 participants concluded that for most healthy people saturated fat influences blood cholesterol levels more than dietary cholesterol.

So tomorrow morning, whip up a couple of eggs and dig in. After all, with news this good, you're going to be real hungry.

Of course, not all the experts agree. So ask your doctor or a registered dietician about the best way to include eggs in your diet. One large egg has 215 mg of cholesterol and 1.5 grams of saturated fat (4.5 grams of total fat). An egg is also an inexpensive source of high-quality protein.

To find out more information about eggs, cholesterol and other topical issues, send for our free booklet, "Eggs and Good Health." Mail a stamped, self-addressed envelope to: American Egg Board, . . .

52. Conscious experience is a widespread phenomenon. It occurs at many levels of animal life, though we cannot be sure of its presence in the simpler organisms, and it is very difficult to say in general what provides evidence for it. (Some extremists have been prepared to deny it even of mammals other than man.) No doubt it occurs in countless forms totally unimaginable to us, on other planets in other solar systems throughout the universe. But no matter how the form may vary, the fact that an organism has conscious experience *at all* means, basically, that there is something it is like to *be* that organism. There may be further implications about the form of the experience; there may even (though I doubt it) be implications about the behavior of the organism. But fundamentally an organism has conscious states if and only if there is something that it is like to *be* that organism—something it is like *for* the organism.

Thomas Nagel, "What Is It to Be a Bat?"

53. Put a line through every slanter in the following, either eliminating it or rewriting neutrally. Then evaluate the argument.

Letter to the editor:
I am writing this letter to complain about the stupid, ridiculous $4 fee they are trying to impose on people using Snow Canyon [a large state park recreational area near St. George where there had previously been no fee]. It is getting harder and harder to find forms of recreation that don't cost money in this area. Now you have to pay $4, even if it's just to sit on the sand for a few minutes and collect some rays.

I've never really had a problem paying $5 to get into Zion's Park [a national park nearby], because going to Zion is an all day event. However, going to Snow Canyon is not. It's a place you go to after work or school when you only have a couple of free hours and a case of spring fever. Being charged for it would be comparable to charging $4 to enter the city park.

I don't feel that my presence in Snow Canyon is costing the state any extra expense that needs to be covered. The only facility I ever use is the road that goes through the park. It is my understanding that the fee isn't new, but they haven't had the staff to collect it until now. So in other words, they need the $4 to pay for the bigger staff, and the reason they need a bigger staff is to collect the $4 (a slight case of circular logic).

It just seems like we are losing more and more freedom all the time. Next they'll probably start charging us $4 to go on to the Sugar Loaf on the red hill. Who knows, maybe some day they will have government officials waiting on the streets to collect money from us every time we leave the house–to pay for the air we breathe–or has that already happened?

Shawn Williams, *The Spectrum,* March 24, 1996

54. Bring to class a letter to the editor. Read it to the class. Then read it with all the slanters replaced with neutral language.

Key Words

slanter	downplayer	weaseler
loaded question	up-player	proof substitute
euphemism	hyperbole	burden of proof
dysphemism	qualifier	innuendo

Further Study   Courses on rhetoric and advertising spend a lot of time looking at slanters in non-argumentative persuasion.

10   Too Much Emotion

Emotion has a place in our deliberations. But too much emotion is a way to convince without argument, the method of the unscrupulous and the demagogue. We need to learn how to distinguish appropriate and inappropriate uses of emotion in arguments.

A. Appeal to Pity

> Zoe: You should vote for Ralph for school vice-president.
> Dick: Why?
> Zoe: Because he doesn't have many friends, and it would make him feel good.

Zoe has some reason for voting for Ralph. But to construe it as a strong argument we need to add "You should vote for someone you feel sorry for."

Appeal to Pity   An argument is called an *appeal to pity* if it uses or can be repaired only by putting in a premise that says, roughly:

You should believe or do _____ if you feel sorry for _____ .

    We might want to consider whether doing something will make us feel good by alleviating our pity. But that's a lousy reason for *believing* a claim.

B. Appeal to Fear

On the cover of a free three-minute video mailed to voters' homes in Las Vegas there is a picture of bearded young man in sweatshirt pointing a gun directly at the reader:

At 14 Years Old He Stole A Car.
At 16 He Raped.
At 17 He Killed.
And He Still Doesn't Have A Record.
We Cannot Continue To Allow Violent Criminals To Terrorize Our Neighborhoods.

| Las Vegas Review Journal Tuesday, June 25, 1996 Living in Fear "... By many measures, the threat of youth related crime and its fallout are on the rise in Las Vegas Valley ..." | Reuter News Service Friday, June 18, 1996 Nevada Rated Most Dangerous State "... Nevada is the most dangerous state in the nation this year ..." according to an independent midwest research firm. | Reno Gazette Journal Sunday, July 14, 1996 Youth-Crime Increase Alarms Officials "The rise in violent crime young people commit is the most serious issue confronting the juvenile system today ..." |

Elect COBB Nevada State Senate

This is an argument. The conclusion is:

You should vote for Cobb.

It is a bad argument. The only reason it gives for electing Cobb is fear. And in this particularly egregious example it doesn't even link the fear to the conclusion.

Appeal to Fear An argument is called an *appeal to fear* or **scare tactics** if it uses or can be repaired only by putting in a premise that says, roughly:

You should believe or do _____ if you are afraid of _____ .

An appeal to fear substitutes one legitimate concern for all others, clouding our minds to alternatives. But fear can be a legitimate factor in making a decision.

Dick: You shouldn't drive so quickly in this rain.
Zoe: Why not?
Dick: The roads are very slippery after the first rain of the season, and we could get into a serious accident.

This is not a bad argument. It appeals to Zoe's fears, but appropriately so. The unstated and quite plausible premise would be:

You should slow down below the speed limit if you are afraid of getting into a serious accident.

Compare that to an advertisement in which it seems that fear is, again, relevant:

A lonely road. Your car breaks down. It's dark. Aren't you glad you bought a Dorkler brand cellular phone?

Rewriting we have:

Because your car might break down at night on a lonely road, you should buy a Dorkler brand cellular phone

What's needed is a premise like: "Dorkler brand cellular phones will save you from the dangers of the night." That's not too implausible. But it isn't enough. Also needed is "Your only consideration in deciding whether to buy *this* brand of cellular phone is your concern about your safety." That's implausible.

C. Appeal to Spite

Dick: Hi Tom, what's wrong with your car?
Tom: The battery's dead. Can you help me push it? Harry will steer.
Dick: Sure.
Zoe: (whispering) What are you doing Dick? Don't you remember Tom wouldn't help you fix the fence last week?

What Zoe said isn't an argument, but we can rewrite it as one:

You shouldn't help Tom start his car, because he wouldn't help you last week.

The premise needed to make this a strong argument is "You shouldn't help anyone who has refused to help you (recently)."

> *Appeal to Spite* An argument is called an *appeal to spite* if it uses or can be repaired only by putting in a premise that says, roughly:
>
> You should believe or do _____ if you are mad about what _____ has done or believes.

Appeals to spite are based on the principle that *two wrongs make a right*. An appeal to spite is bad if it ignores all other reasons for a course of action except revenge.

> When a new national monument was declared in Utah just before the 1996 election, some who were opposed to it complained there was no consultation before the decision, no "due process." Here's what the Southern Utah Wilderness Alliance, strong lobbyists for the monument, said in its November, 1996 *Bulletin*:
>
> Q: What about due process?
>
> A. Due process meant nothing to Utah politicians last year when they tried to ramrod their anti-wilderness proposal down the throat of not only Utahns, but all Americans; their intransigence only proved to the President that rational negotiation on land protection issues in southern Utah is not possible.

The reverse of an appeal to spite is an argument that **calls in your debts**, which relies on a premise like:

You should believe or do _____ if you owe _____ a favor.

For example,

How can you go to the movies with Harry and not watch the game with me? Don't you remember how I helped you wash your car last week?

D. Feeling Good

I really deserve a passing grade in your course. I know that you're a fair grader, and you've always been terrific to everyone in the class. I admire how you handle the class, and I've enjoyed your teaching so much that it would be a pity if I didn't have something to show for it.

Gee, I guess I should have passed her . . .   No, wait, she hasn't given me any reason to change her grade. The premise that's missing is "You should give a passing mark to (almost) anyone who thinks you're a great person."

Feel-Good Argument   An argument is called a *feel-good argument* if it uses or can be repaired only by putting in a premise that says, roughly:

You should believe or do _____ if it makes you feel good.

We might want to consider whether doing something will make us feel good. But it's a lousy reason for *believing* a claim.

When someone appeals to our vanity, as in the example above, we call a feel-good argument **apple polishing**.

But not every comment on what may seem to be vanity is a bad argument:

> To Have and to Hold
> Get healthy, shiny hold with Pantene® Pro–V® Hairspray. The pro-vitamin
> formula penetrates to make your hold strong and your shine last. Now, spray
> your way to all-day hold and all-day shine. With Pantene Pro-V Hairsprays.
> PANTENE PRO-V For Hair So Healthy It Shines

Whatever may or may not be wrong with this attempt to convince you to buy hair-
spray, it isn't an appeal to vanity. It relies on an unstated premise that you want to
look good with shiny, well-kept hair. That may be true.

Wishful thinking is what we call a feel-good argument you use on yourself.

If your reaction to an argument is "Keep on dreaming," you know it's not going to
get any better by adding unstated premises.

E. Is This a Bad Argument?

In applying the labels of this section keep in mind that we can automatically classify
an appeal to emotion as a bad argument only if:

- The appeal to emotion is the only claim supporting the conclusion.
- The appeal to emotion isn't enough to justify the conclusion.

For example,

> We should give to the American Friends Service Committee. They help
> people all over the world help themselves, and don't ask those they help
> whether they agree with them. They've been doing it well for nearly a
> century now. All those people who don't have running water or health
> care deserve our help. Poor little kids.

This is an appeal to pity. But it is a legitimate one. The appeal to pity is only
part of the support for the conclusion. In any case, pity is a legitimate concern in
whether to give to charity. Compare this to the ad on television that shows a little
girl they say they've helped, and they ask, "Wouldn't you like to help her, too?"

That's using pity as the sole motive for giving to a charity, with no concern for whether the charity uses your money well.

Exercises for Chapter 10

1. Write a *bad* argument in favor of affirmative action that is only an appeal to pity.

2. Find an advertisement that uses apple polishing.

3. Find an advertisement that uses an appeal to fear.

4. How would you classify an appeal to common practice among the types of arguments in this chapter?

5. Make up an appeal to some emotion for the next time a traffic officer stops you.

6. Report to the class on a "calling in your debts" argument you've heard.

7. Give an example of an appeal to spite that invokes what someone believes.

8. Define and give an example of an *appeal to patriotism*.
    (Samuel Johnson: "Patriotism is the last refuge of a scoundrel.")

9. Define and give an example of an *appeal to guilt*.

10. The opposite of an appeal to fear is an *appeal to bribery*. Define it and give an example.

For each of the following, decide if it is an argument. If it's an argument and fits one of the categories of this chapter, state the generic premise. Then say if it's a bad argument.

11. Zoe: We should stop all experimentation on animals right now. Imagine, hurting those poor doggies.
    Dick: But there's no reason why we shouldn't continue experimenting with cats. You know how they make me sneeze.

12. Before you buy that Japanese car, ask whether you want to see some Japanese tycoon get rich at your expense, or whether you'd prefer to see an American kid get a meal on his plate next week.

13. Vote for Harry. He knows how important your concerns are.

14. Dear Dr. E,
    I was very disappointed with my grade in your critical thinking course, but I'm sure that it was just a mistake in calculating my marks. Can I speak with you this Tuesday, right before I have lunch with my uncle, Dr. Jones, the Dean of Liberal Arts, where we plan to discuss sexual harassment on this campus?

    Sincerely, *Wanda Burnstile*

15. Go ahead. Live with your girlfriend. Who am I to say "No"? I'm just your mother. Break my heart.

16. Sunbathing does not cause skin cancer. If it did, how could I enjoy the beach?

17. Democracy is the best form of government, for otherwise this wouldn't be the greatest country in the world.

18. Smoking can't cause cancer or I would have been dead a long time ago.

19. (Advertisement)
    Impotent? You're not alone.
    Men naturally feel embarrassed about any sexual problem, but the fact is, impotence is a treatable medical symptom. Virtually every one of the twenty million men in America struggling with this problem could overcome it with the proper treatment from our physician, David Owensby, MD, The Diagnostic Center for Men in Las Vegas. We offer:
    –Medically effective, nonsurgical treatment in over 95% of all men.
    –Trained and certified male physicians and staff.
    –Strictly confidential & personalized care.
    –Coverage by most private insurance and Medicare.
    –More than 25,000 successfully treated men nationwide.

    When men find out how effectively we treat impotence, their most frequent comment is, "If I would have known, I would have worked up the courage to call sooner."
    Call us. We can help.

20. Dear Senator:
    Before you make up your mind on how to vote on the abortion bill, I'd like to remind you that those who support abortion rights usually have small families. A few years from now all my six children, and the many children of my friends, all of whom believe abortion is morally wrong, will be voting.

21. Out? Out? That can't be a strike. You're always picking on me.

22. You mean that after we flew you here to Florida, paid for your lodging, showed you a wonderful time, all for free, you aren't going to buy a lot from us?

23. You shouldn't vote for gun control. It'll just make it easier for violent criminals to take advantage of us.

24. I know this diet's going to work because I have to lose 20 pounds by the end of this month.

25. (In Dr. E's class, if a student has to miss an exam, then he or she has to petition to be excused. If the petition is granted for a midterm, then the final counts that much more. If the petition is denied, the student fails the exam. Here's an excuse petition from one of his students, written before the exam. Is it a good argument? Should Dr. E grant the petition?)

    October seventeenth through the twenty-first I will be out of town due to a family function. I am aware that my philosophy midterm falls on the seventeenth and, unfortunately, my flight leaves at 7 a.m. that morning. I am asking to please be excused from the midterm.
    My boyfriend of two and a half years is standing as the best man in his brother's

wedding. Being together for two years, I have become as much a part of his family as he is. This wedding is a once in a lifetime event and I want to be there to share it with him.

I am a 100% devoted student and would never intentionally miss an exam. However, this is something beyond my control. I understand that if my request is granted I will have to put forth extra effort and prepare myself for the final. With the only other alternative being to drop the course, I am fully prepared to do whatever it takes.

I have attached a copy of my flight reservation as well as a copy of the wedding invitation for verification. I am aware that many teachers would not even give me the opportunity to petition to be excused when the midterm is the case, but I would more than appreciate it if you would grant my request.

Key Words

appeal to pity	calling in your debts
appeal to fear	feel-good argument
scare tactics	apple polishing
appeal to spite	wishful thinking
two wrongs make a right	

11   Fallacies

A summary of
bad arguments

A. Fallacies

Starting with the Principle of Rational Discussion, we learned how to repair arguments.

> ***The Guide to Repairing Arguments***   Given an (implicit) argument that is apparently defective, we are justified in *adding* a premise or conclusion if it satisfies all three of the following:
>
> 1. The argument becomes stronger or valid.
> 2. The premise is plausible and would seem plausible to the other person.
> 3. The premise is more plausible than the conclusion.
>
> If the argument is then valid or strong, yet one of the original premises is false or dubious, we may *delete* that premise if the argument remains valid or strong.

Using this guide required some judgment. After looking at some examples, we found that not every argument is repairable. We noted when it isn't reasonable to repair an argument:

> ***Unrepairable Argument***   We can't repair an argument if any one of the
> following hold:
> - There's no argument there.
> - The argument is so lacking in coherence that there's nothing obvious to add.
> - The premises it uses are false or very dubious and cannot be deleted.
> - The obvious premise to add would make the argument weak.
> - The obvious premise to add to make the argument strong or valid is false.
> - The conclusion is clearly false.

We've seen lots of bad arguments. Each fits *at least* one of the conditions for
not repairing an argument or else directly violates the Principle. We picked out and
labeled a few types of these as clearly unrepairable.

> ***Fallacy***   A *fallacy* is a bad argument of one of the types that have been
> agreed to be so bad as to be unrepairable.

We can classify fallacies according to three broad categories:

- *Structural fallacies*
  The argument has one of the forms of bad arguments.

- *Content fallacies*
  The argument uses or requires, via the Guide to Repairing Arguments,
  a particular kind of premise that is false or very dubious.

- *Violations of the rules of rational discussion*
  There's no argument there, or it's so lacking in coherence there's
  nothing obvious to add, or a premise is more dubious than the
  conclusion, or it's not even the right argument.

B. Structural Fallacies

Some arguments are bad just because of their form. It doesn't matter if they are
about dogs and cats, or numbers, or truth and beauty. The form alone tells us the
person isn't reasoning well. These are the bad arguments we learned about when we
studied compound claims and general claims.

- *Affirming the consequent*
  $$\underline{\textit{If A then B} \ + \ B}$$
  $$\downarrow$$
  $$A$$

- *Denying the antecedent*
  $$\underline{\textit{If A then B} \ + \ \textit{not A}}$$
  $$\downarrow$$
  $$\textit{not B}$$

- *Arguing backwards with "all"*

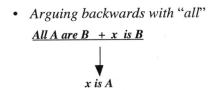

- *Reasoning in a chain with "some"*

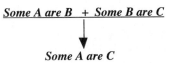

- *Arguing backwards with "almost all"*

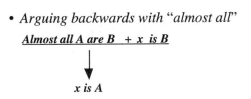

- *Arguing backwards with "no"*

$$\underline{All\ A\ are\ B\ +\ No\ C\ is\ A}$$

↓

No C is B

When someone presents an argument that fits one of these forms, we assume that he or she is confused about how to reason. The argument is invalid and almost always weak. We don't try to repair it.

C. Content Fallacies

Many arguments are bad because they use or require for repair false or very dubious premises. Usually we have to spend some time analyzing the argument, isolating the dubious premises.

But some arguments look like ones we are always suspicious of. When we spot one of those, we look for the *generic premise* the argument uses or needs for repair. If it's false, the argument is a fallacy. Here's a list of the ones we've studied, along with their generic premises.

- *Confusing objective and subjective*
    This claim is subjective. / This claim is objective.

- *Drawing the line*
    If you can't make this difference precise, there is no difference.

- *Mistaking the person (group) for the claim*
    (Almost) anything that _____ says about _____ is false.

- *Mistaking the person (group) for the argument*
    (Almost) any argument that _____ gives about _____ is bad.

- *Appeal to authority*
    (Almost) anything that _____ says about _____ is (probably) true.

- *Appeal to Common Belief*
    If (almost) everyone else (in this group) believes it, then it's true.

- *Appeal to Common Practice*
    If (almost) everyone else (in this group) does it, then it's O.K. to do.

- *Phony refutation*
    1. _____ has done or said _____, which shows that he or she does not believe the conclusion of his or her own argument.
    2. If someone does not believe the conclusion of his or her own argument, the argument is bad.

- *False dilemma*
    The use of any "or" claim that is false or very dubious. (Sometimes an equivalent conditional is used.)

- *Slippery slope*
    (This is reasoning in a chain with conditionals where one of them is false or enough of them are dubious so that the conclusion doesn't follow.)

- *Appeal to pity*
    You should believe or do _____ if you feel sorry for _____ .

- *Appeal to fear* (*scare tactics*)
    You should believe or do _____ if you are afraid of _____ .

- *Appeal to spite*
    You should believe or do _____ if you are mad about what _____ has done or believes.

- *Calling in your debts*
    You should believe or do _____ if you owe _____ a favor.

- *Feel-good argument* (*apple polishing*, *wishful thinking*)
    You should believe or do _____ if it makes you feel good.

An argument that uses one of these generic premises isn't necessarily bad. Sometimes the premise is plausible or even clearly true. *The argument is a fallacy only if the premise is very dubious or false.*

D. Violating the Rules of Rational Discussion

Sometimes it seems the other person doesn't understand what's involved in rational discussion or is intending to mislead. And sometimes there's not even an argument.

- *Begging the question*
    The point of an argument is to convince that a claim is true. So the premises of an argument have to be more plausible than the conclusion.

- *Strawman*

    It's easier to knock down someone's argument if you misrepresent it, putting words in the other person's mouth.

- *Shifting the burden of proof*

    It's easier to ask for a disproof of your claims than to prove them yourself.

- *Relevance*

    Sometimes people say a premise or premises aren't relevant to the conclusion. But that's not a category of fallacy, just an observation that the argument is so weak you can't imagine any way to repair it.

- *Slanters*

    Concealing claims that are dubious by misleading use of language.

- *Ridicule*

    Making someone or something the butt of a joke in order to convince.

Really only begging the question and strawman fit the definition of "fallacy." Especially with slanters we can often repair the argument by recasting it in neutral language. But these are all irrational ways of trying to convince.

E. Is This Really a Fallacy?

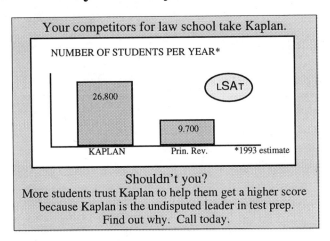

This advertisement is an attempt to convince. Its unstated conclusion is: "If you plan to take the LSAT, you should enroll at Kaplan."

It can be seen as an appeal to fear, with an unstated premise: "If you are afraid that your competitors will gain an advantage by enrolling at Kaplan, then you should enroll at Kaplan."

Or it can be seen as an appeal to common practice: "If this is the most popular way to prepare for the LSAT, and you wish to prepare for the LSAT, then you should enroll at Kaplan."

Either way the unstated premise is very dubious. So the argument is bad. It's a fallacy no matter which analysis you use.

Often an unstated premise is required to make an argument valid or strong. And the richness of most arguments will allow for various choices. The argument is a fallacy only if for *each* (obvious) choice of premise, the premise is one of the generic kinds and is clearly false or dubious. *There is no reason to believe that a bad argument can be bad in only one way.*

Sometimes an argument can be one of the types we call a fallacy while there is still some more or less obvious premise that will save it. But that's so rare we feel confident that the types we've labeled here are arguments that are beyond repair.

The labels you've learned here are like names that go on pigeon holes: This bad argument can go in here. That argument there. This one fits into perhaps two or three of the pigeon holes. This argument, no, it doesn't fit into any, so we'll have to evaluate it from scratch.

> If you forget the labels, you can still remember the style of analysis, how to look for what's going wrong. That's what's important.
> *If you can describe what's going wrong, then you understand.*
> The labels are just shorthand for doing the hard work of explaining what's bad in an argument.

F. So It's Bad, So What?

You've learned a lot of labels and can manage to make yourself unbearable to your friends by pointing out the bad arguments they make. That's not the point.

We are seekers of wisdom—or at least we're heading in that direction. We want to learn, to exchange ideas, not to stifle disagreements. We want to convince and educate, and to that end we must learn to judge bad arguments.

Some arguments are so bad there's no point in trying to repair them. Start over.

Some arguments are bad because the other person intends to mislead you. In that case the Principle of Rational Discussion is violated. There's no point continuing the discussion. These labels and analyses are then prophylactics against being taken in.

But often enough the person making the bad argument isn't aware that he or she has changed the subject or brought in emotions where they don't belong. Be gentle. Point out the problem. Educate. Maturity isn't pointing a finger at someone and laughing—Ha. Ha. Ask the other person to fill in the argument, to add more claims. Then you can, perhaps, learn something, and the other person can, too.

Exercises for Chapter 11

The exercises here are a review of this chapter and some of the basic parts of earlier chapters. Your real practice in using this material will come in evaluating the Arguments for Analysis that follow.

1. What is a good argument?

2. What are the three tests an argument must pass for it to be classified as good?

3. State the Principle of Rational Discussion.

4. State the Guide to Repairing Arguments.

5. State the conditions under which an argument is unrepairable.

6. Is every valid or strong argument with true premises good?
   Explanation and/or counterexample.

7. If a very strong argument has twelve true premises and one dubious one, should we accept the conclusion?

8. What does a bad argument tell us about its conclusion?

9. What is our most reliable source of information about the world?

10. Why isn't a slippery slope argument classified as a structural fallacy?

11. Why isn't a false dilemma classified as a structural fallacy?

12. What is the generic premise for a common practice argument?

13. What is the generic premise for an appeal to common belief?

14. How can you distinguish between ridicule and an attempt to reduce to the absurd?

15. a. Give an example of affirming the consequent.
    b. What is the valid form of arguing that is similar?

16. a. Give an example of denying the antecedent.
    b. What is the valid form of arguing that is similar?

17. a. Give an example of arguing backwards with "all."
    b. What is the valid form of arguing that is similar?

18. a. Give an example of arguing backwards with "almost all."
    b. What is the strong form of arguing that is similar?

19. Give an example of reasoning in a chain with "some." Is it valid?

20. a. Give an example of arguing backwards with "no."
    b. What is the valid form of arguing that is similar?

21. Give an example of confusing objective and subjective. Is it a bad argument?

22. Give an example of drawing the line. Is it a bad argument?

23. Give an example of mistaking the person for the argument. Is it a bad argument?

24. Give an example of mistaking the person for the claim. Is it a bad argument?

25. Give an example of an appeal to authority that is not a bad argument.

26. Give an example of a phony refutation. Is it a bad argument?

27. Give an example of a false dilemma. Is it a bad argument?

28. Give an example of a slippery slope. Is it a bad argument?

29. Give an example of an appeal to pity. Is it a bad argument?

30. Give an example of an appeal to spite. Is it a bad argument?

31. Give an example of an appeal to fear. Is it a bad argument?

32. Give an example of a feel-good argument. Is it a bad argument?

33. Give an example of an argument that uses the generic premise of one of the types of content fallacies but which is not a bad argument.

34. Give an example of an argument that falls into more than one category of fallacy.

35. Give an example of begging the question. Is it a bad argument?

36. Give an example of an argument that someone might criticize as having an irrelevant premise or premises.

37. What's a strawman? Give an example.

38. Why are slanters included in the discussion of fallacies?

Key Words	fallacy	generic premise
	structural fallacy	violating the rules of
	content fallacy	rational discussion

Writing Lesson 12

Here is your chance to show that you have all the basic skills to write an argument. Compose an argument either for or against the following:

"Cats should be legally prohibited from roaming freely in cities."

Check whether your instructor has chosen a *DIFFERENT TOPIC* for this assignment.

This time, write only a (maximum) one-page argument. It should be clear and well structured, since you will have written out the premises and conclusion for yourself first. You can recognize slanters and fallacies, so don't use any in your argument. And you know to include possible objections to your argument.

By now you should have learned a lot about writing arguments. You don't need more examples, just practice using the new ideas presented in the chapters. You can use as a guide Composing Good Arguments (p. 339), which summarizes many of the lessons you've learned.

Arguments for Analysis

Here's your chance to put together all you've learned in analyzing arguments. But first let's see how Tom is doing.

I'm not going to vote, because no matter who is president I still won't get a job.

Argument? (yes or no) Yes.

Conclusion (if unstated, add it): I shouldn't vote.

Premises: No matter who is president I still won't get a job.

Additional premises needed (if none, say so): Either I get a job when a new president is elected, or I shouldn't vote.

Classify (with the additional premises): <u>valid</u>   very strong ————————— weak

Good argument? (yes or no, with an explanation—possibly just the name of a fallacy)
   No. It's kind of a false dilemma. I think there was an exercise where it was called a perfectionist fallacy.

   Excellent!

I hear that Brigitte Bardot is campaigning for animal rights. Isn't she the one who used to do advertisements for fur coats?

Argument? (yes or no) Yes—when rewritten.   *Good*

Conclusion (if unstated, add it): You shouldn't listen to Brigitte Bardot about animal rights.

Premises: Brigitte Bardot used to do advertisements for fur coats. (rewriting)

Additional premises needed (if none, say so): Don't listen to anything Brigitte Bardot says about fur coats.

Classify (with the additional premises): valid   very strong ————————X— weak

Good argument? (yes or no, with an explanation—possibly just the name of a fallacy)
   No. I think it's mistaking the person for the argument.

   At least you spotted that something was wrong. But you've forgotten that the only reason to add a premise is to make an argument valid or strong. The premise you added was just restating the conclusion. That would have made it valid, all right, but also would have been begging the question.

   This is an example of a phony refutation. The premises that are needed are: "Brigitte Bardot doesn't believe the conclusion of her own arguments about animal rights if she was in ads for fur coats" and "If Brigitte Bardot doesn't believe the conclusion of her own argument, her argument is bad." Those will make the argument valid, but are clearly false.

—**Kelly is a moron.**
—**Why do you say that?**
—**Because she's so stupid**

Argument? (yes or no) Yes.
Conclusion (if unstated, add it): *Kelly is a moron.*
Premises:
Additional premises needed (if none, say so):
Classify (with the additional premises): valid   very strong ———————X— weak
Good argument? (yes or no, with an explanation—possibly just the name of a fallacy)
This is just begging the question and a bad argument. Do I really need to fill in all the blanks in your form when it's this obvious?

> *No, you don't need to fill in all the steps. As long as you're sure you've got it right. And you do—except that this begging the question is* <u>valid</u>. *You've confused "bad argument" with "weak argument."*

Wash your car? Sure, and the next thing you know you'll want me to vacuum the upholstery, and fill up the gas tank, and maybe even make a car payment for you.

Argument? (yes or no) Yes.
Conclusion (if unstated, add it): I shouldn't wash your car for you.
Premises:
Additional premises needed (if none, say so):
Classify (with the additional premises): valid   very strong ———————X— weak
Good argument? (yes or no, with an explanation—possibly just the name of a fallacy)
> This is a bad argument. I could rewrite it as a slippery slope, but it's pretty clear that the premises aren't plausible. It really borders on ridicule.
> *Good.*

For Exercises 1–64, fill in the following:
Argument? (yes or no)
Conclusion (if unstated, add it):
Premises:
Additional premises needed (if none, say so):
Classify (with the additional premises): valid   very strong ——————— weak
Good argument? (yes or no, with an explanation—possibly just the name of a fallacy)

1. Smoking must be O.K. All my parents' friends do it, and the guys I hang out with all smoke.

2. Mom: Well, what do you think? Did man evolve from cells and apes, or did God create man?
   Dick: I don't know.
   Mom: C'mon. You've got to have thought about it.
   Dick: Oh, I guess I have, just never very hard. Beats me.
   Mom: You've got to believe one side or the other. Which is it?

3. How can you not believe in God? Could your parents, friends, your family all be wrong?

4. Zoe: The reason girls can't throw balls as well as boys is because their elbows are constructed slightly differently.

   Dick: Sure, that explains it. And the reason men can't wash dishes well is because their wrists are constructed differently.

5. My opponent says he is against tightening the immigration laws and posting more guards along the Mexican border. That's easy for him to say, living in an expensive home in San Francisco.

6. Dan was clever but he couldn't go to college. His father disappeared leaving a lot of debt, and his mother was terminally ill. So Dan had to take care of his mother and work full-time.

7. Fingerprinting may intimidate crooks, but businesses don't want to scare off law-abiding customers, too. So they're trying to put a positive spin on a procedure long used mainly on criminals.

   When customers at Food Lion supermarkets object to the "Authentiprint" program, cashiers are instructed to say, "It's for your own protection."

   Even the word "fingerprint" is taboo in some circles. The preferred terms are "finger image" or "finger minutiae."

   When MasterCard International Inc. announced last year it was considering the use of biometrics for identifying cardholders, it took pains to explain that when customers pressed their dye-coated fingertip against a card, they shouldn't consider that being fingerprinted.

   "One of the most important factors to be aware of with finger minutiae is that we are not talking about fingerprinting," a company news release quoted senior Vice President Joel S. Lisker as saying.   Associated Press, July 13, 1997

8. Stop mowing my lawn in the morning? Just because you want to sleep? Next thing you know you'll want me to stop playing my radio. And not leave my car running in the driveway.

9. —I know that there is ESP.
   —How?
   —If there weren't, there'd be too much left unexplained.

10. She looks asleep. But she's not been breathing for over an hour and her body is very cold. Even if I tickle her, she doesn't move. When a person is not breathing, the body is cold and doesn't move, the person is dead. So she is dead.

11. Parking is still difficult on campus. They said they'd build a parking garage, but that'll take ages. They should get rid of the fees they started charging us for parking on campus.

12. Unprotected sex is O.K. I know lots of people who do it, and what's the worst that can happen? You get pregnant.

13. Psychiatrist: You are suffering from delusions of grandeur.
    Dr. E: What? What? There's nothing wrong with me.
    Psychiatrist: It is not normal to think that you are the smartest man in the world.
    Dr. E: But I am.
    Psychiatrist: Certainly you think so.
    Dr. E: Look, if Arnold Schwarzenegger came in and said he was the strongest man in the world, would you think he's crazy?
    Psychiatrist: Crazy? I did not say you were crazy. You are suffering from delusions of grandeur.
    Dr. E: O.K. Would Arnold Schwarzenegger be suffering from delusions of grandeur?
    Psychiatrist: Possibly not.
    Dr. E: So someone has to be the smartest person in the world.
    Psychiatrist: That's true.
    Dr. E: Why not me?
    Psychiatrist: Because you are not.
    Dr. E: How do you know?
    Psychiatrist: Trust me.
    Dr. E: You can't even define "delusions of grandeur," can you?
    Psychiatrist: I am trained to spot it when it occurs.

14. Usually grocery stores have salt. I haven't been to Von's grocery, but they must have salt, too.

15. [After a chemical explosion at a plant, a man was interviewed who worked in the section where one man was killed by the explosion and four were injured. He had been on vacation at the time.]

    Powell said the idea of working every day in a plant filled with toxic chemicals hasn't worried him, and he plans to return when his vacation is over.

    "There are toxic chemicals in your house under your sink," he said. "There is constant training on how to handle them, and if you follow those guidelines, you're OK. Every job has a potential hazard."

    Tyson Hiatt, in *The Spectrum,* July 31, 1997

16. Tom: Everyone I know who's taken the critical thinking course has really enjoyed and profited from it.
    Harry: Suzy took that course, so she enjoyed it, too?

17. Tom: Everyone in the U.S. should have to speak English. Everyone's got to talk the same, so we can communicate, and it'll unify the country.
    Lee: Sure. But I have real trouble understanding people from New York. So why not make everyone speak just like you, with a midwestern accent?

18. Zoe: Here in the newspaper it says that some of those fraternity guys were crazy enough to swallow goldfish.
    Dick: Stands to reason. Lots of football players are in the fraternities, and they're wild.

19. (Summarizing a discussion heard on National Public Radio)

    An experiment is being conducted to study temperature changes in the ocean using very low frequency sound waves that will be generated in the South Pacific and picked up near the Arctic Circle. The sound waves will be generated two times per day for ten years.

    The interviewer, speaking to one of the people involved in the experiment, said that perhaps we shouldn't do this, since we don't know the effect of the sound on whales. The experimenter replied that the ocean is already so full of sound, if you count all the acousticians vs. all the supertankers, the supertankers would win hands down.

20. Reggie: Look, I deserve at least a C in this course. By your own standards I earned a C. Here, I did all my homework and contributed in class, just like you said. I know I only got a D+ on the final, but our other work was supposed to be able to outweigh that.

    Dr. E: Perhaps I did say that, but I can't go back and change your grade. I'd have to change a lot of grades.

    Reggie: That's unfair and unethical. I'll take it to the chairman.

    Later in the chairman's office

    Dr. E: So this student is going to come in and see you to complain about his grade. He thinks that just because he showed up regularly and handed in some homework he should pass the course.

21. Tom: Suzy said that Chapter 6 won't be on the final.

    Harry: You'd believe that ditsy cheerleader?

22. Fred is a doctor who has been working in this hospital as a chief of surgery for 10 years. So he graduated from medical school.

23. Chris finds most women with dark hair more attractive than women with light hair. Marissa has dark hair and Erika has light hair. Therefore, Chris finds Marissa more attractive.

24. There's only one way to stop Las Vegas from being choked on smog and traffic, and that's to stop migration to the city by limiting the number of building permits.

25. I read that the county wants to start registering dogs. We've got to resist it. The next thing you know they'll make owning a dog illegal.

26. Ms. Fletcher is a good teacher. She gives great parties.

27. The incumbent is going to win the election. She's way ahead in the opinion polls, and the opinion polls are seldom wrong.

28. Tom: Everyone I know who's passed the critical thinking course has really enjoyed and profited from it.

    Harry: Suzy enjoyed that course.

    Dick: So she must have passed it. Amazing.

29. Raise tuition? That's wrong. It's already so expensive to go to school, what with the cost of books, and food, and rent. It's really wrong to raise tuition.

30. You say you want to raise tuition again? Why not raise the parking fees, too? And the dorm contracts. And raise prices at the cafeteria, while you're at it. Or maybe even charge students for using the library. You could balance the university's budget for sure that way.

31. You shouldn't keep a gun in the house. If an intruder breaks in, it could be used against you.

32. You should take your cousin to the dance because she's shy, and doesn't go out much, and is really sad since her cat died. It would make her feel good.

33. The U. S. Attorney General said that there was no need to investigate the president's campaign financing. So the president didn't do anything wrong.

34. I've got to get new clothes, Mom. You don't want me to look like a slob, do you?

35. Rice is good for you. A billion Chinese can't be wrong.

36. Dick: If Suzy doesn't pass her critical thinking class, she can't be a cheerleader unless she goes to summer school.
    Zoe: She's going to fail that course for sure.
    Dick: Looks like she'll be going to summer school.

37. Of course the Mayor is arguing against limiting the number of building permits. He's got his own real estate office.

38. Dick: Very few of the cheerleaders fail courses. They're too motivated.
    Lee: Suzy's a cheerleader. So she passes all her courses. Hmmm.

39. Letter to the editor:
    Governor Pete Wilson signed a law making California the first state to require chemical castration of repeat child molesters. . . . This is one law that should be enacted in every state in the United States. I see the American Civil Liberties Union has called this procedure barbaric. However, the ACLU doesn't consider how barbaric it is when an adult molests a child.
    Roger E. Nielsen, *The Salt Lake Tribune,* October 6, 1996

40. I'm going to give up smoking because I read that the Surgeon General says it's bad for your health.

41. I'm now in favor of allowing abortions, since the Surgeon General said that it should be legal.

42. —Our kids should be allowed to pray in schools.
    —What? If they're not allowed to pray, maybe God won't exist?

43. Maria: Dr. E's course is just great.
    Suzy: It's easy for you to say—you just got an A on the midterm.

44. Suzy: Either Dr. E doesn't like me or he misgraded my test, because I got a D.

45. Zoe: If you don't stop sleeping around you're going to catch a venereal disease.
    Suzy: That's just your opinion.

46. Dick: I can't believe that *Failing in Atlanta* didn't win an Oscar.

    Zoe: Nobody understands what art is.

47. Zoe: It's not healthy to eat a lot of cholesterol.

    Dick: Why?

    Zoe: Because it's not good for your body.

48. You say we should legalize drugs. So you want everyone running around doped up, kids whacked out, and everybody being unproductive members of society.

49. Dick: If Freud was right, then the only things that matter to a man are fame, riches, and the love of beautiful women.

    Zoe: But Ralph is poor, single, never married and uninterested in women (or men), and certainly not famous. Yet he's happy. So Freud was wrong.

    Dick: Freud wasn't wrong. If we take into account the possibility of sublimation, we can see that Ralph is only happy because he has sublimated his desire for beautiful women into caring for his dogs. And he puts so much time into caring for his dogs because he hopes, unconsciously perhaps, to become famous as a great dog lover. And maybe rich, too. Though if you ask him, he'll say he's content.

50. Zoe: Dr. E, you have to pass Suzy.

    Dr. E: Why?

    Zoe: She said if you don't she's going to light herself on fire in the student union.

51. (Contributed by a student)

    Student athletes should not be given special leniency in assigning course marks. Student athletes who do receive special leniency turn out to be failures. They are not given the mental challenge that regular students are given. All student athletes that I have ever met or seen that have received special leniency have not graduated from college. In order to make something of yourself, you must first graduate from college. Everyone that I have ever met or seen wants to make a good living and make something of themselves. On the other hand, all of the student athletes I know that do not receive special leniency have graduated and have been successful in life. Therefore, student athletes that want to be successful in life must not receive special leniency.

52. I resent that. Our company is not racist. We give a donation to the NAACP every year.

53. Professor Zzzyzzx: I am surprised you vas failing dat Suzy kid. She doesn't vork too hard, but I vasn't thinking she vas *so* bad.

    Dr. E: Maybe not. But she deserved to fail. When I joked that the first thing that goes when you get older is your memory . . . You know the one?

    Professor Zzzyzzx: Maybe, but, alas, mine memory is not so goot, now.

    Dr. E: So I say, "And the second thing, the second thing is . . ." Then I pause and usually everyone laughs.

    Professor Zzzyzzx: Jah, so? Is dat a goot joke?

    Dr. E: But Suzy said, "Your looks." No way she deserved to pass.

54. Lee: Every computer science major is a nerd.
    Maria: None of the cheerleaders are majoring in computer science.
    Lee: Right. So none of them are nerds.

55. We should not support Jerry's Kids. After all, many gay organizations try to get us to support that charity.

56. Suppose this patient really does have hepatitis. Well, anyone who has hepatitis will, after a week, begin to appear jaundiced. Yellowing of the eyeballs and skin will proceed dramatically after two weeks. So if he has hepatitis now, since he's been feeling sick for two weeks, he should be jaundiced. But he isn't. So he doesn't have hepatitis.

57. I've got three choices: I can major in accounting and spend my life behind dusty account ledgers and computers, or I can major in finance and spend all my time talking to stuffy bankers and hot-shot brokers, or I can drop out of school and become a waiter and earn $30,000 a year in Las Vegas. Those are the choices, since I'm too far along on a business major to change to another. I'd really prefer to be a nurse. But it's best to settle on being a waiter.

58. (Monday) Zoe: If you eat that candy bar, then you'll gain weight.
    (Friday) Dick: I gained weight this week.
              Zoe: So you ate that candy bar.

59. Dick: I can't stand Siamese cats. Ugh. They all have those strange blue eyes.
    Suzy: Mary Ellen's got a kitten with blue eyes. I didn't know it was Siamese.

60. Zoe: If you don't start helping around the house, doing the dishes and cleaning up, then you don't really understand what it means to be a part of a couple.
    Dick: O.K., O.K., look, I'm vacuuming. I'll do the dishes tonight.
    Zoe: So you do understand what it means to be part of a couple.

61. Zoe: I wear a size 7 blue jeans.
    Dick: J.C. Penney's carries Levi's in all sizes.
    Zoe: So I don't need to worry about finding my size when I go shopping at Penney's.

62. How can sunbathing be bad for you? Lying out in the sun is very relaxing. How can that be bad?

63. Suzy (to Tom): Will you work on an extra credit assignment with me? You're very articulate and have a wonderful grasp of the English language. I know we would get the assignment right if we worked on it together.

64. Tom: I can't believe you're an hour late!
    Suzy: What are you talking about?
    Tom: You said you'd meet me here at 7 to work on the English assignment.
    Suzy: I am not late.
    Tom: It's almost 8.
    Suzy: I said I'd be here a little after 7.

Here are some longer arguments. You'll need to use everything you know to analyze these. Eliminate the slanters and pay attention to unstated premises. To give you an idea of what's involved, I've included a long exercise that Tom did.

Morass of value judgments

Well-intentioned DUI law chips away at individual rights.

When a new state law goes into effect today, police will be allowed to use "reasonable force" to obtain blood samples from first-time drunken driving suspects who refuse to take a breath test. *1*

Defense attorneys plan to challenge this law, citing the potential for unnecessary violence resulting from attempts to enforce it. *2* The law's proponents say it is necessary to obtain adequate evidence to lock up violators of drunken driving laws and force is already allowed against repeat offenders. *3* One supporter of the law was quoted on television recently saying that people who are suspected of driving drunk give up their rights. *4*

There is a hidden danger with laws that chip away at the Fourth Amendment prohibition against unreasonable searches and seizures. *5*

Yes, we need to vigorously fight drunken driving, take away driver's licenses of those who refuse breath tests, and lock up repeat offenders who are obviously impaired according to eyewitness testimony. *6* But our hard-won individual rights, freedoms and protections should not be flippantly squandered, even in the name of public safety. *7*

The danger is that once we begin to buy into the concept that the rights of society as a whole are superior to the rights of the individual, then we begin to slide into a morass of value judgments. *8* If it is more important for society to stop drunken driving than for the suspected driver to be free from unreasonable search of his blood veins and seizure of his blood, then might it not be argued that it is more important for elected officials and sports heroes to get organ transplants than mere working stiffs? *9*

If rights can be weighed against societal imperatives, what next? *10* Our rights against self incrimination? *11* Freedom of religion? *12* Speech? *13* Fair trial? *14* The vote? *15*

Having personally experienced the heavy hand of tyranny, the Founding Fathers wrote: "The right of the people to be secure in their persons, houses, papers, and effects, against unreasonable searches and seizures, shall not be violated, and no Warrants shall issue, but upon probable cause, supported by Oath or affirmation, and particularly describing the place to be searched, and the person or things to be seized." *16*

Rather than slug it out in the courts, we would hope that our various police forces would give a second thought or more before resorting to constitutionally questionable exercises. *17* What difference is there between a hypodermic needle and a battering ram? *18*

If we vigilantly guard and revere the rights of individuals, society in general will be better off. *19*

Editorial, *Las Vegas Review-Journal,* October 1, 1995

Conclusion: Police should not be allowed to use reasonable force to obtain blood samples from first-time drunken driving suspects who refuse to take a breath test.

Premises: 1. This is just stating the background. The editor uses a downplayer in putting quotes around "reasonable force." *It's not a downplayer. It's a quote. It might also show that he doesn't believe the words have a clear meaning.*

2. I suppose this is true. It shows that someone other than the editors think there's a problem. But so what?

3. Gives the other side. Counterargument.

4. Big deal. So one nut said that. Doesn't really contribute to the argument. He'd have to show that a lot of people thought that. Otherwise it's probably a strawman.

5. "Chip away" is a slanter. Dysphemism. Anyway, he hasn't shown that this law goes against the Fourth Amendment. Apparently the lawmakers didn't think so. If it does, it'll be declared unconstitutional, and that's that. Doesn't really help his conclusion. Waving the flag, sort of.

6. Sets out his position. Sort of a counterargument to the supporters of the bill. Shows he's not unreasonable. Giving a bit to the other side, I guess. Doesn't seem to help get to his conclusion.

7. "Hard-won" is there without proof. Perhaps it was hard-won. Possibly adds to the argument by adding a premise: "Whatever is hard-won should not be given up." But that's false. There'd never be peace treaties then without unconditional surrender. "Flippantly squandered" is a dysphemism, and he hasn't shown that they are flippantly squandered. But worst is that when he talks about rights, protections, etc. It's not clear what "right" he is talking about. If it's the one in the Fourth Amendment, he's got to prove that this law is giving that up, which he hasn't. Otherwise he's just waving the flag.

8. He's got to prove this. It's crucial to his argument.

9. This is supposedly support for 8, but it doesn't work. I think the answer is "No." He's got to show it's "Yes."

11.–15. These are rhetorical questions, too. As premises they seem very dubious. Altogether they're a slippery slope.

16. The first part is just there like "hard-won" was before. Quoting the Fourth Amendment doesn't make it clear to me that this law violates it.

17. "Slug it out in the courts" is a dysphemism. He hasn't shown that the law is constitutionally questionable.

18. Another rhetorical question with a stupid comparison. My answer is "Plenty." He's got to convince me that there's no difference. The old slippery slope again.

19. Vague and unproved. Can't be support for the conclusion, and it's not the conclusion, either. Does nothing.

It's a bad argument. Too many slanters, and there's really no support for the conclusion.

Very, very good. Only you need to expand on why it's a bad argument. What exactly are the claims that have any value in getting the conclusion?

All that 2 elicits is, "So?" We can't guess what's the missing premise that could save this support. He doesn't knock off 3 (perhaps 4 is intended to do that, sort of reducing to the absurd?). The support for 8 is a worthless slippery slope (9–15), plus some one person's comments that we'd have to take to be exemplary of lots of peoples (there's a missing premise: "If one person said this on television, then lots of people believe it," which is very dubious). Number 16 is crucial, but he hasn't shown that 7 follows from it. That's the heart of the argument that he's left out (as you noted): He's got to show that this law really violates the Fourth Amendment and, for 19, that it isn't a good trade-off of personal rights vs. society's rights. So there's really no support for his conclusion. That's why it's bad. The use of slanters is bad, but it doesn't make the argument bad. We can eliminate them and then see what's wrong. I'd give B+/A– for this. Incorporate this discussion in your presentation to the class and you'll get an A.

65. (Reputed to come from a Howard Stern show in April, 1996. They're discussing Howard Stern's investment in tobacco/cigarette industry stocks.)

Caller: Howard, how can you invest in killing people?

Stern: What do you mean? I made a good business investment.

Caller: You invested in killing kids.

Stern: Listen buddy, there are laws that say you have to be eighteen to buy cigarettes. If store owners sell to underage kids, that's their own greedy fault; that's not my fault or the fault of the tobacco company.

Caller: But you invested in the tobacco company that lies to the government, and cigarettes kill.

Stern: What's this lie to the government? . . . I don't care–everybody lies–you lie. If someone is so stupid they want to smoke, that's their problem, we all know it's bad to smoke. That's why I don't smoke, I'm not stupid. But if someone else wants to smoke, that's his right, he has the right to be stupid, and I have the right to invest my money in a company that will make me money.

Caller: Howard, it's not right, next thing you know you'll be investing in AIDS.

Stern: You idiot, you can't invest in disease. I invested in a company. You don't know what you're talking about, get off my phone line you jerk. (Hangs up)

66. **St. George doesn't need a $30,000 a year mayor**

Letter to the editor:

The proposal by city officials to give themselves a generous raise has caused much concern among St. George residents, especially the ones who are barely getting by on the notoriously low salaries paid in Dixie [the southwest corner of Utah].

Even if Dan McArthur were to become a full-time mayor, how could he justify $30,000 a year? Since City Manager Gary Esplin is "handling everything from budgets and water treatment to planning and zoning disputes," why do we even need a mayor? And where would St. George find the money to give the proposed salary increases precedence over more critical municipal needs?

The people of St. George have approved bond issues for new schools because we've been convinced of the need for them. However, we see no reason to spend more money on a mayor and councilmen who are living comfortably on incomes from other sources. When they campaigned for their city positions, they were promised no increases in salary. If they really believe they're worth more than they're getting, they could at least lower their sights to a more realistic level!   Sally Jacobsen, *The Spectrum*, July 14, 1996

67. **Proof That God Does Not Exist**

(Several philosophers have become famous for their proofs that God exists. All those proofs have been theoretical. Here is a practical proof supplied by Dr. E that God does not exist. It can be repeated—try it yourself!)

I go into the Sahara Hotel and Casino in Las Vegas. I go up to the Megabucks slot machine at which you can win at least five million dollars on a $3 bet if you hit the jackpot. I put in three one-dollar coins. I pull the handle. I win nothing, or just a little, and when I continue I lose that, too. Therefore, God does not exist.

68. **Pascal's Wager**

(Pascal was a 17th Century mathematician and philosopher who had a religious conversion late in his life. His argument was roughly as follows.)

We have the choice to believe in God or not to believe in God. If God does not exist, you lose nothing by believing in him. But if He exists, and you believe in him, you have the possibility of eternal life, joyous in the presence of God. If you don't believe in him, you are definitely precluded from having everlasting life. Therefore, a prudent gambler will bet on God existing. That is, it is better to believe that God exists, since you lose nothing by doing so, but could gain everlasting life.

69. **Betting on the Lottery**

The lottery pays millions of dollars. This is more than you can earn with a college degree. The money you spend on tuition could buy lots of tickets. The more tickets you buy, the better your odds of winning. So, invest in lottery tickets, not in a dead-end diploma.

70. **On the plans being made to move some of the nearly extinct condors that have been bred in captivity to a wild area in the south of Utah**.

Letter to the editor:

I do not know why we do not leave things alone. Probably environmentalists must have something to show for their reason to exist; often as stupid as wilderness laws by government to make us think they care, for what? Easy money? Now they intend to move condors to Utah. Our over-taxed taxpayers should be getting weary of financing so much for the amusement of idiots.

As long as I can remember, the wolves, elk and now the condor and other nonhuman species have been pawns on the environmental checkerboard for no reason except the whim of a loon to change the order of the universe. I would think all creatures have the instinct to move if they so desired without any help. I am sure the place of their choice would be better for them if not made by us. Let us grow up and leave the elk, wolves and condors alone and mind our own business.

Kenneth S. Frandsen, *The Spectrum,* March, 1996

71. **America's Next Hostage Crisis?**

According to the latest figures, America is now importing almost 50 percent of all the oil we use. If our oil imports continue to rise, another energy crisis could be triggered, one that could hold America's economy hostage again.

But the more we use nuclear energy, instead of imported oil, to generate electricity, the less we have to depend on foreign nations.

Our 112 nuclear electric plants already have cut foreign oil dependence by 4 billion barrels since the oil embargo of 1973, saving us more than $115 billion in foreign oil payments. But 112 nuclear plants will not be enough to meet our growing electricity demand. More plants are needed.

We can help keep America from being held hostage and maintain our energy independence by relying more on our own resources, like nuclear energy.

For a free booklet on nuclear energy, write to the U.S. Council for Energy Awareness, P.O. Box 66103, Dept. RF07, Washington, D.C. 20035.

Nuclear energy means more energy independence.
©1989 USCEA

A Basketball Star . . . (Exercises 72–75)
(During the 1995-1996 professional basketball season, a player for the Denver Nuggets, Mahmoud Abdul-Rauf, chose not to stand during the playing of the national anthem. No one noticed for a long time during the season, but when it was brought to the attention of the management, Abdul-Rauf was given the choice of standing for the anthem or being suspended. He chose to be suspended from playing. He explained that he would not stand for religious reasons. Later in the season he was convinced by Muslim religious authorities that it would not contravene his religious principles to stand during the anthem, and he chose to do that while silently praying. His suspension was lifted.)

72. To the editor:
The former Chris Jackson, now known as Mahmoud Abdul-Rauf, refuses to stand for the national anthem. He claims "The Star-Spangled Banner" is a symbol of oppression and tyranny. He insists on discrediting our country even though he is being paid more than $2.5 million a year ($31,707 per game) to play professional basketball.

This young man should really show his disdain for our tyrannical country by giving up his millionaire status and moving to the Middle East where he can seek empathy for his beliefs and he won't have to worry about hearing our beloved national anthem!

Robert E. Haynes, *Las Vegas Review-Journal,* March 24, 1996

73. To the editor:
If Denver Nuggets player Mahmoud Abdul-Rauf feels he is oppressed in the United States he should go play for one of the famous Muslim basketball teams such as the Iranian Jackals, the Bangladesh Bengals or the Bosnian Rockets, etc.

Maybe we should do what they would do if he made comments there, such as he is allowed to do in our "oppressed" country–cut his tongue out.

William J. Musso, *Las Vegas Review-Journal,* March 24, 1996

74. To the editor:
Mahmoud Abdul-Rauf will now stand for the national anthem. Can anyone out there tell me they believe something has happened in this country that has caused a change of heart in this young man where he now wishes to show respect for the flag and national

anthem? It is my belief that Mr. Abdul-Rauf has no more respect today than the day he decided to take his stance.

While Mr. Abdul-Rauf has become the focus of this issue, I believe the NBA and its rule should be. Flag-burners show no less respect for the flag than the NBA rules. While a flag-burner expresses contempt for the freedom that allows his expression, the NBA rule shows the same contempt for freedom by forcing an expression of respect.

This conjures up images of the dark side of nationalism–the dark side being forced nationalism. In the 20th century this country has fought two world wars against a form of forced nationalism.

While the government cannot and should not interfere here in any way with the NBA and its rules, we as private citizens should make our voices heard. The next time I see players and coaches standing for the national anthem, the image of the NBA will be more of a Nazi Germany than of a free society.

Terry E. Peele, *Las Vegas Review-Journal,* March 24, 1996

75. **Local radio plays national anthem at mosque**

Islamic leaders were angered Wednesday after a local radio personality played the national anthem on a trumpet at a mosque during a live broadcast to mock a Denver Nuggets basketball player who is a convert to Islam.

Islamic worshippers were praying at the mosque when the radio personality, who donned a turban, wore an Abdul-Rauf T-shirt and carried a trumpet, entered the Colorado Muslim Society Islamic Center on Tuesday with two other employees.

"One of the intruders held a microphone as they were broadcasting live on a local radio station," the report from the sheriff's office said.

The intruders tried to place earphones on two worshippers at the mosque and force them to be part of a live interview.

Reuters Ltd., March, 1996

(What implicit argument were the DJs making?)

76. **Sailors imprisoned for rape**

(Concerning the rape of a school girl by three U.S. sailors in Okinawa)

Letter to the editor:

Judging by your opinionated editorial about the Navy, it appears your paper is entirely governed by women for you do not have the slightest conception of what men are all about. But several points need emphasizing:

1. All human beings are animals, and sex is an integral part of their well-being.

2. When a man meets a woman, his thoughts go quickly past the beauty of her eyes and the color of her hair, certainly the capabilities of her brain. That comes later! In 1995, many women have the same thoughts about men.

3. Soldiers, especially sailors who have been at sea for a long time, have a libido that's healthy and must be sustained in order to function normally. Ask any veteran to confirm what precedes.

4. A prostitute has never been called a decent woman in any language. She is still a whore who gets paid for a job well-done. Thank you! It's her choosing, not that of the men at large.

Now, rape is another thing. It is strictly about sex but it is perpetrated by devious minds who could not care about whom they violate, man or woman. Subjugation of the female . . . my foot! What counts is sexual satisfaction, nothing else.

Admiral Macke was honest when he declared it was stupid of his sailors to have raped the Japanese girl when they could have afforded a girl for the price of the rented car. His remark was not unbelievable; it was just. It had nothing to do with the act itself. It was a statement of fact.

This society encourages hypocrisy. The admiral was right and brave enough to declare his assumption in public. He should have been commended for his fortitude in viewing the world the way it really is, not what it portrays.

Rene Vergught, The Spectrum, December 21, 1995

77. Timber wars: Even rotting logs have rights, don't they?

The stars came out in Carlotta, Calif., as protesters yipped and screamed about plans to salvage rotting timber from beneath a privately owned grove of ancient redwood trees.

Millionaire celebrities, including singers Bonnie Raitt and Don Henley, joined perhaps 1,000 others to raise a major ruckus outside the gates of Pacific Lumber Co.'s Carlotta mill, north of San Francisco. A bunch of them got arrested, some chained themselves to gates, one guy stuck his hand in a bucket of cement, and many engaged in a species of ululating they call "wailing women."

At issue is Pacific Lumber's plan to remove dead logs and diseased trees from the 3,000 acres that it owns in the Headwaters Forest. The company has no designs on the old-growth redwoods on its property. It wants only to clean out the dead and dying stuff and mill the lumber. All the relevant authorities have approved the salvage operation.

But the greens are having none of it. Dragging out the dead stuff might endanger living trees, they claim, and it might disrupt the lifestyles of some woodland creatures.

The protesters have managed to delay Pacific's salvage operation.

Question: If dead wood cannot be harvested on private land because doing so would disrupt the habitat of animals that are not even endangered—can dead trees be salvaged anywhere? Can live trees on private land be cut anywhere? Every tree is a habitat for some critter or other.

It should be obvious by now that hard-core environmentalists want no forests anywhere touched for any commercial reason—ever. If, as a consequence, the timber industry dies completely, lumber becomes rare and you end up paying $3 million for a $100,000 house, $40 a copy for a newspaper or $25,000 for a kitchen cabinet—tough.

If these millionaire celebrities care so deeply about rotting logs on Pacific Lumber's land, why don't they buy it?

Editorial, Las Vegas Review-Journal, September, 1996

78. High School Wrestling

Pine View High School officials chose the only reasonable position when they decided to deny a 17-year-old girl's petition to join the school's all-male wrestling team. Technically, the school was within its legal rights to deny the request, according to the U. S. Office of Civil Rights. While the federal law involved, known as Title IX, requires equality in a school's overall athletic program, it also permits schools to keep girls out of "contact" sports such as football and wrestling.

Wrestling is, without question, a contact sport. Lots and lots of body contact. That's kind of the point of the sport—to wrestle and pin your opponent to the mat. You can't do that unless you do a lot of grabbing, clutching, poking, holding, groping, flipping, and generally, having some really solid, personal, one-on-one contact with someone else's body.

Common sense tells us this is one sport where girls and boys should compete separately.

Pine View High School Principal David Broadhead said the school has a strong girl's athletics program, giving girls the chance to earn a letter in various sports. One sport denied to girls, however, is wrestling.

And with good reason. Until there are enough girls who indicate they want to participate in such a sport—and enough to set up girls-only teams to compete against each other—it only makes sense to keep girls out of this male-dominated field.

It's a shame that this particular student won't have the chance to pursue her dream of lettering in wrestling at Pine View High School.

We sympathize and certainly understand the desire to follow a dream. It's an admirable quality and shouldn't be lightly dismissed.

But, the greater question in this debate isn't whether a girl should be allowed on a boy's wrestling team, but whether the girl's athletic programs here are treated equally and given the same kind of support within the school system.

Editorial, *The Spectrum,* July 13, 1997

79. **Prairie Dogs**

Just about every time the word "prairie dog" is mentioned anymore in Iron County, there is heated debate.

Biology professor Jim Bowns discussed prairie dogs during a meeting sponsored by the Color Country Chapter of People for the West in Cedar City Thursday night. Bowns is a professor for both Southern Utah University and Utah State University.

Prairie dogs are a threatened species in Southern Utah. There has been quite a bit of argument in Iron County over how to preserve the little critters without creating chaos.

Iron County is working on a Habitat Conservation Plan (HCP) otherwise known as the Prairie Dog Plan. The HCP will serve as a blanket application for people to safely remove prairie dogs from their land without all the red tape.

Bowns dissected the HCP page by page, voicing his concerns and explaining jargon to the audience. Several discussions ensued during the process.

Bowns said he is especially concerned with prairie dog habitat.

"Finding ideal habitat for prairie dogs is not simple," he said.

The prairie dogs usually have about a 6 percent survival rate, a 94 percent loss, he continued, reading from the HCP.

Lin Drake appeared unhappy at this statement. He is a developer and an officer for the Color Country Chapter of People for the West.

If he lost 94 percent of his business, Drake explained that the bank sure wouldn't be accommodating.

"Yet they're expecting Iron County to put millions of dollars into a project that is a losing cause," he said. . . .

Throughout the discussion, the topic of government distrust surfaced and resurfaced.

"Eighteen people came to me this week to talk about the plan," Jack Hill said. Hill is president of the Color Country Chapter of People for the West.

"They have a lack of faith in the federal government and they don't have any trust," Hill said. "The whole issue is with the government."

Drake agreed, saying the HCP appears to weaken his rights to his land. He would prefer the government back off and worry about more important things, he said.

"We've got fathers beating babies and drugs on the streets and we're spending money on this," Drake said. "Tell them to get the hell out of Iron County." . . .

Drake was disappointed at the turnout of the meeting. Only a dozen people attended, though the meeting was advertised adequately.

"They'll wake up when we don't have a community left," he said.

(Note: June 26, 1997 Lin Drake was fined $15,000 by the U.S. Fish and Wildlife Service for putting a subdivision on a prairie dog habitat.)

The Spectrum, April 18, 1997

80. **Inmate Phone Center**

The Utah Travel Council's recent announcement that it plans to hire inmates housed at the Utah State Prison to field travel questions and take orders for brochures sounds like an idea destined to fail.

Spencer Kinard, assistant director for the travel council, had the audacity to make a tasteless joke about the proposal, saying, "You're going to have your favorite serial killer giving you information about where to go."

If that comment isn't enough to put a bad taste in your mouth, consider the fact that since the first of the year, inmates have been typing into computers the names and addresses of recorded requests for brochures and travel guides.

Raise your hand if you want your name and address given to a convict. It's unanimous. There are no takers.

Another poorly thought-out comment came from the travel center director, Dean Reeder, who said using inmates for a labor pool was a good idea because of their low turnover and their untapped work skill.

That's not a good enough reason to let inmates have access to personal information. It's hard to imagine a dumber idea.

Both Kinard and Reeder are employees of the State Department of Community and Economic Development. That means their salaries are paid with public money and that they are using public funds to conduct this mindless experiment.

Taxpayers should revolt over this one.

Five states have apparently experimented with such an idea and have reported mixed results. Oklahoma ended a similar program when prisoners became adept at giving out the 1-800 information lines to family and friends.

Kinard, on the other hand, thinks the idea constitutes a grand experiment and should ferret out some smart criminals who are fairly bright and who were involved in white collar crime. As if those types of crimes don't involve victims, too.

So far, the Travel Council has kept a tight lid on its plans and has not sought the feedback of regional partners whose attractions would be touted by the inmate phone centers.

Big mistake.

The plans call for a slow start and possible expansion. All inmates who are not in lock down status or considered security risks would be eligible to apply for the job. The Travel Council says the idea is a creative solution to a simple problem of not enough money and too much work. It handles nearly 100,000 information requests a year.

It's doubtful those callers will approve of the Travel Council's grand experiment to solve its money woes. Reed and Kinard say they're bracing themselves for raised eyebrows as details of the plan take shape next month.

Anyone with a brain the size of an ant should do more than raise an eyebrow at this half-baked idea. The Utah Travel Council should confine this idea to solitary and leave it locked up there . . . forever.

Editorial, *The Spectrum,* June 3, 1997

81. **Police chief's dumping a dumb deed by North Las Vegas**

North Las Vegas cannot afford to lose any IQ points—especially in the area of law enforcement—and that's exactly what happened with the forced retirement of city Police Chief Alan Nelson. A 25-year veteran, Nelson was arrested Friday on a drunken driving charge. Rather than battle it out in the courts and attempt to play politics with the North Las Vegas City Council, Mayor James Seastrand and City Manager Linda Hinson, Nelson cleared off his desk and turned in his badge.

That's a shame.

If I may be so presumptuous, the people of North Las Vegas—hard-working people who live in one of the nation's high-crime areas—need police officers of Nelson's experience and level. I'm not condoning driving while legally impaired—although it would be refreshing to read the department's official lab findings before seeing the Northtown political machine bury the chief's career without even playing "Taps."

It makes painfully little sense to force him out of office in the name of political correctness and image enhancement. Holding a top police officer to a higher standard is fine, but this presses the point to the extreme.

If the man has a drinking problem, he should be treated with compassion—not a pink slip. After all, it's not as if he is the first cop to drive drunk, if he did.

Fact is, if he were anyone but the chief and were arrested and later convicted, of driving while intoxicated, Nelson probably would have received a 40-hour suspension and, like almost everyone else similarly situated, would have been ordered by the court to attend alcohol-awareness classes and seek rehabilitation.

Imagine the image Nelson might have enhanced had he been asked to cut a few public-service announcements for anti-DUI groups?

That's not possible now.

Nelson has plenty of critics these days, but he also has his share of friends. North Las Vegas Police Lt. Bob King is one of them. With nearly 26 years on the department, King is the Narcotics Division commander. He knows sticking up for his ousted comrade is unlikely to win him any points with the city's political hierarchy.

"He's not a high-profiler. He's one of those guys who has been in the trenches, kind of a worker bee," King says. "It just breaks my heart, the whole thing. He was really beginning to move the department forward. He was doing all these good things. And he has one transgression, if you will, four blocks from his house."

Be honest. If you were the top cop in one of the nation's roughest communities, wouldn't you be tempted to drink?

Arsenic.

That doesn't mitigate the seriousness of the offense, but neither should the offense wipe out a quarter century of hard work.

As chief, Nelson was implementing the progressive Safe Streets 2000 community policing program and, King says, was a fair-minded administrator who had a mature grasp of the budget realities the small department faced. He also understood the convoluted federal government grant-writing process, an essential component in the budget mechanism in many departments. North Las Vegas has fewer than 200 cops on the street.

"Those talents are gone," King says. "When he gave his word, you knew he was there for you. You knew exactly where he stood day to day. He has my respect, appreciation and admiration."

In an open letter, King adds, "I see a man whose entire 25-year professional career of personal contributions and accomplishments as both an outstanding policeman and administrator are totally overshadowed and will be measured by a single regrettable incident. . . . He neither asked for nor received any preferential treatment. He practiced and demonstrated this ethic his entire career. With eloquence and dignity he has left the job he dearly loves."

For all his human frailties, Chief Nelson was a hard-working cop who was dumped in the name of political correctness. In North Las Vegas, yet.

And that's just plain dumb.

John L. Smith, March 20, 1997, *Las Vegas Review-Journal*

82. **Dumb deed**

In his March 20 column ("Police chief dumping a dumb deed by North Las Vegas"), John L. Smith used sarcastic remarks to assess the situation pertaining to North Las Vegas and its former chief of police, Alan Nelson.

But the only "dumb deed" in North Las Vegas was created by its former police chief when he chose to drink and drive. And let's not forget the "dumb deed" was further enhanced by the fact he was driving a city vehicle. It is also dumb for people to mini-mize the seriousness of drinking and driving by singing the praises of a potential killer. How potential? If a driver's blood-alcohol level is .10 the risk of a fatal crash is increas-ed by 300 percent. Mr. Nelson's chemical test revealed his BAC level to be at .12.

And consider this: The profile of a drunken driver includes the fact that DUI offen-ders drive drunk an average of 80 times per year.

The "dumb" continues—"He wasn't drunk," "It's only a misdemeanor," "A single regrettable incident," "He has one transgression" . . . these are the reasons I have heard and read in defense of Mr. Nelson. This mentality is nearly as frightening as the crime of DUI. "A single regrettable incident" and "one transgression" on the part of drinking drivers was all it took in 1996 to cause the death and injury of more than 1,600 people in Clark County.

Mr. Smith suggested certain IQ points were lost by North Las Vegas and he also alluded to that city's need for police officers of Mr. Nelson's experience. Based on the numerous calls I received from the citizens of North Las Vegas, I believe they want officers at that experience level to also possess an IQ that would not allow jeopardizing a 25-year career nor permit conduct that would endanger the citizens.

Mr. Smith agreed that holding "top police officers" to a higher standard is fine—but he said "political correctness" has gone too far in this instance. Political correctness? Has our society strayed so far from the realm of social, moral and ethical responsibilities that when these standards are utilized, they are scoffed at as "political correctness"?

As far as Mr. Nelson's "forced retirement" is concerned, I can only say that if I had dedicated a quarter of a century of my life to a career and was wrongly accused of a crime that would have a negative effect on that career, I would fight like hell to vindicate myself. Again, that is only if I were wrongly accused.

I question whether Mr. Smith's commentary would have been as generous and compassionate if he and his beautiful child whom he wrote so eloquently about not so long ago had been in the path of Mr. Nelson the night he was arrested (assuming they lived to write about it). Never forget there is only one thing that separates a felony from a misdemeanor—it's called luck.

Mr. Smith stated that if Mr. Nelson has a drinking problem he should be treated with compassion. If he has a "drinking problem," why wasn't it recognized by his friends and co-workers? How could he be treated if the stale, antiquated "drinking problem" excuse is deemed not to be applicable?

If you want to hear "Taps," Mr. Smith, come to our next DUI Victims Candlelight Vigil. You have attended before—however, it appears you may have forgotten the victims who were there. Let me refresh your memory. They were the people who were sobbing their guts out in memory of their loved ones who had been killed by people like Alan Nelson. Your seat is reserved.

Sandy Heverly, president of Stop DUI, a Nevada non-profit organization.

Las Vegas Review-Journal, April 9, 1997

Writing Lesson 13

For each of the following write the best argument you can that has as conclusion the claim below the cartoon. List only the premises and conclusion. If you believe the best argument is only weak, explain why. Do not make up a story about the cartoon. Use what you see in the cartoon and your common knowledge.

1.

Manuel is in an Olympic race for the handicapped.

2.

Flo is lying.

3.

Professor Zzzyzzx hit the wasps' nest.

4.

An adult who is not a fireman opened the fire hydrant.

REASONING ABOUT

OUR EXPERIENCE

12 Reasoning by Analogy

 IS TO AS IS TO ?

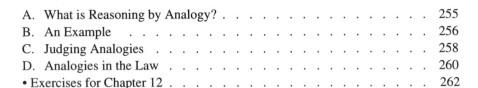

A. What is Reasoning by Analogy?

We have a desire to be consistent in our lives, to see and apply general principles. "Why shouldn't I hit you? You hit me," says the first-grader, invoking the principle that whatever someone does to me that's bad, I'm justified in doing back to her.

Since it was O.K. there, it should be O.K. here. This situation is like that situation. Since we concluded here, we can conclude there. That's arguing by analogy.

Should we let people who are HIV-positive remain in the military? Sure, after all, Magic Johnson is playing in the NBA.

This is an argument: Magic Johnson is allowed to play in the NBA, so people who are HIV-positive should be allowed to remain in the military.

We should legalize marijuana. After all, if we don't, what's the rationale for making alcohol and tobacco legal?

Alcohol is legal. Tobacco is legal. Therefore, marijuana should be legal. They are sufficiently similar.

DDT has been shown to cause cancer in rats. Therefore, there is a good chance DDT will cause cancer in humans.

Rats are like humans. So if rats get cancer from DDT, so will humans.

Reasoning by analogy starts with a comparison. But not every comparison is an argument.

> ***Analogy***   A comparison becomes ***reasoning by analogy*** when it is part of an argument: On one side of the comparison we draw a conclusion, so on the other side we should conclude the same.

"My love is like a red, red rose" is a comparison. Perhaps your English teacher called it an analogy. But it is not an argument—what conclusion is being drawn by Robert Burns?

Analogies, as we will see, are often only suggestions for arguments. But they have to be taken seriously, for they are used in science, law, and ethics. You probably use them yourself every day—how often have you heard or said, "But last time . . ." And there are lots of times when an analogy is just what's needed.

How can we tell if an analogy is good?

B. An Example

Example 1   Blaming soldiers for war is like blaming firemen for fires.

(Background: Country Joe MacDonald was a rock star who wrote songs protesting the war in Vietnam. In 1995 he was interviewed on National Public Radio about his motives for working to establish a memorial for Vietnam War soldiers in Berkeley, California, his home and a center of anti-war protests in the 60s and 70s. This claim was his response.)

Analysis   This is a comparison. But it's meant as an argument:

We don't blame firemen for fires.
Firemen and fires are like soldiers and wars.
Therefore, we should not blame soldiers for war.

This sounds pretty reasonable.

But in what way are firemen and fires like soldiers and wars? They have to be similar enough in some respect for Country Joe's remark to be more than suggestive. We need to pick out important similarities that we can use as premises.

Firemen and fires are like soldiers and war.
  wear uniforms
  answer to chain of command
  cannot disobey superior without serious consequences
  fight (fires/wars)
  work done when fire/war is over

> until recently only men
> lives at risk in work
> fire/war kills others
> firemen don't start fires—soldiers don't start wars
> usually drink beer

That's stupid: Firemen and soldiers usually drink beer. So?

When you ask "So?" you're on the way to deciding if the analogy is good. It's not just any similarity that's important. There must be some crucial, important way that firemen fighting fires is like soldiers fighting wars, some similarity that can account for why we don't blame firemen for fires that also applies to soldiers and war. Some similarities listed above don't seem to matter. Others we can't use because they trade on an ambiguity, like saying firemen "fight" fires.

We don't have any good guide for how to proceed—that's a weakness of the original argument. But if we're to take Country Joe MacDonald's remark seriously, we have to come up with some principle that applies to both sides.

The similarities that seem most important are that both firemen and soldiers are involved in dangerous work, trying to end a problem/disaster they didn't start. We don't want to blame someone for helping to end a disaster that could harm us all.

(‡)
>
> Firemen are involved in dangerous work.
> Soldiers are involved in dangerous work.
> The job of a fireman is to end a fire.
> The job of a soldier is to end a war.
> Firemen don't start fires.
> Soldiers don't start wars.

But even with these added to the original argument, we don't get a good argument for the conclusion that we shouldn't blame soldiers for wars. We need a general principle, some glue:

> You shouldn't blame someone for helping to end a disaster that could
> harm others, if he didn't start the disaster.

This claim, this general principle seems plausible, and it yields a valid argument.

But is the argument good? Are all the premises true? This is the point where the differences between firemen and soldiers might be important.

The first two premises of (‡) are clearly true, and so is the third. But is the job of soldiers to end a war? And do soldiers really not start wars? Look at this difference:

> Without firemen there would still be fires.
> Without soldiers there wouldn't be any wars.

Without soldiers there would still be violence. But without soldiers—any soldiers anywhere—there could be no organized violence of one country against another ("What if they gave a war and nobody came?").

So? The analogy shouldn't convince. The argument has a dubious premise.

We did not prove that soldiers should be blamed for wars. As always, *when you show an argument is bad you haven't proved the conclusion false.* You've only shown that you have no more reason than before for believing the conclusion.

Perhaps the premises at (‡) could be modified, using that soldiers are drafted for wars. But that's beyond Country Joe's argument. If he meant something more, then it's his responsibility to flesh it out. Or we could use his comparison as a starting place to decide whether there is a general principle, based on the similarities, for why we shouldn't blame soldiers for war.

C. Judging Analogies

Why was the example of firemen and soldiers so hard to analyze? Like many analogies, all we had was a sketch of an argument. *Just saying that one side of the analogy is* like *the other is too vague to use as a premise.* Unless the analogy is very clearly stated, we have to survey the similarities and guess the important ones in order to find a general principle that applies to both sides. Then we have to survey the differences to see if there isn't some reason that the general principle might not apply to one side.

Example 2   Magic Johnson was allowed to play in the National Basketball Association. So people who are HIV-positive should be allowed to remain in the military.

Analysis   This doesn't seem very convincing. What has the NBA to do with the military? We can list similarities (uniforms, teamwork, orders, winning, penalties for disobeying orders) and differences (great pay/lousy pay, game/not a game), but none of these matter unless we hit on the basis of the argument.

> The only reason for eliminating someone who is HIV-positive from a job is the risk of contracting AIDS for others who work with that person.
> Magic Johnson was allowed to play basketball when he was HIV-positive.
> So in basketball the risk of contracting AIDS from a fellow worker is considered insignificant.
> Basketball players have as much chance of physical contact and contracting AIDS from one another as soldiers do (except in war).
> Therefore, the risk of contracting AIDS from a fellow soldier should be considered insignificant.
> Therefore, people with AIDS should be allowed to remain in the military.

Here it is not the similarities between basketball players and soldiers that supports the conclusion. Once we spot the general principle (the first premise), it is the differences that support the conclusion (basketball players sweat and bleed all over one another every day, soldiers normally do not, except in war). Whether the analogy is good depends on whether these premises are true, but it's certainly a lot better than it seemed at first glance.

Example 3   (From Chapter 7.B)

> Dick: It's useless to kill flies. The ones you kill will be the slowest, because the fast flies will evade you. So you will be killing off the slowest ones, and the fastest ones will remain. Over time, then, the genes for being fast will predominate. Then with super-fast flies, it will be impossible to kill them anyway. So it's useless to kill flies.
>
> Zoe: Your argument against killing flies is bad. I could use the same argument against killing bacteria, or against killing chickens from Aunt Margery's henhouse. Those conclusions would be absurd.

Analysis Zoe is showing that Dick's argument is bad. She shows that another argument "just like" his is obviously bad. Whatever general principle that makes his argument work must also apply in the other case. So Zoe has refuted Dick. *An analogy of one argument to another can be a powerful way to refute.*

Example 4

Analysis Dick is reasoning by analogy, though it's just a sketch:

> The last time Dick and Zoe went to Suzy's for dinner, Suzy cooked a concoction she'd read about in a cook book, and Dick had the runs for two days.
> This time will be like the last time.
> Dick doesn't want to get the runs.
> So Dick shouldn't go to Suzy's for dinner.

The general principle that Dick seems to need is:

> Anytime Suzy serves dinner it will be cooked badly and give Dick the runs.

The general claim that Dick needs for this analogy is based on just one experience. Is that enough? We'll discuss in Chapter 14 how to judge whether a generalization is good.

Evaluating an analogy

1. Is this an argument? What is the conclusion?
2. What is the comparison?
3. What are the premises? (one or both sides of the comparison)
4. What are the similarities?
5. Can we state the similarities as premises and find a general principle that covers the two sides?
6. Does the general principle really apply to both sides?
   What about the differences?
7. Is the argument strong or valid? Is it good?

D. Analogies in the Law

Most analogies are not made explicit enough to serve as good arguments. But in the law analogies are presented as detailed, carefully analyzed arguments, with the important similarities pointed out and a general principle stated.

> The basic pattern of legal reasoning is reasoning by example. It is reasoning from case to case. It is a three-step process described by the doctrine of precedent in which a proposition descriptive of the first case is made into a rule of law and then applied to a next similar situation. The steps are these: similarity is seen between cases; next the rule of law inherent in the first case is announced; then the rule of law is made applicable to the second case.
>
> Edward H. Levi, *An Introduction to Legal Reasoning*

Laws are often vague, or situations come up which no one ever imagined might be covered by the law: Do the tax laws for mail-order purchases apply to the Internet? Similarities or differences have to be pointed out, general principles enunciated. Then those principles have to be respected by other judges. That's the idea of precedent or common law.

But why should a judge respect how earlier judges ruled? Those decisions aren't actually laws.

Imagine getting thrown in jail for doing something that's always been legal, and the law hadn't changed. Imagine running a business and suddenly finding that something you did, which before had been ruled safe and legal in the courts, now left you open to huge civil suits because a judge decided differently this week. If we are to live in a society governed by laws, the law must be applied consistently. It's rare that a judge can say that past decisions were wrong.

Only a few times has the Supreme Court said that all rulings on one issue, including rulings the Supreme Court made, are completely wrong. Brown v. the Board of Education said that segregation in schools, which had been ruled legal for nearly a hundred years, was now illegal. Roe v. Wade said that having an abortion, which had been ruled illegal for more than a century, was now legal. Such decisions are rare. They have to be. They create immense turmoil in the ways we live. We have to rethink a lot. And we can't do that regularly.

So what does a judge do when he's confronted by fifteen cases that were decided one way, the case before him falls under the general principle that was stated to cover those cases, yet his sense of justice demands that he decide this case the other way? He looks for differences between this case and those fifteen others. He tweaks the general principle just enough to get another principle that covers all those fifteen cases, but doesn't include the one he's deciding. He makes a new decision that now must be respected or overthrown.

Example 5   The Supreme Court has decided that it is a constitutional right for a doctor to terminate medical treatment that prolongs the life of a terminally ill or brain-dead person, so long as the doctor acts according to the wishes of that person (*Cruzan vs. Director, Missouri Department of Health*, 497 U.S. 261). Therefore, the Supreme Court should decide that assisting someone to commit suicide, someone who is terminally ill or in great suffering, as Dr. Kevorkian does, is a constitutionally protected right (*Compassion in Dying vs. State of Washington*).

Analysis   The question here is whether the two situations are similar. The court should decide with respect to the actual incidents in these cases. The court can decide narrowly, by saying this new case is not sufficiently like *Cruzan*, or broadly, by enunciating a principle that applies in both cases or else distinguishes between them. Or it can bring in more cases for comparison in trying to decide what general principle applies. (In the end the court was so divided that it ruled very narrowly, sidestepping the whole issue. Look it up on the Web.)

Summary   Comparisons are very suggestive. When we draw a conclusion from a comparison, we say we are reasoning by analogy.

Analogies are usually incomplete arguments. Often they are best treated as motive for finding a general principle to govern our actions or beliefs by surveying similarities and differences between two cases. When a general principle is made explicit, an analogy can be a powerful form of argument. When no general principle is made explicit, an analogy can be a good place to begin a discussion.

Exercises for Chapter 12

1. Some indicator words that suggest an analogy is being used are "like," "just as," "for the same reason." List three more.

2. What do you need to make a comparison into reasoning by analogy?

3. Are analogies typically complete arguments? Explain.

4. What should you do first in evaluating an analogy? Second?

Tom's caught on to the idea of how to evaluate analogies pretty well. Here are some of the exercises he did.

> **You should treat dogs humanely. How would you feel if you were caged up all day and experimented on? Or if you were chained to a stake all day? Or someone beat you every time you did something wrong?**

Argument? (yes or no) Yes.

Conclusion: You should treat dogs humanely.

Comparison: I'm not certain, cause they stated most of it as questions. But it seems they're comparing being a dog and being treated badly with you being treated badly, like getting caged up all day, or chained to a stake all day, or someone beating you every time you did something wrong.

Premises: Most of this is unstated. We're just supposed to put down what's actually said here, which I guess would be:
You shouldn't cage up a person all day.
You shouldn't chain a person to a stake all day.
You shouldn't beat someone every time she does something wrong.
People are like dogs.
So you shouldn't do any of that to dogs.

Similarities: I know we're supposed to pick out ones that'll give us a general principle. I've got to figure out how dogs and humans are similar. Well, dogs and humans are both mammals.

Additional premises needed to make it valid or strong (if none, say so): Dogs and humans are both mammals. You shouldn't mistreat any mammal.

Classify (with the additional premises): <u>valid</u>   very strong ———— weak

Good argument? I don't know. I guess the added premises are O.K. So probably it's pretty good.

Good. You've got the basis of the analogy right. You understand the method. You've picked out a general principle. But is it true? Isn't it too broad? After all, cats are mammals—does that mean we should treat them humanely?

There's one clue you overlooked. They said, "How would you <u>feel</u> . . ." I can imagine how it would feel to be a dog and be mistreated, just as I can (sort of) imagine how it would feel to be you and be mistreated. How about:

We can imagine what it would be like to be a dog.
We should treat humanely any creature that we can imagine what it would feel like to be mistreated.

That's more plausible, because it rules out cats. And it might include fish, which some people think should be treated humanely.

But really, you did O.K. We're unsure how to repair the original argument because it's too sketchy.

It is easier for a camel to go through the eye of a needle than for a rich man to enter into the kingdom of God.

Argument? (yes or no) This is from the Bible, right? I think it's supposed to make us think that being rich is bad. But I'm not sure. I can't figure out a conclusion, so I better say it's not an argument.

Conclusion (if unstated, add it):

Comparison:

Premises: *Good work!*

Similarities:

Additional premises (make the comparison explicit, add a general principle):

Classify (with the additional premises): valid   very strong ——————— weak

Good argument? (look for differences or ways the general principle could be false)

Critical thinking is like learning to drive a car. It requires practice—you can't just learn it as theory. That's why I give you so many messy arguments to analyze.

Argument? (yes or no) Yes, but just barely.

Conclusion (if unstated, add it): You should have lots of messy arguments to analyze in doing critical thinking.

Comparison: Critical thinking isn't at all like driving a car. Driving a car is a kind of physical skill, like playing basketball. Critical thinking is something you strain your brain over. Sure you need practice on hard stuff till it gets routine. But I don't see how messy arguments are anything like driving a car.

Premises:

Similarities:

Additional premises (make the comparison explicit, add a general principle):
Classify (with the additional premises):   valid   very strong ——————— weak
Good argument? (look for differences or ways the general principle could be false)

I think it's pretty bad. I can't figure out what general principle you'd want.

Good—you jumped to the punch line. There may be something in this comparison, but it's not clear yet, and you're justified in stopping here.

Here are some comparisons for you to evaluate. Use the following outline. There may be more than one argument in an example.

Argument? (yes or no)
Conclusion (if unstated, add it):
Comparison:
Premises:
Similarities:
Additional premises (make the comparison explicit, add a general principle):
Classify (with the additional premises):   valid   very strong ——————— weak
Good argument? (look for differences or ways the general principle could be false)

5. You wouldn't buy a kitten at a pet store to give to your dog. Why, then, do you consider it acceptable to buy white rats for your boa constrictor?

6. All the world's a stage and the men and women merely players.

7. Dick: Zoe, let's get married.
    Zoe: I've told you before, Dick, I won't get married until we sleep together.
    Dick: But that would be wrong. I won't sleep with you before we get married.
    Zoe: Would you buy a car without a test drive?
    Dick: Why buy the cow when the milk's free?

8. (In Japan in 1996 there was a debate whether the U.S. military bases should be allowed to remain on the island of Okinawa. Just a few years previously, the U.S. closed its base in the Philippines after the Philippine government requested it to do so.)

    U.S. and Japanese leaders have stressed the necessity of keeping U.S. troops on the island to assure security in the region.

    But [Governor of Okinawa Masahide] Ota disagrees. "When the U.S. had bases in the Philippines, they used to emphasize that they were [militarily] indispensable," he said. "But they abandoned them, and nothing happened."

    Associated Press, March 6, 1996

9. If killing is wrong, why do you punish murderers by killing them?

10. Maria: The college is collecting parking fees from us as part of our student fees, but we're not getting anything for it. We have to park a long way from our classes, so far we might as well park in the free lot. And the parking garage they promised us won't be built while we're here. We're not getting our money's worth. It would be wrong if you went to a mall and paid for a CD and then they didn't give it to you, or if you paid for a

carwash and they left the car dirty. The college should discontinue the fee and refund what we've already paid.

11. All the conspicuous features on the surface of the moon are the result of impacts. These features include not only the craters, which plainly advertise their origins, but also the great maria, or "seas," which are craters that filled with lava following the impact of very massive objects. Most of the impacts took place during a relatively brief period about four billion years ago, when debris left over from the formation of the solar system was swept up by the planets and their satellites. The earth probably received as heavy a pelting as the moon did, and it therefore must have been densely cratered.

"Science and the Citizen," *Scientific American,* June, 1976

12. A ban on handguns won't deter crime. After all, making drugs illegal doesn't work.

13. I know I can't really feel a pain you have. But because we're so much alike in so many ways, I'm sure that you feel physical pain in much the same way I do.

14. If we regulate the use of Ebonics, then will we have to regulate Western slang in the school system.

15. Dick: How hard can it be to raise kids? After all, I've trained two dogs.

16. God must exist. The way everything works together in nature, the adaptation of means to ends, the beauty, resembles but far exceeds what men do. Everything works together as a fine piece of machinery. So there must be some maker with intelligence behind all of nature. That is, God exists and is similar to human mind and intelligence.

17. **Bride busted for drinking at her OWN wedding**
Wheatland, Wyo. – A new bride faces up to $750 in fines and six months in jail–for having a drink at her own wedding reception!

Jennifer Windemeir, who was 20 years and 7 months old at the time–under the state's legal drinking age of 21– was charged with being a minor in possession of alcohol after an off-duty cop spotted her taking a sip.

"This is absurd," blasts the bride's attorney Eric Alden. "Why anyone would take what's supposed to be the happiest day of someone's life and try to turn it into a crime is beyond me."

The legal drama unfolded about 9:30 p.m. on February 3, a couple of weeks after Jennifer and new husband David were married in a civil ceremony. "It was a two-phase reception," says Alden.

"The first phase was at a church. Later a party of about 20 of the younger guests headed to the Mine Restaurant and Lounge.

"Guests proposed toasts to the bride and groom, and Jennifer took a sip from what I understand was a glass of white wine."

Sheriff's Deputy John Matthews, who was at the lounge with his wife, recognized Jennifer and thought she was underage, said Alden. "The next day he ran a driver's license check and interviewed the barmaid about what she'd served the table."

Three weeks later Jennifer was notified she was being charged. "She was really upset and came to me in tears," says Alden. "I agreed to represent her for free as a wedding gift." The lawyer argues that politics were behind the charges against Jennifer, who's the daughter of the local sheriff. "Deputy Matthews' uncle had run against Jennifer's dad and lost. I assume he was PO'd and this was a way to embarrass the sheriff."

The officer's wife Rhonda gives a different version of events.

"The reception was over and Jennifer and her husband were just in the bar hanging out and drinking tequila," she insists.

"Everyone else in town has to be 21 to drink. Just because she's the sheriff's daughter doesn't make her above the law."

But Alden vows to battle the charges, which go to trial mid-June. "What's next? Are cops going to kick down church doors and drag kids away from the communion rail for drinking wine?"

Weekly World News, June 11, 1996

Analyze what the attorney Eric Alden said.

18. Answer the questions at the end of this editorial.

Voters in Arizona and California approved ballot measures Nov. 5 allowing prescription of marijuana and other controlled substances for certain patients.

The most prevalent use is to ease the suffering of terminal patients or to counteract the side effects of chemotherapy . . .

The legal effect of the measures' passage is still up in the air, since the uses remain outlawed under federal statute. But retired General Barry McCaffrey, the White House's drug policy director, is quite certain about what the practical effect will be:

"Increased drug abuse in every category will be the inevitable result of the referenda," he said in a speech last week. "There could not be a worse message to young people than the provisions of these referenda . . . They are being told that marijuana and other drugs are good, they are medicine."

Apply this logic to the general's primary area of expertise:

Does the necessity of maintaining a standing army and engaging in war to protect national interests send a message to teens to arm themselves and form street gangs?

. . . There is a line between use and abuse of a necessary evil like lethal force or a powerful narcotic.

Social, economic and political circumstances justify the use of lethal force in war; medical circumstances justify the use of drugs.

But to think that teens or other forms of life lower on the food chain than generals are unable to differentiate between use and abuse may lead directly to the kind of logic under which students are expelled for possession of over-the-counter analgesics like Midol.

Albuquerque Journal, November 19, 1996

a. What is the conclusion?
b. What analogy does the editorial make?
c. How does it use the methods for evaluating analogies?
d. Are there any slanters or bad argument types?
e. Is the argument good?

19. a. Suppose that tomorrow good, highly reliable research is announced showing that oils derived from eyelids removed without anesthetic from healthy cats when applied to human skin reduced wrinkles significantly. Would it be justifiable to do further research and manufacture this oil?

   b. Same as (a) except that the oil is drunk with orange juice and significantly reduced the chance of lung cancer for smokers.

   c. Same as (a) except the oil is mixed with potatoes and eaten and significantly reduced the chance of heart disease and lengthened the lives of women.

   d. Same as (a) except that when drunk the oil killed off all viruses harmful to humans.

20. Do Exercise 19 reading "dogs" for "cats."

Key Words   reasoning by analogy

Further Study   Analogies are important in courses in criminal justice, ethics, and health sciences, among others. The exercise about how we justify treating dogs humanely is typical of the sort of problem and reasoning you'd encounter in a course on ethics. Some philosophy classes on reasoning or philosophy of science look at the nature of analogies more deeply.

Writing Lesson 14

You understand what reasoning by analogy is now. So write an argument *using an analogy* either for or against the following:

> "Just as alcohol and tobacco are legal, we should legalize the use of marijuana."

Check whether your instructor has chosen a *DIFFERENT TOPIC* for this assignment.

There are roughly three ways you can argue:

- Marijuana is no worse than alcohol or tobacco, so we should legalize it. (Arguing from similarities.)

- Marijuana is worse than alcohol and tobacco, so we should not legalize it. (Arguing from differences.)

- Marijuana is no worse than alcohol or tobacco, but it is a mistake to have those legal, and we should not make the situation worse by legalizing marijuana. (Arguing from similarities.)

Write the argument as just a *one page* essay. It should be clear and well structured, since you will have written out the claims and diagrammed it first for yourself. You shouldn't have to do major research for this, but at least be sure your premises are plausible.

13   Numbers?

In this chapter we'll look at some ways you can get confused about numbers in claims. If your eyes are starting to glaze, if your mind is going blank with talk of numbers, relax. Numbers don't lie.

**By the year 2000,
2 out of 3
Americans could be illiterate.**

It's true.

Today, 75 million adults . . . about one American in three, can't read adequately. And by the year 2000, U.S. News & World Report envisions an America with a literacy rate of only 30%.

Before that America comes to be, you can stop it . . . by joining the fight against illiteracy today.

Call the Coalition for Literacy at toll-free 1-800-xxx-xxxx and volunteer.

**Volunteer Against Illiteracy.
The only degree you need
is a degree of caring.**

**There's an epidemic with
27 million victims.
And no visible symptoms.**

It's an epidemic of people who can't read.

Believe it or not, 27 million Americans are functionally illiterate, about one adult in five.

The solution to this problem is you . . . when you join the fight against illiteracy. So call the Coalition for Literacy at toll-free 1-800-xxx-xxxx and volunteer.

**Volunteer Against Illiteracy.
The only degree you need
is a degree of caring.**

Ads on the last two pages of a paperback edition of *The Stand* by Stephen King.

A. Misleading Claims with Numbers

1. Apples and oranges

Zoe has 4 apples and Dick has 2 oranges. Who has more? More *what*?

When they use numbers it looks so exact. But a vague or meaningless comparison gets no better by having a few numbers in it.

There were twice as many rapes as murders in our town.

Yes, that's a claim, but a misleading one: It seems to say something important, but what?

It's getting really violent here. There were 12% more murders this year.

This is also a mistaken comparison. If the town is growing rapidly and the number of tourists is growing even faster, it would be no surprise that the *number* of murders is going up, though the *rate* (how many murders per 100,000 population) might be going down. I'd rather live in a town of one million that had 20 murders last year than in a small town of 25,000 that had 6.

2. Compared to what?

If you don't know where they started, increases or decreases can be deceptive.

Attendance up 50% this week at performances of Othello!
Tickets still available!

Great ad, but what was the attendance last week? 25? 250? 1000?

> ***Two Times Zero Is Still Zero***   A *two times zero is still zero* comparison is one that makes something look impressive, but the base of the comparison is not stated.

A clothing store advertises a sale of sweaters at "25% off." You take it to mean 25% off the price they used to charge which was $20, so you'd pay $15. But the store could mean 25% off the suggested retail price of $26, so it's now $19.50.

Percentages can be misleading. You see a stock for $60 and think it's a good deal. You buy it; a week later it's at $90, so you sell. You made $30—that's a 50% gain! Your buddy hears about it and buys the stock at $90; a week later it goes down to $60, so he panics and sells the stock. He lost $30—that's a $33\frac{1}{3}$% loss. The same $30 is a different percentage depending on where you started.

$$50\% \uparrow \begin{bmatrix} \$90 \\ \$60 \end{bmatrix} \downarrow 33\tfrac{1}{3}\%$$

Or my favorite, the little old lady at the slot machine who warbles, "I just won $75 at this machine!" Wrong, if she put $3 in and $75 came out, she only won $72. (And that's not counting her earlier losses.)

Another confusing report is the one that says unemployment is up 8%. That does not mean unemployment is *at* 8%. It should mean that if unemployment had been 5%, it is now 5.4%. There is a difference between "up" and "up to."

> "For every ounce of muscle you build, you burn 25% more calories."
> From a runners' club newsletter.

3. Phony precision

"Last term 27.5862% of all Dr. E's students received a C."

That's accurate. But it's misleading. Rather say, "8 out of the 29 students who took Dr. E's class last term got a C." Using percentages makes it look more impressive, as if there were a huge number that could only be expressed with percentages and lots of digits after the decimal point.

Just the opposite of phony precision and just as misleading are slanted approximations. In a BBC broadcast I heard that 48 police officers in Turkey were on trial. On a later broadcast the same day I heard that nearly 50 officers were on trial. Why say "nearly 50," unless they want you to remember that higher number?

4. How could they know that number?

On National Public Radio I heard:

> Breast feeding is up 16% from 1989.

How could they know? Who was looking in all those homes? A survey? Who did they ask? Women chosen randomly? But lots of them don't have infants. Women who visited doctors? But lots of women, lots of poor ones, don't visit their doctors.

What does "breast feeding" mean? Does a woman who breast feeds one day and then gives it up classify as someone who breast feeds? Or one who breast feeds two days? A month?

Maybe NPR is reporting on a reliable survey (in the next chapter we'll look at what that means). But what they said is so vague and open to doubt as to how they could know it that we should ignore it as noise.

> **Software piracy losses top $13 billion**
>
> U.S. and foreign companies lost $13.1 billion in 1995 from illegally copied business software programs, according to an industry survey.
>
> Although the piracy rate fell worldwide, revenue losses from piracy went up 9 percent. The study estimated the piracy rate decreased to 46 percent in 1995 from 49 percent in 1994, but dollar losses grew because the volume of software sold worldwide increased.
>
> The study, conducted by International Planning & Research of Redmond, Wash., was released Wednesday.
>
> The Software Publishers Association and the Business Software Alliance commissioned a joint study for the first time. . . .
>
> The report said the countries with the worst piracy records are Vietnam, with a 99 percent rate; El Salvador, 97 percent; China and Oman, 96 percent; and Russia, 94 percent.
>
> As the world's leading producer of business software, the United States suffered the most losses, followed by Japan.
>
> U.S. companies lost an estimated $2.94 billion in 1995. But a drop in the average price of U.S.-made software largely accounted for a nearly 18 percent decline in estimated revenue lost between 1994 and 1995.
>
> Piracy within the United States is decreasing, showing that anti-piracy efforts are proving effective, the report said. The U.S. piracy rate in 1995 was 55 percent, down from 66 percent in 1994.
>
> Associated Press, November 19, 1996
>
> These are meaningless statistics. There's no way to estimate illegal activity: Who are you going to interview? And are you going to trust their answers? What is a "piracy rate"? It sounded impressive, until I called directory information and found there's no listing for "International Planning & Research" in Redmond, Wash.

B. Averages

"It ought to be safe to cross here. I heard that the average depth is only two feet."

Beware: The average is not the maximum or most likely depth.

The *average* or *mean* of a collection of numbers is obtained by adding the numbers and then dividing by the number of items. For example,

The average of 7, 9, 37, 22, 109 is calculated:

Add $7 + 9 + 37 + 22 + 109 = 184$

Divide   184 by 5 $= 36.8$, the average

An average is a useful figure to know if there isn't too much variation in the figures. For example, suppose the marks Dr. E gave for his course were:

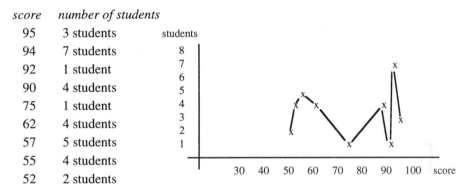

score	number of students
95	3 students
94	7 students
92	1 student
90	4 students
75	1 student
62	4 students
57	5 students
55	4 students
52	2 students

The grading scale was 90–100 = A, 80–89 = B, 70–79 = C, 60–69 = D, 59 and below = F. When Dr. E's department head asked him how the teaching went, he told her, "Great, just like you wanted, the average mark was 75%, a C."

But she knows Dr. E too well to be satisfied. She asks him, "What was the median score?" The *median is the midway mark: the same number of items above as below.* Again Dr. E can reply, "75." As many got above 75 as below 75.

But knowing how clever Dr. E is with numbers, she asks him what the mode score was. The *mode is the number most often obtained.* Dr. E flushes, "Well, 94." Now she knows something is fishy. When she asked that the average score be 75, she was thinking of a graph that looked like:

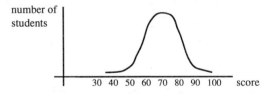

The distribution of the marks should be in a bell-shape: clustered around the median.

> Unless you have good reason to believe that the average mark is pretty close to the median and that the distribution is more or less bell-shaped, the average doesn't tell you anything important.

Sometimes people misuse the word "average" by confusing it with the mode: "The average American enjoys action movies."

> Get your class to stand up. Look around. Do you think the average height is the same as the median height? How can you tell? Come up with a *physical* way to determine the median height and the mode of the heights.
>   Suppose your class had just eight fellows from the men's basketball team and five women gymnasts. Do you think the median and the average would be the same?

Summary   Numbers are our way of measuring. They are important in our reasoning. But it's easy to be misled or use them wrong. A vague claim doesn't get any better by using numbers. Both sides of a comparison must be made clear. The numbers must represent quantities someone could actually know. And often it's not the average that's significant, but the median or the mode.

Exercises for Chapter 13

1. Find an advertisement that uses a claim with percentages that is misleading or vague or ambiguous.

2. Find an advertisement that uses a claim with numbers other than percentages that is misleading or vague or ambiguous.

3. Compare a sundial on a sunny day and a digital watch that is set wrong.
    a.   Which is most accurate at telling the time?
    b.   Which is most precise?

4. Find the average, mean, median, and mode of the scores of Dr. E's students who took his critical thinking final exam: 92, 54, 60, 86, 62, 76, 88, 88, 62, 68, 81.

For Exercises 5–20 point out any use of numbers or percentages that is vague or misleading.

5. Try new Smooth-Glow skin creme, containing a mixture of special oils derived from fava beans. It will reduce your skin's aging by 50%.

6. [Advertisement]   Called home lately? 1-800-Collect® Save up to 44%. Savings based on a 3 min. AT&T operator-dialed interstate call.

7. [Advertisement]   Era® costs up to 1/3 less than those pricey brands and helps remove your toughest stains.

8. [Advertisement for *3 Musketeers*® candy bars]
    The sweetest part is finding out how little fat it has.
    (45% less fat than the average of the 25 leading chocolate brands, to be exact.)*
        *Not a low-fat food. 8 fat grams per serving for single bar vs. 15 gram average for leading chocolate brands.

9. [Advertisement] Studies have shown that three cups of Cheerios a day with a low fat diet can help lower cholesterol.

10. [Advertisement on box of laundry detergent] 25% more free!

11. The Nevada Dance Festival had a great year in 1993. Attendance was up 22%.

12. The rate of inflation went down 2%.

13. (Concerning the way the U.S. Census Bureau operates) In 1990, 65% of the questionnaires that were mailed were filled out and returned. Census counters went back to every household that didn't mail back a form. Even then, the bureau was able to count only 98.4% of the U.S. population.   *USA Today,* April 15, 1998

14. [Television ad] More and more doctors are now recommending Advil®.

15. Hey, I just won $800 at this slot machine!

16. Incredible increase in graduation rates of student athletes at our college! Up by 50%!

17. [Advertisement]
    Official Royal Flush Results!   Fiesta 2,115   Texas 1,735
    It's not even close
    Fiesta backs up its claim:
    "We Pay More Royal Flushes per Machine Than Any Other Casino Hotel in the World!"

    For the month of September, Texas claimed that it paid out a total of 1,735 Royals, with approximately 2,000 machines, but for that same period, Fiesta Casino paid out 2,115 Royal Flushes, with just 1,200 machines. Here's proof, once again, that Fiesta's Slots and Video Poker Machines are the loosest on Earth!

18. **Artery narrowing can be reversed**
    A new study has shown what many researchers have thought all along—cardiovascular disease (i.e., narrowing of the arteries) can be moderately reversed.
        The well-known secret: lifestyle changes.
        In the study, heart patients who had coronary artery (heart) disease—diagnosed through angiograms (X-rays of the arteries)—were: 1) put on a vegetarian diet, 2) told to stop smoking, 3) started on a mild to moderate aerobic exercise program (three hours per week), and 4) told to practice stress management techniques (e.g., meditation) one hour a day.
        Five-year findings: In a *control* group of heart patients who had *not* made the above lifestyle changes, 45% had coronary narrowing that became worse; 50% showed no change; and 5% showed improvement.
        By comparison, 99% of the group who made significant lifestyle changes (see above) had healthier arteries (i.e., improved blood flow) or their condition remained stable.   *From the heart.* Washoe Health System, Fall, 1996

19. Dick: I read that drinking a shot of whiskey a day is good for your health. I didn't drink much last year, so I better make up for it tonight.

20. **S. Korea declares war on leftovers**

    Because of the feeling of bounty and plenty that it gives, Koreans routinely cook more at home than they can eat, and restaurants serve more than any customer could reasonably consume.

    "Koreans are used to thinking 'the more the better,'" said Koh, the restaurant manager.

    It's a philosophy the government is battling to change. In the latest round, the government announced Dec. 6 that it will make a major push in 1997 to cut food waste by half.

    Many Koreans say they are careful at home to eat leftovers the next day. But restaurant waste, which the government says accounts for 42 percent of food garbage, is a tougher problem.

    The government says the country's 45 million people throw away nearly 48,000 metric tons of garbage a day.   Pauline Jelinek, Associated Press, November 23, 1996

21. Dick: I read that on average women think of sex every 18 minutes.

    Zoe: Really? I guess some woman out there is thinking of sex about once a year.

    What is Zoe implying? Does she understand averages correctly?

Which of the following claims should be trusted to give you a good idea of the population as a whole? For which would you prefer to know the median or mode? Explain.

22. The average wage in the U.S. is $28,912.

23. The average wage in one rural county of Utah was $14,117.

24. The average wage of concert pianists in the U.S. is less than the average wage of university professors.

25. The average number of people in a household in Las Vegas is 2.1.

26. The average number of times a 72-year-old man has sex in a week has been determined by surveys to be 1.2 .

27. The average GPA of a graduating senior at this college in 1995 was 2.86, while in 1972 it was 2.41.

28. Dick: Which section of English Lit should I take, Zoe, Professor Zzzyzzx's or Professor Glåsütör's?

    Zoe: It doesn't really matter. You can't understand either, and the department info on the sections said the average mark in both their classes was a C.

29. The average income of a woman in the U.S. was only 82% that of a man.

Key Words	apples and oranges	average
	two times zero is still zero	mean
	phony precision	median
		mode

14 Generalizing from Experience

SPOT!

A. Generalizing

> I think I'll get a border collie. Every one I've met has been friendly and loyal.

> I'd better not visit your home. You've got a cat, and every time I've been around a cat I get a terrific sneezing fit and asthma.

We generalize every day, arguing from a claim about some to a claim about more. It's how we make sense of our world: What's happened before is likely to happen again. My experience is typical, until I learn otherwise. As we gain more experience, we generalize better because we have more examples from which to generalize.

For science, especially the health sciences, generalization along with analogy dominates reasoning from experiments. What makes us think that smoking causes cancer? Because there is a statistical link: A higher percentage of people who smoke get lung cancer than those who do not. To reason well about cause and effect, we have to understand when a generalization is good.

279

> ***Generalizing*** We say that we are *generalizing* if we conclude a claim about a group, the ***population***, from a claim about some part of it, the ***sample***. To generalize is to make an argument.
>
> Sometimes the general claim that is the conclusion is called the ***generalization***; sometimes we use that word for the whole argument.
>
> The knowledge of the sample is called the ***inductive evidence*** for the generalization.

When we generalize from experience, we cannot be certain of our conclusions. Perhaps every cat I've ever encountered has made me sneeze and given me asthma. I'd be wise to avoid cats. But that doesn't mean that every cat will cause me to sneeze and become asthmatic. Perhaps there's a new genetically altered breed of hairless cat that causes no allergies. Highly unlikely, but it's possible.

To evaluate whether a generalization is good, we need to see it as an argument. Since we are generalizing from experience, we know we can't get certainty. Strong arguments—not valid ones—with true premises will be the best.

Examples   Are the following generalizations? If so, what is the sample? What is the population?

Example 1   In a study of 5,000 people who owned pets in Anchorage, Alaska, dog owners expressed higher satisfaction with their pets and with their own lives. So dog owners are more satisfied with their pets and their own lives than other pet owners.

Analysis   Here we know about the 5,000 people who were surveyed in Anchorage. They are the sample. The conclusion is about all pet owners everywhere, and they constitute the population.

Is the generalization good? That is, is the argument good? Unstated premises are needed about how the study was conducted. Is there any reason that we should think that these 5,000 people are representative of all pet owners?

Example 2   I should build my house with the bedroom facing this direction to catch the morning sun.

Analysis   We believe we know where the sun will rise in the future based on where we see it rise today. The sample is all the times in the past when the sun rose: We know that the point where the sun rises varies slightly from season to season, but is roughly east. The population is all times the sun has risen or will rise, which we think will be in roughly the same direction.

Example 3   Of potential customers surveyed, 72% said that they liked "very much" the new green color that Yoda plans to use for its cars. So about 72% of all potential customers will like it.

Analysis   The sample is the group of potential customers interviewed, and the population is all potential customers.

Sometimes the generalization we want and we're entitled to isn't "all," but "most," or "72%": The same proportion of the whole as in the sample will have the property. This is a ***statistical generalization***.

Example 4   Every time the minimum wage is raised, there's squawking that it will cause inflation and decrease employment. And every time it doesn't. So watch for the same worthless arguments again this time.

Analysis   Here the unstated conclusion is that raising the minimum wage will not cause inflation or decrease employment. The reason given is that it hasn't in the past. The sample is all times in the past that the minimum wage has risen, and the population is all times it has risen or will rise.

We need to know how to judge whether the examples are sufficient for the generalization: Do they have enough in common with the situation now? Are there enough examples?

Example 5   The doctor tells you to fast from 10 p.m. Then at 10 a.m. she gives you glucose to drink. Forty-five minutes later she takes some of your blood and has it analyzed. She concludes you don't have diabetes.

Analysis   The sample is the blood the doctor took. It's a very small sample compared to the amount of blood you have in your body, but the doctor is confident that it is representative of all your blood.

Example 6   You go to the city council meeting with a petition signed by all the people who live on your block requesting that a street light be put in. Addressing the city council, you say, "Everyone on this block wants a street light here."

Analysis   You're not generalizing here: There's no argument from some to more, since the sample equals the population. You know what everyone wants, since they told you. It's a valid argument.

Example 7   Should the Yoda plant accept the batch of bolts from its new supplier? Better check them. The inspector chooses 10 from the 20,000 bolts, inspects them under a microscope, finds that all are acceptable, and passes the lot.

Analysis   The sample is the ten bolts studied. The population is the shipment of 20,000. Is the sample big enough? How many is enough? How can we decide?

Exercises for Section A

Here's some of Tom's work on identifying generalizations.

Maria: Every time I've seen a stranger come to Dick's gate, Spot has barked. So Spot will always bark at strangers at Dick's gate.

Generalization? (yes/no) Yes.

Sample: Every time Maria has seen a stranger come to the gate.

Population: Every time a stranger ever comes to Dick's gate when Spot's there.
  Good.

You shouldn't go out with someone from New York. They're all rude and pushy.

Generalization? (yes/no) Yes.

Sample: All the New Yorkers the person has met.

Population: All New Yorkers.

You're too generous. How do you know if the speaker has ever met a New Yorker? Maybe he's just spouting off a prejudice he acquired from his friends. It's not a generalization if you can't identify the sample.

Should we try the new Mexican restaurant on Sun Street? I heard it was pretty good.

Generalization? (yes/no) Yes.

Sample: People who told him it was good.

Population: It will be good food for him, too.

A generalization is an argument, right. But the sample and the population aren't claims— they're groups. The sample here is the times that other people have eaten there (and reported that it was good). The population is all times anyone has or will eat there. It's a past to future generalization.

For each of these exercises, answer the following questions:

Generalization? (yes/no)

Sample:

Population:

1. German shepherds have a really good temperament. I know, because lots of my friends and my sister have one.

2. That blasted paper-boy tossed the paper on the lawn again and the sprinklers got it wet. I'm going to call the newspaper.

3. Suzy: I heard you have a Zitochi CD player.
    Maria: Yeah, and I wish I'd never gotten one. It's always breaking down.
    Suzy: Well, I won't get one then, since they're probably all the same.

4. Maria to Zoe: Don't bother to ask Tom to do the dishes. My brother's a football player and no football player will do the dishes.

5. Suzy: Guys are such nitwits.
    Zoe: What do you mean?

Suzy: Like, they can't even tell when you're down. Emotionally, they're clods. Besides, they just want a girl for her body.

Zoe: How do you know?

Suzy: Duh, it's like a cheerleader like me isn't going to have a lot of dates?

6. Suzy: Are you taking Spot for a walk?

   Zoe: No. I'm getting the leash because I have to take him to the vet, and it will be hard to get him to go. Every time I take him to the vet he seems to know it before we get in the car.

7. You'd better not take the cat in the car with you. She barfed all over your lap last time.

8. Zoe: Do you know a good dry cleaner around here?

   Dick: The one in the plaza north of campus is pretty good. They've always done O.K. with the stuff I take them.

9. Don't go to Mexico in July. It's awfully hot there then.

10. Dogs can be trained to retrieve a newspaper.

11. I want to marry a Japanese guy. They're hard-working and really family oriented.

12. It's incredible how many people in the U.S. watch Baywatch. It got the highest Nielsen ratings of any show on TV.

13. Isabel: I'm so excited. Suzy's arranged a blind-date for me with a football player. I've seen all the games, and the guys on the team are *so* sexy!

14. From our study it appears that the levels of cholesterol in the blood of bald men is lower than that in men with a full head of hair.

15. Write down three examples of generalizations you have heard or made in the last week and one example of a claim that sounds like a generalization and isn't. See if your classmates can pick out the one that isn't. For the generalizations, ask a classmate to identify the sample and the population.

B. When is a Generalization Good?

1. How you can go wrong

Tom's sociology professor has assigned him to conduct a survey to find out the attitudes of students on his campus about sex before marriage. "That's easy," Tom thinks, "I'll just ask some of my friends. They're typical aren't they?"

So he asks all his friends he can reach on Tuesday whether they think sex before marriage is a great idea or not. Twenty of the twenty-eight say "Yes," while eight say "No." That was easy.

Tom takes the results to his professor and she asks why he thinks his friends are typical. Typical? "I guess they are," Tom responds. But aren't they mostly your age? And the same sex as you? How many are gay? How many are married? And is twenty-eight really enough to generalize from? And what about that question? "Is sex before marriage a *great* idea or not?" A bit biased?

O.K., it wasn't such a good job. Back to the drawing board. Tom brainstorms with some of his friends and figures he'll ask 100 students as they leave the student union one question, "Do you approve of sexual intercourse before marriage?"

He goes to the student union at 4 p.m. on Wednesday, asks the students, and finds that 83 said "No," while 17 said "Yes." That's different from what he expected, but what the heck, this is science, and science can't be wrong. There was no bias in the question, and surely those 100 students are typical.

Tom presents the results to his professor and she suggests that perhaps he should find out what was going on at the student union that day. . . . It seems the campus Bible society was having a big meeting there that let out about 4 p.m. Maybe this survey won't give a good generalization.

So Tom and three friends get together, and at 9 a.m., 1 p.m., and 6 p.m. they station themselves outside the student union, the administration offices, and the big classroom building. Each is to ask the first 20 people who come by just two questions: "Are you a student here?" and "Do you approve of sexual intercourse before marriage?"

They get 171 people saying they are students, with 133 saying "Yes" and 38 saying "No" to the second question. That's a lot of responses with no evident bias in the sampling. Tom's sure his professor will be happy this time.

Tom tells his professor what they've done, and she asks, "Why do you think your sample is representative? Why do you think it's big enough?"

Tom's puzzled. It's big enough. Surely 170 out of 20,000 students is a lot, isn't it? How many could she expect us to interview? We're just human.

And representative? What does she mean? "We didn't do anything to get a bias," he says. "But are those students typical?" she asks. "Is not doing anything to get a bias enough to ensure your sample is representative?"

2. Representative samples

Tom's first two attempts to survey students about their attitudes towards sex before marriage used clearly unrepresentative samples. But his third attempt? Can we be sure he has a sample that is just like the population, one that is representative?

> **Representative Sample**   A sample is *representative* if no one subgroup of the whole population is represented more than its proportion in the population. A sample is ***biased*** if it is not representative.

Tom's method was ***haphazard sampling,*** choosing the sample with no intentional bias. Possibly the sample is representative. Maybe not. But we don't have any good reason to believe that it is representative.

There is, however, a way we can choose a sample that is very, very likely to get us a representative sample. Choose it randomly.

> ***Random Sampling***   A sample is chosen *randomly* if at every choice there is an equal chance for any one of the remaining members of the population to be picked.

If you assign a number to each student, write the numbers on slips of paper, put them in a fishbowl, and draw one number out at a time, that's probably going to be a random selection. But there's a chance that slips with longer numbers will have more ink and fall to the bottom of the bowl when you shake it. Or the slips aren't all the same size. So typically to get a truly random selection we use tables of random numbers prepared by mathematicians. Most spreadsheet programs for home computers can now generate tables of random numbers. So for Tom's survey he could get a list of all students; if the first number on the table is 413 he'd pick the 413th student on the list; if the second number is 711, he'd pick the 711th student on the list; and so on, until he has a sample that's big enough.

Why is random sampling better? Suppose that of the 20,000 students at your college, 500 are gay males. Then the chance that *one* student picked at random would be a gay male is:

$$\frac{500}{20,000} = \frac{1}{40}$$

If you were to pick 300 students at random, the chance that half of them would be gay is very, very small. It is very likely, however, that 7 or 8 ($1/40$ of 300) will be gay males.

On the other hand, suppose roughly 50% of the students at your college are female. Then each time you choose a student at random there's a 50% chance it will be female. And if you randomly choose a sample of 300 students the chance is very high that close to 50% will be female.

The ***law of large numbers*** says, roughly, that if the probability of something occurring is X percent, then over the long run the percentage of times that happens will be about X percent. For example, the probability of a flip of a fair coin landing heads is 50%. So, though you may get a run of 8 tails, then 5 heads, then 4 tails, then 36 heads to start, in the long run, repeating the flipping, if the coin is fair eventually the number of heads will tend toward 50%.

IT'S COME UP RED 12 TIMES IN A ROW. IT'S BOUND TO COME UP BLACK SEVERAL TIMES IN A ROW NOW.

Don't bet on it. The times it comes up red and the times it comes up black will even out in the *long run*. But if it came up red 100 times in a row, black could even out by coming up just one more time than red every 100 spins for the next 10,000 spins.

The *gambler's fallacy*: A run of events of a certain kind makes a run of contrary events more likely in order to even up the probabilities.

If you choose a large sample randomly, the chance is very high that it will be representative. That's because the chance of any one subgroup being over-represented is small—not nonexistent, but small. It doesn't matter if you know anything about the composition of the population in advance. After all, to know how many homosexuals there are, and how many married women, and how many men, and . . . you'd need to know almost everything about the population in advance. But that's what you need surveys for.

With a random sample we have good reason to believe the sample is representative. A sample chosen haphazardly may give a representative sample—but you have no good reason to believe it will be representative.

Weak Argument	*Strong Argument*

Sample is chosen *haphazardly*. Therefore,
     The sample is representative.
	Sample is chosen *randomly*. Therefore,
	     The sample is representative.

Lots of ways the sample could turn out to be biased.	Low probability the sample could turn out to be biased.

The classic example that haphazard sampling needn't work, even with an enormous sample, is the poll done in 1936 by *Literary Digest*. The magazine mailed out 10,000,000 ballots asking who the person would vote for in the 1936 presidential election. They received 2,300,000 back. With that huge sample, the magazine confidently predicted that Alf Landon would win. Roosevelt received 60% of the vote, one of the biggest wins ever. What went wrong? The magazine selected its sample from lists of it own subscribers and telephone and automobile owners. In 1936 that was the wealthy class. And the wealthy folks preferred Alf Landon.

When sampling all voters in Mississippi or all the bolts in the shipment from the supplier, surveyors should rely on tables of random numbers to choose which ones to study. But that may not always be feasible: Of the 400 voters in Mississippi that are chosen randomly, 6 are traveling out of the state, 13 have moved with no forwarding address—you can't locate them all. So in practice most sampling is done by dividing up the population into groups that are, you hope, weighted in such a way that they reflect the whole: You choose 50% from the large cities in Mississippi; you choose a few bolts at random from each of the 40 boxes they came in. You can't always get a perfectly representative sample. Like being vague, the right question to ask is: Does the sample seem *too* biased to be reliable?

> Beware of *selective attention*:
> It seems that buttered toast always lands the wrong side down because you notice when it does.

Exercises for Sections B.1 and B.2

1. What is a representative sample?

2. Explain why a good generalization is unlikely to be valid.

3. a. What is the law of large numbers?
    b. How does the law of large numbers justify random sampling as giving unbiased samples?

4. Why does the phone ring more often when you're in the shower?

5. Which of the following seem too biased to be reliable, and why?

    a. To determine the average number of people in your city who engaged in sexual intercourse last week, interview women only.
    b. To determine what kind of cat food is purchased most often, interview only people who have telephones.
    c. To determine what percentage of women think that bald men are sexy, poll students as they leave their classes at your school.
    d. To determine whether to buy grapes at the supermarket, pick a grape from the bunch you're interested in and taste it.

6. a. Suppose you want to find out whether people in your city believe that there are enough policemen. Give four characteristics of people that could bias the survey. That is, list four subgroups of the population that you would not want to have represented out of proportion to their actual percentages in the population.
    b. Now list four characteristics that you feel would not matter for giving bias.

7. A colleague suggested to me that the best way to get a sample is to select one whose relevant characteristics (e.g., gender, age, ethnicity, income, . . .) are known to be in the same proportion as in the population as a whole. Explain why we can't count on that method to give us a representative sample.

8. One of my students was a blackjack dealer at a casino and heard a player say: "I ran a computer simulation of this system 1000 times and made money. So why didn't I win today playing for real?" Can you explain it?

9. Is every randomly chosen sample representative? Explain.

3. Sample size

> Suzy: I've got a couple of Chinese students in my classes.
> Zoe: Really?
> Suzy: They're both hard-working and get good grades. I suppose that all Chinese are like that.

That's generalizing from *too small a sample*—the way stereotypes begin. It's a **hasty generalization** using **anecdotal evidence**.

> Mom: I'm going to start taking Vitamin E.
> Dick: Why?
> Mom: Your cousin Lucy's husband Ed knew about Vitamin E already twenty years ago and started taking it. Look at him now. He's over 65 and in great health.

But how big does a sample have to be? To estimate what percentage of students at your school approve of sex before marriage, is it enough to ask 5? 25? 150? Why is it that opinion polls regularly extrapolate to the preferences of all voters in the U.S. from sampling 1,500 or less?

Roughly, the idea is to measure how much more likely it is that your generalizations are going to be accurate as you increase the number in your sample. If you want to find out how many people in your class of 300 sociology students are spending 15 hours a week on the homework, you might ask 15 or 20. If you interview 30 you might get a better picture, but there's a limit. After you've asked 100, you probably won't get a much different result if you ask 150. And if you've asked 200, do you really think your generalization will be different if you ask 250? It hardly seems worth the effort.

Often you can rely on common sense when small numbers are involved. But when we generalize to a very large population, say 2,000, or 20,000, or 200,000,000, how big the sample should be cannot be explained without at least a mini-course on statistics. In evaluating statistical generalizations, you have to expect that the people doing the sampling have looked at enough examples, which is reasonable if it's a respected organization, a well-known polling company, physicians, or a drug company that's got to answer to the Food and Drug Administration. Surprisingly perhaps, 1,500 is typically adequate for the sample size when surveying all adults in the U.S.

> The popularity of American therapy movements might also explain why all the books mentioned in this review base much of their thinking on interviews and personal stories, or "narratives," as though American readers can no longer follow abstract arguments from ethical or economic or statistical premises. As a result, instead of constructive social policy based on statistical data, we have endless testimonials, diatribes, and spurious science from people who imagine that their personal experience, the dynamics of their particular family, sexual taste, childhood trauma, and personal inclination constitute universals.
>
> Diane Johnson, "What do women want?", *The New York Review of Books,* vol. 43, no. 19.

4. Is the sample studied well?

Choosing a large enough representative sample is important, but it's not enough. The sample has to be investigated well.

The doctor taking your blood to see if you have diabetes won't get a reliable result if her syringe is contaminated or if she forgets to tell you to fast the night before. You won't find out the attitudes of students about sex before marriage if you ask a biased question. Picking a random sample of bolts won't help you determine if the bolts are O.K. if all you do is inspect them visually, not with a microscope or a stress test.

Questionnaires and surveys are particularly problematic. Questions need to be formulated without bias. Even then, you have to rely on your respondents answering truthfully. Surveys on sexual habits are notorious for inaccurate reporting. Invariably the number of times that women in the U.S. report they engaged in sexual intercourse with a man in the last week, or month, or year is much lower than the reports that men give of sexual intercourse with a woman during that time. The figures are so different that it would be impossible for both groups to be answering accurately.

> At the bottom of the barrel: Issues entrepreneurs cared about least in the '96 election
> 1. Electric utility deregulation, 2%
> 2. Superfund reform, 3%
> 3. Pension simplification and reform, 9%
> 4. Estate tax reform, 12%
> 5. Product liability and tort reform, 24%
>
> List of the Week from Arthur Andersen
>
> What questions did they ask? I would have thought windshield wiper standardization laws would have ranked lower.

5. Three premises needed for a good generalization

Here is what a good generalization should have:

> The sample is representative.
> The sample is big enough.
> The sample is studied well.
> *Therefore*: Generalization.

These three premises need to be true for the argument to be good, whether they are stated or not. But you could choose a big enough representative sample, study it well, get a trustworthy generalization, and still have a lousy argument.

A generalization is an argument. You need to examine it as you would any argument: Does the argument rely on slanted or vague language? What unstated premises are missing? Do you have good reason to believe the premises? Does the conclusion follow from the premises? As for other arguments, for some generalizations you will have to rely on "the experts" for whether to believe the premises, which include, "The sample is representative," "The sample is big enough," "The method of investigation was adequate." Even if you have a degree in statistics, you will rarely have access to the information necessary to evaluate those premises.

> Dick: A study I read said that people with large hands are better at math.
> Suzy: I guess that explains why I can't divide!
>
> You don't need a study to know that people with large hands do better at math: Babies have smaller hands, and they can't even add. All people is the wrong population to study.

6. The margin of error and confidence level

It's never reasonable to believe exact statistical generalizations: 37% of the people in your town who were surveyed wear glasses, so 37% of all people in your town wear glasses. No matter how many people in your town are surveyed, short of virtually all of them, you can't be confident that exactly 37% of all of them wear glasses. Rather, "37%, more or less, wear glasses" would be the right conclusion.

That "more or less" can be made fairly precise according to a theory of statistics. The **margin of error** tells us the range within which the actual number for the population is likely to fall.

> The opinion poll says that when voters were asked their preference, the incumbent was favored by 53% and the challenger by 47%, with a margin of error of 2%, and a confidence level of 95%. So the incumbent will win tomorrow.

From this survey they are concluding that the percentage of *all* voters who favor the incumbent is between 51% and 55%, while the challenger is favored by between 45% and 49%. How likely is it that they're right?

The **confidence level** measures that. Here the confidence level is 95%. That means there's a 95% chance it's true that the actual percentage of voters who prefer the incumbent is between 51% and 55%. If the confidence level were 60%, then the survey wouldn't be very reliable: There would be a 4-out-of-10 chance that the conclusion is false. Typically, if the confidence level is below 95%, the results won't even be announced. To summarize:

> Margin of error ± 2% gives the range around 53% in which it is likely that the population value lies. It is part of the conclusion: Between 51% and 55% of all voters favor the incumbent.
>
> Confidence level of 95% says exactly how likely it is that the population value lies in that range. It tells you how strong the generalization is.

The bigger the sample, the higher the confidence level and the lower the margin of error. The problem is to decide how much it's worth in extra time and expense to increase the sample size in order to get a stronger argument.

So will the incumbent win? The generalization that a majority of voters at the time of polling favor the incumbent is strong. But to conclude that the incumbent will win depends on what happens from the time of the polling to the voting. It depends on how fixed people are in their opinions, and on a lot of other unstated premises.

7. Variation in the population

Zoe:　Have you tried getting stuff from the Internet?
Tom:　Yeah, it's easy.
Zoe:　Really? It takes me forever to get anything off websites.
Tom:　What kind of computer do you have?
Zoe:　A PC I got a last year.
Tom:　You should try a Macintosh—I've got a new PowerMac, a 7300 that's 180 MHz. It's really fast.
Zoe:　You reckon it'd work for me, too?
Tom:　Sure.

Tom is generalizing. His conclusion is that any other PowerMac 7300/180 will perform the same as his. But isn't it a hasty generalization?

No. Tom's generalization is good, because any other PowerMac 7300/180 (that's in running order and using the same Internet connections) should perform exactly as his. They're all supposed to be exactly the same.

How big the sample has to be depends on how much **variation** there is in the population. If there is very little variation, then a small sample chosen haphazardly will do. Lots of variation demands a very large sample, and random sampling is the best way to get a representative sample.

8. Risk

With a shipment of 30 bolts, inspecting 15 of them and finding all of them O.K. would allow you to conclude that all the bolts are O.K. But if they're for the space shuttle, where a bad bolt could doom the spacecraft, you'd want to inspect each and every one of them.

On the other hand, suppose that for the first time you try eating a kumquat. Two hours later you get a stomach ache, and that night and the next morning you have diarrhea. I'll bet that you wouldn't eat a kumquat again. But the argument from this one experience that kumquats will always do this to you is pretty weak— it could have been something else you ate, or a twenty-four hour flu, or . . .

Risk doesn't change how strong an argument you have, only how strong an argument you want before you'll accept the conclusion.

9. Analogies and generalizations

Analogies are not generalizations. But they often require a generalization as premise.

The analysis of analogies usually ends in our trying to come up with a general claim that will make a valid or strong argument, as we did in Chapter 12, with "You should never blame someone for ending a catastrophe he didn't start."

Analogies lead us to generalizations. This car is like that one. They both had bad suspension. And here's another from the same manufacturer, which the owner says has bad suspension, too. So if you buy one of these cars, it'll have bad suspension. From two or three or seventeen examples, you figure that the next one will be the same. That's an analogy, all right, but the process is more one of generalization, for it's the unspoken general claim that's got to be proven: All cars from this manufacturer have bad suspension.

Summary   We generalize all the time: From a few instances (the sample) we conclude something about a bigger group (the population). Generalizations are arguments. They need three premises to be good: 1. The sample is representative, 2. The sample is big enough, 3. The sample is studied well.

Often we can figure out whether these premises are true. But it's harder for large populations with a lot of variation. The best way to ensure a sample is representative is to choose it randomly. Haphazardly chosen samples are often used, but we have no reason to believe a sample chosen haphazardly is representative.

Generally we will have to rely on the experts. They should tell us the margin of error and confidence level. Still, we can develop some sense of when a generalization is good or bad. Our best guide is to remember that a generalization is an argument, and all we've learned about analyzing arguments applies.

Exercises for Section B

1. Your candidate is favored by 56% to 44%, with a margin of error of 5% and a confidence level of 94%. What does that mean?

2. You read a poll that says the confidence level is 71%. Is the generalization reliable?

3. a. What do we call a weak generalization from a sample that is obviously too small?
   b. Can a sample of one ever be enough for a strong generalization?

4. The larger the _____ in the population, the larger the sample size must be.

5. What premises do we need for a good generalization?

6. a. You're at the supermarket trying to decide which quart basket of strawberries to buy. Describe and evaluate your procedure as a sampling and generalizing process. (Of course you can't actually taste one.)
   b. Now do the same supposing the basket is covered everywhere but on top.

7. The mayor of a town of 8,000 has to decide whether to spend town funds on renovating the park or hiring a part-time pest exterminator. He gets a reputable polling organization to do a survey.

   a. The results of the survey are 52% in favor of hiring a pest exterminator and 47% in favor of renovating the park, with 1% undecided, and a margin of error of 3%. The confidence level is 98%. Which choice will make the most people happy? Should he bet on that?
   b. The results are 58% in favor of hiring a pest exterminator and 24% in favor of renovating the park, with 8% undecided, and a margin of error of 9%. The confidence level is 94%. Which choice will make the most people happy? Should he bet on that?

8. Suppose you're on the city council and have to decide whether to put a bond issue for a new school on the next ballot. You don't want to do it if there's a good chance it will fail. You decide to do a survey, but haven't time to get a polling agency to do it. There are 7,200 people in your town. How would you go about picking a sample?

9. The president of your college would like to know how many students approve of the way she is handling her job. Explain why no survey is going to give her any useful ideas about how to improve her work.

10. You find a women's magazine in the doctor's waiting-room that has the results of a survey they've done on women's attitudes towards men with beards. They print the questions they asked in the last issue and say that they received over 10,000 responses from their readers, with 78% saying that they think that men with beards are really sexy. Should you tell your brother to grow a beard to improve his chances of getting a date?

11. Flo to Dick: I talked to all the people who live on this street and everyone who has a dog is really happy. So if I get my mom a dog, I'll be happy, too.

    How should Dick explain to Flo that she's not reasoning well?

12. Suppose your friend tells you:

    > "Lanolin is great for your hands—you ought to try it. It's what's on sheep wool naturally. How many shepherds have you seen with dry, chapped hands?"

    What's the first question you should ask?

13. Dr. E was born. Therefore, Dr. E will die.
    a. What generalization is needed to make this a good argument?
    b. What is the population?
    c. What is the sample?

Explain what's wrong with the following two uses of general claims.

14. Most great men are dead. The author of this book is a great man. Therefore, the author of this book is dead.

15. (Ad on Southern California radio station) Cadillac is the most popular selling luxury car in Southern California. (Unstated conclusion) So you should get a Cadillac.

Here are a few of Tom's attempts to use the ideas of this chapter.

Maria: Every time I've seen a stranger come to Dick's gate, Spot has barked. So Spot will always bark at strangers at Dick's gate.

Generalization (state it; if none, say so) Spot will bark at every stranger who comes to the gate.

Sample: All the times Maria has seen a stranger come to the gate.

Sample is representative? (yes or no, with explanation) Who knows?

Sample is big enough? (yes or no) No.

Sample is studied well? (yes or no) Yes—Maria knows if Spot barked when she was there.

Additional premises needed:

Good generalization? No. The sample isn't good.

You almost got it. The generalization shouldn't convince you—that's right. But the problem isn't that the sample isn't "good," but that Maria hasn't given any reason to believe that it's big enough and representative. Is "every time" once? Twice? 150 times? And are those times representative? It's enough that you have no reason to believe that the sample is representative to make this a bad generalization, i.e., a bad argument.

In a study of 5,000 people who owned pets in Anchorage, Alaska, dog owners expressed higher satisfaction with their pets and their lives. So dog owners are more satisfied with their pets and their own lives.

Generalization (state it; if none, say so) Dog owners are more satisfied with their
    pets and their own lives.

Sample: The people surveyed.

Sample is representative? (yes or no, with explanation) No.

Sample is big enough? (yes or no) Don't know.

Sample is studied well? (yes or no) Not sure—I don't know what questions were asked.

Additional premises needed:

Good generalization? No. The sample isn't good.

Right. Once you note that the sample isn't representative, you know immediately that the argument isn't good.

Every time the minimum wage is raised, there's squawking that it will cause inflation and decrease employment. And every time it doesn't. So watch for the same worthless arguments again this time.

Generalization (state it; if none, say so) Raising the minimum wage won't cause
    inflation and decrease employment.

Sample: Every time in the past that the minimum wage was raised.

Sample is representative? (yes or no, with explanation) Yes.

Sample is big enough? (yes or no) Yes—it was all the times before.

Sample is studied well? (yes or no) Yes—assuming the speaker knows what she's
    talking about.

Additional premises needed: None.

Good generalization? Yes.

The sample is big enough, since it can't get any bigger. But is it representative? Is there any reason to think that the situation now is like the situations in the past when the minimum wage was raised? It's like an analogy: This time is like the past times. Until the speaker fills that in, we shouldn't accept the conclusion.

Maria has asked all but three of the thirty-six people in her class whether they've ever used heroin. Only two said "yes." So Maria concludes that almost no one in the class has used heroin.

Generalization Almost no one in Maria's class has used heroin.

Sample: The thirty-four people Maria asked.

Sample is representative? Yes.

Sample is big enough? Yes.

Sample is studied well? (yes or no) Yes.

Additional premises needed:

Good generalization? Yes.

Do you really think everyone who's used heroin is going to admit it to a stranger? The sample isn't studied well—you'd need anonymous responses at least. So the generalization isn't good.

Evaluate Exercises 16–32 by answering the following questions.

    Generalization (state it; if none, say so)

    Sample:

    Sample is representative? (yes or no, with explanation)

    Sample is big enough? (yes or no)

    Sample is studied well? (yes or no)

    Additional premises needed:

    Good generalization?

16. It's incredible how much information they can put on a CD. I just bought one that contains a whole encyclopedia.

17. Don't take a course from Dr. E. I know three people who failed his course last term.

18. What's the IRS doing? It's always picking on us middle-class guys! Both my brother and I got audited this year.

19. (At a health-food store)
    Customer: Have you got anything for this flu?
    Owner: Try this herbal tea. Everyone who's tried it here says it helped
                  with the coughing.

20. Everyone I've met at this college is either on one of the athletic teams or has a boyfriend or girlfriend on one of the athletic teams. Gosh, I guess just about everyone at this college is involved in sports.

21. Dick: Hold the steering wheel.
    Zoe: What are you doing? Stop! Are you crazy?
    Dick: I'm just taking my sweater off.
    Zoe: My Dog, I can't believe you did that. It's *so* dangerous.
    Dick: Don't be silly. I've done it a thousand times before.

22. My grandmother was diagnosed with cancer seven years ago. She refused any treatment that was offered to her over the years. She's perfectly healthy and doing great. The treatment for cancer is just a scam to get people's money.

23. Maria goes out with two bald men and decides that she'll date only bald men in the future, they're so sexy.

24. Maria goes out with two men who smoke and decides that she won't date men who smoke anymore because their breath smells like old ashtrays.

25. Tom: Can you pick up that pro basketball player who's coming to the rally today?
    Dick: I can't. Zoe's got the car. Why not ask Suzy?
    Tom: She's got one of those compact Yodas. They're too small for someone over 6'4".

26. Give the baby his pacifier so he'll stop crying. Every time I give him the pacifier he stops crying.

27. (Overheard at a doctor's office)
    I won't have high blood pressure today because I got enough sleep last night. The last two times you've taken my blood pressure I've rested well the night before and both times it was normal.

28. We will be late for church because we have to wait for Gina. She's always late. She's been late seven Sundays in a row.

29. Gina will be at Club Rio Friday night. She's been going there every Friday night since it opened two months ago.,

30. Maria: I've been searching for jobs on the Internet by description. I didn't look at any jobs called "sales associate" or "sales," because all the sales jobs I've had before didn't work out or I didn't like them.

31. **Biology breeds grumpy old men**
    Men lose brain tissue at almost three times the rate of women, curbing their memory, concentration and reasoning power—and perhaps turning them into "grumpy old men"—a researcher said Wednesday.

    "Even in the age range of 18 to 45, you can see a steady decline in the ability to perform such (attention-oriented) tasks in men," said Ruben C. Gur, a professor of psychology at the University of Pennsylvania.

    Gur said shrinking brains may make men grumpier because some of the tissue loss is in the left frontal region of the brain, which seems to be connected to depression.

    "Grumpy old men may be biological," said Gur, who is continuing to study whether there is a connection.

    However, one researcher not affiliated with the study said Wednesday that other recent studies contradict Gur's findings on shrinkage.

    The findings, which augment earlier research published by Gur and colleagues, are the result of his studies of the brain functions of 24 women and 37 men over the past decade. He measured the brain volume with an MRI machine and studied metabolism rates. From young adulthood to middle age, men lose 15% of their frontal lobe volume, 8.5% of temporal lobe, he said. Women, while they have "very mild" shrinkage, lose tissue in neither lobe. For the brain overall, men lose tissue three times faster.

    Gur found that the most dramatic loss was in men's frontal lobes, which control attention, abstract reasoning, mental flexibility and inhibition of impulses, and the temporal lobe [which] governs memory.   Associated Press, April, 1996

32. **Sex unlikely to cause heart attacks**
    Sexual intercourse is unlikely to trigger a heart attack, even among people who have already survived one, according to a study that is the first to examine this widespread fear.

    Only 1 percent of heart attacks were triggered by sexual activity in a nationwide sample of nearly 900 heart attack survivors who said they were sexually active.

    The odds of suffering a heart attack after engaging in sex are only about 2 in a million, the study found—about twice as high as the average hourly risk of heart attack among 50-year-old Americans with no overt sign of coronary artery disease.

    "It's easy to get the message from movies, and even from Shakespeare, that sexual activity can trigger heart attacks," said Dr. James Muller of New England Deaconess Hospital in Boston, who led the study. "It's part of the mythology, and it's certainly in the minds of many cardiac patients and their spouses."

"What has been lacking in the past are actual numbers. Now the numbers are available, and the risk is quite, quite low."

Furthermore, regular exercise can substantially reduce the risk of a sex-triggered heart attack.

Patients who never engaged in heavy physical exertion, or got vigorous exercise only once a week, had a threefold risk of heart attack in the two hours after sexual activity. But the relative risk dropped to twofold among patients who exercise twice a week, and only 1.2 fold among those who exercised three or more times weekly.

The new figures, which appear in this week's Journal of the American Medical Association, suggest that sexual activity triggers 15,000 of the 1.5 million heart attacks that occur in this nation annually.

"Although sexual activity doubles the risk" of heart attack, the researchers noted, the effect on annual risk "is negligible because the absolute risk difference is small, the risk is transient and the activity is relatively infrequent."

For instance, for an individual without cardiac disease, weekly sexual activity would increase the annual risk of a heart attack from 1 percent to 1.01 percent.

Richard Knox, *Boston Globe,* May 8, 1996

33. Would you try this new procedure? Explain.

Chili peppers a red hot cure for surgical pain
When burning pain lingers months after surgery, doctors say there is a red-hot cure: chili peppers.

In a study, an ointment made with capsaicin, the stuff that makes chili peppers hot, brought relief to patients with tender surgical scars, apparently by short-circuiting the pain.

Patients undergoing major cancer surgery, such as mastectomies or lung operations, are sometimes beset by sharp, burning pain in their surgical scars that lasts for months, even years. Sometimes the misery is so bad that sufferers cannot even stand the weight of clothing on their scar, even though it is fully healed.

The condition, seen in about 5 percent or fewer of all cases, results from damage to the nerves during surgery. Ordinary pain killers don't work, and the standard treatment is antidepressant drugs.

However, these powerful drugs have side effects. So in search of a better alternative, doctors tested a cream made with capsaicin on 99 patients who typically had suffered painful surgical scars at least six months.

Patients preferred capsaicin over a dummy cream by 3-to-1.

"The therapy clearly worked," said Dr. Charles L. Loprinzi, head of medical oncology at the Mayo Clinic. He released his data Monday at the annual meeting of the American Society for Clinical Oncology.

Capsaicin is believed to work by blocking substance P, a natural chemical that carries pain impulses between nerve cells. That same blocking effect may explain why people who eat hot peppers all the time develop a tolerance to the burn.

Dr. Alan Lyss of Missouri Baptist Medical Center in St. Louis called it "a creative, new and very inexpensive way to take care of some kinds of cancer pain."

Capsaicin is sold in drug stores without a prescription, and a tube that lasts a month costs about $16. . . .

In the study, the patients were randomly assigned to capsaicin cream or the look-alike placebo four times a day for eight-week intervals. Until the study was over, no one knew which was which.

Patients kept score of their pain. It went down 53 percent while using capsaicin but only 17 percent while on the placebo. About 10 percent said their pain disappeared completely.

The doctors followed the patients for two months after they stopped using capsaicin and found that pain did not come back. Longer follow-up will be necessary to see if the treatment relieves the pain permanently. . . .

Associated Press, May 21, 1996

For Exercises 34 and 35, identify the analogy and explain how a generalization is required.

34. Dick: What do you think about buying a Yoda sedan?
    Zoe: It's not a good idea. Remember, Suzy got a Yoda and she's had trouble with it from day one.

35. Of chimpanzees fed one pound of chocolate per day in addition to their usual diet, 72% became obese within two months. Therefore, it is likely that most humans who eat 2% of their body weight in chocolate daily will become obese within two months.

Key Words

generalization	random sample
population	law of large numbers
sample	gambler's fallacy
inductive evidence	hasty generalization
statistical generalization	anecdotal evidence
representative sample	margin of error
biased sample	confidence level
haphazard sample	variation in a population

Further Study Courses on statistics will explain the nature of sampling and generalizing. A course on inductive logic in a philosophy department will study more fully the topics of this chapter and the next. A course on philosophy of science will study the role of generalizations in science. Many disciplines, such as sociology, marketing, and the health sciences give courses on the use of sampling and generalizing that are specific to their subject.

A good book with lots of examples you can understand about statistics in reasoning is *Flaws and Fallacies in Statistical Thinking,* by Stephen K. Campbell. Also good is *How to Lie with Statistics,* by Darrell Huff.

15 Cause and Effect

Nancy caused the accident. Smoking causes cancer. Gravity causes the moon to stay in orbit. These are *causal claims*. We make lots of them, though they may not always contain the word "causes" or "caused." For example: "Jogging keeps you healthy" or "Taking an aspirin every other day cuts the risk of having a heart attack." And every time someone blames you, you're encountering a claim that you caused something that was bad and, apparently, avoidable.

What does a claim about causes look like? How do we judge whether it's true?

A. What is the Cause?

1. Causes and effects

What exactly is a *cause*? Consider what Dick said last night:

> Spot caused me to wake up.

Spot is the thing that somehow caused Dick to wake up. But it's not just that Spot existed. It's what he was doing that caused Dick to wake up:

Spot's barking caused
Dick to wake up.

So barking is a cause and waking is an effect? What exactly is barking? What is waking? Let's simplify to something we know. The easiest way to describe the cause is to say:

> Spot barked.

The easiest way to describe the effect is to say:

> Dick woke up.

These are claims. We know a lot about claims: whether they're objective or subjective, whether a sentence is too vague to be a claim, how to judge whether an unsupported claim is true. Let's work with claims. So now we have:

$$\text{Spot barked} \xrightarrow[\text{caused}]{} \text{Dick woke up}$$

What is this relationship of being caused?

It has to be a very strong relation. Once Spot barked it had to be true that Dick woke up. There is no way for "Spot barked" to have been true and "Dick woke up" false.

We know about that relationship—it's the relation between the premises and conclusion of a valid argument. But here we're not trying to convince anyone that the conclusion is true: We know that Dick woke up. What we can carry over from our study of arguments is how to look for all the possibilities—all the ways the premises could be true and conclusion false—to determine if there is cause and effect. But there has to be more to say there's cause and effect.

2. The normal conditions

A lot has to be true for it to be impossible for "Spot barked" to be true and "Dick woke up" to be false:

> Dick was sleeping soundly up to the time that Spot barked.
> Spot barked at 3 a.m.
> Dick doesn't normally awake at 3 a.m.
> Spot was close to where Dick was sleeping.
> There was no other loud noise at the time.
> $\vdots$

We could go on forever. But as with arguments, we state what we think is important and leave out the obvious. If someone challenged us, we could add "There was no earthquake at the time"—but we just assume that.

The "obvious" unstated claims that are needed to establish cause and effect, comparable to unstated premises for an argument, are what we call the ***normal conditions.*** We can take claims as normal conditions only if they are obviously true and make the argument valid.

3. Particular causes, generalizations, and general causes

Spot waking Dick is a ***particular cause and effect.*** This happened once, then that happened once.

To establish the causal claim, we have to consider all the possible ways Spot could have barked, under the normal conditions, and ask whether Dick would have woken up. With a physical situation like this we could even do experiments to look at some of the possible ways the cause could be true, say, getting Spot to bark at 3:23 a.m. on a cloudless night, or getting Spot to bark at 4:18 a.m. on an overcast night. We need that every time Spot barked, Dick woke up. There has to be a ***perfect correlation***: every time this happens, that happens. So to establish a particular cause and effect, we might try to establish a generalization.

Alternatively, we could generalize from this particular cause and effect to any situation like it: "Very loud barking by someone's dog near him when he is sleeping will always wake him, if he's not deaf." That is,

> Very loud barking by someone's dog near him when he is sleeping *causes* him to wake, if he's not deaf.

This is a ***general cause and effect*** claim: for it to be true, lots of particular cause and effect claims must be true. The normal conditions for this general claim won't be specific just to the one time Spot woke Dick, but will be general. Here, too, in trying to survey the possible ways that the cause could be true, we might want to establish a generalization:

Every time that anyone's encountered these conditions—the barking, the sleeper, etc.—the sleeper woke up.

Exercises for Sections A.1–A.3

For each of the following sentences, if appropriate rewrite it as a claim that uses the word "causes" or "caused." If it's a *particular* causal claim, state the cause and the effect as claims. Here are two of Tom's homeworks.

Your teaching made me fail this class.

Causal claim: Your teaching caused me to fail this class.
Particular or *general*? Particular.
Cause (stated as a claim): You taught badly.
Effect (stated as a claim): I failed.

You've got the idea. But why did you say the cause was "You taught badly"? Maybe it should be "You taught well, but didn't slow down for unprepared students." The problem is that the original sentence is <u>too vague</u>.

Drinking coffee keeps people awake.

Causal claim: Drinking coffee causes people to stay awake.
Particular or *general*? General.
Cause (stated as a claim): People drink coffee.
Effect (stated as a claim): People stay awake.

O.K., but remember that with a general causal claim there isn't <u>a</u> cause and effect, but lots of them. So there's no point in filling in after "cause" and "effect." When we try to figure out a particular causal claim that this general one covers, we see the real problem: Maria drank coffee yesterday, Maria stayed awake. How long did she stay awake? What would count for making this true? It's still too vague.

1. The police car's siren got me to pull over.

2. You doing so badly in this class made me teach badly.

3. Because you were late, we missed the beginning of the movie.

4. Dogs make great pets.

5. I better not get the pizza with anchovies, because every time I do, I get heartburn.

6. I would have passed the exam if Dr. E hadn't collected the papers five minutes early.

7. You allowing me to take the final exam a day early made it possible for me to pass.

8. Watching golf makes me want to play golf.

9. Penicillin prevents serious infection.

10. If it weren't for my boyfriend, I'd have no problems.

11. Because of religion, people act more virtuously.

12. The result of watching too much TV is lessened intelligence.

13. Our airplane took off from gate number thirteen. No wonder we're experiencing so much turbulence.

14. Your big mouth led to my getting fired.

15. The garage being under my bedroom makes my room hotter than the rest of the house.

16. Being cold causes people to shiver.

17. Zoe made me lose my virginity.

4. The cause precedes the effect

We wouldn't accept that Spot's barking caused Dick to wake up if Spot began barking only *after* Dick woke up. The cause has to precede the effect. That is, "Spot barked" became true before "Dick woke up" became true.

For there to be cause and effect, the cause has to become true before the effect becomes true.

5. The cause makes a difference

We usually need a perfect correlation to establish cause and effect. But a correlation alone is not enough.

Dr. E has a desperate fear of elephants. So he buys a special wind chime and puts it outside his door to keep the elephants away. He lives in Cedar City, Utah, at 6,000 feet above sea level in a desert, and he confidently claims that the wind chime causes the elephants to stay away. After all, ever since he put up the wind chime he hasn't seen any elephants.

There's a perfect correlation here: "Wind chime up on Tuesday, no elephants," Dr. E notes in his diary.

Why are we sure the wind chime being up did *not* cause elephants to stay away? Because even if there had been no wind chime, the elephants would have stayed away. Which elephants? All elephants. The wind chime works, but so would anything else. The wind chime doesn't *make a difference*.

For there to be cause and effect, it must be that if there were no cause, there wouldn't be the effect. If Spot had not barked, Dick would not have woken up.

6. The cause and effect are close in space and time (tracing the cause backwards)

So Spot caused Dick to wake up. But Dick and Zoe's neighbor tells them that's not right. It was because of a raccoon in her yard that Spot started barking. So really, a raccoon entering her yard caused Dick to wake up.

    But it was no accident that the raccoon came into their neighbor's yard. She'd left her trash can uncovered. So *really* the neighbor's not covering her trash caused Dick to wake up.

    But really, it was because Spot had knocked over her trash can and the top wouldn't fit, so their neighbor didn't bother to cover her trash. So it was Spot's knocking over the trash can that caused Dick to wake up.

    But really, . . .

    This is silly. We could go backwards forever. (If you assume that every action is caused by something, we would have to go backwards forever—right to the start of it all.) We stop at the first step: Spot's barking caused Dick to wake up.

Dick is just wrong. The purported cause—Spot lying next to where Dick walked—was too far away from the effect.

The cause has to be close in time and space to the effect. That is, the objects involved in the cause and the effect were relatively close to each other, and the effect became true relatively soon after the cause became true.

But what do we mean by "relatively close" and "relatively soon after"? That will depend on the circumstances, and you will have to use your judgment. The astronomer is right when she says that a star shining caused the image on the photograph, even though that star is very far away, and the light took millions of years to arrive. The problem isn't how distant in time and space the cause is from the effect. The problem is how much has come between the cause and effect— whether we can specify the normal conditions.

> *When we trace a cause too far back the problem is that the normal conditions begin to multiply.* There are too many conditions for us to imagine what would be necessary to establish that it is impossible for the cause to have been true and effect false. When you get that far, you know you've gone too far.

7. Criteria for cause and effect

> ### Necessary Criteria for Cause and Effect
> 1. The cause precedes the effect.
> 2. It is impossible that the cause could be true and the effect false, given the normal conditions.
> 3. The cause makes a difference.
> 4. The cause precedes and is close in space and time to the effect.

That all these hold, however, is not always sufficient for there to be cause and effect. Worse, there's real difficulty applying them: What exactly are the normal conditions? Why is this particular claim singled out as the cause instead of another? Why do we stop with this claim instead of tracing the cause back further? Why is this one person or object singled out in the cause? Let's look at some examples.

B. Examples

Are the following examples of cause and effect? What more do we need to know?

Example 1 Nancy caused the accident.

Analysis We're interested in who or what was involved in the cause when we go about assigning blame or fault. But it's not just that Nancy exists. Rather:

> *Cause*: Nancy didn't pay attention.
> *Effect*: The cars collided.

Is this really cause and effect? Did the cause make a difference? If Nancy had been paying attention would the cars still have collided? Since she was broadsided by a car running through a red light where a line of cars blocked her vision, we would say that it didn't matter that she was changing a CD at the time: The cars would have collided even if she had been paying attention, or so we all imagine. The purported cause didn't make a difference. It's not cause and effect.

Example 2 Lack of rain caused the crops to fail.

Analysis We've talked about causes as if something active has to happen. But almost any claim that describes the world could qualify as a cause.

> *Cause*: There was no rain.
> *Effect*: The crops failed.

This example was true a couple years back in the Midwest.

Example 3 Oxygen in the laboratory caused the match to burn.

Analysis Harry works in a laboratory where there's not supposed to be any oxygen. The materials are highly flammable, and he has to wear breathing gear. He was joking around with a friend and struck a match, knowing it wouldn't ignite.

It seems there was a leak in his face mask.

The normal conditions don't include "Oxygen is in the laboratory." That, along with Harry striking the match, caused the match to burn. *There may be several claims we want to say jointly are the cause*: Oxygen was in the laboratory; Harry carried matches into the laboratory with him; Harry struck the match. The rest can be relegated to the normal conditions.

Example 4 Running over nails causes your tires to go flat.

Analysis This is a plausible general causal claim. But it's wrong. There's not good inductive evidence. Lots of times we run over nails and our tires don't go flat.
But sometimes they do. What's correct is:

Running over nails *can cause* your tires to go flat.

That is, if the conditions are right, running over a nail will cause your tire to go flat.
The difference between *causes* and *can cause* is the difference between the normal conditions. For "causes" we feel we don't need much that isn't obvious; for "can cause" we feel that we could list claims, but they aren't perhaps "normal" ones we daily expect. We'll learn how to evaluate claims like this in Section D.

Example 5 God caused the universe.

Analysis This is just a way of saying "God created the universe."

Example 6 "When more and more people are thrown out of work, unemployment results." Calvin Coolidge

Analysis You don't have to be smart to be president. This isn't cause and effect; it's a definition.

Example 7 Birth causes death.

Analysis In some sense this is right. But it seems wrong. Why?
What's the cause? What's the effect? The example is a general causal claim covering every particular claim like:

That this creature was born caused it to die.

We have lots of inductive evidence: Socrates died. My dog Juney died. My teacher in high school died. President Kennedy died . . .
The problem seems to be that though this is true, it's uninteresting. It's tracing the cause too far back. Being born should be part of the normal conditions when we have the effect that someone died.

Example 8 Zoe: Fear of getting fired causes me to get to work on time.

Analysis What is fear?

Cause: Zoe is afraid of getting fired.
Effect: Zoe gets to work on time.

Is it possible for Zoe to be afraid of getting fired and still not get to work on time? Certainly, but not, perhaps, under normal conditions: Zoe sets her alarm; the electricity doesn't go off; there isn't bad weather; Zoe doesn't oversleep; . . .

But doesn't the causal claim mean it's because she's afraid that Zoe makes sure that these claims will be true, or that she'll get to work even if one or more is false? She doesn't let herself oversleep due to her fear.

In that case how can we judge whether what Zoe said is true? It's easy to think of cases where the cause is true and effect false. So we have to add normal conditions. But that Zoe gets to work regardless of conditions that aren't normal is what makes her consider her fear to be the cause.

Subjective causes are often a matter of feeling, some sense that we control what we do. They are often too vague for us to classify as true or false. It's subjective whether Zoe is afraid, but whether there is cause and effect is not subjective.

Example 9   Dick: Hold the steering wheel.
　　　　　　Zoe:　　What are you doing? Stop! Are you crazy?
　　　　　　Dick: I'm just taking my sweater off.
　　　　　　Zoe:　　My Dog, I can't believe you did that. It's *so* dangerous.
　　　　　　Dick: Don't be silly. I've done it a thousand times before.
　　　　　　Crash　　　later . . .
　　　　　　Dick: You had to turn the steering wheel!? That made us crash.

Analysis   The purported cause: Zoe turned the steering wheel. The effect: The car crashed. The necessary criteria are satisfied.

But as they say in court, Zoe's turning the steering wheel is a ***foreseeable consequence*** of Dick making her take the wheel, which is the real cause. The normal conditions are not just what has to be true before the cause, but also what will normally *follow* the cause.

Example 10   Dick: Wasn't that awful what happened to old Mr. Grzegorczyk?
　　　　　　　Zoe:　　You mean those tree trimmers who dropped a huge branch on him and killed him?
　　　　　　　Dick: You only got half the story. He'd had a heart attack in his car and pulled over to the side. He was lying on the pavement when the branch hit him—he would have died anyway.
　　　　　　　Zoe:　　But I heard his wife is going to collect from the tree company.

Analysis   What's the cause of death? Mr. Grzegorczyk would have died anyway. So the tree branch falling on him wouldn't have made a difference.

But the tree branch falling on him isn't a foreseeable consequence, part of the normal conditions of his stumbling out of his car with a heart attack. As they say in court, it's an ***intervening cause.*** The courts, usually juries made up of people like you, have to decide what is the cause of Mr. Grzegorczyk's death. There's no clear answer, though these kinds of cases have been debated for centuries. (If you admit that you had a critical thinking course, the lawyers might try to get you disqualified as too intelligent.)

Example 11   Zoe: Every time I wash my car, it rains.

Suzy: Well, don't wash your car today. I want my picnic to be fun.

Analysis Behind Suzy's comment is a general causal claim:

Zoe's washing her car causes it to rain.

We just laugh. Of course there's no connection.

But suppose that it was always clear and forecast sunny for the next two days when Zoe washed her car. And it always rained within twelve hours. And this happened thirty times over two years. We'd have pretty good inductive evidence for the general claim.

But we'd still be suspicious. Inductive evidence alone doesn't seem to be enough to convince us that if the cause weren't true, the effect wouldn't be true. We want a *theory* that connects cause and effect.

Compare this to the claim:

The gas produced by cows' digestion causes the atmosphere to warm up.

Sounds pretty silly. What inductive evidence do we have? There are more cows now than ever before, and it's getting warmer. Pretty slim evidence.

But we have a theory. Scientists estimate the amount of methane produced by cows, calculate how this traps heat in the atmosphere, and say that the gas produced by cows is one of many causes that the atmosphere is warming up, not perhaps sufficient by itself.

Example 12 The Treaty of Versailles caused WWII.

Analysis The cause: The Treaty of Versailles was agreed to and enforced. The effect: WWII occurred.

To analyze a conjecture like this an historian will write a book. The normal conditions have to be spelled out. You have to show that it was a foreseeable consequence of the enforcement of the Treaty of Versailles that Germany would re-arm.

But was it foreseeable that Chamberlain would back down over Czechoslovakia? More plausible is that the signing of the Treaty of Versailles is *a* cause, not *the* cause of WWII.

Example 13 Poltergeists are making the pictures fall down from their hooks.

Analysis To accept this, we have to believe that poltergeists exist. That's dubious. Worse, it's probably not *testable*: How could you determine if there are poltergeists? Dubious claims that aren't testable are the worst candidates for causes.

Exercises for Sections A and B

1. What criteria are necessary for there to be cause and effect?

2. What criteria do we know are sufficient for there to be cause and effect?

3. Why isn't a perfect correlation enough to justify cause and effect? Explain.

4. Comparable to the unstated premises of an argument, what do we call the claims that must be true for a causal claim to be true?

Here's some of Tom's work on cause and effect. He's supposed to fill in after the italics and explain why the causal claim is plausible or clearly wrong.

> **I used Diabolic Grow on my plants and they grew great! I'll always use it.**
>
> *Causal claim*: (unstated) Diabolic Grow caused my plants to grow great.
> *Cause*: The speaker put Diabolic Grow on his plants.
> *Effect*: The plants grew great.
> *Cause before and close in space and time to effect?* Apparently so.
> *Cause makes a difference?* It seems so, but did the cause really make a difference? Maybe they would have grown great anyway. Some years that happens when it rains at just the right time in the spring.
> *Evaluation*: You'd need a lot more evidence to believe the claim.
> *Excellent! You're thinking critically.*

For each of Exercises 5–16 isolate the causal claim. Then evaluate it, explaining why it's plausible or clearly wrong. That is, answer these questions:

> *Causal claim*:
> *Cause*:
> *Effect*:
> *Cause before and close in space and time to effect?*
> *Cause makes a difference?*
> *Evaluation*:

5. Our airplane took off from gate number thirteen. No wonder we're experiencing so much turbulence.

6. Dick: Ooh, my stomach hurts.
   Zoe: Serves you right. You really pigged out on the nachos and salsa last night. They always give you a stomach ache.

7. Zoe: This is horrible. My license was revoked!
   Dick: That's what you get for driving after you drank so much.

8. Suzy: I'm really depressed today because of the dark sky.

9. Marriage is the chief cause of divorce.

10. (OSHA booklet, "Safety with Beef Cattle")
    Hazards are one of the main causes of accidents.

11. Zoe: We've run out of gas.
    Dick: It's 'cause you forgot to fill up before we left town.

12. The emphasis on Hollywood figures in the media causes people to use drugs, because people want to emulate the stars.

13. My instructor's high standards make me work hard in this class.

14. Harry's college education helped him get a high-paying job the year after he graduated.

15. Dick: Every day I run up this hill and it's no big deal. Why am I so beat today?
    Zoe: It's 'cause you stayed out late and didn't get enough sleep.

16. Zoe: My life's a mess. I've never really been happy since all those years ago in high school you told Sally that I killed Puff. She believed your stupid joke, and made sure I wasn't a cheerleader. I'll never be a cheerleader. It's your fault I'm so miserable now.
    Dick: There, there.

17. Make up five causal claims and trade with a classmate to analyze.

18. Judge: I find that Nancy sustained serious injuries in this accident. There is sufficient evidence that the defendant ran a red light and broadsided her car, causing the injuries. But I hold that Nancy was partly responsible for the severity of her injuries in that she was not wearing a seatbelt. Therefore, Nancy shall collect only 50% of the costs associated with this accident.

    Explain the judge's decision in terms of normal conditions and foreseeable consequences.

19. Mickey has taken his four-wheel-drive jeep out into the desert to explore on this hot sunny Sunday. But his two cousins want to see him dead. Bertha has put poison in Mickey's five-gallon canteen. Richard, not knowing of Bertha's plans, has put a very small hole in the canteen.

    Mickey's car breaks down. He's getting hot and thirsty. His cellular phone doesn't work because he forgot to recharge it. He goes to get some water and finds the canteen empty . . . *music swells*

    Overcome by guilt later in the year, both Bertha and Richard confess. Who should be blamed for causing Mickey's death by thirst?

C. Common Mistakes in Reasoning about Causes

1. Reversing cause and effect

Tom: That ecology group is twisting their members' minds around.
Dick: Huh?
Tom: They're all spouting off about the project to log the forest on Cedar Mountain. All in lockstep. What do they do to those guys?

Tom's got it backwards. Joining the group doesn't cause the members to become concerned about the logging on Cedar Mountain. It's the people who are concerned about ecological issues already who join the group. He's reversed the cause and effect.

Suzy: Sitting too close to the TV ruins your eyesight.
Zoe: How do you know?

Suzy: Well, two of my high school friends used to sit really close,
and both of them wear really thick glasses now.

Zoe: Maybe they sat so close because they had bad eyesight.

Even if Suzy had a huge sample instead of just anecdotal evidence, it would be just as plausible to reverse the cause and effect. That doesn't mean Suzy's claim is false. It just shows we have no good reason to believe that sitting too close to the TV ruins your eyesight.

2. Overlooking a common cause

Dick: Zoe is irritable because she can't sleep properly.

Tom: Maybe Zoe's both irritable and unable to sleep because she's been drinking so much espresso.

We don't show a causal claim is false by raising the possibility of a common cause for both cause and effect. But we do put the claim in doubt. Then we have to use our judgment about which causal claim seems most likely.

3. Looking too hard for a cause

Every Tuesday and Thursday at 1:55 p.m. a tall red-headed lady walks by the door of Professor Zzzyzzx's classroom. Then he arrives right at 2 p.m. When Suzy says the lady walking by the door causes Professor Zzzyzzx to arrive on time at his class she's jumping to a conclusion: It happened after, so that's the cause. We call that kind of reasoning *post hoc, ergo propter hoc* (after this, therefore because of this).

Zoe belched loudly in the shower with the bathroom window open, and she and Dick haven't seen Spot since. He must have run away because she belched.

That's just *post hoc ergo propter hoc*. A possible cause is being overlooked: Perhaps someone left the gate open, or someone let him out, or . . .

We look for causes because we want to understand, to explain, so we can control our future. But sometimes the best we can say is that it's *coincidence*.

I scored well on that last exam and I was wearing my red striped shirt. I'd better wear it every time I take an exam.

I hit the jackpot on the slot machine and got $5,000 just after I prayed I would. So praying caused me to win.

Before your jaw drops open in amazement when a friend tells you that a piano fell on his teacher the day after your friend dreamt that he saw him in a recital, remember the law of large numbers: If it's possible, given long enough, it'll happen. After all, most of us dream—say one dream a night for fifty million adults in the U.S. That's three hundred and fifty million dreams per week. With the elasticity in interpreting dreams and what constitutes a "dream coming true," it would be amazing if a lot of dreams *didn't* "accurately predict the future."

But doesn't everything have a cause? Shouldn't we look for it? For much that happens in our lives we won't be able to figure out the cause—we just don't know enough. We must, normally, ascribe lots of happenings to chance, to coincidence, or else we have paranoia and end up paying a lot of money to phone psychics. I'm not against mysticism and religion as possible paths to truth. But these tawdry interpretations aren't on that road.

Contributed by a student with an unusual first name:
While I was parking my car before school one day, I was hit in the rear by another car. The campus police came and the so-called incident was both our faults because the other driver was not looking while backing up, and I was on the wrong side of the road because I wanted to back into my parking space. The strange thing is after the matter was handled, the person who hit me said, "Isn't it weird that we got into an accident and we both share the same birthdate?"

Another time, while driving the same car, I was picking my mother up at work and another car hit me while I was driving past her. She said it was my fault, and I did not agree, how could I hit her with the back side of my car while I was driving ahead of her as she was backing out? The scare came when she found out the car wasn't mine. And as my mother came onto the scene she asked if I got the other driver's name. To my surprise, we both share the same first name.

Is this coincidence or are cosmic forces bringing us together?

What cosmic force? What cause? Every time you say, "Why me God, why me?" you are looking for a cause where it's pretty much hopeless to look for a cause. That way leads to superstition and bad theology.

Sometimes our best response to a causal claim is:
- Did you ever think that might just be coincidence?
- Just because it followed doesn't mean it was caused by . . .
- Have you thought about another possible cause, namely . . .
- Maybe you got the cause and the effect reversed.
- Not always, but maybe under some conditions . . .

4. How to look for the cause

I have a waterfall in my backyard in Cedar City. The pond has a thick rubberized plastic pond liner, and I have a pump and hose that carry water from the pond along the rock face of a small rise to where the water spills out and runs down more rocks with concrete between them. Last summer I noticed that the pond kept getting low every day and had to be refilled. You don't waste water in the desert, so I figured I'd better find out what was causing the loss of water.

I thought of all the ways the pond could be leaking: The hose that carries the water could have a leak, the valve connections could be leaking, the pond liner could be ripped (the dogs get into the pond to cool off in the summer), there could be cracks in the concrete, or it could be evaporation and spray from where the water comes out at the top of the fountain.

I had to figure out which (if any) of these was the problem. First I got someone to come in and use a high pressure spray on the waterfall to clean it. We took the rocks out and vacuumed out the pond. Then we patched every possible spot on the pond liner where there might be a leak.

Then we patched all the concrete on the waterfall part and water-sealed it. We checked the valve connections and tightened them. They didn't leak. And the hose wasn't leaking because there weren't any wet spots along its path.

Then I refilled the pond. It kept losing water at about the same rate.

It wasn't the hose, it wasn't the connections, it wasn't the pond liner, it wasn't the concrete watercourse. So it had to be the spray and evaporation.

I reduced the flow of water so there wouldn't be so much spray. There was a lot less water loss. The rest I figured was probably evaporation, though there might still be small leaks.

In trying to find the cause of the water leak I was using the method scientists often use:

> *Conjecture possible causes, and then by experiment eliminate them until there is only one. Check that one: Does it make a difference? If the purported cause is eliminated, is there still the effect?*

Not much spray, not much water loss. I couldn't be absolutely sure, but it seemed very likely I had isolated the cause.

The best prophylactic against making common mistakes in reasoning about causes is experiment. Often we can't do an experiment, but we can do an imaginary experiment. That's what we've always done in checking for validity: Imagine the possibilities.

Jumping to conclusions about causes isn't a sign of a rich imagination. ("Gee, I'd never have thought the red-haired lady caused Professor Zzzyzzx to arrive on time.") It's a sign of an impoverished imagination.

Exercises for Section C

For Exercises 1–4, come up with a method to determine whether there's cause and effect.

1. Pressing the "Door Close" button in the elevator causes the doors to close.

2. Zoe's belching caused Spot to run away.

3. The red-head walking by the classroom causes Professor Zzzyzzx to arrive at class on time.

4. Reducing the speed limit to 55 m.p.h. saves lives.

5. When should we trust authorities rather than figure out a cause for ourselves?

6. Explain: The way to answer a charge of *post hoc ergo propter hoc* is to show that the purported cause does make a difference.

7. Explain why a *post hoc* argument is just a bad generalization.

8. Explain why it's not amazing that every day a few dream predictions come true.

Tom was asked to bring in a causal claim he made recently and evaluate it. Here's his work:

> **The only time I've had a really bad backache is right after I went bicycling early in the morning when it was so cold last week. Bicycling never bothered me before. So it must be the cold weather that caused my back to hurt after cycling.**
>
> *Causal claim*: The cold weather caused my back to hurt after cycling.
>
> *Cause*: It was cold when I went cycling.
>
> *Effect*: I got a backache.
>
> *Evaluation* (Criteria satisfied? Common mistake? How could you determine if true?):
>> The criteria seem to be satisfied. But now I'm wondering if I haven't overlooked some other cause. I also had an upset stomach. So maybe it was the flu. Or maybe it was tension, since I'd had a fight with Suzy the night before. I guess I'll have to try cycling in the cold again to find out.
>>
>> *Good. But you're still looking for the cause, when it may be a cause. Another possible cause: Did you warm up first? Another possibility: You'll never know for sure.*

9. Write down a causal claim that you made recently and evaluate it like Tom's example. Have a classmate critique your evaluation.

Evaluate Exercises 10–22 in the same way that Tom did above, answering the following:

> *Causal claim*:
> *Cause*:
> *Effect*:
> *Evaluation* (Criteria satisfied? Common mistake? How could you determine if true?):

10. Dick: (*Bending over, sweating and cursing*) There's something wrong with my bike.
    Zoe: What?

> Dick: Something's going "click," "click," "click" all the time.
> Zoe: Must be something that's moving.
> Dick: Duh. Here, hold it up while I turn the pedals.   *click, click, click, . . .*
> Zoe: Yup, there it is.
> Dick: It must be in the pedals or the wheels.
> Zoe: Stop pedaling. . . . It's gone away.
> Dick: It must be in the pedals, then.

11. Sex, drugs, and rock 'n roll are the causes of the decline in family values.

12. I've got to go to the game. The only time I wasn't in the bleachers this season, they lost.

13. Just look at all the sex and violence on TV. That's why we're such a violent society.

14. Flo: Isn't it amazing that of all the houses in this town, I was born in one where the people look so much like me!   (What is Flo overlooking?)

15. My neighbor said it's been the worst season ever for allergies this spring, but I told her I hadn't had any bad days. Then today I started sneezing. Darn it—if only she hadn't told me.

16. Dick: Normally my pulse rate is about 130 after exercising on this bike.
    Zoe: I can't believe you actually measure your heart rate! You're so obsessive.
    Dick: But for the past week or so it's been about 105. That's odd.
    Zoe: You stopped drinking coffee two weeks ago, remember?

17. Satan causes evil.

18. He's stupid because his mother dropped him on his head when he was young.

19. Grey clouds cause rain.

20. (From a public service ad)
    Untreated depression is the #1 cause of suicide.

21. A recent study showed that everyone who uses heroin started with marijuana. So smoking marijuana causes heroin use.

22. Dr. E: My students don't like the material at the end of this course. That's why so many have missed class the last two weeks of the course.

D. Cause and Effect in Populations

When we say, "Smoking causes lung cancer," what do we mean? If you smoke a cigarette you'll get cancer? If you smoke a lot of cigarettes this week, you'll get cancer? If you smoke 20 cigarettes a day for 40 years you'll get cancer?

   It can't be any of these, since we know smokers who did all that yet didn't get lung cancer. And the cause always has to follow the effect. So what do we mean?

   Cause in populations is usually explained as meaning that given the cause there's a higher probability that the effect will follow than if there were not the cause. In this example, people who smoke have a much higher probability of getting lung cancer.

That's how it's explained. But really we are talking about cause and effect just as we did before. Smoking lots of cigarettes over a long period of time will cause (inevitably) lung cancer. The problem is that we can't state, we have no idea how to state, nor is it likely that we'll ever be able to state the normal conditions for smoking to cause cancer. Among other factors, there's diet, where one lives, exposure to pollution and other carcinogens, and one's genetic inheritance. But *if we knew exactly* we'd say: "Under the conditions _____, smoking _____ number of cigarettes every day for _____ years will result in lung cancer."

Since we can't specify the normal conditions, the best we can do is point to the evidence that convinces us that smoking is a cause of lung cancer and get an argument with a statistical conclusion: "People who continue to smoke two packs of cigarettes per day for ten years are ___% more likely (with margin of error of ___ %) to get lung cancer."

What kind of evidence do we use?

1. Controlled experiment: cause-to-effect

This is our best evidence. We choose 10,000 people at random and ask 5,000 of them never to smoke and 5,000 of them to smoke 25 cigarettes every day. We have two samples, one composed of those who are administered the cause, and one of those who are not, the latter called the ***control group***. We come back 20 years later to check how many in each group got lung cancer. If a lot more of the smokers got lung cancer, and the groups were representative of the population as a whole, and we can see no other ***common thread*** amongst those who got lung cancer, we'd be justified in saying that smoking causes lung cancer.

But we don't do such an experiment. It would be unethical. It's not acceptable to do an experiment on humans that has a (major) potential for doing them harm.

So we use some animals sufficiently like humans that we feel are "expendable," say cats. We fit them with little masks and have them breathe the equivalent of 25 cigarettes per day for a few years (20 years of human life is about 4–5 of cat life I guess). Then if lots of them get lung cancer, while the ones who don't smoke are still frisky, we can conclude with reasonable certainty that smoking causes cancer in laboratory cats.

So? We then argue that since cats are sufficiently similar to humans in their biological processes, we can extrapolate to say that smoking can cause cancer in humans. We argue by analogy.

2. Uncontrolled experiment: cause-to-effect

Here we take two randomly chosen, representative samples of the general population for which we have factored out other possible causes of lung cancer, such as working in coal mines. One of the groups is composed of people who say they never smoke. One group is composed of people who say they smoke. We follow the groups and 15–20 years later check whether those who smoked got lung cancer more often. Since we think we've accounted for other common threads, smoking is the remaining common thread that may account for why the second group got cancer more often.

This is a ***cause-to-effect*** experiment, since we start with the suspected cause and see if the effect follows. But it is uncontrolled: Some people may stop smoking, some may begin, people may have quite variable diets—there may be a lot we'll have to factor out in trying to assess whether it's smoking that causes the extra cases of lung cancer.

3. Uncontrolled experiment: effect-to-cause

Here we look at as many people as possible who have lung cancer to see if there is some common thread that occurs in (almost all) their lives. We factor out those who worked in coal mines, we factor out those who lived in high pollution areas, those who drank a lot, . . . If it turns out that a much higher proportion of the remaining people smoked than in the general population, we have good evidence that smoking was the cause.

This is uncontrolled because how they got to the effect was unplanned, not within our control. And it is an ***effect-to-cause*** experiment because we start with the effect in the population and try to account for how it got there.

How do we "factor out" other possible causes? How do we determine whether the sample of people we are looking at is large enough to draw conclusions about the general population? How do we determine if the sample is representative? How do we decide how many more cases of the effect—lung cancer —have to occur before it can be attributed to some cause rather than just to chance? These are the problems that arise whenever we generalize (Chapter 14). I can only suggest you use your common sense and register soon for a course on statistics.

Until you do take such a course and have access to actual write-ups of the experiments—not just the newspaper or magazine accounts—you'll have to rely on "the experts." So if the experiment was done by a reputable group, without bias, and what we read passes the obvious tests for a strong generalization, a good analogy, and a good causal argument, then we can assume that they know statistics well enough to conduct proper experiments. At least until some other reputable group challenges their results.

Summary   A lot that we worry about every day can be interpreted as claims about cause and effect. The cause, a claim, and the effect, another claim, have to be related by the same relation as between the premises and conclusion of a valid argument. As with arguments, there will be unstated claims needed: the normal conditions. But more is required for there to be cause and effect.

The cause has to be prior to the effect, and close in space and time to it. Usually there will also be a general claim that establishes the relation. Anecdotal evidence isn't good enough—that could just be *post hoc ergo propter hoc.* Getting the cause and effect reversed, or overlooking a common cause are other common mistakes in reasoning about causes.

Correlations are needed, but they're not enough. The cause has to make a difference. Often coincidence or chance is the best explanation we can find.

When we can't specify the normal conditions because of too much variation in the population, we rely on statistical arguments to establish that there is some causal link. Three kinds of experiments are important for those arguments: controlled cause-to-effect, uncontrolled cause-to-effect, and uncontrolled effect-to-cause.

Exercises for Section D

Describe what evidence you have for the claims in Exercises 1–5 and what experiments you would devise to try to prove or disprove them. [Don't do the experiments yourself! Some of them are dangerous without adult supervision.]

1. Universities cause students to become smarter.

2. Hedonistic life styles cause premature death.

3. Money brings happiness.

4. Drinking alcohol causes promiscuous behavior.

5. Unprotected sex causes disease.

6. **Study: Better primary care increases hospitalization**
   Researchers set out to show that giving sick people better access to family doctors keeps them out of the hospital. But to the surprise of everyone involved, the study found just the opposite.

   Doctors apparently end up diagnosing more ills, including ones that probably would otherwise go unnoticed.

   "I went in knowing that primary care could help keep these patients out of the hospital. That was my passion. I was exactly wrong," said Dr. Eugene Z. Oddone of the Veterans Affairs hospital in Durham, N.C.

   He and Dr. Morris Weinberger of the VA hospital in Indianapolis had thought the experiment would prove the obvious: Better primary care keeps people healthier, reducing hospital admissions by about one-third and saving money.

   Working with nine VA hospitals, they offered poor, seriously ill veterans the kind of care available in most HMOs—ready access to a nurse, a family doctor in charge of their case, reminders of appointments and follow-up calls.

   After six months of this attention, hospitalizations actually rose by one-third.

   "We were more surprised than anybody," Weinberger said.

   The doctors said their study, published in Thursday's issue of the New England Journal of Medicine, illustrates one of the difficulties of refashioning the health care system: Even common-sense ideas need to be tested to make sure they work.

Furthermore, for some, it raises doubts about an article of faith among doctors—that catching and treating diseases early will make people healthier in the long run.

In an accompanying editorial, Dr. H. Gilbert Welch of Dartmouth Medical School said the study forces doctors to consider a "heretical view."

"Instead of conferring benefit, closer scrutiny of the patients simply led to more medical care and perhaps to harm," he said. "We can no longer assume that early intervention is always the right thing to do."

Associated Press, May 30, 1996

a.   What causal claim is at issue?
b.   Which type of causation-in-population experiment was done?
c.   Evaluate whether it looks like it was done well.
d.   How would you further test the claim?

7. **Saliva may spread deadly virus**

A virus linked to skin cancer occurring in many AIDS patients may be spread by saliva, University of Washington scientists say.

The virus KSHV, which is linked to the cancer Kaposi's sarcoma, does not cause AIDS, but it probably must be present for the cancer to occur.

The University of Washington researchers found it in the saliva of 17 out of 23 men who had both the cancer and the AIDS-causing HIV (human immuno-deficiency virus), which makes the body more susceptible to many diseases.

"It (KSHV) may be capable of spreading to others by saliva contact," said David Koelle, a University of Washington assistant professor of medicine who presented his team's research findings in New Orleans this week at the 36th Interscience Conference on Antimicrobial Agents and Chemotherapy.

KSHV was first identified in 1994. Up to one-third of HIV-infected gay or bisexual men develop Kaposi's sarcoma before death. They may carry KSHV for some time before the body's immune system becomes weak and susceptible to the cancer.

The cancer is not found in patients who were infected with HIV exclusively through blood—injection drug users, hemophiliacs or transfusion recipients. Kaposi's sarcoma commonly spreads to the gastrointestinal tract or lungs, causing death.

The University of Washington scientists also found KSHV in two gay men who had HIV but not Kaposi's sarcoma, and in one patient who had Kaposi's sarcoma but not HIV. They did not find it in any of the 24 heterosexual adults who were not infected with HIV.

Outside of HIV patients, Kaposi's sarcoma is rare. But it also occurs in men without HIV, especially elderly men in southern Europe, and in Africa, both in adults and as an aggressive form in infants.

Koelle said KHSV is genetically similar to the Epstein-Barr virus, which is spread by saliva and causes infectious mononucleosis, with symptoms of fatigue, fever and swollen lymph nodes.

"While the relationship between KSHV infection and Kaposi's sarcoma has not been formally proven, it is highly likely that infection with the virus is required for development of the disease," Koelle said.

Koelle said more research needs to be conducted on KSHV.

Seattle Times, September 19, 1996

    a.   What is the argument here?

    b.   What experiment was done?

    c.   Explain whether the experiment proves the claim.

8. **Vitamin E in moderation may protect heart**

Eating a moderate amount of food rich in vitamin E, such as nuts, vegetable oils and margarine, reduces the risk of death from heart disease, says a study in today's New England Journal of Medicine.

    This supports a growing body of evidence that links vitamin E to a healthy heart.

    Researchers surveyed 34,486 postmenopausal women about their eating habits in 1986 and followed up about seven years later. They studied women but say the results apply to men, too.

    They found women with the diets highest in vitamin E-rich foods had half the risk of death from heart disease compared with those eating diets low in these foods. The highest group got more than 10 IUs of vitamin E from food daily, the equivalent of about an ounce of almonds. Those in the lowest group got about half that amount.

    Margarine and salad dressings are high in fat and calories, so people should use common sense when eating them. "I wouldn't go overboard with these things, but I wouldn't necessarily cut them out entirely," says the study's lead author, Lawrence H. Kushi of the University of Minnesota School of Public Health. The women who did the best in the research did not eat "outrageous amounts" of vitamin E foods.

    Dr. Walter Willett, Harvard School of Public Health, says "one of the unfortunate parts of the fat phobia is that people eliminate major sources of vitamin E in their diets."

    This study didn't come to a definitive conclusion on supplements, but other studies indicate they are beneficial.

    Other rich sources of vitamin E: hazelnuts, sunflower seeds, wheat germ, mayonnaise, peanut butter, avocados.   Nanci Hellmich, *USA Today,* 1996

    a.   What causal claim is at issue?

    b.   Which type of causation-in-population experiment was done?

    c.   Evaluate whether it looks like it was done well.

    d.   How would you further test the claim?

9. **Every breath you take**

It's not muscles alone that get you up the road. Breathing supplies the oxygen that makes those well-trained quads work. But many cyclists can't control the simple act of respiration. They don't know how to breathe efficiently, and they waste energy and gasp uncomfortably on climbs.

    At the bike camps in Colorado where I'm an instructor, many campers fly in from sea level and the next day they're laboring up Tennessee Pass at 10,000 feet, gasping like beached fish. That's when I ride alongside and explain how to get the most out of every breath. This approach, called "switchside breathing," produces almost miraculous increases in climbing speed and comfort—and it's easy to learn. I picked it up from Ian Jackson, author of the book *BreathPlay,* when we used to go snowshoe running around Aspen. Then I started to use it on the bike.

    No one is quite sure why switchside breathing helps. When I was a mountain runner, I noticed that a runner's injuries would often be on the same side. For example, his right knee, ankle and hamstrung all hurt. And the injuries often coincided with his dominant breathing side. But when we taught him to switchside breathe, the injuries went away. Apparently, if you always breathe on one side, you may subconsciously exert more force on that side. Switchside breathing balances out the effort of the legs and makes climbing easier. Give it a try!

Start by practicing correct athletic breathing off the bike. Lie on your back on the floor with a book on your stomach. Breathe in slowly and fully, expanding your diaphragm, not your chest. The book should move toward the ceiling. Then exhale steadily so it moves down toward the floor.

Most people think they should expand their chests, as a drill sergeant does. But if you look at side view photos of professional riders like Miguel Indurain or Tony Rominger, they almost look fat. Their diaphragms are expanded like bullfrogs in full voice. It may look funny—but it leaves more room for air to get into your lungs.

Now try it on the bike. Most riders exhale, every time, on the same side of the pedal stroke. If you're right-handed, you probably breathe out when the right pedal starts the downstroke. You can check by climbing a flight of stairs and paying attention to your pattern of in- and out-breaths. Once you get a rhythm going, I bet you exhale each time the same foot hits a step.

The easiest way to break out of this pattern of same-side breathing is simply to take an extra-long out-breath every five to ten pedal strokes. That will automatically switch your out-breath to the other down-stroke. Try it a couple of times on long climbs and it will become second nature. You can even practice off the bike by climbing stairs in a tall building. While stair climbing, the footstrike is slower and more pronounced, so it's easier to coordinate with breathing.

Finally, emphasize the out-breath. If you force air out of your mouth, you won't even need to think about breathing in. It will happen automatically. Some riders make a guttural sound as they breathe out, like weight lifters. Ex-pro Davis Phinney jokes about sounding like a pen full of pigs when we climb, but it works.

Skip Hamilton, *Bicycling,* June, 1997

    a. What causal claim is at issue?
    b. Which type of experiment was done?
    c. Evaluate whether it looks like it was done well.
    d. How would you further test the claim?
    e. Would you use this technique yourself?

10. Letter to the editor:

In case you missed it, the cost of getting your car's air conditioner serviced shot up like a rocket this summer. Whereas just a few short years ago you could buy a pound of Freon for a dollar or two, today the price has climbed to more than $20 a pound. And why?

Because environmentalists have sold us a lie. They have told us that unless we get rid of the CFC's we use in our air conditioners and refrigerators, we will punch a hole in the ozone layer and fry like bacon from the sun's UV rays. But the facts don't support their doomsdayism.

For one thing, there has never been any decline in atmospheric ozone. As noted by Dr. Ken Towe of the Smithsonian Institute, NASA data over the past 40 years has shown no downward trend in ozone thickness—a direct refutation of the theory.

Secondly, there is no documented increase in UV-B radiation. In fact, as demonstrated by the UV monitoring network that existed in this country from the early 1970s to the mid-1980s, there has been a slight decrease in UV-B—exactly the opposite of what the theory maintains.

And finally, as for the so-called ozone hole over Antarctica, well, that was discovered by none other than Dr. Gordon Dobson, the "father" of modern atmospheric research, in 1956—years before CFCs came into widespread use!

So, remember who to thank when you receive an enormous bill to "fix" your car's air conditioning system this year.   J. C. Marcelli, *Las Vegas Review-Journal*, 1996

a.   What causal claim is at issue?

b.   Evaluate the evidence for it.

11. **Prozac, pregnancy woes linked**
Women who take the widely prescribed anti-depressant Prozac in the final months of pregnancy may be doing harm to their babies, according to a new study.

California researchers followed hundreds of women taking the medicine, generically known as fluoxetine, during all stages of pregnancy and found that the risk of prematurity, admission to special-care nursery and poor outcome were more common in babies exposed to the drug in the last trimester.

But researchers from several laboratories caution that the study, to be published today in the New England Journal of Medicine, lacks the proper controls, and that the effects could be due to the mother's depression and not to the medication.

"I do not think that fluoxetine or tricyclic anti-depressant drugs have been clearly proved unsafe for pregnant women," Dr. Elisabeth Robert, a researcher at the Institut Europeen des Genomutations in France, wrote in an accompanying editorial. "It seems unjustified to use these new results as a reason to withhold fluoxetine from women who require an anti-depressant during pregnancy."

Christina Chambers and her colleagues at the California Teratogen Information Service and Clinical Research Program at the University of California, San Diego, studied 228 pregnant women taking fluoxetine, and compared the birth outcomes with another 254 women not taking the anti-depressant. Thirty percent of the women on Prozac were also taking another mind-altering medication.

According to the study, babies whose mothers took Prozac during the first trimester had no greater percentage of miscarriage, stillbirth or major birth defects than those unexposed to Prozac.

Among those mothers who continued to take Prozac, a drug that alters the brain chemical serotonin, well into the last trimester, there was a higher incidence of premature delivery and their babies were twice as likely to be placed in special-care nurseries. These babies were more jittery, suffered more respiratory problems and even the full-term babies were smaller than the comparison groups.

"Depressed women need to know what the risks might be so that they can discuss them with their doctors and be ready to deal with complications should they occur," Chambers said in an interview.

Dr. David Goldstein, clinical research physician at Eli Lilly, maker of Prozac, said the study did not control for the fact that depression itself has been associated with premature births and neonatal complications.

Patricia Whitaker-Azmitia, associate professor of psychiatry at the State University of New York at Stony Brook, has been studying the effects of Prozac and other anti-depressants on the developing animal in utero. Her animal studies have shown that serotonin, the major brain chemical altered by these drugs, is a key developmental hormone. Changes in the hormone during development of the central nervous system led to many problems in animals, she said. "They had learning deficits, were extremely aggressive and never formed social attachments. At birth, they were very much like the babies in this study, hyper-reactive and suffering from respiratory problems."

"To say not to worry is irresponsible," she said. On the other hand, there have been a handful of human studies that did not find any obvious physical problems of premature births in women exposed during the third trimester to antidepressants, Goldstein said. He worries that depressed women may prematurely decide to stop taking their medicine, and could suffer a rebound depression and hurt themselves.

Goldstein said that physicians should be as conservative as possible when prescribing any drug during pregnancy.

The March of Dimes Birth Defects Foundation recommends that pregnant women try to avoid taking the drug until its effects have been studied better. It added that pregnant women should not stop taking Prozac without first consulting their doctors.

Newsday, October 3, 1996

a. What causal claim is at issue?
b. Describe the experiment. What type is it?
c. What flaw in the experiment is described? Which of the mistakes in reasoning about causes does it fall under?
d. Devise a study that doesn't have that flaw. Would it be ethical to do?
e. How does risk factor into your evaluation of whether to advise pregnant women to stop taking Prozac? Relate that to the strength of the causal arguments.

Here are two pairs of arguments or descriptions of experiments for you to analyze. Each involves some causal claim. Prepare a full analysis of each in the style of the long argument analysis on pp. 239–241. They'll take all the skills you've learned in this course.

12. **Power lines and leukemia: beware of scientists bearing glad tidings**
"No Adverse Health Effects Seen From Residential Exposure to Electromagnetic Fields," said the press release from the National Academy of Sciences (NAS). "Study Fails to Link EMFs With Illnesses," repeated the *Los Angeles Times.* "Panel Sees No Proof of Health Hazards From Power Lines," "Electromagnetic research review finds no danger," "Power lines cleared as cause of cancer," "Power Line Hazard Called Small," echoed the *New York Times, Boston Globe, San Francisco Examiner,* and *Washington Post.*

Feel better now? No need to worry about buying or renting a home near high-voltage electric power lines. Forget the scare stories about your children getting leukemia (cancer of the blood), and worry about real problems like the kids being abducted by aliens.

But the headlines lie. Digging a bit deeper reveals that the study issued last October by a panel of 16 distinguished experts does not exonerate power lines, nor electromagnetic fields (EMFs), from being a danger to human health. In fact, the report itself (as opposed to the press release) summarizes the many existing epidemiological studies as saying that proximity to high-voltage lines raises a child's chances of contracting leukemia by 50%—hardly a negligible figure.

While making this admission, the report goes on to emphasize that childhood leukemia is "a rare disease." This means about one case per 30,000 children in a year, says committee vice-chair David Savitz of the University of North Carolina. Since about one-quarter of homes are exposed to power lines, a bit of arithmetic shows that raising this rate by 50% could cause hundreds of additional deaths per year in the United States!

Perhaps not as frightening as destruction of the ozone layer, but far worse than some other current scares, such as passenger-side air bags. How to reconcile the headlines with the 50% increase? It seems that although statistical studies of humans demonstrate an *association* between EMF strength and cancer, laboratory research has not found the mechanism by which EMFs actually cause cancer. So while the epidemiologists believe there is a problem, the physicists [sic] don't buy it.

The report, rather than focusing on this association, instead centers on the lack of physical proof: "No clear, convincing evidence exists to show that residential exposure to electric and magnetic fields are a threat to human health." Yet in a dissenting statement three committee members point out that, "Even in the case of cigarette smoking, it took nearly 50 years after the demonstration of a statistical association with lung cancer for scientists to define a cellular mechanism by which compounds in smoke could definitely cause the cellular changes associated with lung cancer."

The report's executive summary, and chair Charles Stevens, argue that the association of power lines with cancer could be pure coincidence. Other factors, such as "age of home, housing density, and neighborhood traffic density," could be the cause of the higher rates of leukemia.

But epidemiologists say that these other factors have been investigated and no relationship has been found. "There is no good evidence to suggest that it is something else [other than EMFs]—socioeconomic status, traffic density, or the type of neighborhood," says committee member Larry Anderson of Pacific Northwest Labs. And member Daniel Driscoll of the New York State Department of Public Services agrees.

By adopting an extremely high standard of proof to reach a conclusion of "guilty" the committee ensured that it would exonerate the defendant, says Louis Slessin, editor of *Microwave News*. Stevens also used "the oldest trick in the book," by issuing a press release that did not reflect the more balanced comments in the full report, adds Slessin.

Whose interests would be threatened by a conclusion that EMFs cause leukemia? The conventional view, seconded by Larry Anderson, is that the electric utilities have the most at risk, since their power lines criss-cross the nation, entering every community.

But, claims Slessin, "We are talking about all the technologies of the 21st century. The number one interest group is the military." The modern military, he argues, is fully dependent on electromagnetic fields, for weapons, reconnaissance and communications. Physicists, such as those on the committee, whose work is heavily funded by the military, "are doing the work of the Department of Defense, either consciously or unconsciously," says Slessin.

So don't believe the reassurances from the National Academy of Sciences. Until further notice, if you can avoid living near a power line, do so. And while you're at it, stay away from military bases.

Resources: Possible Health Effects of Exposure to Residential Electric and Magnetic Fields, National Research Council (National Academy of Sciences), October, 1996; "NAS Finds No EMF-Cancer Link; Report Stirs Controversy," *Microwave News,* Nov/Dec 1996.

Marc Breslow, Dollars and Sense, May/June 1997

13. **Power lines not a cancer risk for children**

Children who live near high voltage power lines appear to be no more likely to get leukemia than other kids, doctors report today in the most extensive study of the controversial issue ever done.

Researchers in nine states studied 629 children with leukemia and 619 healthy children. No child was admitted to the study unless the investigators could measure the electromagnetic fields (EMF) in homes where the children had lived 70% of the time. In addition, the researchers:

• Measured EMF in all homes where children under 5 had lived more than 6 months.

• Measured the EMF in homes where the mothers of 460 children—half of whom had cancer—lived for 5 months of their pregnancy.

• Placed dose meters in the children's bedrooms for a day.

They found that children without cancer were exposed to the same levels of electromagnetic energy as children with cancer, effectively ruling out EMF as a cause.

"Overall, I believe this study demonstrates that exposure to electromagnetic fields does not increase a child's risk of leukemia," says Leslie Robinson, of the University of Minnesota and a co-author of the report in today's *New England Journal of Medicine.*

The study, sponsored by the National Cancer Institute, is the latest of hundreds to examine EMF and cancer. Parents nationwide have been alarmed and concerns have cost the nation an estimated $1 billion a year in diminished real estate prices and stalled power-transmission projects.

All of the studies, including the 1979 report that triggered these worries had drawbacks. Indeed, the National Research Council, an arm of the National Academy of Sciences, reported eight months ago that 500 studies over 17 years yielded no conclusive evidence that household EMF causes cancer.

The overall finding comes with a caveat. A handful of children exposed to moderately elevated EMF appeared to be 1.7 times more likely to develop cancer. In contrast, smokers face a 20-fold increase in cancer risk.

However, the children's risk increase was so small—14 of the 19 had cancer—that researchers believe it's a matter of chance.

Even more telling was evidence indicating that children exposed to much more powerful energy fields faced no risk. USA Today, July 3, 1997

Should AIDS exhibit be OK'd as school field trip?

(Arguments 14 and 15 are from the *Las Vegas Sun,* March, 1996)

14. **Yes: Information is not false; trustees should reconsider their decision**

    Sandra Thompson, managing editor of the *Las Vegas Sun*

    The message is written in a teenage scrawl: "A friend of mine is always having unprotected sex. I hope she doesn't have AIDS."

    One of many comments in a book at the AIDS exhibit in the Lied Discovery Children's Museum, it sums up one of the purposes of the exhibit: To inform people that if they have sex, they can get AIDS.

    And that message is causing a ruckus in the community.

    The School Board—without having seen the exhibit—on February 13 voted against approving it as a field trip for students. Members may reconsider their decision at a March 12 board meeting since several have seen the exhibit since their vote.

    All members should see the exhibit for themselves and then approve it as a field-trip option.

    The operative word here is "option."

    By its vote, the School Board in effect made the decision for every parent. Critics counter that parents still have the choice—they can take their kids to the museums themselves.

    Sure. And they could do other things with them, spend time with them and get involved in their education and extracurricular activities.

    The reality is that many parents don't even attend their own children's school activities let alone take them to a museum.

    I agree with Nevada Concerned Citizens that parents should take a more active role in their children's lives, especially education. They should know what their children are learning.

    The furor over students seeing the traveling national AIDS exhibit centers on a perception that it does not stress abstinence, and talks about the risks of unprotected sex. Nevada Concerned Citizens objects to wording in the exhibit literature that says to protect yourself against AIDS, don't share needles and wear a condom during sex.

    Members say that's misinformation because just doing that won't protect you, won't prevent AIDS. After all, condoms break.

    The objection is based on semantics. The exhibit does not say taking such precautions will protect you 100 percent. And several times it mentions abstinence as the safest and best way to avoid AIDS.

    I'm a great believer in youths abstaining from sex. But look around you: Kids are sexually active. They need information contained in the exhibit. They need to know what can happen if they fool around.

    The exhibit does not promote sex. Nor does it promote a certain lifestyle connected with AIDS such as homosexuality, promiscuity or drug use.

    "Whenever you deal with issues like this you set up alarms," Emily Newberry says of the "What About AIDS?" exhibit. "These are touchy issues. It's not the easiest topic to bring up."

Newberry is the public affairs coordinator for the Lied Discovery Children's Museum. She says the exhibit, which opened Feb. 3, is a national touring exhibit that does not contain any misinformation. A local advisory board of health-care professionals, educators and others reviewed the exhibit to ensure that.

"We got this exhibit because we were the only science museum in the state," she says, adding that it contains strong science content "with a compassionate side."

If school field trips were approved for the AIDS exhibit, Newberry says students would be accompanied by teachers and a school nurse who could clear up any perceived misinformation.

High school students should see the exhibit. And just because it's a field trip does not mean ALL students should attend. Parents who don't want their children to view such an exhibit should have the option to say no. Likewise, those parents who do should have the option to say yes.

15. **No: Amid questions about HIV virus, trustees were right to reject trip**
Kris Jensen of Nevada Concerned Citizens

Contrary to accusations, the School Board acted responsibly and wisely when it voted not to allow the AIDS exhibit to be a school-sponsored field trip. The five board members each had individual concerns which were all valid reasons as to why they would not endorse the AIDS exhibit and send busloads of school children to the museum.

Nevada Concerned Citizens had attended meetings and had fully reviewed the materials (all 65 pages), when finally provided in the School Board back-up material. Within the panels on display in the exhibit is a statement that we found to be untruthful and were concerned about given the fact that they were seeking permission for Clark County School District students to view this display on school time.

It reads: "*HIV is spread only by sexual intercourse, contact with blood or from a pregnant mother to her unborn child. By not sharing needles and not having sexual intercourse without a condom, we can protect ourselves from infection with HIV.*"

This is a blatant lie. Risk may be reduced, but there is no 100 percent assurance that we will be protected from infection by using a condom. What would happen when the first student who read and believed that statement contracted AIDS?

After we read this statement, we raised the concern to the School Board that this is inaccurate information and that we need to be totally honest with the students. There is no room for error in contracting AIDS, it is 100 percent fatal. We must be completely straight and say that the *only safe* way for protection from infection is abstinence. Other methods may reduce risk, but don't tell people that they are protected and imply they are safe.

Perhaps the fact that 230 million AIDS viruses can fit on the head of a pin and certain condoms allow passage should tell us that there is no fail-safe way to protect ourselves from infection with HIV other than abstinence.

Condoms leak. Perhaps the fact that dentists double and even triple glove when dealing with AIDS patients, and their actions are nowhere near as risky, should send us a message. So don't lead Clark County school kids down the primrose path with a false assurance.

Former Secretary of Education William Bennet stated: ". . . 'safe sex' or even 'safer sex' was no way to prevent AIDS, that people had to re-learn the value of traditional morality or play a dangerous game."

Dr. Theresa Cranshaw, former member of the Presidential AIDS Commission, said: "Saying that the use of condoms is 'safe sex' is in fact playing Russian roulette. A lot of people will die in this dangerous game."

What about the three women out of 18 who contracted AIDS from their husbands while using condoms during intercourse in Dr. Margaret Fischl's extensive study (that's a 17 percent failure rate)!

Best yet, there's the report how an Australian man's sperm, frozen for months at temperatures that would kill other viruses, infected four of the eight women impregnated.

The point is that the jury is still out as to the "only" methods of transmission of AIDS. Why would we put children at greater risk by telling them half-truths and giving them false assurances?

We commend the five School Board members who had a concern with misinformation that could cost a student his/her life and voted not to lend their endorsement. We encourage them to hold firm for the protection of Clark County school children.

Furthermore, we challenge the Lied Discovery Children's Museum and the National Aids Exhibit Consortium to give their patrons honest and accurate information. Don't ask the School Board to endorse false statements and contradictory information. Do not risk lives by spreading inaccurate information that could have deadly results.

Key Words

causal claim	reversed cause and effect
cause	common cause
effect	*post hoc, ergo propter hoc*
normal conditions	coincidence
particular cause and effect	cause in populations
general cause and effect	control group
perfect correlation	common thread
foreseeable consequence	controlled cause-to-effect experiment
intervening cause	uncontrolled cause-to-effect experiment
	uncontrolled effect-to-cause experiment

Further Study   Many disciplines study the role of cause and effect in their area. But for a general view of the nature of cause and effect take a course on metaphysics. A course on the philosophy of science will consider the role of cause and effect in scientific explanations.

Mills

① Agreement

$$ABCD \rightarrow WXYZ$$
$$AEFG \rightarrow Wtuv$$
_____
$$A \rightarrow W$$

② Difference

$$ABCD \rightarrow WXYZ$$
$$BCD \rightarrow XYZ$$
_____
$$A \rightarrow W$$

③ Joint method of Agreement ∧ difference
$$① + ②$$

④ method of residues
→ process of elimination

⑤ → concomitant
variation, Flu, story! run down, left window open, blah etc

Writing Lesson 15

You understand the basics of how to reason about cause and effect. And you know a lot about critical thinking and why there's a course on this subject. So write a *one page* argument either for or against the following:

"Reading this book has caused me to become a better student."

Check whether your instructor has chosen a DIFFERENT TOPIC for this assignment.

Writing Lesson 16

For each cartoon below there is a sentence that can be understood as a causal claim. Argue either for or against that causal claim, based on what you see in the cartoon and your common knowledge: Check that the necessary conditions for cause and effect are satisfied and that you have not made any of the common mistakes in reasoning about cause and effect.

1.

The falling apple knocked Dick unconscious.

2.

The wasps chased Professor Zzzyzzx because he hit their hive.

3.

Dick got burned because he put too much lighter fluid on the barbecue.

4.

Suzy failed because she
stayed up late dancing.

Review Chapters 12–15

In Chapters 1–5 we established the fundamentals of critical thinking. In Chapters 6–8 we looked at the structure of arguments. In Chapters 9–11 we considered ways that people make bad arguments. In this section we looked at particular ways to reason from experience.

Generally, when we reason from experience we cannot get certainty. Judging arguments is more often weighing up the possibilities.

Analogies are common: We note similarities and draw conclusions. Often that's all that's done, and then an analogy is more a suggestion for discussion than an argument. When analogies are taken seriously as arguments, the similarities will have to be spelled out clearly and a general principle drawing the conclusion from those similarities will be needed.

Analogies lead to generalizations. We generalize when we start with a claim about some and conclude a claim about more. Generalizations often involve numbers, and we looked at a few common problems when using numbers in arguments. Then we saw that, though we don't always know the details of how a generalization was made, we can often judge whether it is good by reflecting on whether the sample is big enough, whether the sample is representative, and whether the sample is studied well.

How big the sample needs to be and whether it is representative depend on the variation in the population. When there is a lot of variation, random sampling—not to be confused with haphazard sampling—is the best way to get a representative sample. With polls and surveys an estimate of the likelihood of the conclusion being right and the margin of error should be given.

Analogies and generalizations play a role in perhaps the most important kind of reasoning we do every day: figuring out cause and effect. We don't know sufficient conditions for establishing cause and effect, but we can set out necessary conditions. And we can survey some of the common mistakes made when reasoning about cause and effect. The most pernicious is *post hoc* reasoning (after this, therefore because of this). Often the best we can say with our limited knowledge is that it's a coincidence.

When we reason about cause and effect in populations with large variation, it's hard, if not impossible, to specify the normal conditions. Typically a statistical causal link is established. We looked at the kind of experiments used for those arguments and found that, as with generalizations, a little common sense allowed us to make judgments about the truth of the conclusion.

Review Exercises for Chapters 12–15 ———————————————

1. What is an argument?

2. What is the definition of "good argument"?

3. What is the difference between a valid argument and a strong argument?

4. Is every valid or strong argument with true premises good? Explain.

5. What is reasoning by analogy?

6. What are the steps in evaluating an analogy?

7. Define, for a collection of numbers:
   a. The average.
   b. The mean.
   c. The median.
   d. The mode.

8. What is a "two times zero is still zero" claim? Give an example.

9. Give an example of phony precision.

10. a. What is a generalization?
    b. What do we call the group being generalized from?
    c. What do we call the group being generalized to?

11. What is a representative sample?

12. Is every randomly chosen sample representative? Explain.

13. Is it ever possible to make a good generalization from a sample of just one? Explanation or example.

14. A poll says that the incumbent is preferred by 42% of the voters with a margin of error of 3% and confidence level of 97%. What does that mean?

16. What are the three premises needed for a good generalization?

17. What do we call a weak generalization from a sample that is obviously too small?

18. List the necessary conditions for there to be cause and effect.

19. What are sufficient conditions for there to be cause and effect?

20. What do we call the unstated claims necessary to establish cause and effect?

21. List three common mistakes in reasoning about causes and give an example of each.

22. List the three common types of experiments used to establish cause in populations and give an example of each.

23. Why is it better to reason well with someone even if you could convince him or her with bad arguments?

24. a. What did you find most valuable in this course?
    b. What did you find least valuable in this course?
    c. Would you recommend this course to a friend? Why?

Composing
Good Arguments

From the grading and discussion of your arguments in class, you will have learned a great deal about how to compose an argument. Here is a summary of some of the main points.

- *If you can't spell, if you can't write complete sentences, if you leave words out, then you can't convince anyone. All the reader's effort will be spent trying to decipher what you intended to say.*

- *If you don't have an argument, literary style won't salvage your essay.*

- *If the issue is vague, use definitions or rewrite the issue completely to make a precise claim to deliberate.*

- *Don't make a clear issue vague by appealing to some common but meaningless phrase, such as "This is a free country."*

- *Beware of questions used as claims. The reader might not answer them the way you do.*

- *Your premises must be highly plausible, and there must be glue, something that connects the premises to the conclusion. Your argument must be impervious to the questions:* So? Why?

- *Don't claim more than you actually prove.*

- *There is a trade-off: You can make your argument strong, but perhaps only at the expense of a rather dubious premise. Or you can make all your premises clearly true, but leave out the dubious premises that are needed to make the argument strong. Given the choice, opt for making the argument strong. If it's weak, no one should accept the conclusion. And if it's weak because of unstated premises, it is better to have those premises stated explicitly so that they can be the object of debate.*

- *Your reader should be able to follow how your argument is put together. Indicator words are essential.*

- *Your argument won't get any better by weaseling with "I believe that" or "I feel that." Your reader probably won't care about your feelings, and they won't establish the truth of your conclusion.*

- *Your argument should be able to withstand the obvious counter-arguments. It's wise to consider them in your essay.*

- *For some issues, the best argument may be one which concludes that we should suspend judgment.*

- *Slanters turn off those you might want to convince—you're preaching to the converted. Fallacies just convince the careful reader that you're dumb.*

You should be able to distinguish a good argument from a bad one. Use the critical abilities you have developed to read your own work. Learn to stand outside your work and judge it, as you would an exercise in the text.

Writing Lesson 17

Let's see how much you've learned in this course. Write an argument for or against the following:

"Student athletes should be given special leniency when the instructor assigns course marks."

Making Decisions

The skills you've learned in this course can help you make better decisions.

Making a decision is making a choice. You have options. When making a decision you can start as you would on a writing exercise: Make a list for and against the claim—all the pros and cons you can think of. Make the best argument for each side. Then your decision should be easy: Choose the option for which there is the best argument. Making decisions is no more than being very careful in constructing arguments for your choices.

But there may be more than two choices. Your first step should be to list all the options and give an argument that these really are the only options, and not a false dilemma.

Suppose you do all that, and you still feel there's something wrong. You see that the best argument is for the option you feel isn't right. You have a gut reaction that it's the wrong decision. Then you're missing something. Don't be irrational. You know when confronted with an argument that appears good yet whose conclusion seems false, you must show that the argument is weak or a premise is implausible. Go back to your pro and con lists.

Now at the end of this course your reasoning has been sharpened, you can understand more, you can avoid being duped. And, I hope, you will reason well with those you love and work with and need to convince. And you can make better decisions. But whether you will do so depends not just on method, not just on the tools of reasoning, but on your goals, your ends. And that depends on virtue.

Exercises on Making Decisions

1. Decide whether you should cook dinner at home tonight.

2. Decide whether and what kind of dog you should get.

3. Decide whether you should buy a car during this next year.

4. Decide whether you should recommend this course to a friend.

5. If you don't have a job, decide whether you should get one next semester. If you have a job, decide whether you should quit.

6. Decide what career you should have.

7. If you're not married, decide whether you should ever get married. If you're married, decide whether you should get divorced.

8. If you have children, decide whether you should have more. If you don't have children, decide whether you ever should.

9. If you're doing drugs, decide whether you should stop.

10. If you have slept with your friend's lover, decide whether you should tell your friend.

11. Decide whether you should be honest for the rest of your life.

12. Decide whether you should believe in God.

13. Decide whether you should keep this book or sell it back at the end of the term.

Key Words   virtue
              the love of wisdom

APPENDICES

Using Examples in Reasoning

A. Examples for Definitions and Methods

When I defined "valid argument" in Chapter 3 I gave an example of a valid argu-ment. So there really are such things. Then I showed that not every argument is valid by giving another example. So the definition wasn't vacuous: Some arguments fit the definition, some don't.

Then I gave examples so you could see the difference between valid arguments and similar notions, such as strong arguments and good arguments.

We need examples when we make definitions in order to be sure we've got the right definition. Something fits the definition, some archetypal example. If you are asked to define "school cafeteria," you'll have to show that the place you always called the "cafeteria" at your school fits the definition. And some things don't fit. You might think that "place to eat at a school" would do as a definition of "school cafeteria," but we can show that's not right by giving as an example, say, a snack bar. It's hard to come up with a definition that also excludes a fast food restaurant on campus, since that is not what we mean by "school cafeteria."

We need examples with *definitions* to:

- Show something fits the definition.
- Show not everything fits the definition.
- Show the difference between the definition and other notions we already know.

The first two points are essential when the term we're defining, like "school cafeteria," is one we supposedly all understand. We want to be sure the definition fits our usual way of talking. Getting definitions of ordinary words is very important in insurance policies and law courts.

On the other hand, suppose we want to make a vague term precise:

A *classic car* is one that was built before 1959 and is in mint condition.

So a 1956 Chevy Bel Air in mint condition would be a classic car. A 1965 Corvette in perfect condition would not be a classic car by this definition, even if some people might call it one. And a classic car might not be an *antique,* for no car built in the 50's would normally count as an antique. Nor would a 1942 Ford in lousy condition, which is an antique, be called a classic car.

I've shown that there are classic cars that aren't antiques, and antiques that aren't classic cars. That is, I showed that neither definition included the other.

Note what I did after listing the three reasons for using examples with definitions above: I showed how to use the method. I showed that the method made sense and gave you an idea how to use it *by giving an example.* Whenever I've introduced a new method in this book, I've given you an example of how to use it.

B. Showing a Universal Statement is False

Dick: All dogs hate cats.
Zoe: No way. Remember Jane on Elm Street when we were growing up? She had a dog and cat that got along fine.

Zoe has shown that Dick's universal claim is false by providing an example.

Harry: No car built before 1992 had an airbag.
Tom: That's not right. My buddy's 1991 Volvo has an airbag.

Tom's example shows the universal negative is false.

Suzy: Almost all students at this university live on campus.
Harry: No they don't. I know lots of guys who go to night classes who don't.
Suzy: Well, anyway, all my friends live on campus.

For Harry to show Suzy's "almost all" claim is false he has to give not one, but a lot of examples.

People often generalize badly, too quickly from too few examples (see Chapter 14). You can bring them back to earth with well-chosen examples.

C. Showing an Argument is Not Valid

How do we show an argument is invalid? Consider:

Dick is a bachelor.
Therefore, Dick was never married.

We could say, no, that's not valid because Dick could be divorced, and we call a divorced man a bachelor. That's giving an example of a *possible* case where the premises are true and conclusion false.

Or we could say the argument's not valid because I know someone, Ralph, who's a bachelor and he was married. And his name could have been "Dick." That's giving an *actual* example (with the names changed).

When we want to show an argument is not valid we give a possible or actual example in which the premises are true and conclusion false.

We do the same when we want to show that an argument is not strong.

> Zoe and Dick have gone out for the day. Dick returns, sees that Zoe is gone, and finds that there's a roast cooking in the oven. So (he thinks) Zoe has started dinner.

Viewing the first three sentences as premises, we can say that Dick's argument is not valid: A burglar might have broken in and left a roast in the oven. That's preposterous, but it will do to show that the argument isn't valid.

But is the argument strong? Well, Zoe's mom often comes over, and perhaps Zoe was expecting guests Dick didn't know about, and Zoe asked her mom to come over and start dinner. That's not preposterous. So the argument is not *very* strong.

On the other hand, if Tom's been visiting them for a week, maybe he decided to help out and started dinner. We've got enough examples then that aren't preposterous that we can say the argument is weak.

That's how we show an argument is weak: We look for enough (possible) examples that aren't preposterous where the premises are true and conclusion false.

Summary   We've reviewed some of the ways we can use examples in reasoning:

- To make sure we've given a good definition and to clarify how to use the definition.
- To show how to use a new method.
- To show that a general claim is false.
- To show that an argument is not valid.
- To show that an argument is weak.

You should get good at using examples, because theory without examples isn't understood—it's unusable, and sometimes just plain wrong.

Exercises on Examples

1. Detail how examples were used in making the definition of "argument" in Chapter 1 (look at the three reasons for making examples with definitions).

2. Define "professional athlete." Use examples to contrast professional athletes with college athletes who receive scholarships and amateur athletes who are supported by governments to participate in the Olympics.

3. Define "school cafeteria" and use examples to show that you've got the definition right.

4. Define "student financial aid" and use examples to make your definition clear.

5. Detail how examples were used in Chapter 4 to show how to use the Guide to Repairing Arguments.

6. Show the following are false or at least dubious:
   a. All dogs bark.
   b. All cats kill songbirds.
   c. Nearly everyone who's at this college is on financial aid.
   d. No teacher at this university gives good lectures.
   e. No fast-food restaurant serves healthy food.

7. Say "preposterous" ten times. Does it begin to sound like a nonsense word?

For each argument below, if it is meant to be valid but is invalid, give an example to show that. If it's meant to be strong but it's weak, give enough examples to show that. If the argument is valid but not good, give an example to show why.

8. All good teachers give fair exams. Professor Zzzyzzx gives fair exams.
   So Professor Zzzyzzx is a good teacher.

9. If this course were easy, the exams would be fair. The exams are fair. So this course is easy.

10. President Clinton didn't inhale marijuana. So President Clinton never got high from marijuana.

11. Almost all teachers at this school speak English as their first language. So your instructor speaks English as his or her first language.

12. Dr. Zzzyzzx was late for class. He's never been late for class before. He's always conscientious in all his duties. So he must have been in an accident.

Diagramming

A. Diagrams

This appendix will provide a way to visualize the structure of the longer arguments we studied in Chapter 7.

> If a claim A is meant to support another claim B then we draw an arrow from A to B, putting A above B.

Here *support* just means that it's a reason to believe the other claim. For example:

Dogs are mammals. *1*
Mammals are warm blooded. *2*
Therefore, dogs are warm blooded. *3*

To picture this argument, we number the premises and conclusion. Then we ask which claim is meant to support which other. The conclusion will have to be at the bottom, since all the premises are supposed to support it. And both do. The picture we'll draw is:

Neither *1* supports *2*, nor does *2* support *1*. So there is no arrow from one to the other. But both support *3*, so we have arrows there. That's simple.

Now consider:

Dogs are mammals. *1*
Cats are mammals. *2*
Some dogs hate cats. *3*
Therefore, some dogs hate mammals. *4*

We number the claims. It's easy to see which is the conclusion (it's labeled with the word "therefore"). Which claims are meant to support which others? We need *2* and *3* to get the conclusion *4*. But what's *1* doing? Nothing. The argument doesn't get any better by adding it, since it doesn't support any of the other claims. So our picture is:

We need a way to represent premises that are dependent.

> In a diagram we indicate that premises are dependent by putting '+' between them and drawing a line under them.

Dogs are loyal. *1*
Dogs are friendly. *2*
Anything that is friendly and loyal makes a great pet. *3*
Hence, dogs are great pets. *4*

Recall the argument:

Whatever you do, don't take the critical thinking course from Dr. E. *1*
He's a really tough grader *2*, much more demanding than the other professors that teach that course. *3*   You could end up getting a bad grade. *4*

We rewrote *1* as "You shouldn't take the critical thinking course from Dr. E." And we rewrote *3* as "He's much more demanding than the other professors that teach that course." It wasn't clear which claim was supposed to support which other. We had two choices:

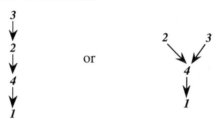

We chose to repair this argument with:

If you take critical thinking from someone who's more demanding than other professors who teach that course and who is a really tough grader, then you could end up getting a bad grade. *a*

That makes the second diagram a better choice, though we still need to get from *4* to *1*. We can use:

You shouldn't take any course where you might get a bad grade. *b*

We can see that the argument is only as good as the unsupported premise *b*.

Finally, let's see how adding a series of unstated premises can affect the picture. Here's an example from the exercises of Chapter 4:

My buddies John, Marilyn, and Joe all took Dr. E's critical thinking class and did well. *1*   So I'm going to sign up for it, too. *2*   I need a good grade. *3*

First, we need to rewrite *2* as a claim "I should sign up for Dr. E's critical thinking class." I take this to be the conclusion (try the other possibilities, asking where you could put "therefore" or "because"). Initially we might take the diagram:

But we need some glue for this to be even moderately strong. To begin with, why do *1* and *3* yield *2* ? A (fairly weak) assumption might be:

Usually if John, Marilyn, and Joe all do well in a class, I'll do well. *a*

But even that plus *3* won't give us *2*. We need some further assumption like:

I should sign up for classes in which I know I'll get a good grade. *b*

Then the argument becomes:

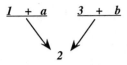

Still, there's something missing. We need:

I'll do well in Dr. E's course. *c*

And that changes the picture entirely:

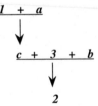

We have a strong argument, in which we see a dependence between *3* and what we get from *1*. Whether this is a good argument depends on whether the premises are true.

Exercises for Section A

Diagram the following arguments. Repair them as necessary.

1. Dr. E is a teacher. All teachers are men. So Dr. E is a man.

2. No one under sixteen has a driver's license. So Zoe must be at least sixteen.

3. Sheep are the dumbest animals. If the one in front walks off a cliff, all the rest will follow him. And if they get rolled over on their backs, they can't right themselves.

4. I'm on my way to school. I left five minutes late. Traffic is heavy. Therefore, I'll be late for class. So I might as well stop and get breakfast.

5. Pigs are very intelligent animals. They make great pets. They learn to do tricks as well as any dog can. They can be housetrained, too. And they are affectionate, since they like to cuddle. Pigs are known as one of the smartest animals there are. And if you get bored with them or they become unruly, you can eat them.

6. ¹Smoking is disgusting. ²It makes your breath smell horrid. ³If you've ever kissed someone after they smoked a cigarette you feel as though you're going to vomit. Besides, it will kill you.

7. You're good at numbers. You sort of like business. You should major in accounting—accountants make really good money.

8. Inherited property such as real estate, stocks, bonds, etc. is given a fresh start basis when inherited. That is, for purposes of future capital gains tax computations, it is treated as though it were purchased at its market value at the time of inheritance. Thus, when you sell property which was acquired by inheritance, tax is due only on the appreciation in value since the time it was inherited. No tax is ever paid on the increase in value that took place when the property belonged to the previous owner.

1994 Tax Guide for College Teachers

B. Counterarguments

We looked at the role of counterarguments in Section A of Chapter 7. We need a device to represent that a claim is an objection, not support, for another claim.

↓ means "therefore"   ⟊ means "therefore, not"

For example,

We ought to get another dog. *1*
(objection) We already have Spot. *2*
The other dog will keep Spot company. *3*
(objection) Spot already has us for company. *4*
We are gone a lot. *5*
He is always escaping from the yard. *6*
He's lonely. *7*
We don't give him enough time. *8*
He should be out running around more. *9*
(objection) It will be a lot of work to have a new dog. *10*
(objection) We will have to feed the new dog. *11*
(objection) It will take a lot of time to train the new dog. *12*
Dick will train him. *13*
We can feed him at the same time as Spot. *14*
Dog food is cheap. *15*

How can we diagram this? First, it seems that Dick intends but never says:

Spot needs company. *a*

That with *3* will be what gets the conclusion.

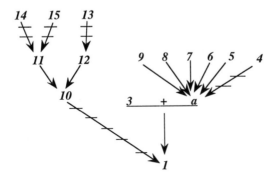

Claim *4* is an objection to *a*. That is, it's an attempt to show that a crucial
premise of Dick is false. It must be answered. And Dick answers it by amassing
enough other evidence for *a*. Claim *10* is a direct challenge to the conclusion. If it
is true, the conclusion is in doubt. So it must be answered. Dick doesn't try to show
that it is false directly. Rather he shows that the two claims Zoe uses to support *10*
are false. So there is no reason to believe *10*.

When we finish diagramming we can see at a glance whether the argument has
left some objection to a premise or objection to the conclusion unanswered. Either
the objection is knocked off with a counterclaim above the support for it (as with
13–15 against *10*) or other claims are amassed as evidence (as with *5–9* against
4). Of course you'll still need to evaluate whether the various claims are plausible.

Exercises for Section B

Diagram and evaluate the following arguments:

1. You should not take illegal drugs. They can kill you. If you overdose, you can die. If you share a needle, you could get AIDS and then die. If you don't die, you may end up a vegetable or otherwise permanently incapacitated. Using drugs runs the risk of getting arrested and possibly going to jail. Or at least having a hefty fine against you. Although some think the "high" from drugs is worth all the risks, the truth is that they are addicted and are only trying to justify supporting their habit.

2. Zoe: I think sex is the answer to almost everyone's problems.
   Dick: How can you say that?
   Zoe: It takes away your tensions, right?
   Dick: Not if you're involved with someone you don't like.
   Zoe: Well, anyway, it makes you feel better.
   Dick: Not if it's against your morals. Anyway, heroin makes you feel good, too.
   Zoe: But it's healthy, natural, just like eating and drinking.
   Dick: Sure, and you can catch terrible diseases. Sex should be confined to marriage.
   Zoe: Is that a proposal?

3. Dick: Nixon was a crook.
   Zoe: No he wasn't. Remember that famous "Checkers" speech where he said so?
   Dick: That was just political evasion. Anyway, you can't just take someone's word that he's not a criminal, especially if he's a politician. He directed the break-in at the Democratic Party Headquarters.
   Zoe: They never showed that he did that.
   Dick: That's because his accomplices like Haldemann were covering up. That's why they got pardoned. And he used the FBI against his enemies. He was a criminal. It was stupid for Clinton to make a speech honoring him when he died.
   Zoe: Maybe Clinton was doing it so that when he dies someone will make a speech for him, too.

Truth-Tables

A. Symbols and Truth-Tables

The ancient Greek philosophers were the first to analyze arguments using compound claims. From then until the mid-19th century the analysis of compound claims was much as in Chapter 6. Many more valid and invalid argument forms had been catalogued, with Latin names attached, but the explanations of why they were valid were very much the same.

At the beginning of this century a simple method was devised for checking whether an argument form using compound claims is valid. Using it we can easily justify the validity and invalidity of the argument forms we studied in Chapter 6.

We will do so by concentrating on how compound claims can be built up from just four English words or phrases:

and,   or,   not,   if . . . then . . .

These will be enough to help us analyze many arguments using compound claims.

These words are used in many different ways in English, too many for us to investigate every possible way that they could be used in arguments. We will concentrate on just one aspect of them: *How compound claims that use them depend on the truth or falsity* (truth-value) *of the claims they are built from.* We won't care just how plausible a claim is, or how we might happen to know it, or its subject matter, or any other aspect of it. We make the following assumption.

The Classical Abstraction The only aspects of a claim we'll pay attention to are whether the claim is true or false and how it is compounded out of other claims.

So long as the argument we are analyzing makes sense in terms of this assumption, the methods we develop here will allow us to check for validity. To remind us that we're making this assumption, we are going to use special symbols to represent the words we are interested in.

∧	∨	¬	→
and	or	not	if . . . then . . .

Now we can be precise about how we will understand these words in arguments, relative to the Classical Abstraction. Let's start with "and."

Spot is a dog and Puff is a cat.

When is this true? When both "Spot is a dog" is true and "Puff is a cat" is true. That's the only way it can be true. Let's summarize that in a table, where A and B stand for any claims:

A	B	A∧B
T	T	T
T	F	F
F	T	F
F	F	F

> A *conjunction* (∧-claim) is true (T) when both parts are true. Otherwise it is false (F).

What do we mean by "not"?

Spot is not a dog.

This is true if "Spot is a dog" is false, and false if "Spot is a dog" is true. That's simple to formalize:

A	¬A
T	F
F	T

> A *negation* (¬-claim) is true if its part is false; it is false if its part is true.

How about "or"?

London is the capital of England or Paris is the capital of France.

Is this true? There's going to be disagreement. Some say it isn't, because "London is the capital of England" and "Paris is the capital of France" are both true. Others say the compound is true. The question is whether an "or" claim can be true if both parts are true.

It turns out to be simplest to use ∨ to formalize "or" in the *inclusive* sense:

One or the other or both parts are true. Later we'll see how to formalize "or" in the *exclusive* sense: One or the other but not both parts are true.

A	B	A∨B
T	T	T
T	F	T
F	T	T
F	F	F

A *disjunction* (∨-claim) is false if both parts are false. Otherwise it is true.

Finally, we have "if . . . then . . .". These words have so many connotations and uses in English that it's hard to remember that we're going to pay attention only to whether the parts of the compound claim are true or false. The following table is the one that's best:

A	B	A→B
T	T	T
T	F	F
F	T	T
F	F	T

A *conditional* (→-claim) is false if the antecedent is true and consequent false. Otherwise it is true.

Why do we choose this table? Let's look at it row by row.

We said the direct way of reasoning with conditionals is valid:

If A then B,   A,   so B .

So if A→B is true, and A is true, then B is true (*the first row*).

Suppose A is true and B is false (*the second row*). In a valid form we can't get a false conclusion from true premises. Since there are only two premises, it must be that A→B is false.

But why should A→B be true in the last two rows? Suppose Dr. E says to Suzy,

"If you get 90% on the final exam, you'll pass this course."

It's the end of the term. Suzy gets 58% on the final. Dr. E fails her. Can we say that Dr. E lied? No. So the claim is still true, even though the antecedent is false and the consequent is false.

But suppose Dr. E relents and passes Suzy anyway. Can we say he lied? No (remember he said "if" not "only if"). So the claim is still true, even though the antecedent is false and the consequent is true.

The formalization of "if . . . then . . ." in this table is the best we can do so long as we adopt the Classical Abstraction. We deal with cases where the antecedent "does not apply" by treating the claim as vacuously true.

B. The Truth-Value of a Compound Claim

With these tables to interpret "and," "or," "not," and "if . . . then" we can calculate the truth-value of a complex claim fairly easily. For example,

> If Dick goes to the movies and Zoe visits her mother, then no one will walk Spot tonight

We can formalize this as:

> (Dick goes to the movies ∧ Zoe visits her mother) →
> no one will walk Spot tonight

I had to use parentheses to mark off the antecedent. They do the work that commas should do in ordinary English.

When is this claim true? Let's look at the form of it:

> (A∧B) → C

We don't know which of A, B, and C are true and which are false. We have to look at all possibilities to decide when the compound claim is true. We can construct a table:

A	B	C	A∧B	(A∧B)→C
T	T	T	T	T
T	T	F	T	F
T	F	T	F	T
T	F	F	F	T
F	T	T	F	T
F	T	F	F	T
F	F	T	F	T
F	F	F	F	T

In the table we first list all possible values for A, B, and C. Then we calculate the value of A∧B. With the truth-value of A∧B we can use the truth-value of C (to its left) to calculate the truth-value of (A∧B)→C.

We can see now that the original claim can be false only if both "Dick goes to the movies" is true and "Zoe visits her mother" is true, and "No one will walk Spot tonight" is false. For example, if Dick doesn't go to the movies (A is F) and Zoe doesn't visit her mother (B is F), then the whole claim is true—the antecedent of (A∧B)→C is false, so the claim is vacuously true.

Perhaps you could have figured out when this claim was true without using a table. But it's equally routine to analyze a complex claim with the complicated form (¬(A∧B) ∨ C) → (¬B∨(C∧¬A)).

Some compound claims are true for every way that their parts are true or false.

For example:

Ralph is a dog or Ralph isn't a dog
A∨¬A

A	¬A	A∨¬A
T	F	T
F	T	T

It doesn't matter whether A is true or false: Any claim with the form A∨¬A is true.

> **Tautology**   A compound claim is a *tautology* if it is true for every possible assignment of truth-values to its parts.

The form (A∨B) → (B∨A) is a tautology, which reflects that the order of the parts of an "or" claim doesn't matter.

A	B	A∨B	B∨A	(A∨B)→(B∨A)
T	T	T	T	T
T	F	T	T	T
F	T	T	T	T
F	F	F	F	T

> A claim is a tautology if in the table for its form
> *the last column of the table has only* T.

Using the tables we can also verify the equivalences of informal claims we noted in Chapter 6:

A→B   is the same as   ¬B→¬A   *contrapositive*

¬(A→B)   is the same as   A∧¬B   *the contradictory of a conditional*

¬A∨B   is the same as   A→B   *conditional form of an "or" claim*

For example, no matter what truth-values A and B have, A→B is going to have the same truth-value as ¬B→¬A. They have the same tables:

A	B	A→B	¬B	¬A	¬B→¬A
T	T	T	F	F	T
T	F	F	T	F	F
F	T	T	F	T	T
F	F	T	T	T	T

Exercises for Sections A and B

1. What are the four fundamental English words or phrases that we will analyze in studying compound claims?

2. What is the first big assumption about claims we made (the Classical Abstraction) when we decided to use the symbols ∧, ∨, ⌐, → ?

3. Explain why using symbols makes you nervous. Suggest a way you can overcome your distaste for them. (If they don't make you nervous, answer this question for your classmates who are bothered by them.)

4. What is a tautology?

5. What is the method for checking whether a claim is a tautology?

6. Explain the method for checking whether two forms of claims are equivalent.

Here's an example of a way Tom devised to check whether a claim is a tautology. It's a little long-winded, but it made it clear to him.

Decide whether (A ∧ B) → ⌐(A ∨ B) is a tautology.

A	B		A	∧	B		⌐	(A	∨	B)		(A∧B)	→	⌐(A∨B)
T	T		T	T	T		F	T	T	T		T	F	F
T	F		T	F	F		F	T	T	F		F	T	F
F	T		F	F	T		F	F	T	T		F	T	F
F	F		F	F	F		T	F	F	F		F	T	T
1	2		3	4	5		6	7	8	9		10	11	12

Columns 1 and 2 are all the possible combinations of truth-values of the claims.
Columns 3 and 5 are just 1 and 2 repeated to see how to get column 4
   (the table for A ∧ B).
Columns 7 and 9 are just 1 and 2 repeated so as to see how to get column 8
   (the table for A ∨ B).
Then column 6 is the table for ⌐ applied to column 8, which gives the table
   for ⌐(A ∨ B).
Column 10 is just column 4 repeated. And column 12 is just column 6 again.
   That lets us see how to get column 11 using the table for →.
Column 11 gives the truth-values for (A ∧ B) → ⌐(A ∨ B). Since there's an F in
that column, this isn't the form of a tautology.

Use the truth-table method to show that the following are tautologies:

7. ⌐⌐A → A

8. ⌐(A ∧ ⌐A)

9. ((A → B) ∧ (⌐A → B)) → B

10. ⌐(A ∧ B) → (⌐A ∨ ⌐B)

Decide whether the following are tautologies by the truth-table method. Then explain why in your own words.

11. A → (A∨B)

12. ((A∨B) ∧ ¬B) →A

13. (A∨B) → (A∧B)

14. ((A→B) ∧ ¬B) → ¬A

15. (¬(A∧B) ∧ ¬A) → B

16. ((A→B) ∧ (¬A→C)) → (B∨C)

Show that the following are equivalent.

17. ¬(A→B)   is the same as   A∧¬B

18. A→B   is the same as   ¬A∨B

19. ¬(A∧B)   is the same as   ¬A∨¬B

20. ¬(A∨B)   is the same as   ¬A∧¬B

C. Representing Claims

To use truth-tables we have to be able to represent ordinary claims and arguments.

Examples   Can the following be represented in a form that uses ¬, →, ∧, ∨ ?

Example 1 Spot is a dog or Puff is a cat and Zoe is not a student.

Analysis   What's the form of this? (A∨B)∧¬C ? or A∨(B∧¬C) ? Without a context, we have to guess. We analyze the argument on one reading, then on the other, and see which is stronger. Our formal analyses help us see ambiguities.

Example 2 Puff is a cat or someone got swindled at the pet store.

Analysis   This one's easy:

   Puff is a cat ∨ someone got swindled at the pet store

Example 3 London is in England or Paris is in France.

Analysis   We can represent this using *exclusive* "or":

   (London is in England ∨ Paris is in France) ∧
            ¬(London is in England ∧ Paris is in France)

In the exercises I ask you to show:

$(A \lor B) \land \lnot (A \land B)$ is true when exactly one of A is true or B is true.

Example 4   Harry is a football player if he plays any sport at all.

Analysis   We're used to rewriting conditionals. This one is:

If Harry plays any sport at all, then Harry is a football player.

Harry plays any sport at all $\to$ Harry is a football player

Example 5   Zoe loves Dick although he's not a football player.

Analysis   This is a compound claim, with parts "Zoe loves Dick" and "Dick is not a football player." But "although" isn't one of the words we're formalizing.

When is this compound claim true? If we stick to the Classical Abstraction, then "although" doesn't do anything more than "and." It shows that the second part is perhaps surprising, but that isn't what we're paying attention to. We can formalize the claim as:

Zoe loves Dick $\land$ Dick is not a football player

If all we're interested is whether the argument in which this appears is valid, this representation will do.

There are a lot of words or phrases that can sometimes be represented with $\land$:

and	even if
but	even though
although	despite that

Sometimes, though, these serve as indicator words, suggesting the roles of the claims in the overall structure of the argument. "Even though" can indicate that the claim is going to be used as part of a counterargument. We can represent these words or phrases with $\land$, or we can just represent the parts of the sentence as separate claims. That's what we did in Chapter 6, and we can do that because the table for $\land$ has that the compound will be true if and only if both parts are true.

Example 6   Spot thinks that Dick is his master because Zoe doesn't take him for walks.

Analysis   Can we represent "because" using $\land$, $\lor$, $\lnot$, $\to$? Consider the following two claims:

Spot is a dog because Las Vegas is in the desert.

Spot is a dog because Las Vegas is not in the desert.

Both of these are false. Spot is a dog, and that's true whether Las Vegas is or is not in the desert. The truth-value of "Las Vegas is in the desert" is irrelevant to the truth-value of the whole compound. All we've got to work with in representing "because" are compounds that depend on whether the parts are true or false. We can't represent this example as a compound claim.

Example 7 Zoe took off her clothes and went to bed.

Analysis We shouldn't represent this compound as:

Zoe took off her clothes ∧ Zoe went to bed

That has the same truth-value as:

Zoe went to bed ∧ Zoe took off her clothes

Example 7 is true most nights, but "Zoe went to bed and took off her clothes" is false. In this example "and" has the meaning "and then next," so that *when* the claims become true is important. But if we use these symbols we can only consider whether the claims are true, not when they become true. So we can't represent this claim.

Example 8 (On the playground): Hit me and I'll hit you.

Analysis We don't represent this as: You hit me ∧ I hit you. The example is a conditional, and we represent it as:

You hit me → I hit you

We can't blindly represent every use of "and," "or," "not," and "if . . . then" as ∧, ∨, ⌐, →. We have to ask what the words mean in the way they're used. Does the use accord with the Classical Abstraction?

Exercises for Section C

1. Make up the table for (A ∨ B) ∧ ⌐(A ∧ B) and show that it is true when exactly one of A is true or B is true.

For each of the following, either represent it using ∧, ∨, ⌐, →, or explain why it can't be represented.

2. If critical thinking is hard, then mathematics is impossible.

3. If you don't apologize, I'll never talk to you again.

4. Dick prefers steak, while Zoe prefers spaghetti.

5. Dick was shaving while Zoe was preparing dinner.

6. Either Dick loves Zoe best, or Zoe will cook dinner tonight.

7. Even if you do whine all the time, I love you.

8. Spot is a good dog even though he scared the living bejabbers out of your cat.

9. Spot is a good dog because he scared the living bejabbers out of your cat.

10. We're going to go to the movies or go out for dinner tonight.

11. Since 2 + 2 is 4, and 4 times 2 is 8, I should be ahead $8, not $7, in blackjack.

12. If Dick has a class and Zoe is working, there's no point in calling their home to ask them over for dinner.

13. If it's really true that if Dick takes Spot for a walk he'll do the dishes, then Dick won't take Spot for a walk.

14. If Dick goes to the basketball game, then he either got a free ticket or he borrowed money from somebody.

15. Either we'll go to the movies or visit your mom if I get home from work by 6.

16. Whenever Spot barks like that, there's a skunk or racoon in the yard.

17. I'm not going to visit your mother and I'm not going to do the dishes, regardless of whether you get mad at me or try to cajole me.

18. Every student in Dr. E's class is over 18 or is taking the course while in high school.

19. No matter whether the movie gets out early or late, we're going to go out for pizza.

20. Suggest ways to represent:

   a.   A only if B

   b.   A unless B

   c.   When A, B

   d.   A if and only if B

   e.   B just in case A

   f.   Neither A nor B

D. Checking for Validity

We have an argument. If we show its form in terms of compound claims, we can check to see whether its structure alone guarantees that it's valid.

   An argument is valid if for every possible way the premises could be true, the conclusion is true, too. So suppose we have an argument of the form:

   $A \rightarrow B$, $\neg A \rightarrow B$
   So, B

For an argument of this form to be valid, it has to be impossible that $A \rightarrow B$ and $\neg A \rightarrow B$ are both true, and B is false. We need to look at all ways that $A \rightarrow B$ and $\neg A \rightarrow B$ could be true:

A	B	$A \rightarrow B$	$\neg A$	$\neg A \rightarrow B$
T	T	T	F	T
T	F	F	F	T
F	T	T	T	T
F	F	T	T	F

We list all the values of A and B. Then we calculate the truth-values of A→B and ¬A→B. In the first row both of those are true, and so is the conclusion, B. Ditto for the third row. In the second row A→B is false, and we don't care about that. In the last row ¬A→B is false, and we can ignore that. So whenever both A→B and ¬A→B are true, so is B. Any argument of this form is valid.

Valid Argument Form   To say an argument form is *valid* is to say that every argument of that form is valid.

We can show that an argument form is valid by making a table that includes all the premises and conclusion. If every row in which all the premises are true, the conclusion is true, too, then the form is valid.

Let's look at the indirect way of reasoning with conditionals:

A→B, ¬B
———————
¬A

I've drawn a line rather than write "so" or "therefore" to indicate the conclusion.

Again, we have to look at every way the premises could be true.

A	B	A→B	¬B	¬A
T	T	T	F	F
T	F	F	T	F
F	T	T	F	T
F	F	T	T	T

Only in the last row are both premises A→B and ¬B true. There we find that ¬A is true, too. So every argument of this form is valid.

The third row of this table also shows that, in contrast, denying the antecedent is invalid:

A→B, ¬A
———————
¬B

Both A→B and ¬A are true, but ¬B is false. It is possible to have the premises true and conclusion false.

Reasoning in a chain provides a more complicated example.

A→B, B→C
———————
A→C

We have the table:

A	B	C	A→B	B→C	A→C
T	T	T	T	T	T
T	T	F	T	F	F
T	F	T	F	T	T
T	F	F	F	T	F
F	T	T	T	T	T
F	T	F	T	F	T
F	F	T	T	T	T
F	F	F	T	T	T

I've circled the rows in which both premises are true. In each of them the conclusion is also true. So every argument of this form is valid.

This table also shows that the following form isn't valid:

$$A \rightarrow B, \quad A \rightarrow C$$
$$\overline{ B \rightarrow C }$$

The third row from the bottom has both A→B and A→C true, with B→C false.

So far this has been just a game, playing with symbols. It's only when we can apply these tables to real arguments that we're doing critical thinking. Consider:

If Tom knows some logic, Tom is either very bright or he studies hard. Tom is bright. Tom studies hard. So Tom knows some logic.

First we represent these claims. Only the first is compound:

Tom knows some logic → (Tom is very bright ∨ Tom studies hard)

So this argument has the form:

$$A \rightarrow (B \vee C), \quad B, \quad C$$
$$\overline{ A }$$

A	B	C	B∨C	A→(B∨C)
T	T	T	T	T
T	T	F	T	T
T	F	T	T	T
T	F	F	F	F
F	T	T	T	T
F	T	F	T	T
F	F	T	T	T
F	F	F	F	T

I've circled a row in which all of A→(B∨C), B, and C are true, yet the conclusion A is false. So the argument isn't valid.

That alone does not make it a bad argument. We still have to see if it could be strong. But it fails that, too, since though Tom is very bright and studies hard, and the first premise is true too, it's not at all implausible that Tom could have been majoring in art history and know no logic at all.

You might not have needed a table to figure out this last one. But you will for some of the exercises. Have fun.

Summary   By concentrating only on whether claims are true and the structure of arguments that involve compound claims, we can devise a method for checking the validity of arguments. We introduced symbols for the words "and," "or," "not," and "if . . . then" and made precise their meaning through truth-tables. We learned how to use the symbols and tables in representing claims. Then we saw how to use truth-tables to check whether the structure of an argument relative to the compound claims in it is enough to guarantee that the argument is valid.

Exercises for Section D ————————————————————————

1. What does it mean to say an argument form is valid?

2. If an argument has a form that is not valid, is it necessarily a bad argument?

Use truth-tables to decide whether the following argument forms are valid.

3. A→B, B
    —————————
        A

4. A→B, A→¬B
    ——————————————
         ¬A

5. A, ¬A
    ————————
       B

6. A∨B
    ———————
    A∧B

7. A∨B, ¬A
    ——————————
         B

8. B∨D, B→C, D→E
    ————————————————————
           C∨E

9. A→¬B, B∧¬C
    ——————————————
         A→C

10. A→¬¬B, ¬C∨A, C
_____
   B

Represent the arguments in Exercises 11–17 and decide whether they are valid. Use truth-tables or not as you wish.

11. If Spot is a cat, then Spot meows. Spot is not a cat. So Spot doesn't meow.

12. Either the moon is made of green cheese or 2 + 2 = 4. But the moon is not made of green cheese. So 2 + 2 = 4.

13. Either the moon is made of green cheese or 2 + 2 = 5. But the moon is not made of green cheese. So 2 + 2 = 5.

14. The students are happy if and only if no test is given. If the students are happy, the professor feels good. But if the professor feels good, he won't feel like lecturing, and if he doesn't feel like lecturing, he'll give a test. So the students aren't happy.

15. If Dick and Zoe visit his family at Christmas, then they will fly. If Dick and Zoe visit Zoe's mother at Christmas, then they will fly. But Dick and Zoe have to visit his family or her mother. So Dick and Zoe will travel by plane.

16. Tom is not from New York or Virginia. But Tom is from the East Coast. If Tom is from Syracuse, he is from New York or Virginia. So Tom is not from Syracuse.

17. The government is going to spend less on health and welfare. If the government is going to spend less on health and welfare, then either the government is going to cut the Medicare budget or the government is going to slash spending on housing. If the government is going to cut the Medicare budget, the elderly will protest. If the government is going to slash spending on housing, then advocates of the poor will protest. So the elderly will protest or advocates of the poor will protest.

Key Words

classical abstraction	conjunction
truth-table	negation
∧	disjunction
¬	conditional
∨	tautology
→	valid argument form

Glossary

Ad Hominem   A general name for any of the ways of mistaking a person or group for a claim or argument.

Affirming the Consequent   Reasoning in the form: If A then B, B, so A. Usually weak.

"All"   Usually means "every single one, no exceptions." Sometimes best understood as "every single one, and there is at least one."

Alternatives   The claims that are the parts of an "or" claim.

Ambiguous Sentence   A sentence that can be understood in at least two clear ways.

Analogy   A comparison becomes reasoning by analogy when it is part of an argument: On one side of the comparison we draw a conclusion, so on the other side we should conclude the same.

Anecdotal Evidence   A sample of one, or two, or very few used as evidence for a generalization. The claims about the sample in a hasty generalization.

Antecedent   In a conditional claim (possibly rewritten as) "If A, then B", the part A.

Appeal to Authority   An argument that uses or can be repaired only by putting in a premise that says, roughly: (Almost) anything that _____ says about _____ is true.

Appeal to Common Belief   An argument that uses or can be repaired only by putting in a premise that says, roughly: If (almost) everyone else (in this group) believes it, then it's true.

Appeal to Common Practice   An argument that uses or can be repaired only by putting in a premise that says, roughly: If (almost) everyone else (in this group) does it, then it's O.K. to do.

Appeal to Fear   An argument that uses or can be repaired only by putting in a premise that says, roughly: You should believe or do _____ if you are afraid of _____.

Appeal to Pity   An argument that uses or can be repaired only by putting in a premise that says, roughly: You should believe or do _____ if you feel sorry for _____.

Appeal to Spite   An argument that uses or can be repaired only by putting in a premise that says, roughly: You should believe or do _____ if you are mad about what _____ has done or believes.

Apple Polishing   A feel-good argument that appeals to vanity.

Arguing Backwards with **All**   Reasoning in the form: All S are P, *a* is P, so *a* is S. Usually weak.

Arguing Backwards with **Almost All**   Reasoning in the form: Almost all S are P, *a* is P, so *a* is S. Usually weak.

Arguing Backwards with **No**   Reasoning in the form: All S are P, no Q is S, so no Q is P. Usually weak.

Argument   A collection of claims one of which is the *conclusion* whose truth the argument attempts to establish. The others are called the *premises,* which are supposed to lead to, or support, or convince that the conclusion is true. *See also* Good Argument.

Assertion   A sentence used as a claim.

Average (or Mean) of a collection of numerical values   The number obtained by adding all the values and then dividing by the number of items.

Begging the Question   An argument that uses a premise that is at least as dubious as the conclusion. *See also* Circular Argument.

Biased Sample   A sample that is not representative.

Burden of Proof   The side of a debate that must be proved.

Calling in Your Debts   An argument that uses or can be repaired only by putting in a premise that says, roughly: You should believe or do _____ if you owe _____ a favor.

Causal Claim   A claim that can be rewritten as one that uses the word "causes" or "caused."

Cause   *See* Necessary Criteria for Cause and Effect.

Cause in a Population   A claim that given the cause there is a higher probability that the effect will follow than if there were not the cause.

Circular Argument   An argument that uses the conclusion, possibly in modified form, as a premise.

Claim   A declarative sentence that we can view as either true or false (but not both).

Classical Abstraction   The only aspects of a claim we'll pay attention to (in formalizing) is whether the claim is true or false and how it is compounded out of other claims.

Compound Claim   A claim made up of other claims, but which has to be viewed as just one claim.

Conclusion   The claim whose truth an argument is meant to establish.

Conditional   The formalization of a conditional claim using $\rightarrow$.

Conditional Claim   A compound claim that can be rewritten as an "if . . . then . . ." claim that must have the same truth-value. A contradictory of "If A then B" is "A but not B."

Confidence Level   The percentage of the time that the same sampling method would give a result that is a true generalization.

Confusing Objective and Subjective   Calling a claim objective when it is really subjective, or vice-versa.

Conjunction   The formalization of an "and" claim using $\wedge$.

Consequent   In a conditional claim (possibly rewritten as) "If A, then B," the part B.

Content Fallacy   An argument that uses or requires for repair a particular kind of premise which if false or dubious classifies the argument as a fallacy.

Contradictory of a Claim   The contradictory of a claim is one that always has the opposite truth-value. Sometimes called the *negation* of a claim.

Contrapositive   The *contrapositive* of "If A, then B" is "If not B, then not A." The contrapositive is true exactly when the original conditional is true.

Control Group   *See* Controlled Experiment: Cause-to-Effect.

Controlled Experiment: Cause-to-Effect   An experiment to establish cause in a population. Two randomly chosen samples are used. One is administered the cause, and the other, called the *control group,* is not administered the cause.

Correlation   *See* Perfect Correlation.

Criteria for Accepting or Rejecting a Claim   In the order in which they should be applied:

      Reject: The claim contradicts our personal experience.

      Accept: The claim is known by personal experience.

      Reject: The claim contradicts other claims we know to be true.

      Don't accept: The claim contradicts one of the other premises.

      Accept: The claim is given as personal experience by someone we know and trust, and the person is an authority on that kind of claim.

      Accept: The claim is offered by a reputable authority whom we can trust as an expert about this kind of claim and who has no motive to mislead.

      Accept: The claim is put forward by a reputable journal or reference source.

      Accept: The claim is in a media source that's usually reliable and has no obvious motive to mislead.

Critical Thinking   Evaluating whether we should be convinced that some claim is true or some argument is good, as well as formulating good arguments.

Deductive Argument   An argument for which the best analysis of its strength can be made solely in terms of its form and the meaning of the words in it.

Definition   An explanation or stipulation of how to use a word or phrase. A definition is not a claim. *See also* Good Definition, Persuasive Definition.

Deliberation   The use of arguments to try to establish true claims or decide on a course of action.

Denying the Antecedent   Reasoning in the form: If A then B, not A, so not B. Usually weak.

Dependent Premises   Two or more premises that are meant together to support another claim, in the sense that if one is false, the other(s) do not give any support.

Direct Way of Reasoning with "All"   Reasoning in the form: All S are P, *a* is S, so *a* is P. Valid.

Direct Way of Reasoning with "Almost All"   Reasoning in the form: Almost all S are P, *a* is S, so *a* is P. Strong.

Direct Way of Reasoning with Conditionals   Reasoning in the form: If A then B, A, so B. Valid. Also called *modus ponens*.

Direct Way of Reasoning with "No"   Reasoning in the form: All S are P, no Q is P, so no Q is S. Valid.

Disjunction   The formalization of an inclusive "or" claim using ∨ .

Disjunctive Syllogism   *See* Excluding Possibilities.

Downplayer   A word or phrase that minimizes the significance of a claim. *See also* Up-player.

Drawing the Line   A type of bad argument which assumes that if you can't make the difference entirely precise, then there is no difference.

Dubious Claim   A claim that we do not have good reason to believe is true, yet we're not sure is false. Also called an *implausible* claim.

Dysphemism   A word or phrase that makes something sound worse than a neutral description. *See also* Euphemism.

Effect   *See* Necessary Criteria for Cause and Effect.

Euphemism   A word or phrase that makes something sound better than a neutral description. *See also* Dysphemism.

Evidence   A claim or claims that give some reason to believe another claim.

Excluding Possibilities   Reasoning of the form: A or B, not A, so B. (Can use fewer or more alternatives.) Valid. Also called *disjunctive syllogism*.

Exclusive "Or" Claim   An "or" claim that is true if exactly one of the alternatives is true.

Existential Claim   A claim that can be rewritten as a "some" claim that must have the same truth-value.

Fallacy   An argument of one of the types that have been agreed to be so bad as to be unrepairable. *See also* Content Fallacy, Structural Fallacy.

False Dilemma   An argument that uses an "or" claim that seems to be true but isn't because it misses some possibilities.

Feel-Good Argument   An argument that uses or can be repaired only by putting in a premise that says, roughly: You should believe or do _____ if it makes you feel good.

Foreseeable Consequence of a Cause   A claim that becomes true after the cause, and which is part of the normal conditions of the cause, and which does not itself count as a cause.

Gambler's Fallacy An argument using as premise that a run of events of a certain kind makes a run of contrary events more likely in order to even up the probabilities.

General Cause and Effect A causal claim that covers many particular cause and effect claims.

Generalizing To conclude a claim about a group, the *population*, from a claim about some part of it, the *sample*. To generalize is to make an argument. Sometimes the general claim is called the *generalization*; sometimes that word is used for the whole argument. The knowledge of the sample is called the *inductive evidence* for the generalization. *See also* Three Premises Needed for a Good Generalization.

Good Argument One in which the premises give good reason to believe the conclusion is true. *See also* Tests for an Argument to be Good.

Good Definition A definition in which the word or phrase being defined and the words doing the defining work interchangeably: It's correct to use the one exactly when it's correct to use the other.

Guide to Repairing Arguments Given an (implicit) argument that is apparently defective, we are justified in *adding* a premise or conclusion if it satisfies all three of the following:
   1. The argument becomes stronger or valid.
   2. The premise is plausible and would be plausible to the other person.
   3. The premise is more plausible than the conclusion.
If the argument is then valid or strong, yet one of the original premises is false or dubious, we may *delete* that premise if the argument remains valid or strong.
   See also Unrepairable Arguments.

Haphazard Sampling Choosing a sample with no intention to be biased, but not randomly. Not usually reliable for generalizing. *See also* Random Sampling.

Hasty Generalization Generalizing from a sample that is much too small.

Hyperbole A gross exaggeration.

Implausible Claim *See* Dubious Claim.

Implying *See* Inferring and Implying.

Inclusive "Or" Claim An "or" claim that is true if at least one of the alternatives is true.

Independent Premises Premises that are not dependent. Each gives support to the conclusion regardless whether the other(s) are true.

Indicator Word A word or phrase added to a claim telling us the role of the claim in an argument or what the speaker thinks of the claim or argument. Not part of a claim.

Indirect Way of Reasoning with Conditionals Reasoning in the form: If A then B, not B, so not A. Valid. Also called *modus tollens*.

Inductive Argument An argument that is not deductive: The best analysis of its strength requires knowing more than just its form and the meaning of the words in it. *See also* Generalizing.

Inductive Evidence   *See* Generalizing.

Inferring and Implying   When someone leaves a conclusion unstated, he is *implying* the conclusion. When you decide that an unstated claim is the conclusion, you are *inferring* that claim. We also say someone is *implying* a claim if in context it's clear he believes the claim. In that case we *infer* that the person believes the claim.

Innuendo   A concealed claim that is particularly unpleasant.

Intervening Cause   A claim that becomes true after the cause and before the effect, which is not a foreseeable consequence of the original cause, and which would qualify as a cause, too.

Invalid Argument   An argument that is not valid.

Irrelevant Premise   A premise that can be deleted from an argument without making the argument any weaker. *See also* Relevance.

Issue   A claim that is being debated.

Law of Large Numbers   If the probability of something occurring is X percent, then over the long run the number of occurrences will tend toward X percent.

Loaded Question   A question that conceals a claim that is dubious.

Margin of Error   In a generalization, the range within which the actual number for the population is likely to fall.

Mean   *See* Average.

Median *of a collection of numerical values*   The midway mark: the value such that there are as many values above it as below it in the collection.

Mistaking the Person for the Argument   An argument that uses or can be repaired only by putting in a premise that says, roughly: (Almost) any argument that _____ gives about _____ is bad.

Mistaking the Person for the Claim   An argument that uses or can be repaired only by putting in a premise that says, roughly: (Almost) anything that _____ says about _____ is false.

Mode *of a collection of numbers*   The number that appears most often in the collection.

Modus Ponens ("way of putting")   *See* Direct Way of Reasoning with Conditionals.

Modus Tollens ("way of taking")   *See* Indirect Way of Reasoning with Conditionals.

Necessary and Sufficient Conditions   For a conditional "If A then B" that is always true, A is a sufficient condition for B to be true, and B is a necessary condition for A to be true.

Necessary Criteria for Cause and Effect
  1. The cause precedes the effect.
  2. It is impossible that the cause could be true and effect false, given the normal conditions.
  3. The cause makes a difference.
  4. The cause is close in space and time to the effect.

Negation   The formalization of a "not" claim using ⌐. *See also* Contradictory of a Claim.

Negative Universal Claim   A claim that can be rewritten as a "no" claim or an "all not" claim that must have the same truth-value.

No Matter What   Reasoning in the form: If A then B; if not A, then B; so B. Valid.

Normal Conditions   The (usually unstated) claims needed to establish that there is cause and effect.

Objective Claim   A claim that is true or false independently of what anyone or anything may believe or think or feel.

Oxymoron   A phrase in which contradictory terms are combined, e.g., square circle.

Particular Cause and Effect   A claim that this particular cause caused this particular effect. *See also* General Cause and Effect.

Perfect Correlation   Every time this happens, that happens.

Perfectionist Dilemma   An argument with (possibly unstated) premise: Either the situation will be completely perfect if we do this, or we shouldn't do it.

Persuasive Definition   A claim masquerading as a definition. An attempt to close off debate by stating the conclusion as a definition.

Phony Refutation   An argument that uses or requires as premises roughly:
    1. _____ has said or done _____, which shows that he or she does not believe the conclusion of his or her own argument.
    2. If someone does not believe the conclusion of his or her own argument, the argument is bad.

Plausible Claim   A claim we have good but not certain reason to believe is true.

Population   The group we are generalizing to. *See* Generalizing.

Post Hoc Ergo Propter Hoc   "After this, therefore because of this." Claiming that there is cause and effect because one claim became true after another.

Premise   The claims in an argument that are meant to establish that a particular claim, the conclusion, is true.

Principle of Rational Discussion   We assume that the other person who is discussing an issue with us or whose arguments we are reading:
    1. Knows about the subject under discussion.
    2. Is able and willing to reason well.
    3. Is not lying.

Proof Substitute   A word or phrase that suggests the speaker has a proof, but no proof is actually offered.

Qualifier   A word or phrase that restricts or limits the meaning of other words.

Random Sampling   Choosing a sample so that at every choice there is an equal chance for any of the remaining members of the population to be picked. *See also* Haphazard Sampling.

Rationality and Arguments   If you recognize that an argument is good, then it is irrational to believe the conclusion is false.

***Reasoning in a Chain with* All**   Reasoning in the form: All S are P, all P are Q, so all S are Q. Valid.

Reasoning in a Chain with Conditionals   Reasoning in the form: If A then B; if B then C; so if A then C. Valid. *See also* Slippery Slope.

***Reasoning in a Chain with* Some**   Reasoning in the form: Some S are P, some P are Q, so some S are Q. Usually weak.

Reducing to the Absurd   Proving a claim or claims false or dubious by drawing out consequences of them that are false or dubious.

Refuting an Argument Directly   Showing an argument is bad by doing one of the following: Showing one of the premises is false. Showing the argument isn't valid or strong. Showing the conclusion is false. *See also* Reducing to the Absurd, Phony Refutation, Strawman.

Relevance   The premises of an argument are irrelevant just means that the argument is so bad you can't see how to repair it. *See also* Irrelevant Premise.

Repairing Arguments   *See* Guide to Repairing Arguments, Unrepairable Arguments.

Representative Sample   A sample in which no one subgroup of the whole population is represented more than its proportion in the population.

Sample   The group we generalize from. *See* Generalizing.

Scare Tactics   *See* Appeal to Fear.

Slanter   Any literary device that attempts to convince by using words that conceal a dubious claim.

Slippery Slope Argument   An argument that uses a chain of conditionals, some of which are false or dubious. A bad form of reducing to the absurd.

Some   Usually means "at least one." Sometimes best understood as "at least one, but not all."

Sound Argument   A valid argument with true premises.

Statistical Generalization   A generalization that says that the same proportion of the whole as in the sample will have the property.

Strawman   Pretending to refute a claim or argument by arguing against a claim that's easier to show false or an argument that's easier to show weak.

Strong and Weak Arguments   Invalid arguments are classified on a scale from very strong to weak. An argument is *very strong* if it is almost impossible for the premises to be true and the conclusion false (at the same time). An argument is *weak* if it's not unlikely that the premises could be true and conclusion false (at the same time).

Structural Fallacy An argument whose form alone guarantees that it is a bad argument.

Subjective Claim Any claim that is not objective.

Sufficient Condition *See* Necessary and Sufficient Conditions.

Support A claim or claims that gives some reason to believe another.

Tautology A compound claim that is true for every possible assignment of truth-values to its parts.

Tests for an Argument to be Good The argument must be valid or strong. There must be good reasons to believe its premises are true. The premises must be more plausible than the conclusion.

Three Premises Needed for a Good Generalization The sample is representative. The sample is big enough. The sample is studied well.

Two Times Zero is Still Zero A comparison that makes something look impressive, but whose basis of comparison is not stated.

Two Wrongs Make a Right *See* Appeal to Spite.

Unbiased Sample *See* Representative Sample.

Uncontrolled Experiment: Cause-to-Effect An experiment to establish cause in a population. Two randomly chosen samples are used. In one the cause is (apparently) present, in the other (apparently) not, and they are followed over time.

Uncontrolled Experiment: Effect-to-Cause An experiment to establish cause in a population. A sample of the population in which the effect is present is examined to see if the cause is also present and other possible causes are not present.

Universal Claim A claim that can be rewritten as an "all" claim that must have the same truth-value. *See also* Negative Universal Claim.

Unrepairable Arguments We can't repair an argument if any one of the following hold:
- There's no argument there.
- The argument is so lacking in coherence that there's nothing to add.
- The premises it uses are false or very dubious and cannot be deleted.
- The obvious premise to add would make the argument weak.
- The obvious premise that would make the argument strong or valid is false.
- The conclusion is clearly false.

Up-player A word or phrase that exaggerates the significance of a claim. *See also* Downplayer, Hyperbole.

Vague Sentence A sentence is vague if it is unclear what the speaker intended. Sentences that are too vague are not claims.

Valid Argument An argument in which it is impossible for the premises to be true and conclusion false (at the same time).

Valid Argument Form   A form of argument such that every argument that has that form is valid.

Weak Argument   *See* Strong and Weak Arguments.

Weaseler   A claim that is actually much weaker than it seems to be.

Wishful Thinking   A feel-good argument used on oneself.

Answers to Selected Exercises

Chapter 1

1. Convincings/arguments.
3. We can convince others; others can convince us; we can convince ourselves.
4. b. Yes, but truth-value depends on who says it (looking forward to Chapter 2)
   e. No, a command.
   g. I could never figure out who was supposed to be in need. It's too unclear for me to classify it as a claim.
   i. Sentences that become true when the right person says them, like this claim or "I now pronounce you man and wife" aren't clearly claims. That's what makes it so hard to argue with an umpire: It's strike three if he says so—that's all there is to it.
   l. Yes, assuming that "Juney" and "Ralph" are indeed names of some things.
   n. Yes, but it might not have the same truth-value as (m).
   o. Yes.
   p. Yes.
   q. Yes.
   s. Depends on your view of what "true" means. Some might say "No," thinking that there's no way we could ever determine whether it is true or false. Others will argue it is true or false, independently of us. That's philosophy.
7. To convince (establish) that a claim, called "the conclusion," is true.
9. *Given an argument,* the conclusion is the claim that someone is attempting to establish is true, while the premises are the claims that are used in trying to establish that.
10. Command, threats, entreaties ("Dr. E, Dr. E, please, please let me pass this course"), etc., are not arguments.
13. *Argument*? No.
    Can be recast as one, but it's not clear whether the conclusion is "You're dumb to like the movie" or "The movie was bad."
14. *Argument*? Yes.
    Conclusion: Cats are nasty.
    Premises: Cats smell bad. Cats urinate in the house. Cats kill songbirds. Cats cause allergies so your friends can't come over.
15. Not an argument. Moreover, it can't be recast as one: What's the conclusion, "It's O.K. to buy white mice for your cat to play with," or "It's not O.K. to buy white mice to feed a boa constrictor"? Illustrates the pitfalls of using questions to advance an argument.
16. *Argument*? Yes.
    Conclusion: You shouldn't eat at Zee-Zee Frap's restaurant.
    Premise: I heard they did really badly on their health inspection last week.

NOTE: The premise isn't "They did really bad on their health inspection last week." Someone hearing that's so and its being so aren't the same claim.

21. Not an argument.

22. What Zoe says isn't an argument, it's only a claim.
What Dick says is an argument. Conclusion "You do love me." ("Of course you do" is elliptical and good English for "Of course you do love me.")
Premise: Yesterday you said you couldn't live without me.

23. Second paragraph is an argument, though there are two good choices for what the conclusion is: the first sentence or the last one. First paragraph isn't, since there's no even remotely clear conclusion for it.

24. Yes, an argument. Conclusion: Homosexuality can't be hereditary. Premise: Homosexual couples can't reproduce. Homosexuality would have died out long ago.
In the next chapter we'll see what's wrong with this.

25. *Argument*? Not as stated. There is no conclusion.
It seems obvious what is intended: Homosexuals should have the right to marry.
In Chapter 4 we'll discuss when it's O.K. to add a conclusion.

28. No, since there's no language. This does not deny that the dog may be reasoning, but if you believe that then you need a notion of reasoning that doesn't require language.

29. Depends on whether she's talking to herself. We can't tell. Arguments use language.

31. **Virtue**

Chapter 2

Section A

1. It is unclear what the speaker intended.

4. a. Too vague—"irritable" might be O.K., but what's "cold"?.
   c. O.K.—subjective.
   f. O.K.—just because you don't know what the entire cost is doesn't mean that phrase isn't precise.
   h. Too vague.
   l. Too vague.
   n. Too vague or subjective.
   p. Too vague: What's "official language" mean?

5. Ask him or her to make it more precise.

7. She could have some objective standards, but you can't imagine what they are. So you'd best not take it as a claim. Or she could just be saying, "I like Picasso's paintings better than Rembrandt's," in which case it's a subjective claim. Or she could have no clear idea at all, in which case it isn't a claim.

10. It's an example of the drawing the line fallacy.

11. Objective: its truth-value does not depend on what anyone or anything thinks/believes/feels. Subjective = not objective.

13. When describing our own feelings we don't have awfully precise language to use. So "It's hot" may be the best we can do in describing how we feel. But it's inadequate as an objective claim.

14. a. Objective.
    d. Subjective (even though Dr. E thinks it's objective and true).
    g. Subjective.
    j. Objective in the Middle Ages, when people believed demons existed. Now probably understood as demons in his mind, so subjective.
    k. Objective, since "insane" is now a technical term of the law.
    n. It had better be objective or there's no point in arguing about a grade.
    q. Objective. "I believe that God exists" (subjective) ≠ "God exists" (objective, since you don't mean that He's just someone's thought or feeling). That there is debate about whether a claim is true doesn't make the claim subjective.

Section B

1. a. No, a sentence can, but we wouldn't classify it as a claim.
   b. Yes, especially if it's subjective.
2. b. I was invited one week ago to go to the movies then.
      I was invited one week ago to go to the movies now.
   c. Americans—individually or collectively? Compare Example 4.
   g. Each player on the team had a B average. The average of all the grades of the members of the team was B.
   j. Vague, not ambiguous.
3. None.
6. c. Ambiguity of the word "protect": Anything that's valuable should be kept from harm or loss.

Section C

1. c. Persuasive definition.
   d. Definition. But no longer classifies correctly, though it once did.
   f. Not a definition.
   g. Persuasive definition. May work for the Pope, but others think it's not just wrong, but an attempt to convince.
4. The definition and the original phrase can be used interchangeably.
6. Because they settle a debate before it's started. They are concealed claims.
8. Ms. Hathaway is (implicitly) arguing that she was justified in allowing her 7-year-old daughter to fly across the country. You might believe her, until you realize she is trading on the vagueness of the words "freedom," "choice," and "liberty" (try to pin down exactly what you think those words mean).

For 9–19, at least two terms will apply to each.

10. Definition, not a claim.
11. Persuasive definition, a claim.
12. Either: too vague and not a claim; or subjective claim.
16. Objective claim.
19. Subjective claim (not ambiguous: it's obvious what's intended).

Chapter 3

Sections A–C

2. One which gives us good reason to believe the conclusion is true.

5. No. The premises could be false. Even if the premises are true, they might be less plausible than the conclusion.

6. Come up with a (possibly imagined) situation in which the premises are true and conclusion false.

8. Nothing.

14. No. A false conclusion shows the argument is bad. But it could still be valid (it would have false premises then).

16. No. *Invalid* arguments are classified from very strong to weak.

17. Bad. (Not necessarily weak—it could be valid.)

19. d.   22. c.
20. d.   23. c.
21. c.   24. d.

Chapter 3

1. No. See Section D.

4. The claim he was using as a hypothesis is false, since mathematicians always (try to) use valid arguments. A mathematician would be laughed out of his profession if he gave strong but not valid proofs.

6. No. See the parakeets example in Section D.

8. *Conclusion*: You cut your hair.   Premises: Your hair was long. Now your hair is short. "So" is not part of the claim.   Invalid: Might have got hair caught in a lawn mower. But it's strong. Good if premises are true.

9. *Conclusion*: My bicycle is a car.
   Premise: All cars have wheels. My bicycle has wheels.
   Weak, bad. Premises are true, conclusion false.

Below are just sketches of the answers. You should do the full exercise.

11. Weak, bad. Spot could be a seal, or a fox, or a philosophy professor.

14. Valid and good.

15. Weak, bad. Spot could be a penguin, or a cockroach.

17. Valid, but begging the question.

20. Weak, and the first premise is false. Bad.

22. Not an argument.

24. Weak, bad. They might want to hire conservatives for balance. Or they always hire conservative, but they become liberal over time. Or Maria just hasn't met enough professors.

25. Valid, good if premises are true.

30. Strong, though surely the premise is false, so bad.

32. The argument is strong, but *not* valid. The laws of nature might change tomorrow and your instructor turns out to be immortal.

33. Valid. But no improvement on Exercise 32, since that's the only way you could get the first premise.

Chapter 4

Sections A–D

2. If the principle doesn't apply there would be no reason to hold deliberations. Detailed explanation given under the Principle.

4. Addicts are notoriously incapable of reasoning well about their addictions. So the Principle of Rational Discussion won't apply. Take her to AA.

5. Because it's ineffective in the long run, and it's unethical. See the discussion below the presentation of the Principle.

6. a. The doctor should assume the Principle when you describe your symptoms, because you want to reason well and are certainly knowledgeable about how you feel.
   b. The doctor shouldn't assume the Principle in telling you how you should deal with your illness unless you are knowledgeable about medicine. (S)he should educate.

8. If any of the following hold:
   The obvious premise to add to make the argument strong or valid is false.
   The obvious premise to add would make the argument weak.
   The premises it uses are false or very dubious and cannot be deleted.
   The argument is so lacking in coherence there's nothing obvious to add.
   There's no argument there.

13. a. i. premise, ii. premise, iii. premise, iv. conclusion
    b. i. conclusion, ii. premise, iii. premise, iv. premise
    f. i. premise, ii. premise, iii. conclusion
    g. i. premise, ii. premise, iii. premise, iv. conclusion
    h. i. premise, ii. premise, iii. conclusion
    i. i. premise, ii. conclusion, iii. premise, iv. premise

15. Deleting it does not make the argument weaker, and there is no obvious way to link it to the conclusion.

The most common errors in the following exercises :

•Repairing arguments that are unrepairable.

•Adding premises that don't make the argument stronger, or make a whole new argument.

•Adding a premise and then marking the argument moderate or weak.

  The only reason to add a premise is to make the argument valid or strong.

•Marking both "valid" and "strong", or both "valid" and "weak."

•Marking an argument "weak", when it's bad (valid or strong with a dubious premise).

In the answers I only note what premise(s) are needed, though you should do the complete exercise. When a premise is added, the argument is good (if the premises are true), unless noted otherwise.

21. The person who shows symptoms of the flu first got the flu first. If you get the flu first, you can't have gotten it from someone who didn't have it. Then valid.

    The first added premise is probably false, but it's the only way the argument could be repaired. So the argument is unrepairable.

    You *can't* add: "The person who shows symptoms of the flu first *probably* got the flu first." The word "impossible" indicates the speaker thinks he/she is making a valid argument, so you can't repair it as a strong argument.

23. This is an argument: You can't ignore what the speaker intends, and "sop" shows that the speaker meant it as an argument. Can't be repaired (see Example 2).

24. Too much missing. Can't be repaired without making a new argument entirely. But it is an argument. See the comments for Exercise 23.

28. Ralph barks.

29. "You can only inherit blue eyes if both your parents are blue-eyed" is the obvious premise to add to make the argument valid ("must be" shows you want to make it valid). But that's false. So it's unrepairable.

30. *Conclusion*: Dr. E is required to have office hours. (*Not*: Dr. E. has office hours.)

34. Only the Lone Ranger has silver bullets in his gunbelt, has a horse called Silver, a friend called Tonto, and goes around saving people.

   You can't drop "Only". Someone from Istanbul might think that everyone in San Francisco has silver bullets in his gunbelt, has a horse called Silver, a friend called Tonto, and goes around saving people.

37. One of the most important duties of a president of a college is to spend time with students. A college president should not neglect one of her most important duties.

   But we don't know if it's good, because we don't know if the first added premise is true.

38. Not an argument.

Chapter 5

Sections A *and* B.1

2. Accept as true, reject as false, suspend judgment.

4. Because if the premises were true, the conclusion would have to be true, too.

7. No. It's just the experience of other people.

10. We have good reason to doubt our memory, or the claim contradicts experiences of ours and there is a good argument (theory) against the claim. Also, beware of confusing memory with deductions from experience.

16. Memory.

17. Nothing.

18. The same attitude we had before we heard the argument. An argument with a false premise tells us nothing about the conclusion.

Sections B.2–B.5

8. b. If you suspend judgment, then the defendant probably will be found innocent.

Section B

3. See the box on page 96 of the text

4. Personal experience. Memory is the greatest limitation.

5. Because the conclusion of an argument is true, the person thinks there's good reason to believe the premises.

6. The criteria go from ones closest to our own experience to those furthest.

9. Tom is making a classic example of a bad appeal to authority. The experts he is

relying on have motive to mislead and should not be relied on.

11. Reject (not expert, common knowledge it's false).
12. Reject—if you know anything about toads and warts. Change doctors.
13. Reject (personal experience. You *did* notice it rises in the east?).
16. Suspend judgment (if it's even a claim, since it's so vague).
18. Accept if you haven't been looking at your speedometer, or if you have and you know you were speeding. Reject if you've been monitoring your speed, saw the speed limit sign, and you weren't speeding. (But don't sass back.)
20. Suspend judgment (biased source).
21. Yes, he should accept it, but not be content, since he needs to *understand* why it's valid.
22. Suspend judgment (not reliable source).
25. ACCEPT!!! You can't reject this on personal experience, since no personal experience you have will tell you who got sick worst from which pets in the U.S. during the last year. And to reject it because of the source is a serious error (see Section C.2).
26. Accept (usually reliable source).
35. None. If you think you should judge ads more critically, you're not judging other arguments critically enough.
37. Be sure you list the criteria.
39. Why would anyone who can make $250,000 per year playing craps share his secret?

Section C

1. a. Accepting a claim because of a supposedly authoritative source.
    b. No. The surgeon general saying smoking is bad for your health.
2. Whether an argument is good or bad does not depend on who said it.
5. A bad appeal to authority.
6. It may smack of hypocrisy, yet not really be a contradiction. Just because the person who states the argument apparently doesn't believe the conclusion, doesn't mean the argument is bad. See the answer to Exercise 2.
7. He's confused the person with the argument, thinking that if a person apparently doesn't believe the conclusion of his own argument, the argument is bad.
8. Suzy really blew it! She's taking the word of an authority over her own experience. Above all you should trust your own experience.
12 and 13. The first of these is not a bad argument: We add the unstated premise "The Surgeon General is a specialist in epidemiology and is hired by the President to advise the public on health concerns. So if the Surgeon General says smoking is bad for you, it probably is bad for you." The conclusion follows.

   But the second of these is a bad argument, for it requires an unstated premise like, "The Surgeon General is well-qualified to decide on what laws should govern our behavior." That seems dubious: A Surgeon General is a physician without special training in law, public policy, or moral judgments.
15. Suzy is right! She says that she has no good reason to believe me, since I'm not an expert on virtue (I'm a logician, after all). She's not suggesting that I'm wrong, but only that she has no reason to accept the claim. (Of course if Suzy knew me better, she'd revise her opinion . . .)
20. Just a comment on the speaker's apparent inconsistency.

Review Exercises for Chapters 1–5

1. A collection of claims intended to show that one of them, the conclusion, is true.
2. A declarative sentence we can view as true or false.
3. a. A claim whose truth-value does not depend on what anyone or anything thinks/believes/feels.
4. There are at least two clear ways to understand it.
5. Yes. All communication is to some extent vague. The question is whether the sentence is *too* vague to be a claim.
6. No. A definition is an instruction how to use a word or words.
7. a. A claim masquerading as a definition.
8. An argument in which the premises give good reason to believe the conclusion is true.
9. The premises must be true or highly plausible.
   The argument must be valid or strong.
   The premises must be less dubious than the conclusion.
10. a. A valid argument is one in which it is impossible for the premises to be true and conclusion false (at the same time).
11. a. A strong argument is one in which it is almost impossible for the premises to be true and conclusion false (at the same time).
12. Yes. See the answer to Exercise 9.
13. Give an example (possibly imagined) where the premises are true and conclusion false.
14. No. From a false premise you can prove anything.
15. Nothing.
16. No. It could beg the question. Or a premise could be false or dubious.
17. No. See the parakeets example in Chapter 3.
18. When someone recognizes that an argument is good but believes the conclusion is false.
19. We assume that the other person who is discussing with us or whose arguments we are reading: 1. Knows about the subject under discussion; 2. Is able and willing to reason well; 3. Is not lying.
20. Given an (implicit) argument that is apparently defective, we are justified in adding a premise or conclusion if: 1. The argument becomes stronger or valid, and 2. The premise is plausible and would seem plausible to the other person, and 3. The premise is more plausible than the conclusion. If the argument is valid or strong, yet one of the premises is false or dubious, we may delete the premise if the argument remains valid or strong.
21. There's no argument there. The argument is so lacking in coherence that there's nothing obvious to add. The premises it uses are false or dubious and can't be deleted. The obvious premise to add would make the argument weak. The obvious premise to add to make the argument strong or valid is false.
22. a. A word or phrase added to a claim telling us the role of the claim in an argument, or what the speaker thinks of the claim or argument.
    b. No.
23. Our personal experience.
24. Accept as true, reject as false, suspend judgment.
25. The claim is known by personal experience.
    The claim is given as personal experience by someone we know and trust and the person

       is an authority on that kind of claim.

     The claim is offered by a reputable authority whome we can trust as being an expert about this kind of claim and has no motive to mislead.

     The claim is put forward in a reputable journal or reference source.

     The claim is in a media source that's usually reliable and would have no obvious motive to mislead.

26. It contradicts our personal experience (with exceptions).

     It contradicts other claims we know to be true.

     It contradicts one of the other premises.

27. He or she believes the argument is good because the conclusion is true.

28. He accepts the claim, "Almost any argument that _____ gives about _____ is bad."

29. Never.

30. Never.

31. Rejecting an argument because the speaker's actions or words suggest that he/she does not believe the conclusion of his/her own argument.

Chapter 6

Section A

1. A single claim that is made up of two or more other claims.

2. Because both parts have to be true anyway for the argument to be good.

3. a. A claim that is reasonable to rewrite as an "if . . . then . . ." claim. b. Yes.

5. The alternatives.

9. Not an or-claim. "Neither A nor B" is the same as "not A and not B."

10. When the conditional is rewritten as an "if . . . then . . ." claim, the claim following "if ."

11. Here are some samples. Come up with your own.

     Don't come home and there'll be hell to pay.

     Ask me nicely and I'll go with you.

     When you get married it means that you can no longer date anyone else.

12. A claim that always has the opposite truth-value.

13. Not A and not B. (Or you could say, "Neither A nor B.")

14. A but not B. (Or, if you prefer, "A and not B." Sometimes it sounds better to say, "not B even though A.")

15. a. Neither inflation will go up nor will interest rates go up.

    d. Manuel will take the exam on Tuesday.

    e. Either Maria won't go shopping or Manuel won't cook.

    f. Maria went shopping, but Manuel didn't cook.

18. *Conditional?* Yes.

    Antecedent: You don't apologize.

    Consequent: I'll never talk to you again.

    Contradictory: You don't apologize and I do talk to you.

19. *Conditional?* No.

    Antecedent:

    Consequent:

    Contradictory: Maria or Manuel will travel at Christmas.

21. *Conditional?* No.

Antecedent:

Consequent:

Contradictory: Sometimes Lee does write to his brother.

24. Not a conditional. Contradictory: Dick didn't say, "If Spot attacked your cat, then I'll pay for the funeral."

26. *Conditional?* Yes.

Antecedent: If Dick takes Spot for a walk he'll do the dishes.

Consequent: Dick won't take Spot for a walk.

Contradictory: If Dick takes Spot for a walk he'll do the dishes and Dick will take Spot for a walk.

27. *Conditional?* Yes.

Antecedent: Dick will go to the basketball game.

Consequent: Dick either got a free ticket or he borrowed money.

Contradictory: Dick will go to the basketball game and he didn't get a free ticket and he didn't borrow money.

Section B

2. A or B, not A, so B. (Also: A or B, not B, so A. And similarly for longer "or" claims.)

10. *Argument?* Yes.

Conclusion : We'll have to get married.

Premises: Either we get married or we should stop living together. Living together is awkward. Dick does not want to live alone. Zoe does not want to live alone.

Additional premises needed: We shouldn't stop living together.

Classify : Valid.

Good argument? Probably not. There doesn't seem to be any way to make strong the inference from "Living together is awkward" to "We should marry or stop living together."

11. *Argument?* Zoe makes one. Dick tries to refute hers.

Conclusion : We should get rid of Spot.

Premises: Either we train him to stop chewing or get rid of him. We haven't been able to train him. Spot keeps chewing on everything in the house.

Additional premises needed If we haven't been able to train Spot, then we won't be able to train Spot.

Classify : Valid.

Good argument? No. Dick shows it's a false dilemma.

12. *Argument?* Yes.

Conclusion : I am leaving you.

Premises: Either you do the dishes and take out the trash or I'm leaving you. Doing the dishes and taking out the trash is not man's work. Dick is a man.

Additional premises needed: If it's not man's work, a man will not do the dishes.

Classify : Valid.

Good argument? Moderate. The added premise is dubious, but does apply to Dick. Not a false dilemma, as Zoe demonstrates by leaving Dick. Don't worry, they'll get back together soon.

Section C.1

6. a. If Flo doesn't have to take a bath, then she didn't play with Spot.
7. Flo came over early to play.
8. None. Appears to be Denying the Antecedent.
11. Dr. E has time to grade a regular exam. (Indirect Way)
12. None. Appears to be Affirming the Consequent.

Sections C.2 and C.3

1. a. If you pass this course, then you studied hard.
      If you don't study hard, then you can't pass this course.
   b. If I'll love you, then you'll love me.
      If you don't love me, I won't love you.
3. (i) is necessary for (ii)
8. Neither.
11. (i) is sufficient for (ii)
12. (i) is necessary for (ii) [(ii) is sufficient for (i)]
17. Being a male.
19. Having a knife, . . .
21. If Spot is to be healthy, then he needs to eat nutritious dog food.
23. If Dick and Zoe go to Mexico for the holidays, then Zoe's mother didn't come.
24. If Suzy gets an A in critical thinking, then Dr. E was drunk when he filled out grades.
26. Neither.

Chapter 6

1. Excluding Possibilities, The Direct Way of reasoning with conditionals, the Indirect
   Way of reasoning with conditionals, Reasoning in a Chain with conditionals, [in an
   exercise: No Matter What].
2. Affirming the Consequent, Denying the Antecedent.
3. Affirming the Consequent, Denying the Antecedent, False Dilemmas, Slippery Slope
   Arguments, [in an exercise: Perfectionist Dilemma].
7. h. Dr. E being rich is necessary when Dr. E wins the lottery.
      Dr. E being rich is necessary when Dr. E marries a rich woman.
      Dr. E being rich is necessary when Dr. E's book sells a million copies.
9. *Argument*? Yes.
   Conclusion : Mr. Ensign is a good congressman.
   Premises: If someone is a good congressman, he shows up for every vote in congress.
      Mr. Ensign is a congressman who shows up for every vote.
   Additional premises needed: None.
   Classify: Weak.
   Good argument? No. Unrepairable: Affirming the consequent.
10. *Argument*? Yes.
    Conclusion: Dick got a free ticket.
    Premises: Dick said he would go to the basketball game only if he could get a free
       ticket. Dick is at the game.
    Additional premises needed: If Dick said he would go to the basketball game only if

he could get a free ticket, then Dick will go to the basketball game only if he can get a free ticket.

Form of argument: Direct Way.

Classify : Valid.

Good argument? If premises are true, then yes.

13. *Argument?* Yes.

Conclusion: Columbus didn't discover America.

Premises: Only if Columbus landed in a place with no people in it could you say that he discovered it. The Americas, especially where he landed, were populated. Columbus met natives.

Additional premises needed: If Columbus met natives, then where he landed was populated.

Classify : Valid.

Good argument? Yes. Indirect way of reasoning with conditionals (rewrite the "only if" claim as an "if . . . then . . ." claim).

15. *Argument* Yes.

Conclusion: I should not allow questions in my class.

Bad argument. Slippery slope.

16. *Argument?* Yes.

Conclusion: Tom should buy Epstein's book.

Premises: The book by Epstein is great. If you have a sense of humor you should buy it. If you don't have a sense of humor you should buy it.

Classify: Valid.

Good argument? Yes. The first premise doesn't help the argument, but the rest is a no-matter-what argument. And the premises are true!

18. *Argument?* Yes.

Conclusion: If Dick has a class and Zoe is working, then there's no point in calling their home to ask them over for dinner.

Premises: Spot can't answer the phone.

Additional premises needed : If Dick has a class and Zoe is working, then Dick and Zoe aren't home. If Dick and Zoe aren't home, then no one can answer the phone if someone calls. If no one can answer the phone, then there's no point in calling their home to ask them over for dinner.

Classify : Valid.

Good argument? Yes. Reasoning in a chain.

20. *Argument?* Yes.

Conclusion : (unstated) Jeffrey Dahmer was guilty of murder.

Premises: If murder is the killing of someone with the intent to kill that person, and Jeffrey Dahmer really did kill all those people they say he did, then Jeffrey Dahmer was guilty of murder. Jeffrey Dahmer intended to kill those people he did kill.

Additional premises needed: None.

Classify : Valid.

Good argument? Yes. But no obvious form we've studied.

21. *Argument?* Yes.

Conclusion : We should get Tom a leash.

Premises: Dick heard that Tom is going to get a pet.

Additional premises needed: If Dick heard that Tom is going to get a pet, then Tom is going to get a pet. Tom is going to get a pet. If Tom gets a dog, then he will need a leash. Tom will get a dog. Tom needs a leash. We should get Tom what he wants.

Classify : Valid.

Good argument? Possibly. Premises are plausible and arguments are valid or strong, except for one unstated premise: "If Dick heard that Tom's going to get a pet, then Tom is going to get a pet."

22. *Argument*? Yes.

Conclusion : If you lock up someone, he should be locked up forever.

Premises: Every criminal is either already a hardened repeat offender or will become one. Criminals learn to be hardened criminals in jail. We don't want any hardened criminals running free on our streets.

Additional premises needed : *First argument*: If a criminal is not a hardened repeat offender and goes to jail, then he will learn to be a hardened repeat offender.* If a criminal goes to jail, then he will be a hardened repeat offender. Every criminal who is locked up will become a hardened repeat offender.

Second argument: If we don't want any hardened criminals running free on our streets, then if we lock up a criminal, we should lock him up forever.

Classify: *First argument*: Valid (No-Matter-What). *Second argument*: Valid. (Direct Way)

Good argument? No. Premises are dubious, especially *. (False Dilemma)

Chapter 7

Sections A and B

1. No. All I've shown is that the student is (apparently) being irrational.
2. Raising objections to parts of an argument to show the argument is bad.
3. Nothing!
4. Answer the objections by showing that they are false or do not destroy the support for your conclusion.

   OR you could say, "I hadn't thought of that. I guess you're right."

   OR you could say, "I'll have to think about that."

7. Sex is the answer to almost everyone's problems.

    Unsubstantiated claim. Dick's "Why?" asks for support. It's an invitation to Zoe to give an argument.

   It takes away your tensions.   *Zoe offers support for her conclusion.*

   It doesn't if you're involved with someone you don't like.

    Dick shows her support is false or dubious.

   Sex makes you feel better.

    Zoe gives up on that support and offers another.

   It doesn't if it's against your morals. Heroin makes you feel good.

    Dick's first comment shows Zoe's claim is dubious. His second comment shows that the relation of Zoe's claim to the conclusion is weak (he's challenging the unstated premise "If it feels good, it's good to do.")

It's healthy, natural, just like eating and drinking.
> *Zoe gives one last try to support her conclusion.*

You can catch terrible diseases. Sex should be confined to marriage.
> *Dick shows that support is dubious, too. Then he asserts his own view, which is somewhat supported by his previous claims.*

Is that a proposal?
> *Zoe shows her true colors.*

10. Unrepairable.
11. Showing that at least one of several claims is false or dubious, or collectively they are unacceptable, by drawing a false or unwanted conclusion from them.
13. Ridicule is not an argument.
16. Putting words in someone's mouth. Refuting an argument or claim that the other person didn't really say.
19. Reducing to the absurd. Whether it's effective depends on what unstated premises are added to make the argument valid or strong. If the other person accepts capital punishment it might be effective.
20. Tom's presented a strawman. Doesn't refute.

Sections C and D

1. a. Premises are dependent if they are meant together to support another claim, in the sense that if one is false, the other provides no support at all. Otherwise, they are independent.
   b. No. The conclusion is not supposed to support another claim.
3. Dr. E is a teacher. *1* All teachers are men. *2* So Dr. E is a man. *3*
   Argument? Yes.
   Conclusion: *3*
   Additional premises needed? No.
   Identify any subargument, stating which claims are dependent: *1* and *2* are dependent.
   Good argument? No, *2* is false.
5. I'm on my way to school. *1* I left five minutes late. *2* Traffic is heavy. *3* I'll be late for class. *4* I might as well stop and get breakfast. *5*
   Argument? Yes.
   Conclusion: *5*
   Additional premises needed? Whenever I'm on my way to school and I'm 5 minutes late and traffic is heavy, I will be late for my classes. *a* If I'm late for classes, I might as well be very late or miss the class. *b*
   Identify any subargument, stating which claims are dependent: *1, 2, 3,* and *a* are dependent and support *4*. *4* and *b* are dependent and support *5*.
   Good argument? Depends on whether *b* is true.
6. Pigs are very intelligent animals. *1* They make great pets. *2* They learn to do tricks as well as any dog can. *3* They can be housetrained. *4* And they are affectionate. *5* They like to cuddle. *6* Pigs are known as one of the smartest animals there are. *7* If you get bored with them or they become unruly, you can eat your pet. *8*
   Argument? Yes.
   Conclusion: *2*

Additional premises needed?   Anything that is intelligent, can be housetrained, and is affectionate is a great pet. *a*

Identify any subargument, stating which claims are dependent: 1, 4, 6 and *a* are dependent and support *2*.

Good argument? First, we can ignore *7*: it duplicates *1* (with exaggeration). There's no plausible premise that will link *8* to the conclusion, so we can delete it. Then *3* gives support for *1*, and *6* gives support for *5*. If those and *a* are true, it's not bad.

9. Las Vegas has too many people. *1* There's not enough water in the desert to support more than a million people. *2* And the infrastructure of the city can't handle more than a million *3*: the streets are overcrowded *4* and traffic is always congested; *5* the schools are overcrowded *6* and new ones can't be built fast enough. *7* We should stop migration to the city by tough zoning laws in the city and county. *8*

    Argument? Yes.

    Conclusion: 8

    Additional premises needed? (You must know what "infrastructure" means to make sense of this argument.)

      Las Vegas has close to a million people. *a* If streets are crowded and schools are crowded, then the infrastructure is inadequate. *b* If infrastructure is inadequate and there is not enough water for more people, there are too many people. *c* If there are too many people, new migration to the city should be stopped. *d* The best way to stop migration is by tough zoning laws. *e* (Can't add: The *only* way to stop migration to the city is by tough zoning laws— you could arm gangs, or raise building fees.)

    Which claims are dependent with the added premises: 4, 5, 6, 7, and *b* are dependent as support for *3*. *2, a, 3,* and *c* are dependent and support *1*.

      1, d, and *e* are dependent and support *8*.

    Good argument? Everything is plausible with the exception of *e*. If that can be shown to be true, it's good.

Chapter 8

Sections A–C

1. Everything that's a car uses gasoline. Every car uses gasoline. Cars uses gasoline.
2. There is a dog that barks. At least one dog barks. There exists a dog that barks.
5. Everything that flies is a bird.
6. Nothing that is a teacher is illiterate. Teachers aren't illiterate. Not even one teacher is illiterate.
7. Dogs and only dogs are canines.
8. Nothing that's a pig can fly. Pigs can't fly. Not even one pig can fly.
15. False. I've seen Crest in some stores.

(There are other correct answers to 20–40.)

20. Some dog doesn't bark.
21. Some teacher is friendly.
22. No dog bites mailmen.
23. There exists a cat that has not clawed its owner.
24. All rats are unpleasant.

25. Some cat owners don't need regular physical examinations.
26. Some dog owner is truly unhappy.
27. Some dog owners like cats and are not mentally unbalanced. (See Chapter 6.)
28. This exam will not be given in some of the sections of critical thinking.
29. Some exam is suitable for all students.
30. All exams really test a student's knowledge.
31. All foxes are red.
32. Some students who play up to their teacher don't get good grades.
33. Some people who know how to teach critical thinking are not philosophy professors.
34. Someone carries a gun that's not a policeman, or some policeman doesn't carry a gun.
35. Something both barks and meows.
36. Some of these exercises aren't boring. [*Not:* These exercises aren't boring.]
37. Some subscribers to this magazine are not gullible. [*Not:* Every subscriber to this magazine is not gullible.]
38. Some decisions about abortions should not be left to the woman and her doctor.
39. Some cowboy had a friend named "Tonto" and the cowboy wasn't the Lone Ranger.
40. Some teacher other than Dr. E knows how to bark.

Section D

1. Invalid.

2. Valid. Only possible picture:

3. Valid. Must have: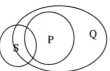

(S could be entirely within P or Q, but still the conclusion would be represented as true.)

4. Invalid.

5. Invalid.

6. Valid.

7. c.   11. d.
8. d.   12. d.
9. c.   13. d.
10. c.

14. Invalid. Zoe could be one of the ones that do attend lectures.
    Not every ≠ every not.

15. Not valid.

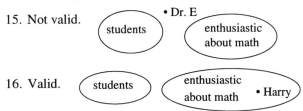

16. Valid.

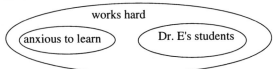

17. Not valid. No picture, but it could be that dogs bite only mailmen who are cowardly and would never bite back, and the mailmen who bite dogs are so tough they never get bitten. So there's no mailman and dog that bite each other.

18. Invalid.

20. Invalid.

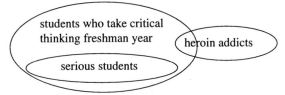

23. Invalid. George could be mute.

25. Invalid.

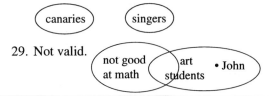

26. Not valid. The premise is *not*: all hogs grunt. Don't mistake your knowledge of the world for what's actually been said. It's reasoning in a chain with "some."

28. Invalid. Don't mistake your knowledge of the world for what's been said. Not every canary can sing = some canaries can't sing, which doesn't rule out that all canaries can't sing. (Unless you go with the other reading of "some" as "at least one but not all.")

29. Not valid.

30. Valid. No picture. Dr. E has a dog. That dog must love its master. So that dog loves Dr. E. So Dr. E is loved.

31. Invalid. Dr. E's ex-wife could have a cat.

32. For example,

If anyone is a good teacher, then he or she gives fair exams.
For anything, if it's a horse, then it loves attention.
If it's a duck, then it likes water.

Section E

1. All but a very few dogs bark. Nearly every dog barks. Only a very few dogs don't bark.
2. Very few cats bark. Almost no cat doesn't bark. Not very many cats bark.
3. Strong.
4. Not strong. Arguing backwards with "very few."
5. Not strong. Here's a picture drawn to scale:
6. Strong.
7. Strong.
8. Strong.
9. Strong.
12. Not strong. Rewrite the conclusion as "Almost all people who like pizza will not eat eggs." Then it's the form discussed in the text.
13. Not strong. It doesn't say "Most ducks quack." Rather, the first claim can be rewritten as "Almost all things that quack are ducks," leaving the possibility that there are lots of ducks that don't quack.

Review Chapters 6–8

1. An argument is a collection of claims, one of which is called the "conclusion," and the others of which, called the "premises," are meant to establish or prove that the conclusion is true.
2. A good argument is one which provides good reason to believe the conclusion is true.
3. A valid argument is one for which it is impossible for the premises to be true and conclusion false (at the same time).
4. A strong argument is one for which it is almost impossible for the premises to be true and conclusion false (at the same time).
5. No. The premises could be false or it could beg the question. You should provide an example of a bad valid argument.
6. Provide an example where the premises are true and conclusion false.
7. No. It could beg the question. You should provide an example.
8. A compound claim is one that is made up of other claims, but which has to be viewed as just one claim.
9. A conditional is a claim that can be rewritten as an "if . . . then . . ." claim that must have the same truth-value.
10. a. The contradictory of a claim is another claim that must have the opposite truth-value.
12. A false dilemma is an "or" claim that seems to be true but isn't, because there is another possibility that it does not state.
17. No. It could be a slippery slope argument.
18. a. "A is a necessary condition for B" means that "If B, then A" is true.
19. It helps you avoid making your argument weak, and it shows others that you have considered the other view.

20. Show that one of the premises is false; show that the argument isn't valid or strong; show that the conclusion is false.
21. Only if the additional premises you have used are all true and the argument is valid. If the additional premises are only plausible, or the argument is only very strong, you've only shown that it's very likely that one of the original premises is false or collectively they lead to an absurdity.
23. A slippery slope argument is bad and doesn't refute.
24. Ridicule is not an argument.
25. a. A universal claim is one that can be rewritten as an "all" claim that must have the same truth-value.
26. a. An existential claim is one that can be rewritten as a "some" claim that must have the same truth-value.
31. Excluding Possibilities.
    The Direct Way of reasoning with conditionals.
    The Indirect Way of reasoning with conditionals.
    Reasoning in a Chain with conditionals.
    The Direct Way of reasoning with "All."
    Reasoning in a Chain with "All."
    The Direct Way of reasoning with "No."
32. Affirming the Consequent.
    Denying the Antecedent.
    Arguing Backwards with "All."
    Arguing Backwards with "No."
    Reasoning in a Chain with "Some."
33. The Direct Way of reasoning with "Almost All."
34. Arguing Backwards with "Almost All."
    Reasoning in a Chain with "Almost All."

Chapter 9
1. a. It eliminates the possibility of debating the claim.
15. Weaseler: Zoe didn't apologize!
17. Euphemism: Watergate was a disaster, not a "downside."
20. Dysphemism (or euphemism these days): "hippies" for demonstrators.
21. Proof substitute: "It has been well documented."
22. Weaseler: He didn't say it was the most important message, but only *if* . . .
26. "Gaming" is a euphemism for "gambling." Sure you'd say, "Honey, let's go out gaming tonight."
27. Qualifier: "for someone his age."
29. Persuasive definition: closes off the debate whether alcoholism is a disease.
30. Tom: Hyperbole: miracle. Innuendo: She's had other miracles.
    Dr. E: Innuendo: Madonna can't sing.
32. Euphemism: unspoiled wilderness area = uninhabited area.
33. Euphemism: passed away = died.
38. Dysphemism: freaks = members. "Nazis" is not a dysphemism, but the actual name of the group that was defended.

39. Dysphemism/politically correct: male chauvinist pig = man.
    Downplayer/innuendo: "complimenting."

41. Qualifier: at present.

42. Hyperbole: Makes you rethink *everything*? Like whether you should study critical thinking?

44. Euphemism: sanitation worker = garbage man.

45. Euphemisms: resettled = forcibly moved to.
    and internment camps = prison camps (it would be a dysphemism to call them "concentration camps").
    Innuendo: At last.

49. Innuendo: seat belts protect from injury / she was lucky not to be injured when not wearing a seat belt. Here the concealed claim is true.

Chapter 10

8. Generic premise: You should believe or do _____ if you love your country.

11. Zoe's argument: appeal to pity. Generic premise: You shouldn't experiment on animals if you feel sorry for the dogs. Great argument.
    Dick's argument: appeal to spite. Generic premise: You should experiment on cats if they make me sneeze. Great argument.

12. False dilemma. Also an appeal to spite and pity. Generic premise: You shouldn't buy a Japanese car if you are mad that some Japanese are rich. Bad.

From here on I'll just list the type of argument and whether it's good or bad.

13. Feel good argument. Bad.

17. Appeal to patriotism (subspecies of feel-good argument). Generic premise: You should believe that democracy is the best form of government if you love the U.S. (and think it's the greatest country). Bad argument.

20. Appeal to fear. You might think it's O.K. because a senator is supposed to worry about how his votes will be perceived by his constituents. *But* it's bad: We have a *representative* democracy, so a senator is supposed to vote as he or she thinks best. And the children whose votes the writer is threatening the senator with aren't voters yet.

23. Appeal to fear. Without more premises it's bad.

24. Wishful thinking. Bad. Except that way of thinking may be useful to motivate the person to lose weight.

Chapter 11

1. One that gives us good reason to believe the conclusion.

2. The argument must be valid or strong; we must have good reason to believe its premises; the premises must be more plausible than the conclusion.

6. No. Begging the question can be bad. Give an example.

7. Only if the false premise can be eliminated and the argument remains strong.

8. Nothing.

9. Our own experience.

10. The argument has a valid form. It's just that some of the premises are false or collectively too dubious.

11. It's a valid argument form. But the "or" claim is false.

14. An attempt to reduce to the absurd is pretty clearly an argument. With ridicule there's no argument at all.
15. b.   The direct way of reasoning with conditionals.
16. b.   The indirect way of reasoning with conditionals.
17. b.   All A are B, *x* is A, so *x* is B.
18. b.   Almost all A are B, *x* is A, so *x* is B.
20. b.   All A are B, no C is B, so no A is C.
37. A strawman is putting words in someone's mouth, attempting to refute an argument by refuting a different one.
38. Because they are also clearly bad ways to convince, though they aren't arguments.

Arguments for Analysis

Below are just sketches of answers, enough for you to see how to fill them out.

1. Common practice. Bad.
2. Mom starts with a loaded question. It's a false dilemma that Dick must either believe true or false. Dick can *suspend judgment*. Bad.
4. Ridicule?
9. Shifting the burden of proof. Bad. But you probably knew that even before reading it.
14. Good.
16. Valid (direct method of arguing with conditionals). (Missing premise: Tom knows Suzy.) Good.
17. Reducing to the absurd. Good refutation.
18. Reasoning in a chain with "some." Bad. (The football players might not have been the ones that swallowed the goldfish.)
19. Perfectionist dilemma, or common practice. ("If I were to stop making noise,that wouldn't solve the problem. So I shouldn't stop making noise.") Bad.
23. Bad. "Most" doesn't work like "almost all."
25. Very dubious premise. Bad. (Not a slippery slope: There's only one step.)
27. Good. More discussion on this in Chapter 14.
28. Reasoning backwards with "All." Bad.
31. Appeal to fear, but not a fallacy. Midway between weak and strong. Needs to consider the other side.
32. Appeal to pity, but not bad.
38. Strong argument, and the premise(s) are true. But not good, since we know that Suzy isn't likely to pass all her courses.
42. Ridicule. Bad.
43. Mistaking the person for the claim. Bad.
46. Mistaking subjective for objective. Bad.
47. Begging the question. Bad.
50. Appeal to fear. (Do you really think she's committed to self-immolation?) Bad.
51. Bad argument. Proved the wrong conclusion! (Compare the last sentence to the first one.) Also bad generalizations, which we'll study in Chapter 14.
56. Valid (the indirect way of reasoning with conditionals). Good.
60. Denying the antecedent. Bad.
64. They're debating a vague sentence that has no truth-value. (Maybe Suzy consistently

thinks that arriving on time means within an hour, like Brazilians do.) Or they're trying to make a subjective claim objective.

Chapter 12

2. We need to draw a conclusion.

3. No. They typically lack a statement of a general principle that would cover both (or all) cases.

4. State the conclusion. Look for similarities that suggest a general principle.

6. This is a comparison, not an argument. What conclusion could we draw? Memorize your lines?

8. Ota is reasoning by analogy. The conclusion is "The base in Okinawa could be closed and nothing bad would ensue." The premises are: The U.S. had a major base in the Phillipines. That base and situation then was very similar to the base and situation in Okinawa. The U.S. said that the base was essential. Nothing bad happened when that base was closed. The U.S. says that this base is essential.

    One crucial difference makes the analogy weak: When the U.S. shut its base in the Philippines, the U.S. still had a few other major bases in the area: Okinawa, mainland Japan, and South Korea. Were the U.S. to close down Okinawa, it would have only two bases left. Reason by analogy: If I were to cut one finger off your hand, you could still use your hand. That finger wasn't indispensable. But I can't cut off two or three or four fingers and still claim you can use your hand.

    Still, Ota would be justified in suspending judgment on whether the base is really indispensable, since the U.S. government has shown itself not to be a reliable source.

10. Yes, this is an analogy, with the last sentence being the conclusion. It depends on the unstated premise "The relationship of a student to the college is that of a consumer to a retail business." That's clearly false: A student only pays for 25–50% of his or her education.

    More generally, the principle might be "A college is a business," which is also false: It's either a government agency or a private foundation. It's not selling something.

13. Challenge: If this isn't a good argument, how would you convince someone that others feel pain? And if you can't, what justification would you have for not torturing people? (We know torture can elicit information or behavior we want.)

16. A lousy analogy because of the differences. We determine that a watch was made by someone because it *differs* from what we find in nature that is not crafted, such as rocks or trees. And we can deduce from its construction that it has a purpose. We can't do that for all of nature.

17. What a bad analogy: You shouldn't bust a kid for drinking at her own wedding party because that's just like busting a kid for drinking communion wine in church. You should be able to spot the differences.

19. If you said "yes" for some and "no" for others, what differences are there? If you said the same for all, did you reason by analogy? What general principle did you use?

20. Did you answer this the same as Exercise 19? If so, what was your reason? Are you arguing by analogy? What's your general principle?

Chapter 13

3. The sundial is more accurate, but the digital watch is more precise.
4. average: 74.27   mean: 74.27   median: 76   mode: 88 *and* 62
6. "Up to 44%" could mean 0%, too. Maybe that's only for that one type of call.
8. It's 45% lower than the *average* of the other brands, but 24 of those other brands could actually have less fat than this candy bar if there's just one of them that has a huge amount of fat. And what are those "leading" brands? Leading where? In Brazil?
10. It ain't free.
12. Down from, say, 5% to 3%? Or from 5% to 4.9%?
18. Funny how they break down the figures in the next-to-last paragraph, but not in the last one. It could be that of the 99%, only 1% actually improved.
    Also, "well-known secret" is an oxymoron.
19. Don't do it Dick. One per day ≠ average of one per day.
22. Meaningless: Too much variation from one area to another. You need to know the cost of living in various areas. Median or mode won't be much more use.
23. A fair indication, since there's not much variation.
24. Terrible comparison: There's little variation in university professors' salaries (almost all between $25,000 and $75,000), but huge variation in concert pianists' income ($15,000 vs. $2,000,000). The mode would be more informative.
26. Worthless: Respondents on surveys about intimate details of their lives are notoriously inaccurate, either because of bad memory, embarrassment, or lying. "I have sexual intercourse 18 times per week." The surveyor has to record that.
27. Curious, but not much you can conclude from it. Could be that it's easier to get good grades now, or the students are smarter, or students are taking a different mix of courses than before, or . . .

Chapter 14

Section A

1. Generalizing.
   Sample: The German shepherds the speaker has met.
   Population: All German shepherds.
2. No generalizing.
3. Generalizing.
   Sample: The CD player that Suzy has.
   Population: All Zitochi CD players.
4. Generalizing.
   Sample: Maria's brother? Others, too?
   Population: All football players.
5. Generalizing.
   Sample: The guys Suzy has dated.
   Population: All guys.
6. Generalizing.
   Sample: The times Zoe has taken Spot to the vet before.
   Population: All times Zoe has or will take Spot to the vet.
7. Generalizing.

Sample: The last time the cat went in the car.
Population: All times the cat ever has or will ever go in a car.
Not such bad generalizing, considering the risk.

8. Generalizing.
   Sample: The times that Dick has taken his clothes to be cleaned.
   Population: All times anyone takes his clothes to that dry cleaner.

9. Possibly generalizing, but could be just repeating a general claim he's heard.
   We can't identify the sample, so it's best not to treat it as a generalization until
   the speaker elaborates.

10. A general claim, but no generalizing is going on, since there's no argument.

11. Hard to say if it's generalizing. Has the speaker met Japanese guys? Or is she
    just repeating a stereotype she's heard?

Sections B.1 and B.2

1. One in which no subgroup of the population is represented more than its proportion in
   the population.

2. There is always a possibility that the members of the population which you haven't
   studied are different from the ones you have studied.

3. a. If the probability of something occurring is X percent, then over the long run the
      number of occurrences will tend toward X percent.
   b. The probability of getting a sample that isn't representative is very small.

7. You can't know in advance what are the "relevant" characteristics. If you could, you
   wouldn't need to do a survey/experiment. You're biasing the sample towards the
   characteristics you think in advance are important. See Exercise 6.b.

9. No. Indeed, the law of large numbers says that eventually a randomly chosen sample of
   students at your college will consist of just gay men. But the likelihood of a randomly
   chosen sample not being representative is small.

Section B

1. There is a 94% chance that between 51% and 61% of the entire population of voters
   actually favors your candidate.

2. No.

3. a. A hasty generalization using anecdotal evidence.
   b. Yes, see the example in Section B.7. There would have to be very little variation in
      the population.

4. Variation.

5. 1. The sample is big enough.
   2. The sample is representative.
   3. The sample is studied well.
   Note well: The second premise is *not* "The sample is chosen randomly."
   That claim can support the second premise, but isn't always necessary.

7. b. Hire the pest exterminator. Even with the huge margin of error and large number of
      undecided, we can be confident that most people prefer that.

8. Remember: You should only ask registered voters.

9. Such a survey would be nonsense because most students don't know what the president

of a college actually does. Do you approve of the way they're sweeping the streets in Timbuktu?

16. *Generalization*: All CDs can hold an encyclopedia's-worth of information.
    Sample: The CD that the speaker just bought.
    Sample is representative? Yes, no variation in population (unless it's broken, and that doesn't count).
    Sample is big enough? Yes, no variation in population.
    Sample is studied well? Yes, the speaker has seen it on his/her computer.
    Good generalization ? Yes.

17. *Generalization*: (unstated) Lots of people fail Dr. E's course.
    Sample: The three people the speaker knows.
    Sample is representative? No reason to believe so.
    Sample is big enough? More like anecdotal evidence.
    Sample is studied well? Yes, they failed.
    Good generalization? No.
    Use: You shouldn't take Dr. E's course. Depends on unstated premise:
        You don't want to fail a course.

19. *Generalization:* This herbal tea can help cure your flu.
    Sample: The people who have told the clerk the tea helped.
    Sample is representative? Almost certainly not. Perhaps the ones that weren't helped didn't come back. Perhaps people who buy herbal medicines at a health-food store are more susceptible to the placebo effect.
    Sample is big enough? Anecdotal evidence.
    Sample is studied well? No. Coughing ≠ flu.
    Good generalization? No.

23. *Generalization*: Bald men are really sexy to Maria.
    Sample is representative? Probably not–the next bald guy might be hopeless.
    Sample is big enough? Anecdotal evidence.
    Sample is studied well? Yes, she found them sexy.
    Good generalization? No. Perhaps a different conclusion might be O.K.:
        "All things equal, bald men are sexier than hairy men."

25. Not a generalization. Use of a generalization: Almost all basketball players are over 6'4" tall and people that tall won't fit into Suzy's car. Therefore (unstated) You shouldn't use Suzy's car to pick up the basketball player.
    Need unstated premise: You shouldn't pick up someone in a car he can't fit into.
    Pretty good argument.

26. *Generalization*: The pacifier will stop the baby from crying.
    Sample: All the times the speaker has given the pacifier to the baby.
    Sample is representative? Who knows?
    Sample is big enough? We don't know how often they've done it.
    Sample is studied well? Possibly, or possibly bad memory.
    Additional premises needed? None.
    Good generalization? Weak, but there's little risk in that course of action.

28. *Generalization*: Gina will be late every Sunday.

Sample: The last seven Sundays.

Sample is representative? More or less (see conclusion).

Sample is big enough? Yes.

Sample is studied well? Yes, she was late, assuming the speaker isn't exaggerating and remembers correctly.

Good generalization? Yes, a pattern has been established, but not a great argument, because people can change, especially if Gina's been nagged to show up on time.

29. *Generalization*: Gina will be at Club Rio every Friday night.

Sample is representative? Hard to say.

Sample is big enough? Yes.

Sample is studied well? Yes, assuming the speaker isn't exaggerating and remembers correctly.

Good generalization? Her tastes might have changed, the sample might not be representative. But probably O.K.

32. *Generalization*: Sexual activity is unlikely to trigger a heart attack.

Sample: The 900 heart attack victims who were studied.

Sample is representative? NO! The sample only includes people who've already had a heart attack and survived. Maybe sexual activity is primarily lethal to those who haven't had a heart attack yet.

Sample is big enough? Possibly.

Sample is studied well? Can't be sure. We have to rely on people being honest about their sex lives.

Good generalization? No. At best we could conclude that sexual activity is unlikely to trigger a heart attack in survivors of heart attacks in the U.S. And then you'd want to study more people from different areas of the U.S.

33. Yes, I'd try it, if I had incurable pain. Little risk, low cost, and probable help. The study seems well-designed. We'll look at cause and effect more in the next chapter.

34. *Generalization*: It's an analogy, with a generalization needed for it:

Suzy has a Yoda sedan that has had lots of mechanical problems.

Therefore, Almost all Yoda sedans will have mechanical problems.

Therefore, A Yoda sedan we buy will have mechanical problems.

Sample is representative? No reason to believe so.

Sample is big enough? More like anecdotal evidence.

Sample is studied well? Yes, it broke.

Good argument? No.

Chapter 15

Sections A.1–A.3

1. *Causal claim*: The police car's siren caused me to pull over.

Particular or *general*? Particular.

Cause (stated as a claim): The police car had its siren going near me.

Effect (stated as a claim): I pulled over.

2. *Causal claim*: You doing so badly in this class caused me to teach badly.

Particular or *general*? Particular, but too vague.

5. Not a causal claim. This is inductive evidence for a generalization that might be used in

establishing a general causal claim.

7. Not a causal claim, or at best *a* cause, not *the* cause. Part of the normal conditions for a causal claim about the effect "I passed this course."

8. *Causal claim*: Watching golf causes me to want to play golf.
   Particular or *general*? General.

11. *Causal claim*: This is *way* too vague.

16. *Causal claim*: Being cold causes people to shiver.
    Particular or *general*? General.

Sections A and B

1. It's impossible that the cause could be true and the effect false, given the normal conditions.
   The cause makes a difference.
   The cause precedes and is close in space and time to the effect.

2. No one knows.

4. The normal conditions.

5. *Causal claim*: Our airplane taking off from gate number 13 caused us to experience turbulence.
   Cause: Our airplane took off from gate number 13.
   Effect: We had a lot of turbulence on the flight.
   Cause before and close in space and time to effect? Doubtful.
   Cause makes a difference? Almost certainly not. We could test this by asking if any other flights from other gates at that or any other airport had turbulence in that area.
   Evaluation: Very implausible.

6. *Causal claim*: Dick pigging out on nachos and salsa caused his stomach ache.
   Cause: Dick pigged out on nachos and salsa last night.
   Effect: Dick got a stomach ache.
   Cause before and close in space and time to effect? Close enough.
   Cause makes a difference? Don't know. Too many other possibilities.
   Evaluation: Suspend judgment.

8. *Causal claim*: The dark sky caused Suzy to be depressed.
   Cause: The sky was dark.
   Effect: Suzy got depressed.
   Cause before and close in space and time to effect? Close in space and time, but do we know for sure which came first? Is Suzy's memory right about when she first got depressed?
   Cause makes a difference? Perhaps, but we need to know what happened to Suzy before that might have made her depressed.
   Evaluation: Possible. Hard to evaluate because it's subjective.

9. Marriage isn't a cause of divorce, it's part of the normal conditions.

11. *Causal claim*: Zoe's forgetting to fill up before they left town caused Dick and Zoe to run out of gas.
    Cause: Zoe forgot to fill up before she and Dick left town.
    Effect: Dick and Zoe ran out of gas.
    Cause before and close in space and time to effect? Close enough.

      Cause makes a difference? Yes.

      Evaluation: It's *a* cause. But it's not *the* cause. Dick's not getting gas the night
before—is that a normal condition or one of the causes?

16. *Causal claim*: Dick telling Sally that Zoe killed Puff caused Zoe to be miserable now.

    Cause: Dick told Sally that Zoe killed Puff.

    Effect: Zoe is unhappy now.

    Cause before and close in space and time to effect? No.

    Cause makes a difference? ???

    Evaluation: Seems to be tracing too far back in time. A psychiatrist might say Zoe's
right. But spelling out what she believes the normal conditions are might show she's
wrong. It's like the Treaty of Versailles example, and on top of that it's so
subjective. Just have broad shoulders, Dick.

Section C

5. Reread Chapter 5.

6. If you can show that the purported cause makes a difference, then all the other criteria
necessary for cause and effect are satisfied. It's not *just* a sequence.

7. This happened once, then that happened. But a general claim is needed: Every time
something this happens, that happens afterwards. All we have is anecdotal evidence.

10. *Causal claim*: The pedals are making a clicking sound on Dick's bike.

    Cause: The pedals are defective. ??

    Effect: There is a clicking sound.

    Evaluation: Good method, but a false dilemma starts it. The clicking could also come
from the gears. Have Zoe put her ear close to the pedals when Dick is turning them.

11. *Causal claim*: As stated.

    Cause: There is a lot of sex, drugs and rock 'n roll around.

    Effect: Family values have declined.

    Evaluation: Too vague. Anyway, it's just as likely that the decline in family values
(whatever those are) caused people to want more sex, drugs, and rock 'n roll. Or
perhaps there's some common cause, like the decline in the economy since the
1960s and the lack of optimism people feel about the future.

14. There isn't a causal claim here. Rather, Flo is overlooking one. Perhaps coincidence is
just our ignorance of real cause and effect. To be sure, our knowledge is limited. But
not commonly as limited as in this example.

15. *Causal claim*: My neighbor talking about allergies caused me to have allergies.

    Cause: My neighbor told me it's been the worst season ever for allergies this spring.

    Effect: I started sneezing.

    Evaluation: Seems like *post hoc* reasoning. But it could be true because of the power
of suggestion . . . Implausible.

21. *Causal claim*: Smoking marijuana causes heroin use. (general claim)

    Evaluation: First of all, it's *can cause* not *causes,* since we all know examples of
people who smoke marijuana and don't use heroin. But it's also *post hoc*
reasoning. They probably all drank milk, too.

22. *Causal claim*: Dr. E's students not liking the material at the end of the course causes
them not to show up for class.

Cause: Some students of Dr. E don't like the material at the end of the course.
Effect: Those students don't show up for class.

This is an example of *egotism*: Dr. E thinks that it's something he does, and he's overlooking another cause, namely, at the end of the term students have a lot of work and cut classes to do that.

Section D

6. a. Giving sick people better health care causes them to be hospitalized more.
    b. Controlled cause-to-effect. The control group is composed of those patients at those hospitals before the experiment, apparently. Or perhaps those that weren't given better care. It's not made explicit.
    c. i. The experiment can't be generalized to anyone other than poor, seriously ill veterans. Very dubious to generalize to all people. Especially dubious to generalize to people who are in good health to begin with.
        ii. Overlooks other possible causes, such as normal deterioration in the patients' health during that period. (They were seriously ill to begin with.) Or the doctors, knowing the patients didn't have to pay, were more willing to hospitalize them. Overall, not much you can conclude from this experiment.
    d. Do the same experiment with other populations throughout the country, ensuring that the samples are taken randomly. Choose control groups better. Screen doctors for their attitudes.

7. a. Viruses linked to cancer are found in the saliva of AIDS patients. Therefore, AIDS patients can infect people with their saliva.
    b. They found the virus in the saliva in 17 of 23 AIDS patients. But no information is given about how often you'd find it in the saliva of healthy people.
    c. The argument is very weak: No evidence that the virus is actually capable of being spread by saliva, just that it's there. It's not clear what "the virus is linked" to the cancer means. Does it cause it?

9. a. Switchside breathing causes you to have more energy when bicycling. (Cause: Cyclists switch the side they breathe on. Effect: Cyclists have more energy and fewer injuries.) Causation in populations.
    b. The experiment is entirely personal experience. Anecdotal. And analogies from anecdotal evidence on runners.
    c. What he did seemed to work for him. It's too easy to say that it wasn't well done because there was no causation in population experiment. By that standard you'd have to throw out the evidence for yoga or zen meditation or the breathing techniques developed over the last century for actors. Certain techniques are more an art that is handed down and are very hard to test.
    d. Best would be to do a controlled cause-to-effect experiment on a representative population of cyclists. Perhaps you could monitor riders' breathing, etc., but that can't fully prove or disprove the claim. The good that people find in meditation is only partially confirmed by noting that their respiration and heartbeat slow.
        But who would sponsor such a study?

Review Exercises for Chapters 12–15

1. A collection of claims which are intended to show that one of them, the conclusion, is *true*.
2. One that gives us good reason to believe the conclusion is true.
3. For a valid argument it is impossible for the premises to be true and conclusion false. For a strong argument it is *almost* impossible.
4. No. It could have a false premise or beg the question.
5. A comparison becomes reasoning by analogy when a claim is being argued for. On one side of the comparison we draw a conclusion, so on the other side we should conclude the same.
6.   1. Is this an argument? What is the conclusion?
   2. What is the comparison?
   3. What are the premises? (one or both sides of the comparison)
   4. What are the similarities?
   5. Can we state the similarities as premises and find a general principle that covers the two sides?
   6. Does the general principle really apply to both sides? What about the differences?
   7. Is the argument strong or valid? Is it good?
7.   a. Add all the numbers in the collection. Divide by the number of numbers in the collection.
   b. Same as the average.
   c. The mid-way number: As many numbers in the collection are greater than it as are less than it.
   d. The number that appears most often in the collection.
8. A comparison where the base is unknown.
10. a. A generalization is an argument concluding a claim about a group from a claim about some part of the group.
   b. The sample.
   c. The population.
11. One in which no one subgroup of the population is represented more than its proportion of the population as a whole.
12. No. You could get a very biased sample by chance, but the likelihood of that happening is very, very small.
13. Yes. The computer example in Section B.7 of Chapter 14.
14. There is a 97% chance that between 39% and 45% of the voters favor that candidate.
16. The sample is big enough. The sample is representative. The sample is studied well.
17. A hasty generalization. The information about the too small sample is called "anecdotal evidence."
18. The cause precedes the effect.
    It's impossible that the cause could be true and the effect false, given the normal conditions.
    The cause makes a difference.
    The cause is close in space and time to the effect.

19. No one knows.
20. The normal conditions.
21. Reversing cause and effect. Overlooking a common cause. Looking too hard for a cause.
22. Controlled cause-to-effect. Uncontrolled cause-to-effect. Uncontrolled effect-to-cause.
23. Because arguing or persuading badly will:
    Undermine your own ability to reason well.
    Help destroy democracy.
    In the long run not work as well as reasoning well.

Appendix: Using Examples in Reasoning

Exercises

6. a. Basenjis don't bark.
    b. I know a cat that always stays indoors in a big city.
    c. I know several students who aren't.
    d. Name some who are good lecturers.
    e. Wendy's has a salad bar.
9. Even if the first premise is true, the argument is bad. This course is a counterexample: the exams are fair, but it's not easy.
10. Unstated premise: You have to inhale marijuana to get high from it. Valid. But that premise is false: You could eat it.
11. Strong, but the first premise is dubious at most schools, which can be shown with some examples.
12. Unstated premise: Almost any professor who's never been late before and is very conscientious and is late for the first time has been in an accident. Unlikely. He could have been ill and the secretary forgot to tell the class. Unstated premise is dubious.

Appendix: Diagramming

Section A

1.

2. No one under sixteen has a driver's license. *1* So Zoe must be over sixteen. *2* Zoe has a driver's license. *a*

3. If an animal is such that *2* and *3*, then it is the dumbest animal in the world. *a*

4. I'm on my way to school. *1* I left five minutes late. *2* Traffic is heavy. *3* I'll be late for class. *4* I might as well stop and get breakfast. *5* Whenever I'm on my way to

school and I'm five minutes late and traffic is heavy, I will be late for my classes. *a*
If I'm late for classes, I might as well be very late or miss the class. *b*

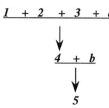

5.   Pigs are very intelligent animals. *1* They make great pets. *2*
They learn to do tricks as well as any dog can. *3* They can be house-
trained. *4* And they are affectionate *5*. They like to cuddle. *6*
Pigs are known as one of the smartest animals there are. *7*
If you get bored with them or they become unruly, you can eat
them. *8* Anything that is intelligent, can be housetrained, and is
affectionate is a great pet. *a* (See the answer to Exercise 6 of
Chapter 7, Sections C and D.)

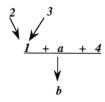

6.   Smoking is disgusting. *1* It makes your breath smell horrid. *2* If you've ever
kissed someone after they smoked a cigarette you feel as though you're going to
vomit. *3* Besides, it will kill you. *4*. You should not do anything that is
disgusting and can kill you. *a* You should not smoke. *b*

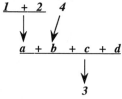

7.   You're good at numbers. *1* You sort of like business. *2* You should major in
accounting *3*—accountants make really good money. *4* If you're good at numbers and
sort of like business, you'll be good at accounting. *a* If you're an accountant you'll
make good money. *b* You should major in something that you'll enjoy, be good at, and
make good money at. *c* Accounting is the *only* thing that you'll enjoy, be good at, and
make good money at. *d*

$$\begin{array}{c} \underline{1 \;+\; 2} \quad\; 4 \\ \downarrow \quad\;\; \downarrow \\ \underline{a \;+\; b \;+\; c \;+\; d} \\ \downarrow \\ 3 \end{array}$$

8.   Not an argument.

Section B

1.   You should not take illegal drugs. *1*
They can kill you. *2*
If you overdose, you can die. *3*

If you share a needle, you could get AIDS. *4*

If you get AIDS, then you die. *5*

If you don't die (not *3*), you may end up a vegetable or otherwise permanently incapacitated. *6*

Using drugs runs the risk of getting arrested and possibly going to jail or having a hefty fine against you. *7*

Some think the "high" from drugs is worth all the risks. *8*

They are addicted. *9*

They are only trying to justify supporting their habit. *10*

You shouldn't do anything that has a high risk of killing you or permanently incapacitating you or putting you in jail or having a fine against you. *a*

People who are addicted to drugs and are trying to justify their habit shouldn't be believed. *b*

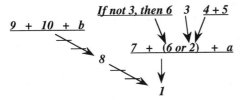

2. Sex is the answer to almost everyone's problems. *1*

    It takes away your tensions. *2*

    It doesn't if you're involved with someone you don't like. *3*

    Sex makes you feel better. *4*

    It doesn't if it's against your morals. *5* Heroin makes you feel good. *6*

    It's healthy, natural, just like eating and drinking. *7*

    You can catch terrible diseases. *8* Sex should be confined to marriage. *9*

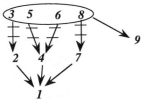

This is an example in which the counterargument is intended to do more than throw doubt on the conclusion: it's meant to establish another claim (though it's missing premises for that).

   Just looking at the diagram, we can see that Zoe has not established her conclusion: Every one of her premises has been brought into doubt (by a plausible claim).

3. Nixon was a crook/criminal. *1*

    He said he wasn't in the famous "Checkers" speech. *2*

    That was just political evasion. *3*

    You can't just take someone's word that he's not a criminal, especially if he's a politician. *4*

    He directed the break-in at the Democratic Party Headquarters. *5*

They never showed that he did that. *6*
His accomplices like Haldemann were covering up. *7*
That's why they got pardoned. *8*
Nixon used the FBI against his enemies. *9*
It was stupid for Clinton to make a speech honoring Nixon when Nixon died. *10*
Clinton was doing it so that when he dies someone will make a speech for him. *11*
It is stupid to make a speech honoring someone who was a criminal. *a*
(Don't add "Clinton is a criminal." There's no reason to believe that Zoe thinks that's plausible.)

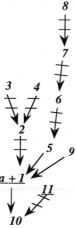

Appendix: Truth-Tables

Sections A and B

1. "and," "or," "not," "if . . . then . . ."
2. The only aspects of claims that we will pay attention to are whether the claim is true or false and how it may be compounded out of other claims.
4. A tautology is a compound claim that is true regardless of the truth-values of its parts.
5. Represent the claim using $\wedge$, $\vee$, $\neg$, $\rightarrow$. Replace the claims with letters. Make a truth-table with the last column the formal claim. If all the entries in that column are T, then it's a tautology. If even one is F, it's not a tautology.
6. Form the table for each. They are equivalent if for every row they are both true or both false.

7.

A	$\neg\neg A$	$\neg\neg A \rightarrow A$
T	T	T
F	F	T

9.

A	B	$A \rightarrow B$	$\neg A$	$\neg A \rightarrow B$	$(A \rightarrow B) \wedge (\neg A \rightarrow B)$	$((A \rightarrow B) \wedge (\neg A \rightarrow B)) \rightarrow B$
T	T	T	F	T	T	T
T	F	F	F	T	F	T
F	T	T	T	T	T	T
F	F	T	T	F	F	T

A	B	A∨B	¬B	(A∨B) ∧ ¬B	((A∨B) ∧ ¬B) → A
T	T	T	F	F	T
T	F	T	T	T	T
F	T	T	F	F	T
F	F	F	T	F	T

12. Tautology.

A	B	A∨B	A∧B	(A∨B) → (A∧B)
T	T	T	T	T
T	F	T	F	**F**
F	T	T	F	**F**
F	F	F	F	T

13. Not a tautology.

14. Tautology.

A	B	A→B	¬B	(A→B)∧¬B	¬A	((A→B)∧¬B) → ¬A
T	T	T	F	F	F	T
T	F	F	T	F	F	T
F	T	T	F	F	T	T
F	F	T	T	T	T	T

15. Not a tautology.

A	B	A∧B	¬(A∧B)	¬A	¬(A∧B)∧¬A	(¬(A∧B)∧¬A)→B
T	T	T	F	F	F	T
T	F	F	T	F	F	T
F	T	F	T	T	T	T
F	F	F	T	T	T	**F**

16. Not a tautology.

A	B	C	A→B	¬A	¬A→C	(A→B)∨(¬A→C)	B∨C	((A→B)∨(¬A→C))→(B∨C)
T	T	T	T	F	T	T	T	T
T	T	F	T	F	T	T	T	T
T	F	T	F	F	T	T	T	T
T	F	F	F	F	T	T	F	**F**
F	T	T	T	T	T	T	T	T
F	T	F	T	T	F	T	T	T
F	F	T	T	T	T	T	T	T
F	F	F	T	T	F	T	F	**F**

17.

A	B	A→B	¬(A→B)	¬B	A∧¬B
T	T	T	F	F	F
T	F	F	T	T	T
F	T	T	F	F	F
F	F	T	F	T	F

19.

A	B	A∧B	¬(A∧B)	¬A	¬B	¬A∨¬B
T	T	T	F	F	F	F
T	F	F	T	F	T	T
F	T	F	T	T	F	T
F	F	F	T	T	T	T

Section C

1.

A	B	A∨B	A∧B	¬(A∧B)	(A∨B)∧¬(A∧B)
T	T	T	T	F	F
T	F	T	F	T	T
F	T	T	F	T	T
F	F	F	F	T	F

4. Dick prefers steak ∧ Zoe prefers spaghetti
   ["While" doesn't mean "at the same time" here.]

5. "While" does mean "at the same time," and when a claim is true can't matter when we use the symbols. So the claim can't be represented.

7. Not compound, just two claims. Or: You whine all the time ∧ I love you

10. We're going to the movies tonight ∨ we're going out for dinner tonight.
    However, if you think the "or" is exclusive:
    (we're going to the movies tonight ∨ we're going out for dinner tonight)
    ∧ (¬ (we're going to the movies tonight) ∧ ¬(we're going out for dinner tonight))

13. (Dick takes Spot for a walk→Dick will do the dishes) →
        ¬(Dick will take Spot for a walk)

16. Spot barks → (there's a skunk in the yard ∨ there's a raccoon in the yard)

17. How you formalize this will depend on how you understand "regardless." Here's one interpretation:
    (You get mad at me)→¬(I will visit your mother) ∧   ¬(You get mad at me)→
    ¬(I will visit your mother) ∧   (You cajole me)→¬(I will visit your mother)
    ∧ ¬(You cajole me)→¬(I will visit your mother)

18. Can't represent it. It's *not*: Every student in Dr. E's class is over 18 ∨ every student in Dr. E's class is taking the course while in high school.
    That could be false and the original true. [Compare: Every student is male or female.]

20. a. A→B
    b. ¬B → A (This is the same as ¬A→B.)

c. A→B   if "when" doesn't mean "at that time."
d. (A→B) ∧ (B→A)
e. B→A
f. ¬A ∧ ¬B

Section D

1. Every argument that has that form is valid.
2. Not necessarily. It might have another valid argument form. Or it might be a strong argument. For example: All cats meow. Puff is a cat. So Puff meows. Truth-tables won't show that this is valid.

4. Valid.

A	B	A→B	¬B	A→¬B	¬A
T	T	T	F	F	F
T	F	F	T	T	F
F	T	T	F	T	T
F	F	T	T	T	T

5. Valid. No row can have both premises true.

6. Invalid. Either circled row shows that.

A	B	A∨B	A∧B
T	T	T	T
T	F	T	F
F	T	T	F
F	F	F	F

8. Valid. Argue that if C∨E were false, then both C and E would be false. Since B→C and D→E are true, both B and D would have to be false. But B∨D is true. So one of B or D is true. A contradiction. So one of C or E is true.

9. Valid.

A	B	C	¬B	A→¬B	¬C	B∧¬C	A→C
T	T	T	F	F	F	F	T
T	T	F	F	F	T	T	F
T	F	T	T	T	F	F	T
T	F	F	T	T	T	F	F
F	T	T	F	T	F	F	T
F	T	F	F	T	T	T	T
F	F	T	T	T	F	F	T
F	F	F	T	T	T	F	T

continued . . .

A	B	C	¬B	¬¬B	A→¬¬B	¬C	¬C∨A
T	T	T	F	T	T	F	T
T	T	F	F	T	T	T	T
T	F	T	T	F	F	F	T
T	F	F	T	F	F	T	T
F	T	T	F	T	T	F	F
F	T	F	F	T	T	T	T
F	F	T	T	F	T	F	F
F	F	F	T	F	T	T	T

10. Valid.

11. Spot is a cat → Spot meows,   ¬ (Spot is a cat)
    So ¬(Spot meows)

    A→B, ¬A   Not valid. Denying the antecedent.
         ¬B

12. The moon is made of green cheese ∨ 2 + 2 = 4
    ¬(the moon is made of green cheese)
    So 2 + 2 = 4

    A∨B, ¬A   Valid. Excluding possibilities.
       B

13. Valid, same as 12. Sure the conclusion is false. It's valid, not good.

14. (The students are happy →no test is given) ∧ (no test is given → the students
    are happy)
    The students are happy → the professor feels good
    The professor feels good → ¬(the professor will feel like lecturing)
    ¬(the professor feels like lecturing) → the professor will give a test
    So ¬(the students will be happy)
    [Identify "the professor will give a test" with "a test is given."]
    (A→¬B) ∧ (¬B→A) , A→C, C→¬D, ¬D→B

                    ¬A

    First note that the last three premises yield, via reasoning in a chain, A→B.
    So we've reduced it to: (A→¬B) ∧ (¬B→A) ,   A→B

                    ¬A

    But from the first premise we get (A→¬B).
    Then from Exercise 4 we have ¬A. So it's valid.

15. Dick and Zoe visit his family at Christmas → they will fly
    Dick and Zoe visit Zoe's mother at Christmas → they will fly
    Dick and Zoe visit his family at Christmas ∨ Dick and Zoe visit Zoe's mother
       at Christmas
    So they will fly [Identify "They will fly" with "Dick and Zoe will travel by plane."]
    A→B, C→B, A∨C
        B

A	B	C	A→B	C→B	A∨C
T	T	T	T	T	T
T	T	F	T	T	T
T	F	T	F	F	T
T	F	F	F	T	T
F	T	T	T	T	T
F	T	F	T	T	F
F	F	T	T	F	T
F	F	F	T	T	F

Valid.

16. ٦(Tom is from NY ∨ Tom is from Virginia)

    Tom is from Syracuse → (Tom is from NY ∨ Tom is from Virginia)

    So: ٦(Tom is from Syracuse)   ["Tom is from the East Coast" isn't needed.]

    ٦(B∨C) , D→(B∨C)

              ٦D

    Valid. If it were possible to have ٦D false, and so D true, with these premises true, then
    by the direct way of reasoning with conditionals, B∨C would be true. But the first
    premise gives us that ٦(B∨C) is true. A contradiction. So D is false. So ٦D is true.

17. The government is going to spend less on health and welfare.

    The government is going to spend less on health and welfare →

        (the government is going to cut the Medicare budget ∨ the government is going to
        slash spending on the elderly)

    The government is going to cut the Medicare budget → the elderly will protest

    The government is going to slash spending on the elderly → advocates of the poor will
        protest

    So: The elderly will protest ∨ advocates of the poor will protest

    A, A→(B∨C) , B→D, C→E

              D∨E

    Valid. From the first two premises we get B∨C. Then if we want we can do a table.
    Or we can argue as follows. Suppose D∨E were false. Then both D and E are false. So
    by the Indirect Way of reasoning with conditionals, both B and C would have to be false.
    So B∨C would have to be false. But B∨C we already have is true. So D∨E isn't false.

Index

Italics indicate a definition.